The State of
Working America

The State of
Working America
2004/2005

LAWRENCE MISHEL

JARED BERNSTEIN

SYLVIA ALLEGRETTO

ECONOMIC POLICY INSTITUTE

ILR Press
an imprint of
Cornell University Press
Ithaca and London

First published 2005 by Cornell University Press
First printing, Cornell Paperbacks, 2005

ISBN 0-8014-4339-3 (cloth: alk. paper)
ISBN 0-8014-8962-8 (paper: alk. paper)

Printed in the United States of America

Recommended citation for this book is as follows: Mishel, Lawrence,
Jared Bernstein, and Sylvia Allegretto, *The State of Working America 2004/2005.*
An Economic Policy Institute Book. Ithaca, N.Y.: ILR Press,
an imprint of Cornell University Press, 2005.

Cornell University Press strives to use environmentally responsible suppliers and
materials to the fullest extent possible in the publishing of its books. Such
materials include vegetable-based, low-VOC inks and acid-free papers that are
recycled, totally chlorine-free, or partly composed of nonwood fibers. For further
information, visit our website at www.cornellpress.cornell.edu.

Cloth printing   10 9 8 7 6 5 4 3 2 1
Paperback printing   10 9 8 7 6 5 4 3 2 1

To Ellen, The Mercury Lady and a wonderful woman
– LARRY MISHEL

To Catherine Ling Bernstein
– JARED BERNSTEIN

To Charlotte Allegretto, who worked over two decades
for the same company and luckily retired just before the plant closed
and relocated; and to Edmond Allegretto, Sr., a lifetime member
of the International Union of Painters and Allied Trades, AFL-CIO
– SYLVIA ALLEGRETTO

VISIT EPINET.ORG

The Economic Policy Institute's web site contains current analysis of issues addressed in this book. The DataZone section presents up-to-date historical data series on incomes, wages, employment, poverty, and other topics. The data can be viewed online or downloaded as spreadsheets.

Table of Contents

Acknowledgments

The preparation of this publication requires the intensive work of many people on EPI's staff and many contributions from other researchers on the topics covered in the text.

Yulia Fungard, Grace Maro, and Adam Hersh provided extensive and enormously valuable research assistance in all of the areas covered in this book by collecting and organizing data and creating tables and graphs. Our programming staff, headed by Danielle Gao and including Jin Dai, provided extensive computer programming and data analysis. Danielle's tireless work (e-mailed SAS output at 1 a.m.!) and deep knowledge of our data are invaluable resources. Gabriela Prudencio also provided helpful assistance.

Among EPI staffers (and former staffers), Josh Bivens, Lee Price, and Elise Gould provided extensive insights and guidance in many areas, including outsourcing research, trade and employment, international comparisons, and analysis of capital and labor incomes. Michael Ettlinger provided helpful comments on the tax section in Chapter 1. We thank all our previous co-authors—Jacqueline Simon, David Frankel, John Schmitt, and Heather Boushey—for their lasting input. Our development staff, headed by Noris Weiss Malvey, provided valuable help in raising funds for this work.

EPI economist Jeff Chapman wrote the regional chapter, and it was a pleasure to work with him. His knowledge of regional data and trends has greatly improved the quality of this chapter.

Joe Procopio, Lisa Goffredi, Pat Watson, and Kim Weinstein provided invaluable production assistance. Their careful editing and layout under considerable time pressure is greatly appreciated. Our readers are the true beneficiaries of their work, as they make us look like far better writers. Nancy Coleman, Karen Conner, and Stephaan Harris work to provide a large audience for our work. We deeply appreciate the energy and creativity they bring to their work.

Many experts were helpful in providing data or their research papers for our use. We are particularly grateful to Ed Wolff and Robert McIntire for the provision of special tabulations. Others who provided data, advice, or their analysis include Carl Brown, Alan Ecks, R. Jason Faberman, Howard Hayghe, Ryan Helwig, David Johnson, Dean Lillard, Robert Manning, Tom Nardone, Chuck Nelson, Steven Sabow, Isaac Shapiro, William Shay, Timothy Smeeding, Gary Solon, Jay Stewart, Paul Swaim, Robert Valletta, Ed Welniak, and Susan Wilson.

We are grateful to the Ford Foundation, the Foundation for Child Development, the Joyce Foundation, the John D. & Catherine T. MacArthur Foundation, the Charles Stewart Mott Foundation, and the Rockefeller Foundation for providing support for the research and publication of this volume.

Executive summary

Despite being two and a half years into an economic recovery, many of the problems that beset working Americans in the 2001 recession and protracted jobless recovery persist today. The 2001 downturn stopped and even reversed most of the positive economic trends that characterized the latter 1990s, a period when historically tight labor markets ensured that the growth of productivity was, for the first time in two decades, broadly shared throughout the income scale. Through the late 1990s, real wages grew rapidly not just for high-wage workers, but also for those in middle- and lower-wage jobs. Incomes rose across the board, poverty rates fell quickly, and the growth of inequality was significantly dampened.

In contrast, since 2000, unemployment has been high (relative to the preceding period of full employment) and not responsive to the productivity growth that has occurred. In fact, the unemployment rate of 5.6% in mid-2004 stood at precisely the same level as that of November 2001, when the recovery began. The great American job machine was uniquely dormant for almost two years into this recovery, with consistent job creation finally occurring in the fall of 2003. Since then, the U.S. economy has added 1.5 million jobs, yet it remains 1.2 million jobs below the last business cycle's peak employment level in March 2001. The United States has been tracking employment statistics since 1939, and never in history has it taken this long to regain the jobs lost over a downturn.

This persistent labor market slack and its negative effect on wages and incomes is a central theme of this book and is explored throughout the chapters that follow. Yet this book's analysis goes far beyond a review of the past few years, as it explores in great detail the history of the U.S. economy from the perspective of working families. As with most economic analyses, the focus is

1

on unemployment, jobs, gross domestic product, productivity—the usual set of indicators of interest to those who follow economics.

The analysis does not stop there, and for a very important reason: the living standards of working families depend not only on overall growth, but also on how that growth is distributed. For that reason, every chapter in this book focuses far less on statistical averages than it does on the richly varied set of economic outcomes that can be viewed through the lenses of race, gender, family type, and wage/salary/wealth status. In this regard, the inequality of economic outcomes is of great concern to us, and we pay particular attention to its evolution, both in the distant past and in recent months.

The book's chapters—summarized below—provide a detailed portrait of the economy and its relationship with working Americans and their families. Each chapter provides a history-in-numbers that focuses on incomes, wages, jobs, wealth, poverty, variations between regions, and comparisons with international peers.

Family income: higher inequality leads to uneven progress

The full employment economy of the latter 1990s ushered in a unique period of fast and broadly shared income growth. Not only did middle-income families get ahead over those years, but the least-advantaged families did the best in terms of income growth. From 1995 to 2000, median family income grew at an annual rate of 2.1% for whites, 2.9% for blacks, and 4.6% for Hispanics.

The 2001 recession and subsequent jobless recovery halted these gains. Real median family income fell by over $1,300 (2.4%) from 2000 to 2002 (in 2003 dollars), and the loss of employment opportunities alone explains 80% of the decline in middle-class family incomes over these years. In percentage terms, lower income families took a bigger hit, as incomes at the 20th percentile (where 80% of families have higher incomes) fell 4.2%. Wealthy families also lost ground, as the bursting of a stock market bubble led to large losses in capital gains. Hours of work fell for married-couple families at all income levels, as did their real incomes.

As noted, the broad-based income growth of the latter 1990s was a unique period given income trends over the past 25 years. Prior to that period of full employment, income growth was highly unequal. Between 1979 and 2000, for example, the real income of households in the lowest fifth (the bottom 20% of earners) grew 6.4%, while that of households in the top fifth (the top 20% of earners) grew 70%, with the top 1% achieving real income gains of 184%. In contrast to this unequal pattern of growth, in the 1950s and 1960s, real incomes just about doubled for each income fifth.

The extent to which middle-class incomes have diverged from productivity growth is intimately related to this historical perspective on income inequality. Between 1947 and 1973 productivity and real median family income both grew 104%, a golden age of growth for both variables. Over this era, there could be no doubt that the typical family fully benefited from productivity growth.

Yet starting in the mid-1970s, this lockstep relationship broke down. From 1973 to 2002, median family income grew at about one-third the rate of productivity (22% versus 65%). That is, while faster productivity growth led to a larger economic pie, growing inequality meant that slices were divided up such that some income classes—those at the top of the income scale—claimed most of the income growth.

Thus, there now exists far more income inequality in the United States than has been the case in earlier periods. Some commentators have downplayed this problem by citing supposedly high levels of income mobility, such that those who begin at the low end of the income scale have a strong likelihood of leapfrogging to the top. The evidence, however, contradicts this contention. Of those who started out in the lowest income fifth in the late 1980s, more than half (53%) were still there in the late 1990s, and another 24% had climbed only to the next fifth, meaning that 77% of those who started out in the low end of the income scale remained there a decade later. Furthermore, the rate of mobility has slowed slightly over time. In the 1970s, 49% of families that started out in the bottom fifth were still there 10 years later.

Once all income sources are taken into account, including capital gains, the extent of income concentration at the end of the last business cycle was remarkably high by historical standards. Using newly available income data that goes all the way back to 1913, income in 2000 was only slightly less concentrated among the top 1% of households than during the run-up to the Great Depression, which was the worst period of uneven income concentration in the last century. In 2000, the top 1% held 21.7% of total income, compared to 22.5% in 1929. Chapter 7, which focuses on international comparisons, shows such high levels of inequality to be uniquely American.

Recent regressive changes in federal taxation will further boost income inequality. For households in the top 1% of the income scale, the full tax savings from the cuts that were made from 2001 to 2003 were about $67,000; for middle-income families, the cuts amounted to just under $600; and for the lowest 20%, the savings was $61. The effect of these cuts has thus been to redistribute after-tax income up the income scale, leading to an inequality-exacerbating transfer of 0.8% of total, after-tax household income from the bottom 99% to the top 1%.

Most recently, profits and capital incomes appear to have recovered from their losses in the early years of the decade. Since the first quarter of 2001, virtually all (98.5%) of the real income growth in the corporate sector has accrued to capital income (profits, interest, and dividend payments), a hugely disproportionate share when considering that capital income comprised just 16.3% of the total corporate income when the recession started in early 2001.

Finally, the necessary strategy for income growth for many middle-income families has been to devote more hours to work in the paid labor market than in the past. Largely due to the increased labor supply of wives, married couples with children in the middle-income fifth, for example, were working 500 hours more per year in 2000 than in 1979—the equivalent of 12 and a half more full-time weeks per year. Because of these wives' contributions, instead of growing only 5% in real terms, middle-class family income grew 24%.

Wages: battered by labor slack

Because wages and salaries make up roughly three-fourths of total family income (the proportion is even higher among the broad middle class), wage trends are the primary determinant of income growth and income inequality trends. This chapter examines and explains the trends in wage growth and wage inequality of the last few decades up through 2003, focusing particularly on the current business cycle, from 2000 to 2003, and the earlier cycles over the 1979-89 and 1989-2000 periods. The most recent wage trends, through early 2004, are examined in this book's Introduction.

The wage story of the last few years is mixed. The strong wage growth of the late 1990s continued into 2002, despite the rising unemployment from 2000 to 2002. However, the high and continuous labor slack of the early 2000s eventually knocked down wage growth, lowering the yearly growth of real median hourly wages over the 2000-03 period by 1.0% among women and 1.5% among men. The persistent labor slack affected lower-wage workers even more—knocking yearly wage growth down 1.5% and 2.2%, respectively, among low-wage women and men. The consequence of this high and persistent labor slack has been to reestablish a growing wage inequality between low- and middle-wage workers, a phenomenon not seen since the late 1980s.

The wage story of the past quarter century has three predominant themes. First, an era of stagnant and falling wages gave way to one of strong wage growth. Wages were stagnant overall and median wages fell from the early 1970s to 1995. After 1995, wages changed course, rising strongly in response to persistent low unemployment and the faster productivity growth relative to the 1973-95 period. Second, the pattern of wage growth has shifted. In the 1980s wage inequality widened dramatically and, coupled with stagnant average wages, brought about widespread erosion of real wages. Wage inequality continued its growth in the 1990s but took a different shape: a continued growth in the wage gap between top and middle earners, but a shrinking wage gap between middle and low earners. Since 1999, however, wage inequality has been growing between the top and the middle but has held steady between the middle and the bottom. A third theme is the critical role played by rising unemployment in raising wage inequality and the role played by low unemployment in boosting wage growth overall, but particularly at the bottom.

The trends in average wage growth—the slowdown in the 1970s and the pick-up in the mid-1990s through the early 2000s—can be attributed to corresponding changes in productivity growth. Productivity accelerated in the mid-1990s, and its growth continued into the current recession, leading to historically high growth in average wages. But as Chapter 1 shows, income shifted from labor to capital in the mid-1990s though labor's income shares rebounded in the last few years of the boom. In the 2000-03 period income shifted extremely rapidly and extensively from labor compensation to capital income (profits and interest), so the benefits of faster productivity growth went disproportionately, in fact completely, to capital (see the Introduction).

Explaining the shifts in wage inequality requires attention to several factors that affect low-, middle-, and high-wage workers differently. The experience of the late 1990s should remind us of the great extent to which a low unemployment rate benefits workers, especially low-wage earners. Correspondingly, the high levels of unemployment in the early and mid-1980s and in recent years disempowered wage earners and provided the context in which other forces—specifically, a weakening of labor market institutions and globalization—could drive up wage inequality. Significant shifts in the labor market, such as the weakening of unions and the severe drop in the real value of the minimum wage, can explain one-third of the growing wage inequality. Similarly, the increasing globalization of the economy—specifically with regard to immigration, trade, and capital mobility—and the employment shift toward lower-paying service industries (such as retail trade) and away from manufacturing can explain, in combination, another third of the total growth in wage inequality. Macroeconomic factors also played an important role: as high unemployment in the early 1980s greatly increased wage inequality, the low unemployment of the late 1990s reduced it. High unemployment has renewed growing wage inequality since 2000.

The shape of wage inequality shifted in the late 1980s as the gap at the bottom—i.e., the 50/10 gap between middle-wage workers at the 50th percen-

5

tile and low-wage workers at the 10th—began to shrink. However, over the last few years, this progress against wage inequality at the bottom has been halted among men, and wage inequality among women has resumed its growth. This reversal partially results from the rise in unemployment and is partially due to the continued drop in the real value of the minimum wage. The greatest increase in wage inequality at the bottom occurred among women and corresponded to the fall in the minimum wage over the 1980s, the high unemployment of the early 1980s, and the expansion of low-wage retail jobs. The positive trend in the wage gap over the 1990s owes much to increases in the minimum wage, low unemployment, and the slight, relative contraction in low-paying retail jobs in the late 1990s. The wage gap at the top—the 95/50 gap between high- and middle-wage earners—continued its steady growth in the 1990s and early 2000s but at a slightly slower pace than in the 1980s. The continuing influence of globalization, de-unionization, and the shift to lower-paying service industries ("industry shifts") can explain the continued growth of wage inequality at the top.

There is a popular notion that the growth of wage inequality reflects primarily a technology-driven increase in demand for "educated" or "skilled" workers. Yet economists have found that the overall impact of technology on the wage and employment structure was no greater in the 1980s or 1990s than in the 1970s. Moreover, skill demand and technology have little relationship to the growth of wage inequality within the same group (i.e., workers with similar levels of experience and education), and this within-group inequality was responsible for half of the overall growth of wage inequality in the 1980s and 1990s. Technology has been and continues to be an important force, but there was no "technology shock" in the 1980s or 1990s and no ensuing demand for "skill" that was not satisfied by the continuing expansion of the educational attainment of the workforce.

The conventional story about technology leading to increased demand for skills and the erosion of wages among the less-skilled does not readily explain the pattern of growth in wage inequality. In particular, the late 1990s are seen as a period of rapid technological change, yet during that period wage inequality diminished at the bottom. Similarly, education differentials grew slowly during most of the 1990s and declined in the early 2000s, a trend incompatible with rapid technological change driving up demand for skills. The decline in the wage payoff for experience in the later 1990s also runs counter to the technology story. Moreover, it was the growth of wage inequality among workers of similar education and experience, not easily linked to technology, which accounted for all of the wage inequality growth since 1995.

Despite the strong wage improvements starting in 1995, it was not until 1997 that the wage level for middle-wage workers (the median hourly wage) jumped above its 1979 level. Wage growth was very strong in the late 1990s, a period of broad-based wage growth (for the first time in several decades) that resulted from faster productivity and persistent low unemployment.

As for benefit coverage, it declined through the early 2000s. In contrast, in the 1990s, there were modest extensions of employer-provided health insurance coverage for the bottom 20%, while erosion of coverage continued for middle- and high-wage workers. Health insurance coverage declined for all wage groups in the 2000-02 period. After rising over the 1990s, pension coverage receded in the 2000-02 recession, leaving overall pension coverage at only 45.5%, or 5.1 percentage points less than the 50.6% coverage of 1979. In other words, less than half the workforce is covered by employer-provided pensions.

Unionized workers earn higher wages, as is well known, but it is also true that they enjoy a premium in every dimension of the compensation package. Unionized workers are 28.2% more likely to be covered by employer-provided health insurance. Unionized employers also provide better health insurance—they pay an 11.1% higher share of single-worker coverage and a 15.6% higher share of family coverage. Moreover, deductibles are $54, or 18.0%, less for union workers. Finally, union workers are 24.4% more likely to receive health insurance coverage in their retirement.

The rising trade deficit was responsible for a major loss of jobs in the 1990s, especially in manufacturing (over 4 million jobs lost between 1989 and 2002). The trade impact over the last 10 years was more evenly spread over the workforce, affecting college and other workers in rough proportions to their share of the workforce. The issue of the offshoring of white-collar technical and professional jobs to low-wage countries has become prominent. Though hard data on these trends are not available, information in software and other industries suggests that these trends are not trivial.

As the wage of the typical worker fell in the early 1990s and rose in the latter 1990s, executive pay soared. From 1989 to 2000, the wage of the median chief executive officer grew 79.0%, and average compensation grew 342%. CEO compensation, however, declined 36.0% between 2000 and 2003, reflecting the fall in stock values and the value of stock options available to CEOs. This decline affected only the very highest paid CEOs, as those at the median and the 25th and 75th percentiles saw increases (16.1% at the median). Nevertheless, CEOs in 2003 still made 185 times as much as a typical worker, whereas in 1965, CEOs made 26 times more than a typical worker. This level of executive pay is a distinctly American phenomenon: U.S. CEOs make three times as much as their counterparts abroad.

7

The jobs of the future will not be far different than the current jobs available. The change in occupation mix will raise annual wages by just 1% over 10 years. Future jobs will require more education credentials but not to any great extent. The occupational composition of jobs in 2012 will require that 27.9% of the workforce have at least a college degree, just one percentage point more than the 26.9% of workers who held college degrees in 2002.

Jobs: persistent jobless recovery follows 2001 recession

The 2001 recession and subsequent prolonged weak recovery brought an end to an expansion that proved historically unique in the extent to which it lifted the economic prospects of American workers. Employment opportunities increased considerably during the tight labor market of the 1990s, especially for traditionally disadvantaged groups, including women, African Americans, and Hispanics. Overall, low unemployment over the second half of the 1990s strengthened workers' bargaining power as many employers had to compete for workers. This in turn spurred strong wage and income gains over the latter half of the 1990s economic boom.

March 2001 marked the official beginning of the last recession, initiating a time of higher unemployment and labor slack that resulted in a substantial amount of underutilized labor. While the unemployment rate was low relative to past recessions, the rate continued to increase two years after the recovery began. In March 2001 the unemployment rate was 4.3%; it trended upward until June 2003 when it reached 6.3%, and it was most recently (June 2004) 5.6%. From December 2003 until June 2004, the unemployment rate has been at an unyielding 5.6% or 5.7%.

Due to the lack of job opportunities, many potential job seekers left the labor market over this period, and were hence not counted in the unemployment rate. Thus, throughout the recession and jobless recovery, there was a persistent decrease in the share of the adult population working or looking for work (known as the labor force participation rate). In March 2001 the labor force participation rate was 67.1%. It trended downward until it hit 65.9% in February 2004—a 15-year low—and it was 66.0% by mid-2004. Factoring in the decreased labor force participation rate and assuming these workers would have been unemployed had they been in the labor force, the unemployment rate would currently be 7.2%—substantially higher than the official 5.6% rate.

The lack of job creation has been unprecedented in this latest recovery—which is why the recovery was deemed a "jobless" one. A jobless recovery occurs when an economy begins to expand (as defined by the National Bureau of Economic Research) but businesses continue to shed jobs as if the economy were still in recession. During the 2001 recession, the economy lost 1.6 million nonfarm payroll jobs. A severe jobless recovery, during which an additional 870,000 jobs were lost, followed the recession and lasted 21 months (November 2001 until August 2003). In June 2004 (the most recent data available) the economy was still down 1.2 million jobs from the March 2001 peak—an unparalleled occurrence this far into a recovery.

The 2001 downturn, as usual, disproportionately affected minorities and workers with less education: in 2001 African Americans had an unemployment rate of 8.7%, compared to the overall average of 4.8%. However, the 2001 downturn also adversely affected other groups usually thought to have some protection against recessions. For example, the employment to population ratio for young college graduates hit a 30-year low during the recovery. The recession and its aftermath affected a broadly diverse contingent of workers: young and old, less educated to highly educated, laborers to professionals. Manufacturing jobs were lost for a record 41 consecutive months. However, significant job loss occurred in other occupations, such as the information technology sector. The stock market bubble burst in 2000, which left many white-collar workers unemployed. In addition, firms' demand for offshoring is increasing. Technological advancements coupled with a supply shock of skilled labor that resulted from the opening up of global labor markets have made this labor practice possible.

The lack of job creation has led to unemployment spells that are much longer than would be expected given the level of unemployment. In 2003, when unemployment was 6.1%, long-term unemployment (i.e., unemployment lasting 27 or more weeks) and the average duration of unemployment spells were at levels historically associated with much higher levels of unemployment. In 2003, for example, the share of long-term unemployed as a percent of total unemployment was 22.1%—the highest since 1983, when the unemployment rate was 9.9%. In addition, the problem of long jobless spells was broad-based, as the number of college-educated workers unemployed for long periods increased by 300% from 2001 to 2003.

Despite the return of job growth in September 2003, the labor market as of mid-2004 remains slack, and the benefits that accompanied the tight labor market of the 1990s remain elusive. As we stress in the Introduction that follows, this persistent weakness has led much of the growth that has occurred over the jobless recovery to flow to profits, leaving little for compensation. Whether we soon return to a more equitable job market remains an open question.

Wealth: persistent inequality

The income data examined in Chapter 1 represent the flow of family's economic resources. Wealth, however, is the stock of a family's income and assets, minus their debt. Its distribution is highly unequal in the United States, far more so than income. For example, in 2001 (the most recent data available) the wealthiest 1% of all households controlled over 33% of national wealth, while the bottom 80% of households held only 16%. The share of average wealth by wealth class shows that wealth inequality is stark and persistent. This skewed distribution is, in part, perpetuated by the passing of wealth from generation to generation. The level of wealth a family acquires is, to a large degree, determined by where it starts on the wealth ladder. Wealth determines how adequately a household can smooth consumption when financial emergencies arise. Those with little wealth can be financially devastated by any economic setback. It is a difficult challenge for middle- and lower-income families to accumulate ample wealth.

Some debt can be acquired for a worthy cause such as home ownership (mortgage debt) or school loans, but such debt can be hard to acquire for those who presumably have the greatest needs for such loans. Other types of debt, such as the use of high-interest-bearing credit cards, can be much more problematic—especially when balances accrue to meet day-to-day living expenses.

Several key features about American wealth stand out. For example, 17.6% of households had zero or negative net wealth in 2001. There are vast differences when race is factored in; for instance, 13.1% of white households versus 30.9% of African American households have zero or negative net wealth. Median wealth for African Americans was $10,700 in 2001, just 10% of the corresponding median for whites.

The ownership of stocks is particularly unequal. Given the increases in stock ownership over the last decade, along with the boom of the 1990s, it may be surprising that roughly half of Americans still do not participate in the stock market, either directly or indirectly through the likes of mutual funds. The top 1% of stockowners held 33.6% of all stocks, by value, while the bottom 80% of stockholders owned just 10.7% of total stock value in 2001. On average, the wealthiest 1% of households owned $3.5 million in stocks, while the bottom 40% of households owned an average of $1,800 in stocks. While 48.1% of households had no stock investment, another 11.8% had less than $5,000 of stock, leaving only 40.1% of all households with $5,000 or more in stock assets.

It follows, then, that the wealthiest households gain the most from the growth in the stock market. From 1989 to 2001, the top 10% of wealth holders reaped 74.9% of the growth in stocks, while the bottom 80% received 11.1%.

Home ownership—the most important source of assets for most American families—continued the upward trend that started in 1994, especially among nonwhite households. In 1994 the rate of home ownership was 64%, and it increased to 68.3% in 2003. However, home ownership rates vary considerably by income and race. Only 50.9% of those in the bottom quarter of the income distribution owned their homes in 2001, while 88% in the top quarter of the income distribution owned homes. Blacks and Hispanics, while slowly increasing home ownership rates, still lag behind whites. In 2003, 72.1%, 48.1%, and 46.7% of whites, blacks, and Hispanics, respectively, owned homes. There is a lot of room for improvement in home ownership rates for racial minorities and those at the bottom of the income distribution.

The aftermath of the 1990s boom left most Americans better prepared for retirement than before: in 2001, almost three out of four Americans will be able to replace at least half of their pre-retirement income with income from Social Security, pensions, and defined-contribution plans. This was a marked improvement from 1998, when 57.5% could expect to replace half of their current income in retirement. It will be interesting to see if this improvement will hold up in the 2004 survey.

Household debt as a share of assets was, on average, 18% in 2003. As expected, debt burdens continued to plague lower-income families disproportionately, although debt burdens for the typical household decreased slightly. By 2001, middle-income families had a slight increase in debt, but experienced larger increases in stocks, assets, and overall net worth. Conversely, the most recent government data show that 16% of households in the $20,000-$39,999 range had debt-service obligations that exceeded 40% of their income, while 11.7% of these households had at least one bill that was more than 60 days past due. Moreover, the official report of debt by the Federal Reserve Board has undoubtedly understated serious financial hardships—akin to debt—incurred by households with high levels of financial insecurity. These households increasingly access loans and money through nontraditional or predatory lending institutions such as pawn shops and check-cashing centers. Additionally, despite the robust state of the economy, personal bankruptcy rates reached all-time highs in 2001. Next year, the Federal Reserve Board's Survey of Consumer Finances will release data from its 2004 survey, at which time we will be able to determine the longer-term impact that the stock market crash of 2000 had on household finances.

Poverty: rising in this business cycle

While America is the richest of the industrialized nations, it has always, to a greater or lesser degree over time, suffered the problem of poverty amidst prosperity. In recent decades, the growth of inequality has meant that much of the economic growth that did occur was channeled to higher income families, while incomes at the bottom stagnated. For example, the official poverty rate—the share of Americans living in households with incomes below the federal poverty threshold—was about the same in 1973 (11.1%) as in 2000 (11.3%), despite the fact that real per capita income grew 66% over that period.

To some, the fact that a bit more than one-tenth of Americans—12.1%, or 34.6 million persons in 2002—face material deprivation may be disheartening, but not particularly alarming. Yet, like many other poverty analysts, we strongly believe that the official poverty statistics underestimate the extent of material hardship in America. The thresholds used to determine poverty status, critiqued in detail below, were developed half a century ago, and they have only been updated for inflation. In 2003, for example, a single parent with two children is considered poor if the family income (before taxes but counting cash transfers like welfare benefits) is below $14,824; for two parents with two children, the income threshold is $18,660.

Various alternative measures are used in this chapter to expand the scope of poverty analysis. One useful measure simply doubles the poverty thresholds. This seems arbitrary—if the official thresholds are so inferior, what is gained by simply doubling them? In fact, the Economic Policy Institute's own work on family budgets reveals that twice the poverty threshold corresponds quite closely to more rigorously defined measures of a family's ability to meet its basic needs. These family budget thresholds are developed by adding up the costs of basic consumption components, including food, shelter, clothing, health care, taxes, and child care.

Regardless of the metric, a few trends clearly emerge. First, after making impressive progress against poverty in the 1960s, the trend stalled and then generally drifted up from the early 1970s to the mid-1990s. The 1995-2000 period was one of dramatic progress, as poverty fell by 2.5 percentage points, and twice-poverty by 4.3 points (corresponding to 4.8 million fewer poor and 8.6 million fewer twice-poor persons). The 2001 recession and jobless recovery partially reversed these gains.

As is always the case in a recession, the ranks of the poor and near-poor expanded in the recent downturn, as poverty rates rose from 11.3% in 2000 to 12.1% in 2002, while twice-poverty rates went from 29.3% to 30.5%. These rate increases translate into about 3 million more officially poor, and 6 million more near-poor over this two-year period. In addition, this chapter examines the extent to which the safety net helped to catch those economically vulnerable families hurt by the recession. Focusing on low-income single-mother families, for example, shows that welfare benefits—which fell steeply throughout the latter 1990s—continued to slide in the recession, thus failing to play their historical countercyclical role. Furthermore, the slowing economy led to a significant reduction in the hours worked by these women, and that, in turn, led to lower earnings and less income from the Earned Income Tax Credit (EITC), a generous wage-subsidy that is key to lifting the incomes of low-income working families. In this regard, the safety net is less countercyclical than it used to be for some groups of poor and near-poor persons (a related finding is that the EITC fails to reach many families between the one and two-times poverty range).

Taking a longer-term view, this chapter examines which factors might best explain the lack of progress in reducing poverty over the past 30 years. The growth of inequality and weak low-wage labor markets have certainly played primary roles. Throughout the 1980s, when poverty rates were particularly unresponsive to growth, the effect of inequality was to drive poverty up by 2.9 percentage points (poverty rose 1.1 points over the decade because other factors, such as the improved education of low-income family heads, offset the inequality effect). That effect was significantly dampened in the 1990s, but as the economy moved into the next business cycle, growing inequality appears poised to return, creating potentially strong headwinds against poverty reduction.

Another factor implicated in much research on this topic is the increase in mother-only families. This view emphasizes the increase in the share of such families since at any given point in time, they have considerably lower income and higher poverty rates than families with two earners. Although this argument may have some merit, the upward pressure on poverty rates by the formation of single-parent families has diminished considerably over time, while the economic determinants—growth, inequality, and unemployment—have, if anything, grown more important. Over the 1970s, for example, had all else remained constant, the shift to more mother-only families would have contributed two percentage points to the poverty rate according to our decomposition of these trends (in fact, poverty fell slightly over the decade). But the effect fell steeply after that, and by the 1990s, this factor contributed only 0.3 points to higher poverty.

Given the policy shift emphasizing work as the primary pathway out of poverty, this chapter focuses closely on the opportunities in the low-wage labor market. In the latter 1990s, fast productivity growth combined with low unemployment to give a significant boost to the earnings of low-wage workers. In fact, by comparing a few different time periods, it is clear that, by itself, fast economic growth is unlikely to move the wages of the lowest-paid workers. In the last five years of the 1980s business cycle, productivity grew 1.5% per year, but average unemployment was a high 6.4%. As a result of a labor market too slack to ensure low-wage growth, the real wages of low-paid workers barely budged, and poverty rates were largely unresponsive to growth. Over the last five years of the 1990s business cycle, productivity grew a point faster per year (2.5%), and, equally important, average unemployment was 4.8%. Under these conditions, 20th percentile real wages grew as employers needed to bid even low wages up to get and keep the workers they needed to meet strong demand in these years. In fact, low wages grew at almost the rate of productivity, an unprecedented trend over the last 30 years, and poverty rates fell more quickly than they had in decades.

The most recent trends of low wages corroborate the view that fast productivity growth alone will not suffice to fuel the growth of low wages. Between 2001 and 2003, productivity grew far more quickly than in the earlier periods mentioned above. Yet unemployment was high, on average, compared to the latter half of the 1990s. Under these conditions, the extra income generated by the fast growth of productivity did not flow to low-wage workers, as earnings at the 20th percentile slowed to 0.5% per year.

Thus, it is reasonable to conclude that it takes a combination of fast growth and very low unemployment to ensure that the benefits of growth are distributed broadly enough to connect the fortunes of the poor with those of the rest of working America. At the same time, we need to be mindful of the historically important role of an effective safety net in a dynamic economy like that of the United States, with business cycle downturns that can do great damage to the living standards of the most economically vulnerable among us.

Regions: labor market slump widespread in most states

While much of this book focuses on information of national scope, this chapter examines the state of the economy in each of the nation's regions, Census divisions (groups of states within regions), and individual states. A regional focus is important because, in many ways, state or regional data more accurately represent the economy faced by workers in a particular area than do broad national data.

This chapter focuses on what happened to state labor markets between 2001 and 2003, a period of weak labor markets in nearly every state. Two years after the recession's official end in November 2001, job growth was worse in

39 states. By 2003, 36 states—spread out in every region and division of the country—had fewer jobs than they did three years earlier.

The manufacturing sector was a key factor in the recession and jobless recovery: making up 13.1% of jobs in 2000, this industry lost 15.9% of its jobs in the next three years, compared to slight job *growth* of 0.8% in the other industries combined. Furthermore, 21 of the 36 states that had fewer jobs in 2003 than in 2000 experienced job growth outside of manufacturing. For example, while Arkansas lost 14.2% of its manufacturing jobs, all other industries grew by 2.1%.

As of mid-2004, the national labor market had finally started to show signs of recovery. While this was welcome news, it comes three years after the recession started and over two years after the economy purportedly entered the recovery. For many states, it will take numerous consecutive months of robust job growth to return to the employment levels of three years ago.

Not surprisingly, the recession and jobless recovery led to increased unemployment. From 2000 to 2001 the unemployment rate of 16 states rose by one percentage point or more, mostly in those states affected strongly by manufacturing losses, including North Carolina, Michigan, Oregon, and Washington. By 2003, all but nine states had unemployment rates of one percentage point or more above their 2000 rates.

Long-term unemployment rose considerably in every state except Hawaii and Delaware between 2000 and 2003. For example, in Georgia, where the 2003 unemployment rate was lower than the national average (4.7% compared to 6.0% nationally), the share of unemployed workers that had been unemployed for more than half a year rose from 7.6% in 2000 to 27.7% in 2003.

A weak labor market affects the living standards of working families directly when workers lose jobs or are unable to find work that pays well and offers enough hours and benefits. Another effect of high unemployment is that workers have less bargaining power and wage growth can either decline or disappear. After rising at an annual rate of 2.3% from 1995 to 2000, the growth in low wages slowed to less than 1% annually from 2000 to 2003.

The federal minimum wage has not been raised since 1997. Once again, some states have stepped in and raised their own state-level minimum wage rates. The number of states with higher minimum wages has more than doubled, from five in 1997 to 13 in 2004. The wage levels set by these states range from $5.50 in Illinois to $7.16 in Washington state.

The contrast between the economy of the late 1990s and that of the last three years was sharp in most states. Expanding payrolls, full employment, and strong, broad-based wage growth were replaced by fewer jobs, higher unemployment, and stagnating wages. A state-by-state analysis of labor markets reveals that the recent slump has been uniquely geographically pervasive, but that the plight of the manufacturing sector has been a central factor in states with the most severe job losses: while most states' economies have suffered in the last three years, states with heavy reliance on manufacturing have generally done worse.

International: beyond the U.S. model

In this chapter, the economic performance of the United States is compared to that of 19 other rich, industrialized countries that, like the United States, belong to the Organization for Economic Cooperation and Development (OECD). This analysis—which compares the U.S. economy with similar economies facing the same global conditions with respect to trade, investment, technology, and the environment—provides an independent yardstick for gauging the strengths and weaknesses of the U.S. economy.

In 2002, per capital income in the United States ($36,102) was greater than that of all 19 other OECD countries ($26,680 on average). However, the gap has been closing, as annual growth rates in per capita income are, on average, higher in the other OECD countries (0.9%) compared to the United States (0.4%) between 2000 and 2002.

OECD countries are also catching up and surpassing the United States in output per hour worked. In 1950, the average of the other OECD countries output per hour was only 41% of the U.S. average; in 2002, the average was 88%. Additionally, the U.S. is no longer a leader in this category, as seven other countries have surpassed the United States in terms of output.

Inequality has been and continues to be a mainstay of the U.S. economic model. Measuring the gap between the richest and poorest workers in each country, U.S. households at the 90th percentile had incomes that were 5.5 times that of those at the 10th percentile. The United States had the largest gap of all the OECD countries. The United States also reported the largest Gini coefficient (0.368), which is another measure of within-country inequality.

Supporters of the U.S. economic model generally acknowledge the relative inequality in the United States but argue that the model provides greater mobility, greater employment opportunities, and greater dynamism than do more "interventionist" economies. The evidence, however, provides little support for this view. First, there was less mobility out of poverty in the United States than in other nations. The U.S. percentage of people who were "always poor" is 9.5%, the highest reported figure for any OECD country. One of the most disturbing statistics is the rate of childhood poverty in the United States: 21.9% of U.S. children lived in households that faced severe financial distress, which was again the highest percentage for any country in this analysis. Poverty was deeper and harder to escape in the United States and much less in the way of adequate social policy was available relative to other OECD countries. Social expenditures in the United States, as a percentage of gross domestic product, were the lowest for any country.

The evidence in this chapter underscores the diversity of international experience in providing wage, income, and employment security. Many OECD countries have economic and social policies that differ from those in the United States and that have not been detrimental to their productivity levels. In fact, in many cases, these alternative policies have been pursued in economies with productivity levels that surpass U.S. levels. Such findings suggest that those formulating policy—in both the United States and abroad—may benefit from looking beyond the U.S. model.

Conclusion

The analyses to be found throughout this edition of *The State of Working America* shed light on the economic conditions facing working families in America today. The lessons are not hard to derive: the U.S. economy is capable of generating tremendous wealth, but there is absolutely no guarantee that this wealth will reach the working families responsible for its growth. In fact, as this book goes to press, the U.S. economy has been consistently expanding for years, yet real wages of the middle-class working Americans have been falling, and virtually all of the growth that has occurred has flowed to profits, not to labor.

Thus, a central goal of this analysis is to identify the necessary and sufficient conditions needed to ensure that economic growth is broadly shared. We have many facts at our disposal, and these are useful in their own right, painting a detailed picture of both the historical and prevailing economic conditions facing working families. But the many tables and figures that follow are also instructive in pointing toward a better economy, one that lifts the living standards of all working Americans.

Introduction: an economy at the crossroads

The persistent weakness of the current recovery

When the previous edition of this book was written in the summer of 2002, the recovery that had begun in late 2001 did not appear to be particularly promising from the perspective of working families. At that point, we had observed that, although the economy was expanding, "the unemployment rate remained well above its level of a few years back, job growth was virtually zero, wage growth was slowing, and the share of the long-term unemployed was hitting historically high rates....early signs indicate a return to the pattern of widening wage inequality seen in the 1980s."

Remarkably, two years later, and after hundreds of billions spent on poorly targeted fiscal stimulus, all those problems remain. A welcome exception is that, by September 2003, employment growth finally got underway. Nevertheless, one critical trend has worsened—the wage growth of many workers has continued to slow and is now falling behind inflation.

Due largely to the decline in employment opportunities over the jobless recovery, the real income of the median family fell in 2002 for the second consecutive year and is down 2.4% from 2000. Based on the fact that unemployment rose in 2003—job growth only appeared in the last third of the year—and wage growth slowed, it is likely that the real median income fell again (or rose only slightly) in 2003. Poverty rates also rose from 2000 to 2002 by 0.8 percentage points, adding three million more to the ranks of the poor; this indicator also may have worsened in 2003.

Unfortunately, there still remains considerable slack in the labor market even though the recovery, which started in November 2001, is nearly three years old. The 5.6% unemployment rate in June 2004 was precisely the same as when the recovery got underway. The unemployment rate, however, has been a particularly poor barometer of labor slack in this business cycle because it has not reflected the employment losses and the millions of workers who are missing altogether from the labor force. The share of the population employed, a reliable indicator of the strength of a labor market, was 62.3% in June 2004, 2.0 points below its level of 64.3% at the peak of the last business cycle in March 2001.

Even with the recent job gains, long-term unemployment remains high by historical standards—and not just for those usually hurt by weak labor markets, such as minorities and those with lower-education levels, but also for college-educated workers. The unemployment rate among computer programmers was 7.6% in the first half of the year, and the employment rate of young college graduates remained near historic lows. Less-advantaged workers have also felt the brunt of the lagging recovery, with African American unemployment at 10.1% in June 2004, slightly higher than at the start of the recovery (9.8% in November 2001). As we highlight below, this persistent weakness in the job market has led to substantially slower wage growth, and real hourly wages (that is, wages adjusted for inflation) in June 2004 that were 1.2% below their year-ago level.

The upside in the economy is that job growth appears to have returned in earnest, with gains of over 200,000 per month through the first half of 2004. As a result, many economic commentators assure the public that various "lags" are in play, and that the recovery will soon reach down and lift the living standards of middle- and working-class families. The last edition of this book cited similar frequently made assurances ("The fundamentals are all in place" was the mantra in mid-2002). We hope, of course, that this prediction will soon bear out.

Yet as of this writing, 31 months into the recovery, the U.S. economy remains more than one million jobs below the last employment peak. By this time in every other recovery on record (going back to 1939) we had surpassed, usually far surpassed, the prior employment peak. This jobs deficit is the primary reason that, after over two-and-a-half years of consistent economic expansion and stellar productivity growth, many working families are either worse off or about where they were at the end of the last business cycle in March 2001.

This introduction presents an overview of the facts that make up the material explored in careful detail throughout the next seven chapters. Here, the goal is to marshal a choice few indicators and trends that best describe how the recovery has evolved from the perspective of working families. These last few years have been a very unique period, one that deserves close scrutiny, particularly because it is not clear at what point the growing economy will begin to lift the living standards of working families, as it did in the latter 1990s.

Looking to the future, the critical question is whether this business cycle will resemble the second half of the 1990s, when full employment ensured that the benefits of fast productivity growth were broadly shared, driving wages up strongly throughout the wage scale, lifting middle and low-incomes, and driving down poverty rates, most strongly among the least advantaged? Or, is the stage set for another period like that of the 1980s, of unbalanced growth, high budget deficits, high average unemployment, stagnant wage growth for many, and increasing inequality?

Labor market slack in the aftermath of the jobless recovery

The labor market shed jobs from the official end of the downturn in November 2001 until September 2003. Although the U.S. economy has had a few strong months in 2004, the overall job growth during the last 10 months has been modest and has yet to significantly diminish the slack in the job market. This "labor slack" remains at the heart of the economic challenges facing working families today. In earlier periods, like the latter 1990s or the 1950s and 1960s, tight labor markets in tandem with strong labor market institutions (such as unions and higher real minimum wages) served as a conduit through which the benefits of growth were broadly shared. Unfortunately, labor market institutions have been weakened over time, which is one of the reasons why the wedge of economic inequality grew so quickly in the 1980s and early 1990s. Thus, at this point, many working families depend more on tight labor markets to raise their living standards.

The importance of tight labor markets is by no means simply about low unemployment and enough job vacancies to meet the needs of job seekers. It is also about creating the conditions that lead employers to increase compensation in order to get and keep the workers they need. As shown in Chapter 1 (see, for example, Figure 1K), such conditions are historically associated with far more evenly spread income growth than occurs in weaker periods. One reason for this positive dynamic is the virtuous cycle engendered by wage-led demand growth, wherein broad-based income gains generate equally broad consumption, triggering greater confidence among investors and producers. This confidence in turn feeds greater investment and sustains further growth. At the same time, these growing incomes boost government coffers, leading to a better fiscal position and other associated benefits, from reassuring financial markets to providing government with more resources to meet social needs.

FIGURE A Percent change in employment 39 months after business cycle peak

Source: Authors' analysis of BLS (2004d).

These conditions are uniformly absent from the present economic environment. Starting with the current jobs deficit, **Figure A** compares the trend in employment growth in this business cycle to the average of all the others (the values are indexed to the peak of the prior cycle, and thus show percent changes), with the early 1990s jobless recovery plotted separately to facilitate a comparison with the current cycle. In the past, employment regained its prior peak by about 20 months past the onset of recession; in the early 1990s jobless recovery, it took 30 months. In the case of the current recovery, 39 months past the peak the U.S. economy remained 1.2 million (0.9%) jobs below the employment level in March 2001. The emergent trend in job growth toward the end of Figure A is clear enough that, if it persists, will soon regain the peak. But in historical terms, the depth of this jobless recovery has been unique.

It should be noted that Figure A tracks net job gains, that is, the difference between the jobs lost and added throughout the labor market. In that regard, this indicator masks the underlying dynamics of job creation, which have had a distinctive characteristic in recent years that is critical to understanding the unusually weak employment performance over this recovery: the lack of job gains. **Figure B** shows total job gains and losses (the difference between the

FIGURE B   Gross job gains and gross job losses, 1990-2003

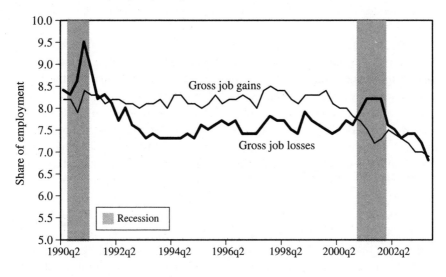

Source: Faberman (2004).

two is net job gains or losses) since 1990. In the early 1990s downturn—and other evidence suggests that this is the usual dynamic—the main factor leading to net job losses is a sharp spike in gross job losses surrounded by fairly steadily paced period of job gains. As the recovery ensues, the gross losses subside and net job growth prevails.

This time, however, the pace of job gains declined through the recession and continued to trend sharply downward throughout the first few years of recovery. Clearly, employers were able to meet the demands for the goods and services they produce and sell without creating many new jobs. Most commentators have attributed this trend to the faster productivity growth that occurred over the period, but this explanation is not particularly informative because growing output in a period of net job losses mechanically amounts to faster productivity growth. In addition, productivity usually grows quickly as a recovery gets underway (though it grew faster this time), but demand usually picks up quickly, too, triggering the virtuous cycle noted earlier. This cycle did not occur this time around, in part due to the absence of wage-led demand growth.

Yet throughout this period of weak job creation and, until recently, net job losses, the unemployment rate stayed relatively low in historical terms, rising as high as 6.3% before falling to 5.6% in June 2004. The level of the unemployment rate, however, belies the extent of remaining labor slack. **Table 1** presents a range of indicators that tell this story.

First, the unemployment rate of 5.6% is 1.3 percentage points above the rate at the start of the recession. So, recent unemployment, though "historically low," is significantly higher than the low rates achieved at the end of the 1990s boom (unemployment bottomed out at 4.0% in 2000). Furthermore, a broader measure of underemployment—which includes unemployment plus involuntary part-time work (people wanting full-time but holding part-time jobs), discouraged job seekers, and those marginally attached to the job market (i.e., those who have looked for work in the last year but are not counted as "officially" unemployed)—has increased since the recession started by 2.3 percentage points to 9.6%.

In addition to the rise of unemployment, there has been an unusually large 2.0 percentage-point erosion in the share of the workforce employed (i.e., the employment rate) since March 2001. The share of the working-age population in the labor force has shrunk since the recession started (and not grown at all in the recovery), a reflection of workers dropping out of the labor force or failing to enter because of disappointing job prospects. As shown in Chapter 3, there is a missing labor force of 2.5 million workers, a facet of labor market slack not captured by the unemployment rate. Had these labor force absentees instead been job seekers, the unemployment rate would have surpassed 7.0% by the middle of 2004.

Finally, another labor market indicator that points up the labor market's current weakness is the increase in the share of the long-term unemployed (i.e., those unemployed that have been looking for work for at least six months). This kind of difficulty in finding work runs counter to expectations during a period of low unemployment (by historical standards).

Labor slack's effect on wages and incomes

High unemployment and extensive labor slack adversely affect family income and cause greater inequality. Chapter 1 shows that middle-class family incomes fell 2.2% from 2000 to 2002. Most of the decline was due to lower annual earnings (2.1% of the 2.2% decline), which is not surprising since most of the income of a middle-class family comes from labor market earnings. The decline in annual earnings, in turn, arose from fewer hours worked in the family (as the result of unemployment and cutbacks in weeks worked and hours worked per week). However, the wages earned per hour fell 0.3%, further contributing to this overall income loss.

TABLE 1 Labor market indicators since the recession and recovery began

Indicator	Beginning of:		Latest month, June 2004	Change since recession began March 2001 to June 2004	Change since recovery began November 2001 to June 2004
	Recession, March 2001	Recovery, November 2001			
Payroll employment (thousands)					
Total	132,507	130,871	131,301	-1,206 [-0.9%]	430 [0.3%]
Private sector	111,564	109,535	109,762	-1,802 [-1.6%]	227 [0.2%]
Government	20,943	21,336	21,539	596 [2.8%]	203 [1.0%]
Unemployment					
All	4.3%	5.6%	5.6%	1.3	0.0
Men	4.3	5.7	5.6	1.3	-0.1
Women	4.2	5.4	5.6	1.4	0.2
Underemployment					
All	7.3%	9.4%	9.6%	2.3	0.2
Employment rate					
All	64.3%	63.0%	62.3%	-2.0	-0.7
Men	71.4	70.0	69.2	-2.2	-0.8
Women	57.7	56.6	55.9	-1.8	-0.7
Labor force participation rate					
All	67.1%	66.7%	66.0%	-1.1	-0.7
Men	74.6	74.3	73.3	-1.3	-1.0
Women	60.2	59.8	59.2	-1.0	-0.6
Share long-term unemployed*					
All	11.2%	14.0%	23.9%	12.7	9.9

* Share of the unemployed who were jobless for at least 27 weeks.

Source: Authors' analysis of BLS data.

Although low inflation and the momentum of the full-employment economy kept real wages rising through the early part of the recession, the growing labor market slack eventually retarded wage growth. This is illustrated in **Table 2,** which shows the inflation-adjusted annualized growth in wages in the final two years of the 1990s recovery, from 1998 to 2000, and compares that to the wage growth from 2002 to 2003. The table presents trends for workers with low, middle, high and very high wages among both men and women. Because labor

TABLE 2 Deceleration of wage growth in 2003

| Wage level* | Inflation-adjusted hourly wage growth | | Deceleration |
	1998-2000**	2003	
Men			
Low	1.0%	0.1%	-0.8%
Middle	1.6	-0.9	-2.5
High	1.8	0.2	-1.6
Very high	2.8	0.5	-2.3
Women			
Low	2.0%	-0.2%	-2.1%
Middle	1.5	0.2	-1.3
High	1.1	-0.1	-1.2
Very high	2.1	1.3	-0.7
Inflation	2.7%	2.3%	-0.4%
Productivity	2.8%	4.4%	1.6%

*   Wage levels correspond to the 20th, 50th, 80th, and 95th percentiles.
** Average annual growth from 1998 to 2000.

Source: Authors' analysis of CPS and BLS data.

slack and unemployment was much greater in the early 2000s through 2003, wages grew substantially slower (roughly one to two percentage points slower in 2003) than in the 1998-2000 period. The result was that wages were essentially stagnant or falling for low-, middle-, and high-wage earners in 2003, among both men and women; only very high earners enjoyed real wage growth in 2003. This slower wage growth for most workers came about despite faster productivity (up 1.6 percentage points from 2.8% to a very high 4.4%) and subdued inflation (down to 2.3% from 2.7%).

Since 2003, wage trends have deteriorated further, as seen in **Figures C** and **D**. The figures present hourly wages and weekly earnings of blue-collar (production) workers in manufacturing and non-managers in services in 2003 dollars through June 2004 (these workers represent about 80% of the employed U.S. workforce). Since November 2003, the trend in real hourly wages has been consistently negative, and by June 2004 hourly wages were 1.2% below their year-ago level. Due to a loss in hours worked per week, weekly earnings fell further over this period, by 1.5%. In fact, as Figures C and D highlight,

FIGURE C   Real hourly wages since recession ended, November 2001-June 2004

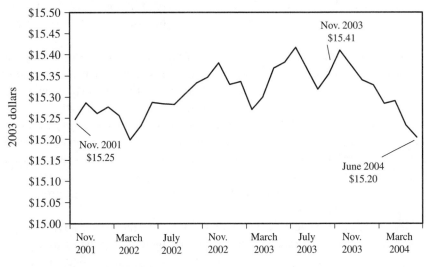

Source: Authors' analysis of BLS data.

FIGURE D   Real weekly wages since recession ended, November 2001-June 2004

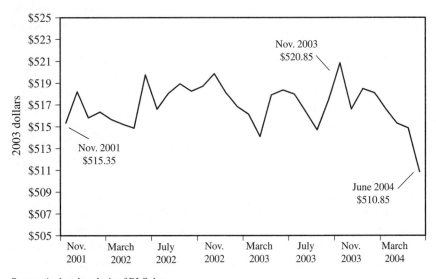

Source: Authors' analysis of BLS data.

these negative trends have taken back any gains in hourly wage or weekly earnings made over the recovery. After adjusting for inflation, both hourly and weekly earnings are below where they were when the current recovery got underway.

One relevant question about these negative trends is to what extent they are largely just a function of faster inflation, and thus less indicative of a labor market weakness. It is, of course, true that faster inflation in recent months has meant that nominal wages need to grow faster to beat price growth. Yet, because of the factors noted throughout this introduction, nominal wage growth has slowed sharply, from an annual average of 2.9% in the second quarter of last year to 2.1% in the same quarter this year. Inflation over this same period has accelerated from 2.2% to 2.8%. Thus, even if inflation was back at its level of a year ago, wages would still be stagnant at best, with real wage growth far behind the growth rate of productivity.

The erosion of wages illustrates that extensive labor slack adversely affects those who remain employed in a downturn, by lowering their earnings, as well as adversely affecting those who lose their jobs or cannot find work.

Job quality

As noted, employment has begun to grow fairly steadily, and, while considerable slack remains, the jobless recovery appears to be safely behind us. Here too, however, there is an arising problem: the quality of the net new jobs, or, more specifically, the wages and compensation in the industries and occupations growing most quickly relative to those growing more slowly.

Table 3 presents a worrisome dimension of changes in job quality: the industries that are expanding (as shares of total employment) pay far less in wages, benefits, and total compensation than industries that are contracting. This trend holds true during both the recession and the recovery. For instance, industries expanding over the recovery paid just $30,368 per year, $20,902 or 42.7% less than the $51,270 paid by contracting industries. The difference in benefits is even larger, with expanding industries paying only half as much in benefits ($5,178) as contracting industries ($10,713).

Other changes in job quality are more positive, such as the continued shift toward higher-paying white-collar occupations. However, the impact of "upscaling" among occupations is smaller than the downward push to jobs in lower-paying industries. For instance, an analysis that takes both occupational and industry shifts into account shows that expanding sectors paid 9.5% less per week than sectors in which jobs were contracting. This analysis would show a much larger pay gap if it could have used more detailed information on indus-

TABLE 3 Compensation, wages, and benefits in expanding and contracting industries, 2001-04

	Since recession's start	Since recovery's start
	March 2001- June 2004	Nov. 2001- June 2004
Expanding industries		
Annual compensation	$37,052	$35,546
Annual wages	31,818	30,368
Annual benefits	5,234	5,178
Contracting industries		
Annual compensation	$57,330	$61,983
Annual wages	47,403	51,270
Annual benefits	9,927	10,713
Difference ($)		
Annual compensation	-$20,278	-$26,437
Annual wages	-15,584	-20,902
Annual benefits	-4,694	-5,535
Difference (%)		
Annual compensation	-35.4%	-42.7%
Annual wages	-32.9	-40.8
Annual benefits	-47.3	-51.7

Source: Authors' analysis.

tries and annual, not weekly, pay (especially full compensation, including benefits). In any case, the severe contraction of jobs in manufacturing and information technology over the last several years has eroded the quality of jobs available to workers in the recovery.

The unbalanced nature of the current recovery

An economy characterized by these sort of unemployment and wage trends is conducive to increasing inequality. Tight labor markets perform a distributional function, that is, they distribute the gains of faster growth among all income classes in the workforce. Unfortunately, over much of the past 25 years, high average unemployment (in tandem with weaker unions, lower real minimum wages, and a diminished manufacturing sector) have contributed to a steady rise in the inequality of economic outcomes. In fact, as documented in Chapter

1, by the end of the last decade, income was only slightly less concentrated among the richest households than it was in the run-up to the Great Depression. Chapter 7 on international comparisons shows such high levels of inequality to be uniquely American.

By ensuring that more of the benefits of growth flowed to middle- and low-income families, the movement toward historically tight labor markets in the latter 1990s helped to partially reverse this pattern for a few years. But with the recent recession and jobless recovery, labor market conditions have produced slower relative growth among those with lower wages and incomes. There was, however, an important countervailing factor that occurred in 2001: the stock market bust and the decline in income from capital sources such as interest and dividends, an income source far more important to those at the very top of the income scale. The sharp capital losses over the recession reduced, but did not eliminate, the large gap that had evolved between the wealthiest families and everyone else (historically large capital losses related to the decline in stock prices are not included in the Census data that follow). Of course, as capital markets rebound, this inequality-dampening factor is likely to be reversed.

In fact, as shown in **Figure E**, the pattern of income growth over the recession and jobless recovery was predictably unbalanced, with larger income losses at the bottom and middle of the income scale than at the top. Each bar in Figure E shows the percent loss in income at different points, or percentiles, in the income scale. The largest declines occurred for the lowest-income families (at the 20th percentile, meaning 80% of families have higher incomes), and the declines grew smaller moving up the income scale, underscoring the point that those most vulnerable to slack labor market conditions tend to fare worse during such periods. The exception is the larger income loss at the 95th percentile than at the 80th (-1.7% versus -1.0%), driven in part by the significant capital income losses among the most wealthy. Even so, the fact that low and middle incomes fell faster than those at the top of the income scale heralds a return to a pattern of unbalanced income growth that has dominated much of the past 25 years.

The data in Figure E focus exclusively on pretax income and thus leave out another source of increased inequality: the unbalanced nature of the federal tax cuts legislated over the past few years. Chapter 1 shows the reduction in tax liabilities resulting from these cuts by income class. For those households in the top 1% of the income scale, the full tax savings from the cuts that were made from 2001 to 2003 were about $67,000; for middle-income families, the cuts amounted to just under $600, and for the lowest 20% the tax cut came to $61. The effect of these cuts has thus been to redistribute after-tax income up the income scale, leading to an inequality-exacerbating transfer of 0.8% of total, after-tax household income from the bottom 99% to the top 1%.

FIGURE E Change in real income by income percentile, 2000-02

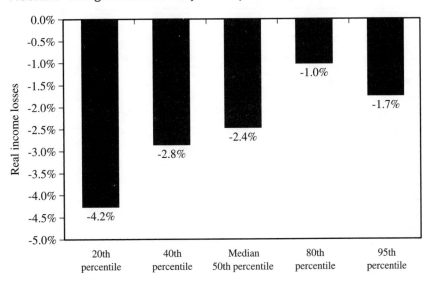

Source: Authors' analysis of U. S. Bureau of the Census data.

Another major indicator of the unbalanced pattern of growth during this downturn and recovery comes from the fact that capital income (profits and interest) has grown very quickly by historical standards, while total compensation has been flat. This development can be examined using a set of aggregate statistics: the total amount of income flowing to profits (including interest and dividend payments) and compensation in the corporate sector of the economy, as distinguished from the hourly and weekly wage series stressed above (we use the corporate sector for this analysis because it does not include proprietors' income, which cannot easily be divided between capital and compensation, or government income, which has employee compensation but no capital income). **Table 4** shows that inflation-adjusted capital income grew 32.2% over the recession and jobless recovery, while real compensation was up only 1.2%. Thus, the vast majority (84.6%) of the real income growth in the corporate sector since the first quarter of 2001 has accrued to capital income, a hugely disproportionate share when considering that capital income comprised just 16.6% of total corporate income when the recession started in early 2001.

Reflecting this shift in income growth, the returns to capital (the amount of capital income per dollar of assets) grew from 10.5% in 2000 to 11.1% in 2003

TABLE 4 Growth of income in corporate sector, 2000:q1 to 2004:q1

Time period	Compensation*	Capital income*	Total corporate income*
Since recession started			
2001:q1	$4,288	$856	$5,143.6
2004:q1	$4,338	$1,131	$5,469.2
Change			
Percent	1.2%	32.2%	6.3%
Dollars	$50	$275	$326
Share of change	15.4%	84.6%	100.0%

* In billions of 2004 dollars.

Source: Authors' analysis.

(**Table 5**). However, because the share of corporate income subject to taxation declined over this same period (from 39.5% to 24.9%), the after-tax return on capital grew three times as much as the pretax returns, up 2.0 percentage points from 6.3% to 8.3%.

The poor growth of total compensation in recent years reflects the lack of job creation and the slowdown in the growth of wages as a result of the extensive labor slack that has characterized this recovery. But how unique is this period compared to past recoveries? As shown in **Figure F**, the division of the economic pie between profits and compensation over this cycle is far more unequal than in past periods. On average over the post-WWII period, 12 quarters after an economic peak, real capital income was up 11.3%, only slightly ahead of compensation growth's 9.4%. Comparable figures for the most recent three years are 32.2% for capital income and little real growth at all for compensation. This extremely unbalanced division of income growth in the corporate sector stands out as historically unique.

Conclusion: a recovery at the crossroads

The recovery that began in late 2001 proved to be the worst on record for jobs, and its lingering effects—the slack that remains a hallmark of our current job market—are amply documented throughout this book. The chapters that follow also stress historical analyses that highlight various periods in the U.S.

TABLE 5   Returns to capital, 2000-03

| | Corporate sector | | |
| | Returns to capital | | Implied tax rate |
Year	Pre-tax	After-tax	
2000	10.5%	6.3%	39.5%
2001	9.0	6.0	33.0
2002	10.0	7.4	26.0
2003	11.1	8.3	24.9

Source: Authors' analysis of NIPA and BEA data.

FIGURE F   Real growth of compensation and capital income in the corporate sector, 12 quarters after peak, current cycle versus average of prior cycles

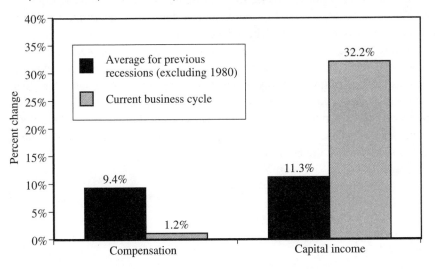

Source: Authors' analysis of BEA data.

economy when full employment in tandem with a set of adequate labor market institutions (e.g., stronger unions, higher real minimum wages) lifted the bargaining power of the millions of workers who depend on such conditions and policies to maintain living standards that rise with productivity.

What does this analysis tell about where we are right now? The evidence suggests that, as of mid-2004, the recovery is at a crossroads. One path leads to a broad-based, balanced recovery, where tight labor markets ensure widely shared real wage and income growth; where the benefits of the faster productivity regime that began in the mid-1990s flow freely to all income classes; where inequality is held at bay and poverty rates are driven down by a growing economy that provides quality jobs to even the least-advantaged worker.

The other path leads to an economy more like that of the 1980s, although with faster productivity growth. Throughout those years—which were characterized by large and growing budget deficits, high average unemployment, sharply growing inequality, and declining real wages and incomes for many in the bottom half—the living standards of far too many working families were stagnant at best.

Although the evolution of the recovery thus far, as documented above, is pushing us in the wrong direction, it is not too late to change course. The question is, of course, what can be done to avoid the wrong path and promote the correct one? First, policy makers, journalists, and most importantly, the electorate need to be well versed in the economic facts that determine the living standards of working families. Those facts are the subject of the seven chapters that follow. Once we have these facts in front of us, we then need a national economic discussion about the type of economy we want, and how to get there.

This framing of the economy as being at a crossroads may sound strange to many policy makers and citizens who believe that the path of the economy is determined by fate, not by fiat. But we firmly reject that notion, and maintain that we can—in fact, we must—wield public policy most effectively to push the economy toward the better path.

Documentation and methodology

Documentation

The comprehensive portrait presented in this book of changes in incomes, taxes, wages, employment, wealth, poverty, and other indicators of economic performance and well-being relies almost exclusively on data in the tables and figures. Consequently, the documentation of our analysis is essentially the documentation of the tables and figures. For each, an abbreviated source notation appears at the bottom, and complete documentation is contained in the Table Notes and Figure Notes found at the back of the book. (In rare circumstances, however, we incorporate data in the discussion that are not in a table or figure.) This system of documentation allows us to omit distracting footnotes and long citations within the text and tables.

The abbreviated source notation at the bottom of each figure and table is intended to inform the reader of the general source of our data and to give due credit to the authors and agencies whose data we are presenting. We have three categories of designations for these abbreviated sources. In instances where we directly reproduce other people's work, we provide an "author-year" reference to the bibliography. Where we present our own computations based on other people's work, the source line reads "Authors' analysis of *author (year)*." In these instances we have made computations that do not appear in the original work and want to hold the original authors (or agencies) blameless for any errors or interpretations. Our third category is simply "Authors' analysis," which indicates that the data presented are from our original analysis of microdata (such as much of the wage analysis) or our computations from published (usually government) data. We use this source notation when presenting descriptive trends from government income, employment, or other data, since we have made judgments about the appropriate time periods or other matters for the analysis that the source agencies have not made.

Time periods

Economic indicators fluctuate considerably with short-term swings in the business cycle. For example, incomes tend to fall in recessions and rise during expansions. Therefore, economists usually compare business cycle peaks with other peaks and compare troughs with other troughs so as not to mix apples and oranges. In this book, we examine changes between business cycle peaks. The initial year for many tables is 1947, with intermediate years of 1967, 1973, 1979, 1989 and 2000, all of which were business cycle peaks (at least in terms of having low unemployment). We also present data for the latest full year for which data are available (2003, when available) to show the changes over the current business cycle.

In some tables, we also separately present trends for the 1995-2000 period in order to highlight the differences between those years and those of the early 1990s (or, more precisely, 1989-95) and earlier business cycles. This departs from the convention of presenting only business-cycle comparisons (e.g., comparing 1979-89 to 1989-2000 trends) or comparisons of recoveries. We depart from the convention because there was a marked shift in a wide variety of trends after 1995, and it is important to understand and explain these trends.

Growth rates and rounding

Since business cycles differ in length, we usually present the annual growth rates in each period rather than the total growth. We also present compound annual growth rates rather than simple annual rates. Compound annual growth rates are just like compound interest on a bank loan: the rate is compounded continuously rather than yearly. In some circumstances, as noted in the tables, we have used log annual growth rates. This is done to permit decompositions.

In presenting the data we round the numbers, usually to one decimal place, but we use unrounded data to compute growth rates, percentage shares, and so on. Therefore, it is not always possible to exactly replicate our calculations by using the data in the table. In some circumstances, this leads to an appearance of errors in the tables. For instance, we frequently present shares of the population (or families) at different points in time and compute changes in these shares. Because our computations are based on the "unrounded" data, the change in shares presented in a table may not match the difference in the actual shares. Such rounding errors are always small, however, and never change the conclusions of the analysis.

Adjusting for inflation

In most popular discussions, the Consumer Price Index for All Urban Consumers (CPI-U), often called simply the consumer price index, is used to adjust dollar values for inflation. However, some analysts hold that the CPI-U overstated inflation in the late 1970s and early 1980s by measuring housing costs inappropriately. The methodology for the CPI-U from 1983 onward was revised to address these objections. Other changes were introduced into the CPI in the mid-1990s but not incorporated into the historical series. Not all agree that these revisions are appropriate. We chose not to use the CPI-U so as to avoid any impression that this report overstates the decline in wages and understates the growth in family incomes over the last few decades.

Instead of the CPI-U, we adjust dollar values for inflation using the CPI-U-RS index. This index uses the new methodology for housing inflation over the entire 1967-2001 period and incorporates the 1990s changes into the historical series (though not before 1978, which makes economic performance in the years after 1978 falsely look better than the earlier years). The CPI-U-RS is now used by the Census Bureau in its presentations of real income data. Because it is not available for years before 1978, we extrapolate the CPI-U-RS back to earlier years based on inflation as measured by the CPI-U.

In our analysis of poverty in Chapter 5, however, we generally use the CPI-U rather than the CPI-U-RS, since Chapter 5 draws heavily from Census Bureau publications that use the CPI-U. Moreover, the net effect of all of the criticisms of the measurement of poverty is that current methods *understate* poverty. Switching to the CPI-U-RS without incorporating other revisions (i.e., revising the actual poverty standard) would lead to an even greater understatement and would be a very selective intervention to improve the poverty measurement. (A fuller discussion of these issues appears in Chapter 5.)

Household heads

We often categorize families by the age or the race/ethnic group of the "household head," that is, the person in whose name the home is owned or rented. If the home is owned jointly by a married couple, either spouse may be designated the household head. Every family has a single household head.

Hispanics

Unless specified otherwise, data from published sources employ the Census Bureau's designation of Hispanic persons. That is, Hispanics are included in racial counts (e.g., with blacks and whites) as well as in a separate category. For instance, in government analyses a white person of Hispanic origin is included both in counts of whites *and* in counts of Hispanics. In our original analyses, such as the racial/ethnic wage analysis in Chapter 2, we remove Hispanic persons from other racial (white or black) categories; using this technique, the person described above would appear only in counts of Hispanics.

CHAPTER 1

Family income:

higher inequality leads to uneven progress

This analysis of working America begins with a detailed look at one of the most important determinants of a family's economic well-being: family income. The chapter examines the most relevant trends and arguments involving the growth of family income over the past half-century, with a central focus on recent trends, such as the impact of the recession that began in 2001, and key historical trends, such as the mid-1970s slowdown in median family income growth and the increase in income inequality.

Two dominant themes that emerge from this analysis relate to income position, or class, and labor market opportunity. First, when it comes to income growth over the previous generation, the extent of a household's prosperity is largely a function of its position in the income scale, with households from higher income classes faring far better than those at the low end of the income scale. Between 1979 and 2000, for example, the real income of households in the lowest fifth (the bottom 20% of earners) grew 6.4%, while that of households in the top fifth (the top 20% of earners) grew 70%, with the top 1% achieving real income gains of 184%.

Second, labor market opportunity is more important than ever in raising or lowering the living standards of American families—an observation based in part on the experience of families in the recent downturn. Economic fortunes have, of course, always been tied to work, but the relationship between income and work opportunity has become even more pronounced over time, as more families work and more family members spend increased amounts of time in the paid labor market.

The increase in income inequality is central to understanding the dynamics of income growth over the past generation. Between 1947 and 1973, incomes nearly doubled for low-, middle-, and high-income families. But between 1973 and 2000 (the most recent economic peak), income growth was far more uneven, expanding 12% for low-income families, 27% for middle-income families, and 67% for high-income families. This post-1973 increase in inequality shows up in measures of both consumption and income. Moreover, the income disparity is not driven by tax changes, although lowering the tax burden on the wealthy has demonstrably exacerbated the problem of inequality. (This is particularly the case with recent tax changes introduced by the Bush Administration, the distributional implications of which are discussed below.)

While the experiences of all income classes are examined in some detail, the initial focus is on those at the middle of the income scale, so as to begin with the income trends affecting typical families. Their experience is especially germane in that it reflects both of the central findings noted above. In terms of income growth, after rising quickly and in lockstep with productivity growth over much of the post-war era, with the onset of inequality, real median family income growth decelerated markedly. The median family income grew at less than half the rate of productivity over the past generation, rising by 2.8% per year between 1947 and 1973 and 0.8% annually across 1973 to 2000.

In the current economy, middle-class incomes have been considerably constrained by the loss of employment opportunities. Middle-income families saw their average income fall by 2.2% in real terms between 2000 and 2003 (the date of the most recent available data), and that loss is fully accounted for by fewer employment opportunities, meaning sustained unemployment for some and fewer hours worked for others. Middle-income families are also devoting more hours to work than in the past. Largely due to the increased labor supply of wives, married couples with children in the middle-income fifth, for example, were working 500 hours more per year in 2000 than in 1979—the equivalent of 12 and a half more full-time weeks per year. What's more, because of these wives' contribution, middle-class family income grew 19% faster than would otherwise have been the case.

More recently, and despite the fact that the economy has been in a recovery since late 2001, middle-income families continue to fall behind. A key reason for the lagging growth in middle-class incomes can be gleaned from the analysis of the distribution of national income between the share accruing to profits and that accruing to compensation, the latter being a much more important determinant of middle-class income growth. This analysis reveals a historically large imbalance in the distribution of national income—one that goes much of the way to explain why most working families have yet to recover from what was billed as a relatively mild recession.

FIGURE 1A Real median family income, 1947-2002

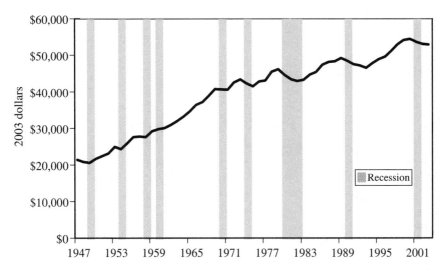

Source: Authors' analysis of U.S. Bureau of the Census data.

Median income: fewer employment opportunities in the recession and jobless recovery drive income losses

While no one variable can paint a complete picture of the living standards of the typical American family, median family income—the income of the family right at the center of the income scale—is a key indicator of their economic well-being. In 2003, the most recent year of available data, the median family's income was $52,680 (in 2003 dollars).

As shown in **Figure 1A**, real median family income usually falls during a recession (see shaded areas in the figure) and recovers with the upturn in the economy. This is because, for most families—especially working families in the middle class—compensation from employment is the main determinant of income growth. In a weak economy, people are less able to find paid work or are forced to work fewer hours than they would like. In a more persistent downturn, hourly wages may fall behind inflation, further dampening income growth (as discussed in the introduction, real hourly wages were falling in 2004 as a result of this phenomenon).

This recessionary drop in income explains the 0.9% annual decline in real median family income that occurred over the 2000 to 2003 period (**Table 1.1**). As the labor market weakened over the recession and jobless recovery (see

TABLE 1.1 Median family income,* 1947-2003 (2003 dollars)

Year	Median family income*
1947	$21,201
1973	43,219
1979	45,989
1989	49,014
1995	48,679
2000	54,191
2003	52,680

Changes	Total dollar changes	Annual growth rates
1947-73	$22,018	2.8%
1973-79	2,770	1.0
1979-89	3,025	0.6
1989-2000	5,177	0.9
1995-2000	5,512	2.2
2000-03	-1,511	-0.9

* Income includes all wage and salary, self-employment, pension, interest, rent, government
  cash assistance, and other money income.

Source: Authors' analysis of U.S. Bureau of the Census data.

Chapter 3), family members worked fewer hours than in prior years. This helped to pull down family incomes such that, by 2002, median family income was down about $1,300 below its 2000 level (in 2003 dollars).

Table 1.2 breaks out the determinants of family income into earnings, employment (annual hours worked by all family members per year), and other income. (Note that, to facilitate the decomposition that follows, the average income of the middle fifth is used instead of the median.) These data reveal the central importance of labor market conditions—i.e., employment and earnings opportunities—to the living standards of middle-income families, an issue that appears as a consistent theme throughout this book, particularly in the chapters on wages and jobs.

Over the 1990s boom, the real income for middle-income families rose 12.7%, driven wholly by increased earnings, as income from other sources actually fell. Both annual hours and hourly wages contributed to the rise in income (here, the family's hourly wage is simply the family's annual earnings divided by their annual hours).

Between 2000 and 2003, income fell 2.0% for middle-income families, driven largely by a drop in the number of hours worked. The decomposition in

TABLE 1.2 Average family income and its components for the middle quintile, 1994-2003 (2003 dollars)

Year	Family income	Family earnings	Other income	Family wage	Family hours
1994	$46,764	$36,859	$9,905	$12.67	2,908
1994	47,684	38,268	9,416	12.86	2,975
2000	54,195	44,572	9,623	14.20	3,138
2003	53,141	42,841	10,300	14.45	2,965
Log percent changes					
1994-2000	12.8%	15.2%	2.2%	9.9%	5.3%
2000-03	-2.0	-4.0	6.8	1.7	-5.7

Decomposition	1994-2000	2000-03
Total change in real family income	12.8%	-2.0%
Earnings*	12.4	-3.2
Wages*	8.1	1.4
Hours*	4.3	-4.6
Other*	0.4	1.3

* These changes represent the contribution of these variables to the growth of family income; thus, the "earnings" and "other" categories sum to the total, within a rounding error. This differentiates these values from the actual percent changes above. See Table Notes for more detail.

Source: Authors' analysis of March CPS data.

Table 1.2 allows for the apportioning of the contribution of wages, employment (annual hours), and other income to the percentage changes in income. Note that the percentage changes in the decomposition do not equal the actual changes reported in the upper panel because the changes in the decomposition are weighted by relevant shares so as to sum up to the overall change (e.g., in the decomposition, earnings is weighted by earnings as a share of family income—see Table Notes).

For the 1994 to 2000 period, earnings growth more than explains the growth in income, with hourly wage growth contributing 8.1% and the growth in hours adding 4.3%. From 2000 to 2002, the decline in annual hours worked explains 1.8% of the 2.0% decline in income. Thus, the decline in employment opportunities (both jobs and hours worked) explains about 80% of the fall in middle incomes from 2000 to 2002.

The real income trends examined thus far actually involve two separate trends: nominal income and inflation. Other insights into the relationship between the

FIGURE 1B Annual growth in nominal median family income and inflation, 1995-2003

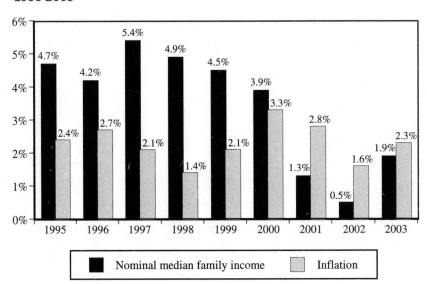

Source: Authors' analysis of U.S. Bureau of the Census data.

labor market and income growth can be gleaned from analyzing these two trends separately. **Figure 1B** provides clear evidence of the slowing of nominal income growth as the economy weakened. For each year, the black bar on the left shows the annual percent change in nominal income, while the grey bar on the right represents price growth. Nominal income growth far surpassed inflation over the latter 1990s, though by 2000 the gap between the two bars had shrunk, meaning real income grew little that year (by only 0.5%; the difference between this result and that in the figure is due to rounding).

Nominal median family income growth slowed a good deal further over the next few years, falling behind inflation in 2001 and 2002. In fact, the 0.5% growth in nominal family income in 2002 was the slowest growth since 1954. The real decline in income was somewhat mitigated that year, since inflation was also relatively low. Nevertheless, the cumulative two-year decline of income amounted to 2.4%, the largest two-year percentage loss since the previous downturn in the early 1990s. In 2003, both nominal income growth and inflation accelerated, with inflation slightly outpacing income, leading to a third consecutive year of income losses.

TABLE 1.3 Length of time to recovery of median family income after recession

Year of prior peak	Year prior peak surpassed	Number of years to recover
1953	1955	2
1957	1959	2
1969	1972	3
1973	1978	5
1979	1986	7
1989	1996	7
2000	?	?

Source: Authors' analysis.

As shown in Figure 1A, when the recovery gets underway and labor market income bounces back, incomes reverse course and start to climb. One measure of how long it takes for families to make up for lost ground after a recession is shown in **Table 1.3**. The first column shows the year of the prior income peak, the second shows the year in the following recovery when the peak was surpassed, and the third shows how many years it took to regain the prior peak. The question mark in the last row is there since we cannot yet know when median income will return to its 2000 peak.

Over time, it has taken longer for real median family income to regain lost ground. Income losses over the downturns of the 1950s and 1960s were quickly replenished in two or three years. But during the last two recoveries, incomes took much longer to climb back—seven years in both cases—and given the protracted jobless recovery after the most recent downturn, it may again be a while before median family income regains its peak.

Table 1.1 and Figure 1A provide a historical view of median family income since 1947. There are two distinct growth periods. The first, from about 1947 to the early 1970s, was the strongest and by far the most sustained. Over the 26 years from 1947 to 1973, median family income grew 104% in real terms; over the next 27 years, it grew 25%. But this latter period can be subdivided into the period of stagnation from the mid-1970s to the mid-1990s (when growth never surpassed 1% per year), and the short but strong growth period from 1995 to 2000, when family incomes expanded by 2.2% per year.

How does this historical record of income growth compare with that of productivity? After all, it is a common mantra among economists that productivity is the main determinant of living standards. But, as **Table 1.4** reveals,

TABLE 1.4 Growth of real median family income and productivity, 1947-2003

Period	Productivity	Median family income
1947-1973	103.5%	103.9%
1973-2003	71.3	21.9
1995-2000	13.2	11.3

Source: Authors' analysis of U.S. Bureau of Labor Statistics and U.S. Bureau of the Census data.

productivity growth does not always reach the median family. Between 1947 and 1973, a golden age of growth for both variables, productivity and real median family income more than doubled, each growing by the same amount. Over this era, there was no doubt that the typical family fully benefited from productivity growth.

Yet starting in the mid-1970s, this relationship broke down. From 1973 to 2003, median family income grew by less than one-third the rate of productivity. As discussed in detail below, relative to the earlier years this was a period of growing income inequality, which served as a wedge between productivity and the living standards of the median family. That is, while faster productivity growth led to a larger economic pie, growing inequality meant that slices were divided up such that some income classes—those at the top of the income scale—claimed most of the income growth.

The last line of the table shows that over the 1995 to 2000 period, productivity and median income once again grew at roughly similar rates, as the very tight labor market ensured that the benefits of productivity growth (which accelerated over this period) were broadly shared. This important topic is revisited in the next chapter's analysis of wages.

It is common practice also to examine measures of family income growth that adjust for changes in family size, since the same total family income shared by fewer family members can be interpreted as improved economic well-being for each family member. However, trends in incomes adjusted for family size can be misleading because the recent decline in the average family's size is partially due to lower incomes (family size is down 14% from its mid-1960s peak, and the number of children per family has dropped by one-third). That is, some families feel they cannot afford as many children as they could have if incomes had continued to rise at early postwar rates. As a result, a family deciding to have fewer children or a person putting off starting a family because incomes are down will appear "better off" in size-adjusted family-income mea-

TABLE 1.5 Annual family income growth for the middle fifth, unadjusted and adjusted for family size, 1967-2003

Period	Unadjusted for family size*	Adjusted for family size**	Difference (adjusted minus unadjusted)
1967-73	2.2%	2.8%	0.6%
1973-79	0.0	0.5	0.5
1979-89	0.2	0.5	0.3
1989-2000	0.6	0.6	0.0
1989-95	-0.6	-0.5	0.1
1995-2000	2.0	2.0	0.0
2000-03	-0.7	-0.6	0.2

* Unlike most other tables in the book, we use the CPI-U to deflate income here to be consistent with the size-adjusted measures, which also use that deflator.

** Annualized growth rate of family income of the middle fifth, divided by the poverty line for each family size.

Source: Authors' analysis of U.S. Bureau of the Census data.

sures. It also seems selective to adjust family incomes for changes in family size and not adjust for other demographic trends such as more hours of work and the resulting loss of leisure.

Nevertheless, even when income growth is adjusted for the shift toward smaller families (as in **Table 1.5**, column 2), the income growth of the 1980s was only slightly higher than the unadjusted measure. In fact, after 1979, the annual growth rates of size-adjusted income are never more than 0.3% higher than the unadjusted numbers. Over the 1990s, the growth trends were identical (0.6%). Thus, putting aside the critique that income growth and family size are themselves closely related, these data offer little evidence to support the notion that the shrinking size of families has been an important factor explaining the slower income growth of middle-class families since 1979.

Recession hits minority families hardest

Growth in median income tends to vary by the race/ethnicity of the head of the family, the age of the family head, and the family type. Typically, growth rates are slower for younger and minority-headed families and for married-couple families where only one spouse works. It is also the case that these families' incomes tend to be more responsive to overall economic trends, both positive and negative. Thus, in the full-employment economy of the latter 1990s, the

TABLE 1.6 Median family income by race/ethnic group, 1947-2003 (2003 dollars)

Year	White	Black*	Hispanic**	Ratio to white family income of: Black	Hispanic
1947	$22,083	$11,290	0	51.1%	n.a.
1967	38,430	22,753	0	59.2	n.a.
1973	45,170	26,069	$31,255	57.7	69.2%
1979	47,990	27,175	33,268	56.6	69.3
1989	51,539	28,952	33,589	56.2	65.2
1995	51,118	31,129	29,451	60.9	57.6
2000	56,645	35,972	36,790	63.5	64.9
2003	55,768	34,369	34,272	61.6	61.5
Annual growth rate					
1947-67	2.8%	3.6%	n.a.		
1967-73	2.7	2.3	n.a.		
1973-79	1.0	0.7	1.0%		
1979-89	0.7	0.6	0.1		
1989-2000	0.9	2.0	0.8		
1995-2000	2.1	2.9	4.6		
2000-03	-0.5	-1.5	-2.3		

* Prior to 1967, data for blacks include all non-whites.
** Persons of Hispanic origin may be of any race.

Source: Authors' analysis of U.S. Bureau of the Census data.

pace of their income growth surpassed that of better-off families, and in the ensuing downturn, they lost relatively more ground.

Table 1.6 compares real median income levels and trends by the race/ethnicity of the family head. African American and especially Hispanic family incomes grew faster than that of whites over the 1995 to 2000 period. Black family income growth surpassed that of whites by 0.8% per year (2.9% versus 2.1%) while Hispanic family income grew more than twice as fast as white income during the five-year interval (4.6%). In both cases, this was their fastest income growth in a generation. However, when the labor market weakened in 2001, these growth rates sharply reversed course, especially compared to that of the median white family. Black families lost 1.5% per year between 2000 and 2003, three times the annual decline for white families, and the gap between white and Hispanic incomes grew even faster.

FIGURE 1C Ratio of black and Hispanic to white median family income, 1947-2003

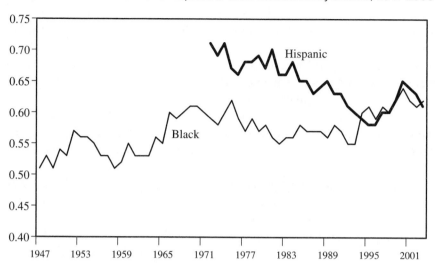

Source: Authors' analysis of U.S. Bureau of the Census data.

This pattern of relative income changes meant a reversal of trend in the racial income gap, which had been closing—implying a smaller income gap between blacks and whites, and Hispanics and whites—in the latter 1990s, as shown in **Figure 1C**. The figure plots the ratio of black-to-white and Hispanic-to-white family income. (Data on Hispanic family income are available only for 1972 and later. Note also that the data for white families include Hispanics who identify their race as white. Data on non-Hispanic whites are available from 1972 forward; using this series for whites does not change the trends shown in the figure.) Throughout the 1960s, the median income of black families increased relative to that of whites, with the ratio peaking in the mid-1970s. Over the 1980s black families lost ground relative to whites, but this trend was reversed in the 1990s, when the black/white ratio rose to its highest level on record (64% in 2000). (The figure reveals a large upward shift in one year: 1994. There are no obvious data reasons, such as a coding or weighting change, that would explain this one-year jump. It is, however, unusual for a trend to change this dramatically in one year, and there may be a non-economic explanation. However, blacks made relative gains in other areas over these years, including poverty and hours worked, so, while the change probably occurs more gradually than reflected in the figure, it likely did occur.)

The 1960s and the 1990s shared certain characteristics that might explain these favorable shifts in relative incomes. First, both the 1960s and the late 1990s were periods of fast productivity growth and low unemployment. Falling unemployment in particular is generally more beneficial to minorities than to white families, in part because, as unemployment falls, labor force activity increases more for minorities than for whites (Chapter 3 shows relative gains in employment rates for minorities in the 1990s).

One notable difference between the two periods is that the relative gains in the 1960s were also driven by geographic and industry shifts by African Americans, with many black families migrating north and finding employment in manufacturing. In fact, by 1970, the share of black men working in manufacturing surpassed that of whites. As manufacturing employment contracted over the 1980s and especially the latter 1990s, this sector ceased to be a venue for relative gains by minorities.

Though the racial income gap compressed in the 1990s, the magnitude of the gap remained. Even with this improvement, black median income never reached two-thirds of white median income. And even if these favorable trends of the latter 1990s that contributed to the narrowing of the racial gap had persisted, it would have taken until 2054 for the black/white income gap to close.

Of course, the trend toward smaller race gaps did not persist. Recessionary contractions and the associated increases in unemployment tend to lower minority income more than that of whites, as can be seen in the last row of Table 1.6, which shows black and Hispanic income falling further than income for whites. As Figure 1C illustrates, the result was a reversal in the trend in relative incomes and a return to wider racial income gaps. As of 2002, minorities had lost only part of their relative gains made in the late 1990s, but unless the very favorable labor market conditions of the latter 1990s return, racial income gaps are likely to widen further.

Unemployment's impact felt most by youngest

The income data examined thus far take no account of age differences, which will be discussed in this section. In fact, as shown in all the years in **Table 1.7**—which describes median income levels by age of the head of the family— the pattern of median family income by age follows an inverted "U." Young families just starting out usually have lower income than older families, who tend to have both higher earning capacity and greater wealth. As families retire and spend down their assets, income tends to decline.

This section addresses three questions related to income and age. First, how have the median incomes of different age groups moved over time? Sec-

TABLE 1.7 Median family income by age of household head, 1979-2002 (2003 dollars)

Year	Under 25	25-34	35-44	45-54	55-64	Over 65	45-54 compared to 25-34 relative incomes
1979	$30,549	$45,334	$53,801	$59,403	$51,455	$26,583	1.31
1989	24,446	44,229	57,594	66,045	53,928	33,069	1.49
1995	22,482	43,176	55,770	65,961	54,256	33,923	1.53
2000	28,345	49,019	62,044	72,724	59,517	35,092	1.48
2002	27,248	47,622	58,875	70,765	60,885	34,536	1.49
Annual growth rate							
1979-89	-2.2%	-0.2%	0.7%	1.1%	0.5%	2.5%	18.3
1989-2000	1.4	0.9	0.7	0.9	0.9	0.5	-1.0
1995-2000	4.7	2.6	2.2	2.0	1.9	0.7	-4.4
2000-02	-2.0	-1.4	-2.6	-1.4	1.1	-0.8	0.2

Source: Authors' analysis of U.S. Bureau of the Census data.

ond, how does the relationship between the labor market and family income vary by age? Finally, how has median family income grown within age co-horts? This analysis illustrates the lifetime income growth for a young worker starting out in, say, the 1950s and compares it to the experience of young workers starting out in later decades.

Starting with the most recent data, Table 1.7 reveals that between 2000 and 2003 real median income fell for all families headed by someone less than 55 years old, with larger losses for younger families. This represents a sharp reversal from the trends in the late 1990s, when the job and wage opportunities associated with full employment lifted the incomes of young families considerably more quickly than those of older families. For example, real median income grew 2.6% per year among families headed by a 25-to 34-year-old and 1.9% for families with a 55-to 64-year-old head. Note that the relative income of middle-age to younger families fell over the 1995 to 2000 period as a result of this pattern of stronger growth for younger families. Nevertheless, the generational income gap remained well ahead of its 1979 level (see the last column of Table 1.7).

Note that for younger families, this 1995 to 2000 period was unique in its strong growth. Between 1979 and 1995, the median income of families headed by young and even middle-age persons was relatively stagnant or falling. For families headed by someone younger than 65, with one exception, real median income either fell or grew less than 1% over these years (the one exception is the 45-54 age group, whose income grew 1.1% per year between 1979 and 1989). The first half of the 1990s was a period of particularly slow growth. The fact that these years hosted a stagnant job market (like the early 2000s, the 1990s recovery was also deemed "jobless") may presage continued weakness in the early 2000s.

Figure 1D provides some statistical evidence of the relationship between unemployment and income growth by age. The figure plots a simple two-variable relationship between the change in real income by age level and unemployment. Each bar represents the impact on income for families headed by someone that age of a one-percentage-point increase in the unemployment rate. Thus, an increase in unemployment from, say, 5% to 6% is predicted to lower the growth of family income among the youngest families by about 1.6% and among the next oldest families by just over 1%. Note the clear step function of the chart, showing the diminished impact of unemployment by age, until with the oldest families, many of whom are retired, the relationship between the two variables is small and statistically no different from zero.

Some income analysts have discounted the importance of the general trend toward slower income growth by noting that families receive higher real incomes as they age, as shown in Figure 1D. But this fact does not solve the problem of the slower growth of income and wages that has persisted since the mid-1970s. The slower growth of median income means that the living standards of today's working families are improving less quickly as a family ages compared to the experience of families in earlier periods. The next table examines how this dynamic has changed over time by tracking and comparing the progress of various age cohorts, offering clear evidence that the economic progress of recent cohorts has lagged behind that of their predecessors.

Table 1.8 tracks various cohorts over time and compares two dimensions of real income growth. The first dimension is how quickly one age cohort's income grows relative to a different cohort's (the second dimension, examined next, evaluates income growth within cohorts). The top section follows five different age cohorts over time, beginning in 1949. Each column contains the median family income of families headed by persons in three different age groups, 25-34, 35-44, and 45-54 (referenced as young, middle, and older, respectively). Note that, although these data do not track the same families over time, this kind of analysis does provide an approximation of what such families would experience.

The real median income of families in the cohort starting out in 1949 grew by more than half as they aged through each period. As they went from young to middle, their income grew by 57.1%; as they grew from middle to older, it grew by 51.5%. For the cohort starting out in 1959 (Cohort 2), income grew by

FIGURE 1D Effect of a one-percentage-point increase in unemployment on median family income by age

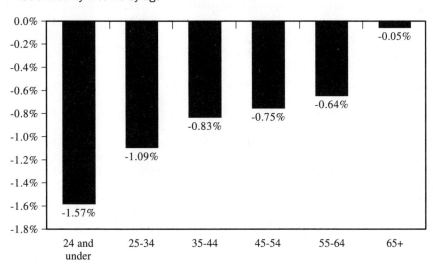

Source: Authors' analysis of U.S. Bureau of the Census and BLS data.

59.3% as they started out, about the same rate as for Cohort 1 (note also that the 1959 cohort started from a higher level; this is discussed below). But as the 1959 cohort passed from middle to older age, its rate of growth decelerated to 26.0%, as compared to 51.5% for the earlier cohort.

The 1969, 1979, and 1989 cohorts saw considerably slower growth as they aged, relative to earlier age groups (because the last cohort started out in 1999, there is only one observation for this group). Families in the 1979 cohort saw their median family income grow by 27.0% as they moved into middle age and by 25.2% as they entered older age. Over the full 30 years, the median income of their cohort grew by 59.0%, less than half as fast as that of the 1949 cohort. The income of the 1989 cohort can only be observed as it moved from young to middle age, and, thanks to the faster growth of the latter 1990s, income for these families grew faster (37.1%) as they aged than it did for either of the two previous cohorts, which saw growth of 31.7% and 27.0% (though slower than for the first two).

With this one exception, each cohort's real income growth has been successively slower than that of the previous cohort. The bottom panel, however, shows that, except for the 1989 cohort, the income starting line was higher for

TABLE 1.8 Median family income growth by 10-year cohorts, starting in 1949 (2003 dollars)

Age of family head	Cohort 1: Young in '49 Middle in '59 Older in '69	Cohort 2: Young in '59 Middle in '69 Older in '79	Cohort 3: Young in '69 Middle in '79 Older in '89	Cohort 4: Young in '79 Middle in '89 Older in '99	Cohort 5: Young in '89 Middle in '99 n.a.	Cohort 6: Young in '99 n.a. n.a.
25-34 (young)	$20,472	$28,935	$39,932	$44,319	$43,239	$46,735
35-44 (middle)	32,167	46,083	52,596	56,304	59,279	n.a.
45-54 (older)	48,748	58,072	64,566	70,469	n.a.	n.a.
Percent growth:						
Young to middle	57.1%	59.3%	31.7%	27.0%	37.1%	n.a.
Middle to older	51.5	26.0	22.8	25.2	n.a.	n.a.
Young to older	138.1	100.7	61.7	59.0	n.a.	n.a.

Addendum:

Growth between cohorts	1949-59 (Cohort 2 compared to Cohort 1)	1959-69 (Cohort 3 compared to Cohort 2)	1969-79 (Cohort 4 compared to Cohort 3)	1979-89 (Cohort 5 compared to Cohort 4)	1989-99 (Cohort 6 compared to Cohort 5)
25-34 (young)	41.3%	38.0%	11.0%	-2.4%	8.1%
35-44 (middle)	43.3	14.1	7.1	5.3	n.a.
45-54 (older)	19.1	11.2	9.1	n.a.	n.a.

Source: Authors' analysis of U.S. Bureau of the Census data.

each successive cohort, but even that trend diminishes over time. For example, the 1959 cohort began its trajectory 41.3% above that of the 1949 cohort, and the 1969 cohort began its journey 38.0% ahead of the previous group. But as the 1979 cohort began, its income was only 11.0% above that of the 1969 cohort, and the next cohort, beginning in 1989, was the first to start out with lower income (by 2.4%) in real terms than its predecessor (though by the time the 1989 cohort reached middle age, it had caught up to the earlier group). The most recent cohort, which started out in 1999, began 8.1% above the previous cohort, but that is a small advantage relative to the much larger gains posted by earlier cohorts.

The data in Table 1.8 confirm that incomes tend to rise as families age, and that, at least through the late 1970s, each cohort started out ahead of the last. But the table also reveals that the rate of income growth of later cohorts has slowed considerably compared to that of earlier ones.

The demographics of the American family are constantly changing shape. While most families are still headed by married couples, over the last 50 years there have been proportionately fewer married-couple families, and, conversely, more single-parent families. Among married couples, far more wives have entered the labor force, a topic examined in more depth in a later section of this chapter. This section examines changes in median income among these different family types.

Table 1.9 focuses both on changes in median family income by family type and changes in the shares of different family types in the overall population. Since 1973, the most consistent income growth has occurred among married couples with both spouses in the paid labor force, as these families (specifically, the wives in these families) have increased their amount of time spent in paid work relative to other families (though single-mother families also made large labor force gains over the 1990s). In 1979, the share of married couples without a wife in the labor force was about equal to that of those with a wife in the labor force (41.9% versus 40.6% of married-couple families). By 2000, married couples with two earners (assuming the husband worked) made up 47.7% of all families, while one-earner married couples were proportionately fewer in number—29.1% of the total.

While this shift toward two-earner families has been a major factor in recent income growth, the shift appears to be attenuating, since the rate at which wives have been joining the labor force and increasing their hours of work has slowed in recent years. For example, among married-couple families, the share of families with wives in the paid labor force increased at an annual rate of about 1% in the 1960s and 1970s, 0.8% in the 1980s, and 0.4% in the 1989-2000 period (numbers not shown in table). It is difficult to know the causes of this deceleration. It could be that, with the share of middle-class working wives

55

TABLE 1.9 Median family income by family type, 1973-2003 (2003 dollars)

Year	Total	Married couples Wife in paid labor force	Married couples Wife not in paid labor force	Single Male-headed	Single Female-headed	All families
1973	$42,177	$49,236	$37,316	$36,145	$20,427	$39,574
1979	50,314	58,372	41,573	39,464	23,198	45,989
1989	55,223	64,849	41,184	39,894	23,555	49,014
1995	56,411	66,913	38,807	36,389	23,603	48,679
2000	63,219	74,199	42,444	40,088	27,553	54,360
2003	62,281	75,170	41,122	38,032	26,550	52,680
Annual growth rate						
1973-79	3.0%	2.9%	1.8%	1.5%	2.1%	2.5%
1979-89	0.9	1.1	-0.1	0.1	0.2	0.6
1989-2000	1.2	1.2	0.3	0.0	1.4	0.9
1989-95	0.4	0.5	-1.0	-1.5	0.0	-0.1
1995-2000	2.3	2.1	1.8	2.0	3.1	2.2
2000-03	-0.5	0.4	-1.0	-1.7	-1.2	-1.0
Share of families						
1951*	87.0%	19.9%	67.1%	3.0%	10.0%	100.0%
1979	82.5	40.6	41.9	2.9	14.6	100.0
1989	79.2	45.7	33.5	4.4	16.5	100.0
2000	76.8	47.7	29.1	5.9	17.3	100.0
2003	75.7	46.0	29.7	6.2	18.1	100.0

* Earliest year available for wives' work status.

Source: Authors' analysis of U.S. Bureau of the Census data.

at 62% (47.7%/76.8%), the country is approaching the "ceiling" of the share of wives that are able or willing to spend time in the labor market (2000 is used as an endpoint here to avoid the cyclical effect of the downturn). Second, wives' willingness to work has generally been found to be more sensitive to both their own and their spouses' earnings than that of most other groups of workers, meaning that they are more likely to cut back their hours when their earnings or their spouses' earnings rise, as occurred in the latter 1990s. However, while this so-called "cross-income effect" has consistently been found to exist, its esti- mated magnitude is small and has shrunk over time. Thus, it can only explain a small part of the flatter trend in wives' labor force participation.

Married-couple families, although still predominant—representing 75.7% of all families in 2003—make up a smaller share of families than they did in the 1950s and 1960s. At the same time, the share of families headed by single women has grown; in 2003, single-mother families represented 18.1% of the total. Although this phenomenon has been the focus of increased critical attention in recent years, the share of families headed by single women grew more quickly in the 1967 to 1979 period than it has since.

After stagnating in the first half of the 1990s, the real median income of mother-only families grew more quickly from 1995 to 2000 than it did for any other family type (3.1% annually). As will be discussed both later in this chapter and in Chapter 5 on poverty, such families sharply increased their annual weeks and hours of paid work over this period, which helped boost their incomes. Still, mother-only family income was about half that of all families in 2000, and it was slightly less than twice the poverty line that year for a family with one parent and two children. (Two times the poverty line is a benchmark for what it takes for working families to make ends meet, including child care costs.) Thus, even with considerable effort in a strong economy, the median single-mother family still faces income constraints.

The increased labor market participation of both mother-only families and married-couple families has made these groups more vulnerable to economic contractions such as those that have occurred since 2000. As shown in the last row of the middle panel of Table 1.9, real income fell for both types of families, although it was up (by 0.4% per year) for married-couple families with wives in the paid labor force. Note the sharp reversal in income growth by family type, derived by subtracting the 1995-2000 change from the 2000-03 change. For all family types, income grew 3.2% per year more slowly in 2000-03 than 1995-2000. For married couples, the annual deceleration of income growth was 2.8% (1.7% for couples with working wives). For single-mother families the reversal in median income growth was particularly sharp, going from a 3.1% annual increase in the latter 1990s to a 1.2% decline in the 2000-03 period, i.e., their income grew 4.3% more slowly in the downturn compared to the boom.

The fact that incomes grew quickly for single mothers over various time periods is important in another light as well. Many analysts of family income trends argue that changes in family structure of the type shown in the bottom panel of Table 1.9 are a major determinant of the overall trend in incomes. Specifically, this argument holds that, more than high unemployment or slow wage growth, the shift to lower-income family types has driven the post-1973 slowdown in income growth. Yet the data in Table 1.9 suggest that the trends in income within each family group are at least as important as the shifts in the types of families.

In fact, analysis of the relative roles of these different factors suggest that the shift to lower-income family types was a relatively minor factor explaining trends in both income growth and inequality in the 1980s and 1990s. For example, when the shift to single-mother families was occurring most quickly, during the 1960s, income inequality was contracting. Conversely, the next section shows that income inequality increased quickly between 1995 and 2000 as the incomes of the richest families far outpaced those of lower income families. Yet this was a period when single-mother family incomes grew quickly and the share of single mothers actually fell slightly, from 18.0% to 17.3%. Clearly, other factors were boosting inequality over this period.

Growing inequality of family income

A dominant theme in the evolution of the American economy over the past few decades has been the increase in the inequality of economic outcomes. After contracting through the 1950s and 1960s, the distribution of income and wealth began to grow wider, with the lion's share of economic growth accruing to families at the top of the income scale (unequal wealth distribution is the focus of Chapter 4). Even the strong, full-employment economy of the late 1990s, which generated large wage gains for workers at the bottom, was unable to reverse that trend. In fact, certain measures that focus on the relative growth of income among the most wealthy suggest that the gap between those at the very top continued to expand at least as quickly as in earlier periods. By other measures—those that focus more on changes in the middle and lower end of the income scale—inequality grew more slowly over the 1990s than over the 1980s. Ordinarily, a sustained period of low unemployment like that of the latter 1990s would have significantly lowered inequality, and it is perhaps a sign of diminished expectations about economic equity that slower growth in income inequality seems like good news.

This analysis of income inequality begins by taking advantage of a unique historical data set created by economists Thomas Piketty and Emmanuel Saez (see figure note for more information). While these data lack detailed information about the components of the income distribution, they provide invaluable data on the share and composition of income going to the wealthiest households since 1913, thus providing a long view of the evolution of inequality at the top of the income scale. Unlike much of the Census data used later in this section, the Piketty/Saez data include realized capital gains (the dollar value of asset appreciation or losses claimed by the owner of the asset), and thus capture the contribution of this important component of inequality trends.

FIGURE 1E Income share of the top 1%, 1913-2002

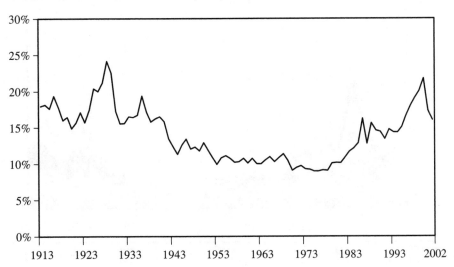

Source: Piketty and Saez (2003).

Figure 1E plots the income share of the top 1%, showing that by the end of the last decade, income was almost as concentrated among the richest households as at any point in the last century. After rising through the 1920s and falling sharply in the Great Depression, income concentration declined in the 1940s through the 1970s before starting to climb in the early 1980s. The growth of income concentration among the top 1% accelerated in the second half of the 1990s, largely due to increased concentration of salary income and realized capital gains. By 2000, the share of income held by the top 1% was at its highest level since the run-up to the Depression. The sharp post-2000 decline in the income share of these wealthy households was largely driven by the steep stock market correction in those years and the ensuing capital losses. As financial markets have since stabilized, we expect this dip to be temporary. As noted in the introduction, by 2003 most of the benefits of the recovery were flowing to profits, not compensation, and this dynamic is likely lifting the income share at the very top of the income scale.

Figure 1F probes even deeper into the upper reaches of the income scale, examining the income shares and composition of the top 0.01%—the very narrow slice representing one one-hundredth of the top percentile. A similar pattern to the last figure is evident here too, suggesting that the inequality trajec-

FIGURE 1F Composition of income share for the top 0.01%, 1916-2000

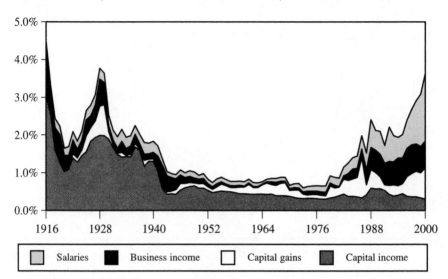

Source: Piketty and Saez (2003).

tory of the top percentile is closely linked to that of the very top of that group. This figure shows the components of income at the very top broken down into capital income (dividend and interest income), capital gains, business income (mostly self-employment income), and salary income.

Most notable about this decomposition is the increase in the salary share in the most recent data. Historically, labor market earnings have played a far less significant role in the concentration of income at the very top of the scale. But over the 1990s, as executive compensation soared, much more of the nation's salary income became concentrated at the top, leaving less to be divided among the larger workforce. At the same time, capital gains and business income grew also, reinforcing the growth of salary income and lifting the share of income going to the very top.

Another useful data series for studying the growth of income inequality (as well as the distribution of federal taxes, which will be presented next) is produced by the Congressional Budget Office (CBO) and covers the years 1979 to 2001. These data have many useful attributes, but most importantly, they are comprehensive, including the value of non-cash benefits like Medicare, Medicaid, employer-paid health insurance premiums, and food stamps, as well as

FIGURE 1G Real income growth by income group, 1979-2001 (comprehensive income data)

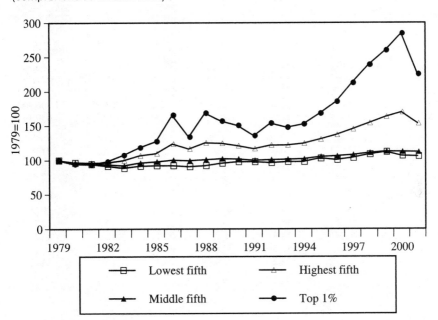

Source: Authors' analysis of CBO data.

realized capital gains (note that all of the above are left out of Census income data). The CBO data also adjust for family size.

Figure 1G plots the trajectory of the average real household income of four income groups between 1979 and 2001: the lowest fifth, the middle fifth, the top fifth and the top 1% (in 2000, the income levels corresponding to these groups were $0-$16,300, $27,600-$39,800, $59,400 and up, and $238,000 and up). To accommodate the wide scale generated by these intervals, each series in Figure 1G is indexed to 100 in 1979. Thus, each data point represents the percent difference between that point and 1979. The average real values for each income group are shown in the top panel of **Table 1.10**, including a more disaggregated look at the top 20%.

The table shows that within the top fifth of households, income grew successively quicker moving into the highest reaches of the income scale, with the faster growth among the top 1%. By the mid-1980s, the top 1% had grown by half while the middle fifth was essentially unchanged and the bottom

TABLE 1.10 Average real income levels and shares, 1979-2001, by income group and share of growth accruing to each group (2001 dollars)

	Lowest fifth	Middle fifth	Highest fifth	80-95%	95-99%	Top 1%
1979	$14,100	$46,000	$119,100	$88,400	$147,300	$466,800
1989	13,500	47,000	148,500	101,767	177,900	731,900
1995	14,500	48,300	155,200	104,833	186,900	783,900
2000	15,000	51,700	202,000	120,533	226,275	1,326,900
2001	14,900	51,500	182,700	117,000	212,225	1,050,100
1979-89	-4.3%	2.2%	24.7%	15.1%	20.8%	56.8%
1989-2000	11.1	10.0	36.0	18.4	27.2	81.3
1979-2000	6.4	12.4	69.6	36.3	53.6	184.3
2000-01	-0.7	-0.4	-9.6	-2.9	-6.2	-20.9
Income shares						
1979	5.8%	15.8%	45.5%	24.8%	11.4%	9.3%
1989	4.3	15.1	49.9	25.1	12.3	12.5
1995	4.6	14.9	50.2	25.1	12.6	12.5
2000	4.0	13.5	54.8	24.1	12.9	17.8
2001	4.2	14.2	52.4	24.9	12.7	14.8
1979-2000	-1.8	-2.3	9.3	-0.7	1.5	8.5
Addendum						
Share of income growth to income group, 1979-2000	0.8%	5.1%	74.0%	21.5%	14.1%	38.4%

Source: Authors' analysis of CBO data.

fifth was slightly down relative to 1979 (Figure 1G). This gap remained fairly constant from the mid-1980s through the early 1990s. Starting in the mid-1990s, the top 1% began to grow quickly, presumably driven, as shown in Figure 1F, by fast-growing high-end salaries and realized capital gains. While the growth in the middle and bottom fifths accelerated as well, their growth rates paled beside that of the top 1%. Note the very sharp decline in the real income of the top 1% in 2001, largely attributable to the correction in the stock market that year, which led to a severe decline in realized capital gains.

The second panel of Table 1.10 shows these real growth rates of household income over business cycle peaks along with the most recent CBO data from 2001. Income growth accelerated over the 1990s, growing by between 10.0% to 11.1% for the bottom and middle quintiles and 36.0% for the top fifth, with most of the latter growth driven by the top 5% within the top fifth. The changes between 1979 and 2000 show the extent of uneven growth over the full period. Low and middle incomes grew 6.4% and 12.4%, respectively, while the top 1% grew 184.3%.

This pattern implies that the benefits of average income growth were very unequally shared during the 1979 to 2000 period, as shown in the addendum to the income section of Table 1.10. The lowest fifth claimed less than 1% of income growth and the middle fifth had 5.1% growth, while 74.0% went to the top fifth. About half of that growth, 38.4%, accrued to the top 1% alone. In this sense, growing inequality serves to funnel growth to a narrow slice of wealthy households, and thus has a profound impact on the living standards of the broad majority of American households.

Interestingly, according to these CBO data (and as shown in Figure 1E), inequality contracted sharply in 2001, as losses were far higher at the top of the income scale. However, this contraction likely relates to the sharp decline in the value of stock holding that occurred in that year (see the Wealth Chapter for more details), and is likely to have been temporary. The stock market has since rallied off these lows, and, more revealingly, since 2002 much of the growth in national income has flowed to profits and little to compensation, as shown below. This pattern obviously tends to exacerbate income inequality. Wages have also grown more unequally in the early years of this decade, as shown in Chapter 2. Finally, it is worth noting that even with this 2001 stock market correction, the income gap between the top households and all others remains at the historically high levels reached by the end of the 1990s.

The bottom panel in Table 1.10 shows similar information using income shares: the share of total household income going to each income group. In 1979, 5.8% of total income was held by households in the bottom fifth, 15.8% in the middle fifth, and so on. Again, the concentration of income at the top is evident as time progresses. The share held by the top fifth grew by 9.3% between 1979 and 2000, with 90% of this gain accruing to the top 1% (8.5% of the 9.3% growth in the top fifth). The 17.8% share held by this wealthiest group in 2000 was the highest on record since this data series began in 1979, though it falls back significantly—by three percentage points—with the large capital losses in 2001.

A final view of the CBO inequality data is shown in **Table 1.11**, which provides income ratios of different income groups for the period spanning 1979 to 2001. Each value in the table shows the multiple of one income group's average over another. For example, the first entry in the table implies that the average income of the middle fifth was 3.3 times that of the bottom, or lowest fifth, in 1979. This ratio grew very slightly such that by the 2000 peak, middle incomes were 3.4 times that of low incomes, an increase of only 0.1.

TABLE 1.11 Income ratios, comprehensive income data, 1979-2001

Year	Middle fifth/ Bottom fifth	Top fifth/ Middle fifth	Top fifth/ Bottom fifth	Top 1%/ Bottom fifth	Top 1%/ Middle fifth
1979	3.3	2.6	8.4	33.1	10.1
1989	3.5	3.2	11.0	54.2	15.6
2000	3.4	3.9	13.5	88.5	25.7
2001	3.5	3.5	12.3	70.5	20.4
Changes					
1979-89	0.2	0.6	2.6	21.1	5.4
1989-2000	0.0	0.7	2.5	34.2	10.1
1979-2000	0.2	1.3	5.0	55.4	15.5

Source: Authors' analysis of CBO data.

The income multiples are, of course, far larger when taking into consideration the top 20%, and especially the top 1%, relative to lower-income groups. Furthermore, these multiples have grown a great deal over the last few decades. The income of the top 1% was 33.1 times that of the bottom 20% in 1979, and 10.1 times that of the middle fifth. By 2000, the average income of the top one percentile was 88.5 times that of the bottom fifth, an increase of 55.4 points (i.e., compared to the bottom fifth, the income of the top 1% was 55 times higher than it was 21 years earlier). Relative to the middle fifth, the top 1% grew 15.5 times over this same period. The sharp decline of high incomes in 2001 in tandem with the relative stability of the bottom and middle fifths led to a large drop in these income ratios in that year.

Inequality data from the Census Bureau lack the comprehensiveness of the CBO data (e.g., the Census data exclude realized capital gains), but they provide a long, consistent time series, which allows for an examination of the evolution of income inequality over the full postwar period. **Figure 1H** plots real family income at the 20th, 50th (median), and 95th percentile. The values are indexed to 100 in 1979, and thus they illustrate long-term developments between high-, middle-, and low-income families.

From the beginning of the postwar period until the mid-1960s, the rate of income growth for middle- and low-income families was remarkably similar— at times the two lines appear to be almost coincident. And high incomes grew slightly more slowly than low and median incomes, suggesting some compression of the income distribution over this period.

All three income groups lost ground in the deep recession of the early 1980s, but the 95th percentile fell the least and quickly began to rebound, pull-

FIGURE 1H Low-, middle-, and high-income growth, 1947-2003

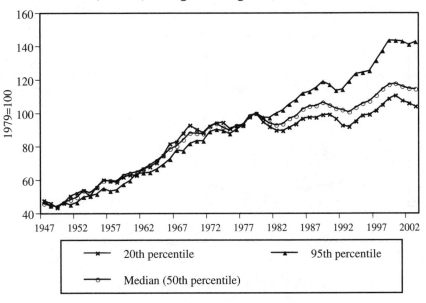

Source: Authors' analysis of U.S. Bureau of the Census data.

ing away from the lower income groups. Income at the 95th percentile grew about 20 percentage points (relative to the 1979 level) in both the 1980s and the 1990s, while the incomes of middle- and lower-income families grew little over the 1980s. Low and middle incomes did better in the 1990s, and in fact have grown at similar rates since the early 1990s, meaning the gap between the bottom and middle has remained relatively constant. But the 95th percentile continued to pull ahead, and by 2003, the last year represented in Figure 1H, the income gap stood at a historically high level.

Another useful means for assessing the pace of the overall trend in inequality is the Gini coefficient (used in **Figure 1I**), wherein higher numbers reveal greater inequality. In 1993, the main survey used by the Census Bureau to measure income changed in such a way as to induce a large jump in the Gini. The smooth trend line (see Figure Notes for details), however, statistically controls for this shift and plots the underlying trend in family income inequality. This trend has been positive since the mid-1970s, rising quickly over the 1980s. Note that unlike some of the other inequality series shown thus far, the trend in the Gini coefficient grows somewhat less quickly

FIGURE 1I Family income inequality, Gini coefficient, 1947-2003

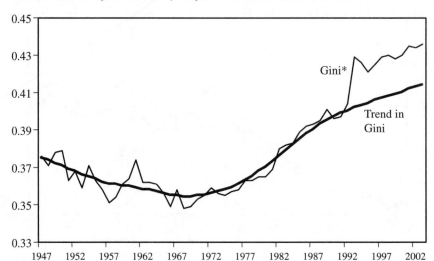

*A change in survey methodology in 1993 led to a sharp rise in measured inequality.

Source: U.S. Bureau of the Census.

in the 1990s relative to the 1980s (the trend actually grows about half as fast between 1989 and 2000 as it does from 1979 to 1989). This is because inequality measures like those shown in Table 1.11 weight sharp increases in high incomes more heavily, while the Gini gives greater weight to movements around the middle of the income distribution. Thus, in order to develop a full understanding of trends in income inequality, it is necessary to examine various measures.

Sorting families into fifths, or quintiles, of the population by income allows an examination of the percentage of total national income that goes to each family (this is the same metric used in the bottom panel of Table 1.10, but here the less comprehensive Census family income data are used because they provide a long, historically consistent time series). Under perfect equality, each fifth would get 20%. In the U.S. economy, income shares at the top far exceed those at the bottom of the income scale (see **Table 1.12**). For example, the 20% of families with the highest incomes claimed 47.4% of all family income in 2000, while the poorest 20% of families held only 4.3%. The 1993 change in Census survey methodology, noted above, has a large effect on these data as well, leading to a sudden increase in the share of income going to the top fifth.

TABLE 1.12 Shares of family income going to income fifths and to the top 5%, 1947-2003

						Breakdown of top fifth	
Year	Lowest fifth	Second fifth	Middle fifth	Fourth fifth	Top fifth	First 15%	Top 5%
1947	5.0	11.9	17.0	23.1	43.0	25.5	17.5
1967	5.4	12.2	17.5	23.5	41.4	25	16.4
1973	5.5	11.9	17.5	24.0	41.1	25.6	15.5
1979	5.4	11.6	17.5	24.1	41.4	26.1	15.3
1989	4.6	10.6	16.5	23.7	44.6	26.7	17.9
1993*	4.1	9.9	15.7	23.3	47.0	26.7	20.3
2000	4.3	9.8	15.5	22.8	47.4	26.6	20.8
2003	4.1	9.6	15.5	23.3	47.6	27.1	20.5
Percentage-point change							
1947-67	0.4	0.3	0.5	0.4	-1.6	-0.5	-1.1
1967-73	0.1	-0.3	0.0	0.5	-0.3	0.6	-0.9
1973-79	-0.1	-0.3	0.0	0.1	0.3	0.5	-0.2
1979-89	-0.8	-1.0	-1.0	-0.4	3.2	0.6	2.6
1993-2000	0.2	-0.1	-0.2	-0.5	0.4	-0.1	0.5
2000-03	-0.2	-0.2	0.0	0.4	0.2	0.5	-0.3

* In 1993, a change in Census survey methodology leading to greater measured inequality. Thus, we include this year in this table to gauge the change in income shares over the 1993-2000 period.

Source: Authors' analysis of U.S. Bureau of the Census data.

The table includes 1993 to allow an examination of the change in income shares over the consistently measured 1993-2003 period.

The top 5% received 20.8% of all family income in 2000, more than the families in the bottom 40% combined (they received 14.1%). In fact, the 2000 share of total income in each of the three lowest-income fifths—the 29.6% of total income going to the bottom 60% of families—was smaller than the 34.5% share this group received in 1979.

The changes in income shares, shown in the bottom section of Table 1.12, show that the two decades following World War II (1947-67) were equalizing in terms of income: 1.6% of national income shifted from the top fifth to the bottom four-fifths. In contrast, the 1980s was the decade with the largest growth in income inequality: 3.2% of income shifted the other way—from the bottom 80% to the top 20%—with most of this (2.6%) going to the top 5% of families.

Such different patterns in the trend of income shares raises the question of whether there was something uniquely different about these two periods that explains such different inequality outcomes. In fact, there were many salient differences. Productivity grew more quickly in the earlier years, but more importantly from a distributional standpoint, the unemployment rate was far lower, averaging 4.8% between 1947-67 compared to 7.1% in the period between 1979 and 1989. Budget deficits were high in the 1980s and GDP growth was relatively sluggish compared to the earlier years. U.S. manufacturers were less exposed to low-wage global competition in the 1950s and 1960s, and a larger share of jobs had union representation. The federal minimum wage rose steeply through the 1947-67 period, hitting its historical high of $7.18 in 2003 dollars in 1968, compared to $5.15 today.

To what extent did these factors play out in the 1990s? The change in the survey makes it difficult to look over the full 1990s cycle, but between 1993 and 2000 there was some evidence of a hollowing out of the middle, with small share gains at the bottom (0.2 points for the bottom fifth) and larger gains at the top. Other evidence shown earlier also supports the finding that there was some degree of income compression in the 1990s, though it largely occurred between middle- and lower-income families. In reference to the factors noted above, unemployment was considerably lower in the 1990s, especially in the second half. The minimum wage was raised twice in the decade, government fiscal conditions were better than in the 1980s, and overall growth was faster. At the same time, however, the manufacturing sector faced increased competition from abroad and unions continued to decline, though at a somewhat slower rate.

The increase in the income gap between upper- and lower-income groups is illustrated in **Figure 1J**, which shows the ratio of the average incomes of families in the bottom 20% to those of the top 5% from 1947 to 2003. The gap between the top and the bottom incomes fell from 1947 to 1979 but grew consistently over the ensuing business cycle peak, and had reached 19.7 by 2000, rising to a record high 20.3 times in 2003.

Another way of viewing the post-1970s surge in income inequality is to compare the "income cutoffs" of families by income group, as in **Table 1.13.** These values, some of which appeared in Figure 1F, represent the income at the top percentile of each fifth. Focusing on this measure allows an examination of income gains and losses for complete groupings of families (e.g., the bottom 40%). Also, since the cases affected by the top-coding change are typically above the 95th percentile, the 1995 and 2000 values in this table are not upwardly biased relative to earlier years.

Note that in this latter period, from 1995 to 2000, income growth accelerated sharply in each percentile shown in the table. For example, after falling or growing very slightly from the 80th percentile and down, real family income

FIGURE 1J Ratio of family income of top 5% to lowest 20%, 1947-2002

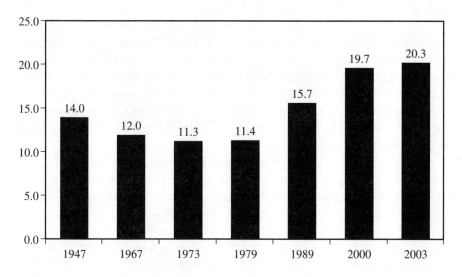

Source: Authors' analysis of U.S. Bureau of the Census data.

TABLE 1.13 Real family income by income group, 1947-2003, upper limit of each group (2003 dollars)

Year	Lowest fifth	Second fifth	Middle fifth	Fourth fifth	95th percentile	Average
1947	$11,080	$17,879	$24,244	$34,400	$56,462	$24,803
1973	21,809	35,985	50,209	69,048	107,644	48,853
1979	23,153	38,072	53,937	74,270	119,149	52,397
1989	22,926	40,113	58,451	85,313	141,776	59,462
1995	22,858	39,538	58,716	86,615	148,221	61,555
2000	25,636	43,625	65,506	97,604	171,037	70,258
2003	24,117	42,057	65,000	98,200	170,082	68,563
Annual growth rate						
1947-73	2.6%	2.7%	2.8%	2.7%	2.5%	2.6%
1973-79	1.0%	0.9%	1.2%	1.2%	1.7%	1.2%
1979-89	-0.1%	0.5%	0.8%	1.4%	1.8%	1.3%
1989-2000	1.0%	0.8%	1.0%	1.2%	1.7%	1.5%
1989-95	0.0%	-0.2%	0.1%	0.3%	0.7%	0.6%
1995-2000	2.3%	2.0%	2.2%	2.4%	2.9%	2.7%
2000-03	-2.0%	-1.2%	-0.3%	0.2%	-0.2%	-0.8%

Source: Authors' analysis of U.S. Bureau of the Census data.

grew faster than 2% per year from 1995 to 2000. Still, inequality continued to grow, as income grew most quickly (2.9%) at the 95th percentile.

Over the recent recession and jobless recovery, incomes were stagnant or fell at each income cutoff, though most quickly at the lower end. The 20th percentile family income fell at an annual rate of 2.0% between 2000 and 2003, close to the rate that incomes at this percentile grew over the latter 1990s boom. Income cutoffs from the 60th percentile were essentially stagnant in 2000-03. However, as shown in earlier figures, more inclusive data sources show larger losses for high-income families, due mostly to the sharp decline in the value of stocks at the end of the last business cycle.

Figure 1K presents a revealing picture of incomes growing together in the first 26 years of the postwar period and thereafter growing apart. The bars in each panel represent the growth rate of average income by income fifth over the periods 1947-73 and 1973-2000. The top panel, covering the years 1947-73, shows strong and even growth, with average incomes either doubling (i.e., growing by at least 100%) or nearly doubling for each income fifth. Note also that over this period growth was faster at the bottom of the income scale than at the top, i.e., growth was equalizing. The bottom panel shows a distinctly different pattern. Since 1973, the annual growth of family income was relatively weak for the bottom fifth, rising only 12.1% through 2000. Income growth was moderate for the second and middle fifths, but much more positive for the top fifth (66.9%) and especially for the top 5% (87.5%, not shown in figure; data for the top 5% are not available for the earlier period). Between 1947 and 1973 income grew 31% more slowly in the top relative to the bottom fifth; between 1973 and 2000, income grew 55% more *quickly* in the top relative to the bottom fifth. Thus, the 1947-73 equalizing pattern of growth was sharply reversed in the post-1973 period.

Some inequality analysts express doubts about measures of income inequality because the incomes of families fluctuate from year to year in response to special circumstances—a layoff, a one-time sale of an asset, and so on. As a result, a family's income may partially reflect transient events and not indicate its economic well-being over the long term. For example, a family experiencing a bad year in terms of income may dip into its savings to continue consuming at the same level as during a better year. In this view, consumption levels of families provide a better measure of inequality, since families typically gear their consumption to their expected incomes over the long term.

Figure 1L shows the trend in the Gini coefficient for consumption along with the Gini ratio for disposable income (basically, after-tax income) from the same data source: the Bureau of Labor Statistics' Consumer Expenditure (CE) Survey (note that these series are adjusted for differences in family size). The

FIGURE 1K Real family income growth by quintile, 1947-2000

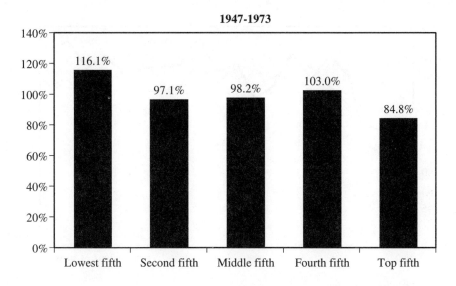

1947-1973

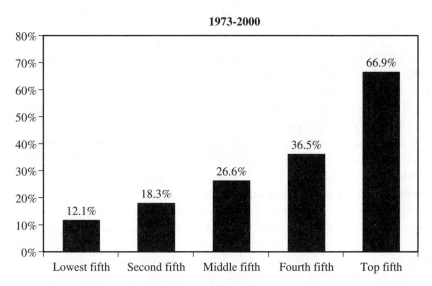

1973-2000

Source: Authors' analysis of U.S. Bureau of the Census data.

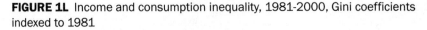

FIGURE 1L Income and consumption inequality, 1981-2000, Gini coefficients indexed to 1981

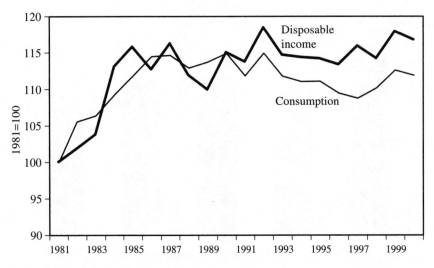

Source: Johnson and Smeeding (1998).

income inequality trends from the Current Population Survey data—the focus of most of this chapter—are considered more reliable in that they come from a larger sample and are based on a more detailed set of questions. Nevertheless, the CE income trend is included in the figure for comparative purposes (in fact, the income inequality trends from the two surveys are similar over the 1980s, while the CE data show less inequality growth over the 1990s). Both series in Figure 1L are indexed to the starting year, 1981, to allow a comparison of their growth rates. (Note that the level of consumption inequality tends to be about 20% below that of income inequality in these data.)

Both inequality measures increased over the 1980s by about 15%. Beginning in the early 1990s, disposable income inequality essentially flattened, while consumption inequality fell for a few years before beginning to climb again at the end of the decade. While these inequality trends do not match those of the Gini shown in Figure 1I, they still reveal an increase in consumption inequality over the 1980s, which has yet to be reversed. It is also well known that household debt increased significantly in the latter 1990s as families boosted consumption through borrowing. While this may show up as diminished consumption relative to income inequality, the debt burden can be a significant negative factor in family living standards.

Has the increase in income mobility offset the growth of inequality?
The data reported so far are cross-sections—essentially snapshots of the income distribution at different points in time. However, since economies are dynamic, with families' economic fortunes changing regularly, such data can miss the extent to which families move up and down the income ladder over the course of their lives (the cohort analysis in Table 1.8 is one attempt to address this critique). Of importance to the inequality debate, there are those who argue that the cross-sectional data overstate the increase in inequality. The validity of that critique is addressed in this section.

Essentially, this inequality counter-argument agrees that the distance from the basement to the penthouse has grown further over time, but it argues that a family that starts out in the basement has a better chance these days of making it to the top floor than it used to. In other words, these critics implicitly argue that an increase in income mobility has served to offset the increase in income inequality such that inequality over a family's lifetime is little changed.

In fact, those who make this mobility argument fail to either articulate or substantiate this claim. Instead, they simply show evidence of economic mobility and leave it at that, as if mobility in and of itself should lessen the concern about increased inequality. But unless the rate of mobility is increasing relative to that of earlier decades, families are no more likely today to span the now-wider income gap. As shown below, there has been no such increase, implying that cross-sectional inequality corresponds to widening income inequality over a lifetime.

The economist Joseph Schumpeter derived a useful analogy to explain the concept of mobility: that of a hotel where the quality of rooms improves the higher the floor. If everyone simply ended up in the same room they started out in, society would be totally immobile, with the poor stuck in the basement and the rich ensconced in the penthouse. The reality, of course, is that some stay where they start while others move up and down.

How does this analogy help explain the interplay between increased inequality and income mobility? The fact that, as this chapter has demonstrated, the income gap between those at the top, middle, and bottom has expanded over time means that the quality of life for a resident of the basement is now worse relative to his neighbor in the penthouse than it was two decades ago.

The proponents of the mobility argument acknowledge this, but they say that this family won't always be in the basement. This is true, but unless their chance of making it to the higher floors has increased over time, the increase in inequality means that they are sure to experience more inequality over the course of their lives. The wider income gap means that the higher floors are further away, and the chance of someone in the basement reaching these uppermost levels has not increased.

These mobility issues are best addressed with longitudinal data, or data that follow the same persons over time. Each person is assigned to an income fifth at the beginning and end of the relevant periods of observation based on his or her family's income. Different income cutoffs are used for each period, meaning that the 20th percentile upper limit in, for example, 1979 will be different than that of 1989. This approach to income mobility examines whether a family becomes better or worse off relative to other families, as opposed to better or worse off in terms of their actual incomes.

In particular, the longitudinal analysis tracks how families are doing relative to others they started with at the beginning of the periods in the same age cohort and income class. If each family's income grew by the same amount (in percentage terms), there would be no change in mobility and therefore no changes in the relative positions of families in the income distribution. If, however, a family that starts out in the bottom fifth experiences faster income growth than other low-income families, it may move into a higher fifth—i.e., this family will experience upward mobility.

Table 1.14 presents three "transition matrices" for three time periods, essentially the 1970s, 1980s, and 1990s. Going across each row in the table, the numbers reveal the percentage of persons who either stayed in the same fifth or moved to a higher or lower quintile. For example, the first entry in the top panel shows that just under half—49.4%—of families in the bottom fifth in 1969 were also in the bottom fifth in 1979 (the family income data are adjusted for family size). About the same share—49.1%—started and ended the 1970s in the richest fifth. The percentage of "stayers" (those who did not move out of the fifth they started out in) are shown along the diagonal in each panel.

Note that large transitions are uncommon. In each of the periods covered, the share of families moving from the poorest to the richest fifth never exceeds 4.3%. Conversely, the share moving from the top fifth to the bottom fifth never exceeds 5%. Those transitions that do occur are most likely to be a move up or down to the neighboring fifth. For example, in both the 1970s and 1980s, about 25% began and remained in the middle fifth. But close to 50% of those who started in the middle ended up in either the second or fourth quintile; for example, summing the relevant percentages in the 1980s panel gives 47.9% (23.3% + 24.6%).

The critical point of relevance to the inequality debate comes from comparing the differences in these mobility matrices over time. Recall that the argument against the evidence presented using this cross-sectional data depends upon an increase in the rate of transitions, particularly from low quintiles to high ones. If anything, Table 1.14 shows the opposite.

TABLE 1.14 Family income mobility over three decades

	Bottom	Second	Middle	Fourth	Top
			Quintile in 1979		
Quintile in 1969					
Bottom	49.4%	24.5%	13.8%	9.1%	3.3%
Second	23.2	27.8	25.2	16.2	7.7
Middle	10.2	23.4	24.8	23.0	18.7
Fourth	9.9	15.0	24.1	27.4	23.7
Top	5.0	9.0	13.2	23.7	49.1
			Quintile in 1989		
Quintile in 1979					
Bottom	50.4%	24.1%	15.0%	7.4%	3.2%
Second	21.3	31.5	23.8	15.8	7.6
Middle	12.1	23.3	25.0	24.6	15.0
Fourth	6.8	16.1	24.3	27.6	25.3
Top	4.2	5.4	13.4	26.1	50.9
			Quintile in 1998		
Quintile in 1989					
Bottom	53.3%	23.6%	12.4%	6.4%	4.3%
Second	25.7	36.3	22.6	11.0	4.3
Middle	10.9	20.7	28.3	27.5	12.6
Fourth	6.5	12.9	23.7	31.1	25.8
Top	3.0	5.7	14.9	23.2	53.2

Source: Bradbury and Katz (2002).

In the 1990s, the entries on the diagonal—i.e., the "stayers"—are larger than in either of the other two decades. For example, 36.3% started and ended in the second fifth in the 1990s, compared to 27.8% in the 1970s and 31.5% in the 1980s. In terms of upward mobility, whereas 12.4% moved from the poorest fifth to the fourth or fifth highest in the 1970s, in the 1980s and 1990s that share was 10.6% and 10.7%. Finally, as highlighted in **Figure 1M**, the share of families staying in the top fifth grew consistently from decade to decade, implying diminished mobility over time.

Data combining all family types mask important differences in mobility by race. Recent work by economist Tom Hertz examines the extent of upward and downward mobility by white and African American families. Some of his findings, presented in **Table 1.15** reveal far less upward (and more downward) mobility among black families relative to whites. The data in Table 1.15 pro-

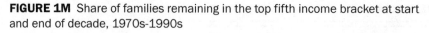

FIGURE 1M Share of families remaining in the top fifth income bracket at start and end of decade, 1970s-1990s

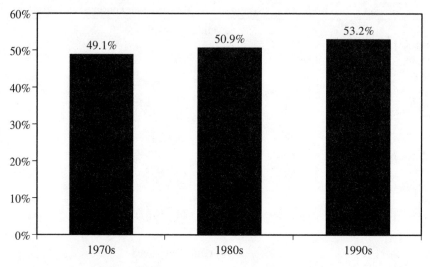

Source: Bradbury and Katz (2003).

vide the percentage of families by race who moved between the bottom and top 25% of the income scale between 1968 and 1998 (income data are adjusted for family size). The share of upwardly mobile families—those moving from the bottom quartile to the top—was 7.3%, slightly lower than the share moving the other direction (9.2%). But this overall measure is quite different by race. For white families, 10.2% were upwardly mobile compared to 4.2% for black families, a statistically significant difference. Note also that far more black families than whites were likely to fall from the top 25% to the bottom quartile: 18.5% compared to 9.0% (though given the small sample size of black families in the top 25%, the difference does not reach statistical significance).

These mobility studies show that while some degree of family income mobility certainly exists in America, it has not accelerated in such a way as to offset the increase in income inequality discussed in the previous section. To the contrary, income mobility appears to have diminished somewhat over the 1990s. In addition, what mobility does exist varies significantly by race, as white families are more than twice as likely as black families to be upwardly mobile.

TABLE 1.15 Income mobility for white and black families: percent moving from the bottom 25% to the top 25% and vice versa

	Bottom to top quartile	Top to bottom quartile
All	7.3%	9.2%
White	10.2	9.0
Black	4.2	18.5
Black-white difference	-6.0%	9.5%

Source: Hertz (2003, Table 9).

What role have federal taxes played in living standards and inequality?

The data up to this point have dealt exclusively with pretax income, raising the question: what role has tax policy played in the trends in income and inequality? This section addresses this question using the same CBO data source noted earlier, but this time accounting for federal income taxes. (An even more inclusive analysis would include the impact of state and local taxation, but such distributional data are not available; however, some information on state tax trends is presented on the following pages and in Chapter 6.)

Figure 1N reveals that post-tax outcomes are no more equal than pretax outcomes. Each bar represents the real growth of household income from 1979 to 2000, with the pretax bar on the left for each income group and the post-tax bar on the right. While post-tax income grew a bit more quickly than pretax for the lowest and middle income groups, it grew far more quickly for the top 1%. For example, for low-income families, the expansion of the Earned Income Tax Credit (EITC, a wage subsidy for low-income earners) helped boost their post-tax income 2.1% more than their pretax income. Similarly, a decline in their effective tax rate (the share of income paid in federal taxes) raised middle-income post-tax income growth 2.6% above that of pretax growth. But the share of income paid in taxes fell more for the top 1%, and their post-tax income outpaced their pretax income growth over this period by 17.0%. Thus, given the pattern of pretax income growth and changes in federal tax policy between 1979 and 2000, the post-tax gap between the richest 1% and middle- and low-income families was greater than the pretax gap, meaning that tax policy exacerbated the growth of income inequality.

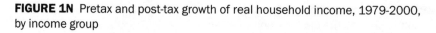

FIGURE 1N Pretax and post-tax growth of real household income, 1979-2000, by income group

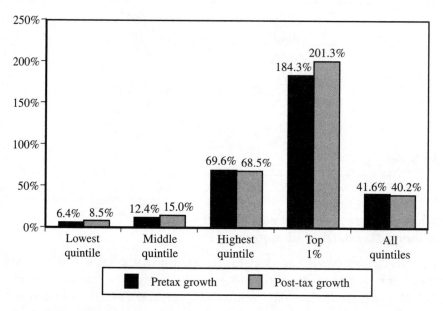

Source: Authors' analysis of CBO data.

In fact, significant changes in federal, state, and local tax rates have been implemented since the 1970s. In general terms, over the 1980s, taxes became more regressive—that is, higher-income families saw their tax payments fall relative to lower-income families—and more progressive during the early 1990s, when higher-income families saw their tax payments rise relative to lower-income families. Changes in tax policy over the 1980s, then, reinforced the overall trend toward inequality, while changes in tax policy during the early 1990s helped to reduce inequality's growth. As shown below, federal tax changes since 2000 have been highly regressive.

Table 1.16 presents the CBO's estimates of effective household tax rates at three cyclical peaks—1979, 1989, and 2000—as well as the most recent year (2001). Note that these 2001 data include the impact of sharp pretax income losses at the top of the income scale (as described in earlier sections) as well as changes in federal tax law legislated that year. Though 2001 data are shown, the focus is on changes between 1979, 1989, and 2000 so as to follow the standard of comparing cyclical peaks.

TABLE 1.16 Effective federal tax rates for all households by comprehensive household income quintile, 1979-2001

Income category	1979	1989	2000	2001
Bottom four-fifths				
Bottom	8.0%	7.9%	6.4%	5.4%
Second	14.3	13.9	13.0	11.6
Middle	18.6	17.9	16.7	15.2
Fourth	21.2	20.5	20.5	19.3
Top fifth	27.5%	25.2%	28.0%	26.8%
Top 10 %	29.6	26.3	29.7	28.6
Top 5 %	31.8	27.2	31.1	30.1
Top 1 %	37.0	28.9	33.2	33.0
All	22.2%	21.5%	23.1%	21.5%

Source: Congressional Budget Office (2004).

On average, federal tax liability as a share of household income—the effective tax rate—changed little over the period, as the average effective rate went from 22.2% in 1979 to 23.1% in 2000. However, some notable changes occurred within the income groups. Over the 1980s, effective rates changed little at the bottom of the income scale, but fell slightly in the middle (from 18.6% to 17.9%) and quite sharply at the top. For example, the rate for the top fifth fell by 2.3 points, led by the top 1%, which fell by 8.1 points.

Changes in the 1990s—including a large expansion of the EITC and the raising of the top marginal tax rates—returned some progressivity to the federal code, but nonetheless the top 1% faced a much lower rate in 2000 than in 1979: 33.2% versus 37.0%. Given the sharp growth in income going to the top 1%, this meant a tax savings in 2000 of about $50,000 (in 2001 dollars) compared to what this group's liability would have been at 1979 effective rates.

It is the nature of a progressive system that effective rates fall in a recession, enabling post-tax income to fall less than pretax, and providing some income stimulus to the economy. This partially explains the lower rates shown in the 2001 column of Table 1.16. That year also saw significant legislative changes in tax policy, and the effective rates in the table reflect both these economic and tax changes (the full impact of the post-2000 federal tax changes are described on the following pages). Effective rates fell fairly uniformly across the quintiles, with the exception of the top 1%. Though the actual tax liability of the top 1% fell sharply in 2001, their income fell quickly as well, leaving their effective rate relatively unchanged.

The data in Table 1.16 also demonstrate how little impact the various tax changes in the 1980s and 1990s have had on typical middle-income households. The effective federal tax rate for the middle fifth of households was 18.6% in 1979, 17.9% in 1989, and 16.7% in 2000. Since effective rates have fallen slightly for the middle fifth, there is no truth to the claims that government taxes (at the federal level, at least) are taking a bigger chunk out of middle-class family incomes.

So far, the analysis of taxes has examined the combined effects of all federal taxes. In fact, federal taxes take a variety of forms, some progressive and some regressive, and the impact of these taxes has changed over time. **Table 1.17** shows the effective tax rate for households at different income levels for the four most important types of federal taxes in 1979, 1989, and 2000. The personal income tax is highly progressive, with effective rates rising smoothly with income. The EITC expansion that occurred over the period heightened the progressivity of the income tax by taking to bottom rate from 0% to -4.6%. Thus, while low-income families simply faced a zero-income-tax burden in 1979, they actually received income through the income-tax system in 2000 ($46 for every $1,000 of income, on average).

Since the federal taxes facing the bottom fifth changed significantly between 1979 and 2000, **Figure 1O** takes a closer look at the composition of taxes paid in this low-income group. As shown in the prior table, their overall federal tax burden fell from 8.0% to 6.4%, but the figure (taken from the data in Table 1.17) shows that this is a result of the decline in their income tax offsetting a significant increase in the share of their income paid in payroll taxes.

The payroll tax, which is capped at $87,900 in 2004, is used primarily to finance Social Security and Medicare. All workers pay the payroll tax at the same rate (15.3%, combining the employer and employee's share) from their first dollar of earnings until the point in the year when they reach the cap. With the lowest earners paying the full rate from the first dollar earned and high earners paying no payroll tax on earnings over the cap, the payroll tax is regressive, as borne out by the effective rates in Table 1.16. The rate rises through the bottom, second, middle, and fourth fifth of households, but falls steeply thereafter. In 2000, for example, households in the middle fifth paid 9.6% of their income in federal payroll taxes, compared to just 1.9% paid by the top 1% of households. Comparing rates in 2000 with those in place in 1979 demonstrates that effective rates rose one percentage point on average as a result of increases in the payroll tax implemented in the 1980s to improve the long-term finances of the Social Security and Medicare systems. Yet, while the payroll tax is re-

TABLE 1.17 Effective tax rates for selected federal taxes, 1979-2000

Income category	Personal income tax			Payroll tax			Corporate income tax			Excise tax		
	1979	1989	2000	1979	1989	2000	1979	1989	2000	1979	1989	2000
Bottom four-fifths												
Bottom	0.0%	-1.6%	-4.6%	5.3%	7.1%	8.2%	1.1%	0.6%	0.5%	1.6%	1.8%	2.2%
Second	4.1	2.9	1.5	7.7	8.9	9.4	1.2	0.8	0.6	1.3	1.2	1.4
Middle	7.5	6	5	8.6	9.8	9.6	1.4	1.1	1.0	1.1	1.0	1.2
Fourth	10.1	8.3	8.1	8.5	10	10.4	1.6	1.2	1.0	0.9	0.9	0.9
Top fifth	15.7%	14.6%	17.5%	5.4%	6.6%	6.3%	5.7%	3.5%	3.7%	0.7%	0.6%	0.6%
Top 10 %	17.4	16.3	19.7	4.2	5.1	5	7.4	4.4	4.5	0.7	0.5	0.5
Top 5 %	19.0	17.7	21.6	2.8	3.7	3.8	9.5	5.3	5.4	0.6	0.4	0.4
Top 1 %	21.8	19.9	24.2	0.9	1.4	1.9	13.8	7.2	6.8	0.5	0.3	0.3
All	11.0%	10.2%	11.8%	6.9%	8.1%	7.9%	3.4%	2.3%	2.5%	1.0%	0.8%	0.9%

Source: Congressional Budget Office (2004).

FIGURE 10 Components of effective federal tax rate, bottom fifth income quintile, 1979 and 2000

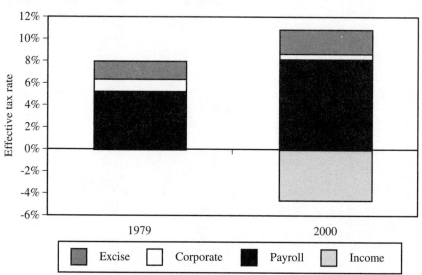

Source: Authors' analysis of CBO data.

gressive, the Social Security and Medicare benefits it funds are progressive. This suggests that the most appropriate way to judge the progressivity or regressivity of a particular tax or tax system should involve looking at the effect of the tax or tax system after accounting for all benefits realized from government activities.

The next set of columns in Table 1.17 displays the effective rates from the corporate income tax, which are portioned out to households according to their estimated income from capital. The corporate income tax is progressive, with effective rates rising sharply with income. However, between 1979 and 1989 corporate taxes declined, with particularly large drops in effective rates among the groups in the top fifth. In practice, the progressivity of the corporate income tax simply reflects the ownership structure of corporations, with few poor and middle-income households holding any substantial amount of stock (see the Wealth chapter for further information on stock ownership).

The last three columns show the effective rates of federal excise taxes (such as those on gasoline, alcohol, and cigarettes). While these taxes claim a small share of income—not more than 1% on average in any year in the table—they are highly regressive because the tax rates on these items do not vary by in-

TABLE 1.18 Composition of federal and state/local tax revenue, by progressive and regressive components, 2000 and 2003

Tax revenue	2000	2003
Federal		
Progressive	60.8%	52.4%
Personal income tax	49.8	42.5
Corporate income tax	10.9	9.9
Regressive	38.9%	47.2%
Excise/customs taxes	4.4	4.9
Contributions for social insurance	34.5	42.4
Other*	0.4%	0.4%
State and local		
Progressive	30.1%	27.0%
Personal income tax	26.2	23.1
Corporate income tax	3.9	3.8
Regressive	64.4%	67.3%
Sales	35.0	34.8
Contributions for social insurance	1.2	1.4
Property taxes	28.2	31.1
Other*	5.5%	5.7%

* For federal, this refers to taxes from the rest of the world; for state and local, it refers to other taxes on goods produced or imported.

Source: NIPA.

come level. In 2000, for example, the bottom fifth of households spent over three times more of its income than did the top fifth on federal excise taxes. This can also be seen in Figure 1O, which shows excise taxes as a larger component of the effective rate of low-income families relative to 1979 (in fact, such taxes went from 20% of their total effective rate to 35%).

The mix of taxes—federal, state, and local—can have an important impact on how the tax burden is shared and thus on after-tax inequality. Federal taxes, driven by the progressivity of the federal income tax, are far more progressive than state and local taxes, which tend to raise revenue from more regressive sources such as sales and property taxes. **Table 1.18** shows the share of federal and state/local tax revenues collected by progressive and regressive taxes in the most recent peak year, 2000, and in the most recent completed year, 2003. This latter year is included partly to show the regressive impact of recent federal tax changes.

TABLE 1.19 Federal and state/local revenue as a share of GDP, 1959-2003

	Federal	State and local	Total
1959	17.1%	6.8%	23.9%
1969	19.2	8.5	27.7
1979	18.5	8.4	27.0
1989	18.2	9.1	27.3
2000	20.4	9.2	29.6
2003	16.4	8.9	25.3

Source: Authors' analysis of NIPA data.

In the peak year, 2000, over three-fifths (60.8%) of federal tax revenue was raised through progressive taxes, compared to less than a third (30.1%) for state and local revenues. The income tax comprises the largest revenue source for the federal government, though the payroll tax for social insurance—a regressive source of revenue—is the next largest federal component. While state income taxes accounted for over a quarter of state revenue in 2000, sales and property taxes were both larger sources, driving the regressive structure of the non-federal tax burden.

Just three years past the peak, in 2003, the composition of taxes at both levels of government change considerably, though more so in the federal case. The federal personal income tax share, for example, fell from 49.8% to 42.5%, the largest three-year decline in this measure since 1950. This is partly due to declines in pretax income, especially among those well-off families with higher income-tax liabilities, but it also reflects regressive changes in the federal tax code explored in a later table. Since these component shares have to sum to 100%, a decline in the share of revenue from progressive sources implies an increase in the share from regressive sources, as can be seen in the case of both federal and state/local taxes.

Table 1.19 focuses on the changes over time in government revenues as a share of GDP, again broken down by federal and state/local. Revenue from all levels of government as a share of GDP remained fairly constant over the 1970s and 1980s, from 27.7% in 1969 to 27.3% in 1989. Over the 1990s, the historically sharp rise in high pretax incomes (which face the highest marginal income tax rates) caused this share to rise to 29.6% in 2000, the highest level on record. The post-2000 drop in these high-level incomes, in tandem with recent tax cuts, have reversed this effect, bringing the overall revenue share down to 25.3% in 2003, the lowest level since 1967.

TABLE 1.20 Impact of recent tax changes on effective rates and after-tax income shares

| Income quintile | Taxes as shares of income before and after 2001-03 tax cuts | | | Average tax cut* | Percent of total after-tax income before and after 2001-03 tax cuts | | |
	Before	After	Change		Before	After	Change
Lowest	9.0%	8.5%	–0.5	$ –61	4.0%	3.9%	–0.1%
Second	13.9	12.5	–1.4	–327	7.8	7.7	–0.1
Middle	18.4	16.9	–1.5	–586	12.1	12.0	–0.1
Fourth	21.6	20.1	–1.5	–967	19.3	19.2	–0.1
Next 15%	24.6	23.2	–1.4	–1,538	24.3	24.1	–0.2
Next 4%	25.9	24.7	–1.2	–2,907	13.8	13.6	–0.1
Top 1%	27.9	22.9	–5.0	–66,601	18.8	19.6	0.8
All	23.0	20.8	–2.1	–1,386	100.0	100.0	—

Notes: Figures show the effects of the post-2001 tax program fully phased-in (including the cuts in taxes on dividends and capital gains). Corporate tax cuts that expire after 2004 are not included. Taxes include virtually all federal taxes (personal and corporate income, Social Security and Medicare, excise and customs, and estate). For calculations of taxes as shares of income, income includes employer-paid FICA taxes (allocated to workers) and corporate profits net of taxable dividends (allocated by capital ownership). After-tax income means income (including corporate profits and employer-paid FICA taxes) less all federal taxes.

* Fully phased-in tax cuts in 2004 dollars.

Source: Institute on Taxation and Economic Policy.

From 1959 to 1989, the 3.4 percentage-point growth in the total share of taxes, from 23.9% to 27.3%, was largely due to an increase in state taxation. The state share's contribution to the increase was twice that of the federal share— 2.3 percentage points (6.8% in 1959 compared to 9.1% in 1989)—versus 1.1 percentage points. The run-up to the peak level in 2000 was driven largely by increased federal income tax liabilities tapping the fast growth of high incomes, including capital gains. Between 1989 and 2000, the state share was virtually unchanged, while the federal share grew by 2.2 percentage points. Conversely, the drop from 2000 to 2003 was almost wholly driven by the reversal of this effect. State revenues as a share of GDP fell only slightly, by 0.3 percentage points, over these three years.

A final table in this section examines numerous changes in federal tax policy introduced by the Bush Administration and legislated between 2001 and 2003. **Table 1.20** shows the cumulative impact of these changes on effective tax rates and on the distribution of post-tax income. The data reveal the regressive nature of the Bush Administration tax cuts.

The first two columns show that while effective tax rates fell for each income group, the decline was largest among the most wealthy. Federal taxes as a share of income fell half a percentage point for the families in the lowest fifth, 1.5 percentage points for middle-income families, and 5.0 points for families in the top 1%. As the next column shows, these changes led to lower tax liabilities throughout the income scale, with tax savings of $1,386 (in 2004 dollars) on average. However, there is tremendous variation around this average tax cut, with very minor savings at the bottom ($61), moderate savings in the middle ($586), and a very large decline of $66,601 for the richest 1%.

The after-tax income share changes shown in the last column have the advantage of isolating the impact of tax changes on inequality, revealing the strongly regressive tilt of the Bush Administration's changes (i.e., the share changes reflect only the impact of the changes in the tax system, not pretax income changes). Taken together, the changes implemented over these years ended up transferring income share from the bottom 99% to the top 1%. Each income group's share of after-tax income falls slightly except that of the top 1%, which increases by 0.8 percentage points, an increase in post-tax income inequality wholly induced by changes in the federal tax code.

Family income changes by income class

Thus far, the analysis of income groups has examined various percentiles in the income distribution, such as fifths (quintiles) or the top 1%. These relative measures—comparisons of where families of different income levels are relative to each other, but without reference to real income levels—are useful ways of assessing questions of inequality and tax progressivity. Another important dimension of living standards comes from an analysis of the proportion of families with low, middle, and high incomes. The analysis turns now to two measures of family income that facilitate this vantage point. The first is an absolute (as opposed to "relative") measure that looks at the percentage of families in a set of real income brackets over time, while the second returns to a more relative approach. Comparing these two sets of results yields an important insight about the trajectory of income classes over the past few decades: while the growth of average income has led to fewer families with low absolute income levels, income growth of families in these lower brackets have not kept pace with that of higher-income families.

There are two main factors that determine the distribution of the population at various income levels: the rate of growth of average income and changes in income equality. As long as average income growth is faster than inflation (as is usually the case) and income inequality is unchanged (which has not been the case in recent decades), there will be a greater proportion of the population at higher income levels over time. For example, the share of families with incomes under $25,000 (adjusted for inflation) will fall under this scenario. However, if inequality grows such that the low-income population fails to receive much of the income growth and the high-income population obtains an unusually large proportion, then a rise in average income is less likely to translate into a general upward movement of the families to higher income levels. The data through 2002 allow for an examination of the impact of the downturn on the share of families at different income levels.

Table 1.21 reveals that economic growth over time has led to a larger share of families with higher incomes. While some analysts have touted this trend as indicative of balanced growth in an economy that "lifts all boats," such a trend is exactly what could be expected to occur. As the economy becomes more productive and expands year in and year out, the general income level rises, the share of families with low incomes falls, and the share with higher incomes rises. The question is, how steady has this progress been, and have certain income groups benefited less than others from overall growth? In fact, when inequality grew quickly, as in the 1980s, fewer families benefited from growth, and the shift toward higher absolute living standards was slowed for many families.

The first section of Table 1.21 shows the proportion of families in various income brackets between 1969 and 2002, broken into brackets of $25,000 (2002 dollars). From 1969 to 1979, when income inequality grew less quickly than in later decades, average income growth lifted a significant proportion of families—9.6%—from the bottom two categories (those earning less than $50,000 in 2002 dollars) to the three highest categories. Over the 1980s, however, the share of families moving out of the lower two categories was smaller (4.4% compared to 9.6%). In fact, the shift out of the lowest income group (those earning less than $25,000) was less than 1%; about 23% of families were in this group in both 1979 and 1989. Clearly, little of the economic growth that occurred over the 1980s reached low-income families, which is one of the reason poverty rates fell much less than expected over the decade, as discussed in Chapter 5. At the same time, the pace at which families were shifting into the highest group—those earning more than $100,000—sped up in both the 1980s and 1990s.

The 2001 recession and ensuing jobless recovery led to a generally uniform shift to the lower income brackets. As the last column of Table 1.21 shows, though the $75-$100,000 group was essentially unchanged (up by 0.1), downshifting occurred in each other category above $25,000 and the lowest

TABLE 1.21 Family income by real and relative income brackets, 1969-2002

Income	1969	1979	1989	2000	2002	Percentage-point changes			
						1969-79	1979-89	1989-2000	2000-02
<$25K	25.5%	23.6%	23.0%	19.7%	21.0%	-1.9	-0.6	-3.3	1.3
$25K-$50K	41.1	33.4	29.6	27.5	27.2	-7.7	-3.8	-2.1	-0.3
$50K-$75K	22.3	24.8	22.5	21.1	20.6	2.5	-2.3	-1.4	-0.5
$75K-$100K	6.8	10.3	12.2	13.4	13.5	3.5	1.9	1.2	0.1
$100K+	4.3	8.0	12.7	18.3	17.8	3.7	4.7	5.6	-0.5
Total	100.0	100.0	100.0	100.0	100.0				
Family income									
relative to the median									
Less than 50% of median	18.0%	20.1%	22.1%	22.0%	22.5%	2.1	2.0	-0.1	0.5
50%-200% of median	71.2	68.0	63.2	61.7	60.7	-3.2	-4.8	-1.5	-1.0
Over 200% of median	10.8	11.9	14.7	16.3	16.8	1.1	2.8	1.6	0.5
Total	100.0	100.0	100.0	100.0	100.0				

Source: Authors' analysis of March CPS data.

FIGURE 1P Change in family income shares over the past two recessions

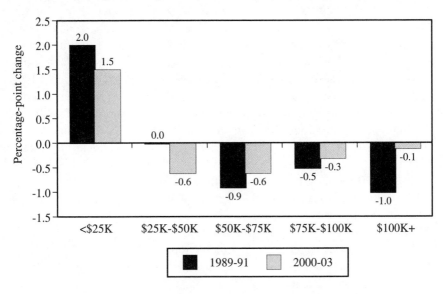

Source: Authors' analysis of U.S. Bureau of the Census data.

category expanded accordingly. This is the expected pattern for recessions (the opposite of the expected pattern during expansions). But how does the recent downturn compare to others?

Figure 1P compares the change in shares over two similar downturns: 1989-91 and 2000-02. Compared to the early 1990s downturn, the most recent recession had a slightly greater impact on the least well-off and a slightly smaller impact on families with incomes greater than $100,000. The earlier downturn saw a similarly sized increase in the share of families in the lowest income group, while the recent downturn was somewhat more concentrated among the lowest income families, the only income group that experienced a significant increase. The share of families in the $25-$50,000 group grew by 0.8 points in the earlier downturn and contracted slightly in the 2000-02 period, while the share of the families with at least $100,000 fell slightly more in the earlier period (-0.9 compared to -0.5). However, earlier data on the sharp income losses among the very wealthy (top 1%) show that there was surely a shift downward in the recent recession within the top bracket shown in Table 1.21.

The second section of Table 1.21 examines the incomes of individuals— single and in families—according to the per capita incomes of their families (size-adjusted), with single persons categorized according to their individual incomes. In this analysis, the income of persons is measured relative to the median. Thus, unlike the top panel of the table, which fixes the income brackets in real dollar terms, the brackets for the income categories in this section move with the median income. This approach provides more important insights into inequality because it measures the relative, as opposed to the absolute, changes in family incomes. Thus, in the first section, the absolute income level of a low-income family may grow such that it crosses from the $25,000 category into the middle group. But if its income grows more slowly than that of the median, then the family will still fall behind relative to more affluent families.

From 1979 forward, more than one-fifth of the population lived in households with income below half of the median income. Over both the 1970s and 1980s, this share grew by about two percentage points and remained at that level in 2000, climbing slightly over the downturn to reach 22.5% by 2002. The difference in this pattern from that in the top panel of Table 1.21 provides interesting information about the impact of growing income inequality. Note, for example, the consistent decline in the share of families with incomes less than $25,000 ($25,000 was about half of the median income in 2002; the median income was about $51,700 in 2002 dollars). Yet the share of persons in families with income less than half the median has grown or remained unchanged since 1969. Thus, while average income growth has helped to diminish the share of low-income families measured in absolute terms, increased inequality has kept them from gaining ground of higher income families. In other words, their incomes have grown in absolute terms, but not relative to that of middle-income or wealthy families.

Meanwhile, the share at the top of the income distribution—over 200% of the median—grew fairly consistently over this period. Since these shares must sum to 100 in each year, and thus the changes in each of the last four columns must sum to zero, this pattern of increased shares on either side of the middle means a declining share in middle-income families (those with incomes from half to twice the median), and this middle-income share fell from 71.2% in 1969 to 60.7% in 2002. Thus, by this measure, America's broad middle class has been shrinking, with shares shifting upward and downward.

Expanding capital incomes

The fortunes of individual families depend heavily on their reliance upon particular sources of income: labor income, capital income, or government assistance. For instance, one significant reason for the unequal growth in family

TABLE 1.22 Sources of household income by income type, 1999

Income group	Share of each group's income				Share of income type by group			
	Wage and salary	Capital*	Government transfer and other	Total	Wage and salary	Capital*	Government transfer and other	Total
Bottom four-fifths	76.5%	10.0%	13.5%	100.0%	45.7%	19.7%	83.6%	42.5%
Bottom	56.6	5.6	37.8	100.0	2.7	0.9	18.3	3.3
Second	71.7	8.0	20.3	100.0	7.4	2.7	21.7	7.3
Middle	76.1	10.9	13.0	100.0	12.9	6.1	23.0	12.1
Fourth	81.8	11.0	7.2	100.0	22.7	10.0	20.6	19.8
Top fifth	67.5%	30.5%	2.1%	100.0%	54.3%	80.9%	16.7%	57.6%
81-90%	82.2	13.5	4.3	100.0	17.2	9.3	9.2	15.0
91-95%	81.9	15.5	2.6	100.0	12.0	7.5	3.9	10.5
96-99%	73.6	24.8	1.6	100.0	14.7	16.3	3.2	14.3
Top 1%	41.6	58.2	0.2	100.0	10.4	47.8	0.4	17.8
All	71.4%	21.7%	6.9%	100.0%	100.0%	100.0%	100.0%	100.0%

* Includes rent, dividends, interest income, and realized capital gains.

Source: Institute on Taxation and Economic Policy.

incomes between 1979 and 1989 and between 1989 and 2000 was an increase in the share of capital income (such as rent, dividends, interest payments, and capital gains) and a smaller share earned as wages and salaries. Since most families receive little or no capital income, this shift generated greater income inequality.

Table 1.22 presents estimates of the sources of income for families in each income group in 1999. These data are from a different source than that used for the earlier analysis of income trends, but they are comparable to the CBO data used to analyze tax trends. The families in the top fifth of the income scale received 30.5% of their income from financial assets (capital). The top 1% received 58.2% of its income from capital assets, and the other income groups in the upper 20% received from 13.5% to 24.8% of their income from capital. In contrast, the bottom 80% of families relied on capital for 11.0% or less of their income in 1999. Turning to the share of each type of income going to different income groups, the top fifth received 80.9% of all capital income, with nearly half (47.8%) accruing to the top 1%. Clearly, fast growth for capital income will disproportionately benefit the best-off income groups.

Those with less access to capital income depend either on wages (the broad middle) or on government transfers (the bottom) as their primary source of income. As a result, any cutback in government cash assistance primarily affects the income prospects of those in the bottom 40% of the income scale, and particularly the bottom fifth. For instance, roughly 40% of the income of families in the bottom fifth is drawn from government cash-assistance programs (e.g., welfare benefits, unemployment insurance, Social Security, Supplemental Security Income) or other income (pensions, alimony). The income prospects of families in the 20th to 99th percentiles, on the other hand, depend primarily on their wages and salaries (which make up at least 70% of their income). Thus, changes in the level and distribution of wages (see Chapter 2) are key to understanding changes in the incomes of the broad middle class.

The shift in the composition of personal income toward greater capital income is shown in **Table 1.23**. Over the 1979-89 period, capital income's share of market-based income (personal income less government transfers) shifted sharply upward, from 15.1% to 20.8%, as interest income expanded. This shift toward capital income was slightly reversed by 2000 as interest rates and, therefore, interest income fell. However, dividend income had expanded by 2000, partially offsetting the decline in interest income. Unfortunately, these data (drawn from the GDP accounts) do not capture realized capital gains as a source of income, and therefore provide only a partial picture of income trends. Adding realized capital gains to the analysis (with data drawn from the Internal Revenue Service) does not affect any conclusions about the 1970s or 1980s, as capital gains were comparably important in 1973, 1979, and in 1989. However, the share of income from capital gains grew to 7.8% of income in 2000, significantly higher than 1989's 3.4% share. Thus, capital income, inclusive of realized capital gains, was clearly a larger share of personal income in 2000 than in the 1980s or 1990s, even with the large drop in interest income. Correspondingly, a smaller share of income was paid out to wages and benefits, with the compensation share falling from 75.8% in 1979 to 71.8% in 2000 (not counting any impact of capital gains).

The shift in personal income toward more capital income did not continue over the 2000-03 period, as interest income fell and realized capital gains diminished after the stock market decline early in the period. Relative to 1979, however, capital incomes and realized capital gains in 2003 were still high. Even higher levels of capital gains will occur as the stock market recovers over the next few years.

This shift away from labor income and toward capital income is unique in the postwar period and is partly responsible for the ongoing growth of inequality since 1979. Since the rich are the primary owners of income-producing property, the fact that the assets they own have commanded an increasing share

TABLE 1.23 Shares of market-based personal income by income type, 1959-2003

Income type	Shares of income					
	1959	1973	1979	1989	2000	2003
Total capital income	13.3%	13.9%	15.1%	20.8%	19.1%	18.1%
Rent	4.2	2.3	1.2	1.0	1.9	1.9
Dividends	3.3	2.8	2.9	3.6	4.7	5.0
Interest	5.8	8.8	11.0	16.3	12.6	11.2
Total labor income	73.5%	75.6%	75.8%	71.0%	71.8%	72.1%
Wages & salaries	67.9	66.0	63.4	58.6	60.0	59.3
Fringe benefits	5.5	9.5	12.4	12.4	11.8	12.8
Proprietor's income*	13.3%	10.6%	9.1%	8.2%	9.1%	9.8%
Total market-based personal income **	100.0%	100.0%	100.0%	100.0%	100.0%	100.0%
Realized capital gains*	n.a.	3.3%	3.6%	3.4%	7.8%	2.7%

* Business and farm owners' income.
** Total of listed income types.
*** Estimate for 2003.

Source: Authors' analysis of NIPA and IRS data.

of total income automatically leads to income growth that is concentrated at the top.

It is difficult to interpret changes in proprietor's income (presented in Table 1.23) because it is a mixture of both labor and capital income. That is, the income that an owner of a business (or farmer) receives results from his or her work effort (labor income) and his or her ownership (capital income) of the business or farm. To the extent that the shrinkage of proprietor's income results from a shift of people out of the proprietary sector (e.g., leaving farming) and into wage and salary employment, there will be a corresponding increase in labor's share of income (e.g., as farm income is replaced by wage income). This shift out of proprietor's income thus helps to explain a rising labor share in some periods, such as from 1959 to 1973. However, there has not been a dramatic shift in proprietor's income over the last few decades (it is roughly equivalent in 1979 and 2003), so it has not been a factor that has shifted the income distribution during that time.

From the point of view of national income (incomes generated by the corporate, proprietor, and government sectors), one can also discern a clear shift away from labor income toward capital income **(Table 1.24)**. Unfortunately, there are no recent data (from the regular GDP accounts) to provide an up-to-date look at this issue (and some definition changes have occurred in these economic variables, as well, in recent years). The general point, however, can be made with the older data, as seen in Table 1.24. For instance, labor's share of national income fell from 73.5% in 1979 to 72.1% in 1989, and then fell further to 71.6 % in 2000. A closer look at the underlying data, however, suggests an even more significant shift away from labor income. First, labor's share of national income rose steadily from 1959 to 1979. One reason for the expanding share of labor income in those years was the steady expansion of the government/nonprofit sector. When the government/nonprofit sector grows, there is a tendency for labor's share of income to grow because this sector generates *only* labor income and no capital income. For example, Table 1.24 shows that the growth of the government/nonprofit sector—from 18.4% to 19.4% of national income between 1979 and 1989—necessarily added 1.0 percentage points to labor's share of national income (other things remaining equal). On the other hand, the shrinkage of the government/nonprofit sector over the 1989-2000 period led to a smaller labor share of income. Thus, the growth of the government sector over the 1980s led to an understatement of the decline of labor's share in that decade; in the 1990s, the decline in the government/nonprofit sector had the opposite effect. The decline in labor's share of national income from 1979 to 2000—a 1.9 percentage-point decline—is not affected by any change in the size of the government/nonprofit sector, which was nearly as big in 2000 as in 1979.

Labor's share of national income also grows as the proprietary sector (farm and non-farm unincorporated businesses) shrinks, as it did from 1959 to 1979, because labor's share of income in that sector is relatively low (about one-third in 1979). When resources shift from a sector with a low labor share of income, such as the proprietor's sector, to sectors with a higher labor share (all of the other sectors), the share of labor income in the economy necessarily rises. The changing composition of income across organizational sectors (expanding government, shrinking proprietorships) is important to examine when studying particular decades. Changes in the proprietor's sector, however, have not materially affected the aggregate labor share over the last few decades.

The clearest way to examine the changes in income shares is to focus on the corporate sector, which accounted for 60% of national income in 2000. Such an analysis is useful because it is not muddied by income shifts among sectors (such as expanding or shrinking government or proprietors' sectors) or the difficulty in defining "proprietor's" income as either labor or capital income. The division of incomes in the corporate sector, using these older data, is

TABLE 1.24 Shares of income by type and sector, 1959-2000

| | Shares of domestic national income | | | | | |
Sector	1959	1969	1973	1979	1989	2000
National income, all sectors						
Labor	68.8%	72.5%	72.8%	73.5%	72.1%	71.6%
Capital	18.6	17.6	16.9	17.5	19.6	19.5
Proprietor's profit	12.7	9.9	10.3	9.0	8.3	8.9
Total	100.0	100.0	100.0	100.0	100.0	100.0
Corporate and business sector						
Labor	44.5%	47.9%	48.3%	50.4%	48.4%	48.9%
Capital	18.3	17.0	15.9	16.1	17.4	18.4
Total	62.7	64.9	64.1	66.5	65.8	67.2
Proprietor's sector						
Labor	9.1%	6.0%	5.2%	4.7%	4.3%	4.7%
Capital	0.3	0.6	1.0	1.4	2.2	1.1
Proprietor's profit	12.7	9.9	10.3	9.0	8.3	8.9
Total	22.0	16.6	16.6	15.1	14.8	14.7
Government/ nonprofit sector						
Labor	15.2%	18.6%	19.3%	18.4%	19.4%	18.0%
Capital	0.0	0.0	0.0	0.0	0.0	0.0
Total	15.2	18.6	19.3	18.4	19.4	18.0
Addendum:						
Shares of corporate-sector income*						
Labor	78.1%	80.3%	81.8%	82.3%	81.8%	80.5%
Capital	21.9	19.7	18.2	17.7	18.2	19.5
Total	100.0	100.0	100.0	100.0	100.0	100.0

* Does not include sole proprietorships, partnerships, and other private non-corporate business. The corporate sector, which includes both financial and non-financial corporations, accounted for 60% of national income in 2000.

Source: Authors' analysis of NIPA data.

shown in the bottom section of Table 1.24. Labor's share fell from 82.3% in 1979 to 81.8% in 1989, and then to 80.5% in 2000. These data suggest that there has been a strong shift away from labor income in the private corporate sector. Fortunately, the revised data (up-to-date and with new definitions) for income shares in the corporate sector are available and shown in **Table 1.25**

TABLE 1.25 Corporate sector profit rates and shares, 1959-2003

	Profit rates*		Income shares			Capital-output
	Pre-tax	After-tax	Profit share**	Labor share	Total	ratio
Business cycle peaks						
1959	14.5%	8.0%	22.7%	77.4%	100.0%	1.56
1969	14.2	7.8	20.3	79.7	100.0	1.43
1973	12.1	6.6	18.8	81.2	100.0	1.55
1979	9.8	5.1	17.9	82.1	100.0	1.83
1989	10.5	6.2	18.9	81.1	100.0	1.80
2000	10.5	6.3	17.7	82.3	100.0	1.69
2003	11.1	8.3	19.4	80.6	100.0	1.76
Business cycle averages						
1959-69	15.6%	9.2%	22.4%	77.6%	100.0%	1.44
1970-73	12.2	6.9	18.9	81.1	100.0	1.55
1974-79	10.5	5.7	18.8	81.2	100.0	1.79
1980-89	9.9	6.0	18.5	81.5	100.0	1.87
1989-95	10.1	6.3	18.2	81.8	100.0	1.80
1996-2000	11.5	7.5	19.7	80.3	100.0	1.71
2001-03	10.0	7.2	17.7	82.3	100.0	1.77

* "Profit" is all capital income. This measure, therefore, reflects the returns to capital per dollar of assets.
** "Profit share" is the ratio of capital income to all corporate income.

Source: Authors' analysis of NIPA and BEA data.

and in **Figure 1Q**. Labor's share had dramatically fallen by the mid-1990s but recovered the lost share in the boom of the late 1990s, gaining four percentage points between 1997 and 2000. This indicator provides further affirmation that low unemployment strengthened workers' hands in the labor market in the late 1990s.

How important is the shift in the shares of labor and capital income? Labor's share in the corporate sector in 2003 was 80.6%, 1.5 percentage points below labor's share in 1979. It would require average hourly compensation to be 1.9% greater (82.1 divided by 80.6, less 1) to return to the previously higher labor share. Thus, the shift toward greater capital income shares has had a non-trivial implication for wage and compensation growth.

An examination of labor and capital income shares, however, cannot fully determine whether there has been a redistribution of income from labor to capital, or vice versa. This type of analysis assumes that, if labor and capital shares remain constant, then there has been no redistribution. Such an analysis is too simple for several reasons. First, in contrast to most topics in economics, such an analysis makes no comparison of actual outcomes relative to what one might

FIGURE 1Q Income shares in the corporate sector, 1947-2003

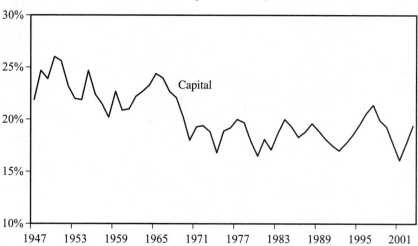

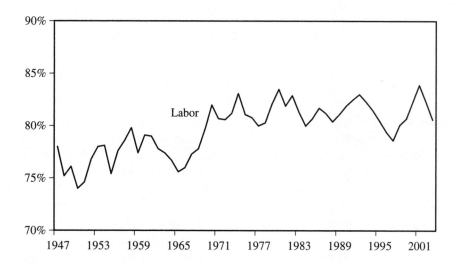

Source: Authors' analysis of NIPA data.

have expected to happen given a model of what drives labor and capital income shares. Accomplishing this requires looking at the current period relative to earlier periods, and examining variables that affect income shares. Several trends suggest that, other things being equal, capital's share might have been expected

FIGURE 1R Before- and after-tax return to capital, 1947-2003

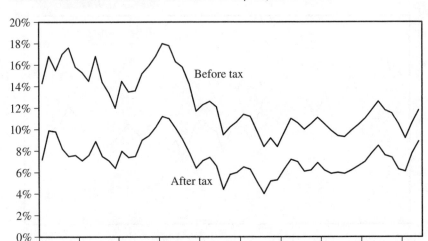

Source: Authors' analysis of NIPA and FRB data.

to decline and labor's share to rise over the last two decades. One reason for this expectation is that there has been a rapid growth in education levels and labor quality that would tend to raise labor's share. The primary trend, however, that would tend to lessen capital's share (and increase labor's share) is the rapid decline in the capital-output ratio since the early 1980s (see Table 1.25). For instance, in 1979 there was $1.83 of corporate capital assets (building and equipment) for every dollar of corporate income generated, a ratio that fell to $1.69 by 2000 but rose to $1.76 in 2003. This fall in the ratio of the capital stock to private-sector output implies that capital's role in production has lessened, suggesting that capital's income share might have been expected to fall in tandem.

Rather than fall, the share of capital income has risen, due to the rapid growth in the return to capital, before and after tax, starting in the late 1980s and continuing steadily through 1997 (**Figure 1R**). That is, the amount of before-tax profit received per dollar of assets (i.e., the capital stock) had grown by 1997 to its highest levels since the late 1960s. The after-tax return on capital is also at historically high levels: since 1947, only the booming years of the mid-1960s and the years at the end of World War II were comparable to the high after-tax returns on capital attained in 1997. The returns to capital declined in the final years of the late 1990s boom until 2001. During the early

RISING PROFIT RATES, CONSTANT PROFIT SHARE

There has been some confusion as to the difference between a rise in the *profit rate,* or return to capital (which has risen dramatically in the last 15 years), and a rise in *capital's share of income,* which has grown less. The following exercise is designed to show how these two rates differ and how each can rise or fall at its own pace.

Income is the sum of the returns to capital and labor. It can be expressed in the following equation:

(K * r) + (W * L) = Y

where K is the capital stock, r is the rate of return on capital (the profit rate), W is the average hourly wage, L is the number of labor hours, and Y is income.

Capital's share of income can be calculated by dividing capital income, K * r, by total income, Y. If the capital share remains constant, then the quantity (K * r)/Y doesn't change (nor does the labor share, (W * L)/Y). Capital's share, (K * r)/Y, can also be written as (K/Y) * r, where the quantity K/Y is equal to the ratio of the capital stock to total income. If K/Y falls, as it has over the last 10 years, then r can rise a great deal, even if capital's share remains constant.

For example, if K = $2,000, r = .05, and Y = $1,000, then the capital share of income would be 10%:

(K * r)/Y = ($2,000 * .05)/$1,000 = $100/$1,000 = .10

If the capital stock fell to $1,000 (so that K′ = $1,000), the profit rate rose to 10% (so that r′ = .10), and income remained unchanged (Y′ = $1,000), the capital share would still be 10%:

(K′ * r′)/Y′ = ($1,000 * .10)/$1,000 = $100/$1,000 = .10

In this example, the profit rate doubles, but the capital share of income remains the same because the capital stock has fallen 50%.

Over the last 15 years, the fall in the capital-output ratio has muted the rise in capital's share of income. From 1979 to 1997 the capital-output ratio fell 25% (from 2.23 to 1.68) while the "profit rate," or return to capital, rose from 6.4% to 10.4% (a 62.5% rise). The combined effect of these two trends was to raise capital's income share from 17.4% to 21.6%.

2000s downturn, however, the after-tax returns to capital surged to 8.3% in 2003, the highest rate since 1969 (except 1997). The relationship between the return to capital and capital's share of income is illustrated in the accompanying sidebar.

This growth in profitability has left less room for wage growth. This might be considered the consequence of businesses successfully restraining wage growth as sales and profits grew in recent years, even in years of low unemployment. If the pre-tax return to capital in the 2000 period (10.5%) had been at the 1979 level (9.8%), then hourly compensation would have been 1.4% higher in the corporate sector. This was equivalent to an annual transfer of $56.8 billion dollars from labor to capital (measured for 2000). If one takes account of the high levels of profitability in the late 1990s, one sees that the average return in the 1996-2000 period of 11.5% (Table 1.25) was significantly higher than the 10.1% profitability in the early1990s. This growing profitability in the late 1990s was equivalent to a 3.1% growth in compensation. Last, one can gauge the impact of the surge in profitability in the 2000-03 period, as pre-tax returns rose from 10.5% to 11.1%. Had profitability not grown over this period, compensation would have been 1.3% or $54 billion higher in 2003. These shifts from labor to capital income are large, comparable in size to the loss of wages for the typical worker due to factors such as the shift to services, globalization, the drop in union representation, or any of the other prominent causes of growing wage inequality discussed in Chapter 2.

Family work hours

Surveys and media accounts suggest that many working Americans experience significant stress in trying to balance the often countervailing demands of work and family. Many of these families report feeling like they are working more hours than their parents did while spending less time enjoying their families. Such a dynamic potentially engenders feelings of stress and guilt that can erode the quality of family life, even as incomes rise. This section examines the evidence behind this sense of overwork, largely focusing on married-couple families with children.

One common trend often cited to disprove the contention that many Americans are working longer is the trend in average hours per week, shown as the relatively flat line in **Figure 1S**. Over the full period from 1975 to 2002, average weekly hours show little upward movement; at their peak in 2000, average weekly hours were 3.1% above their 1975 level. Some argue that an increase of such a small magnitude would not be grounds for the extensive controversy around balancing work and family.

In fact, the trend in average weekly hours tells us little about how much families are working, and is even misleading in regard to the extent of hours that families devote to work. For example, the primary factor driving the flat trend in average hours is the entry of more women into the labor force over this period. Since women are more likely to work part time, their hours worked per week lowers the average of weekly hours, despite the fact that family members are clearly spending more time in the paid labor market.

The upward sloping line in Figure 1S—the average hours worked by all families, summed across the family—captures this trend (these data are only available since 1975). This index, up 11% since 1975, is a more relevant depic-

FIGURE 1S Growth of family work hours compared to average weekly hours

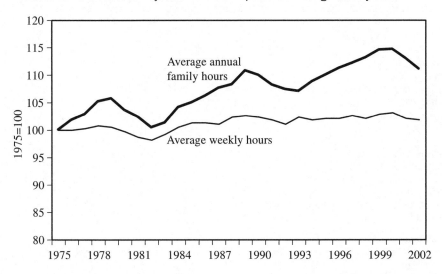

Source: Authors' analysis of March CPS data.

tion of the time spent in the paid labor market by working families as more family members participate in the job market. As shown on the following pages, family work hours are up even more for middle-income families.

The rest of this analysis focuses exclusively on a family type that is at the heart of the work/family balance challenge: prime-age, married-couple families with children. Each spouse in these families is between age 25 and 54, a selection criterion that allows for a focused look at those most likely to be attached to the labor market, avoiding young families just getting started and retirees. **Table 1.26** shows hours worked by the spouses in these families in various peak years as well as the most recent year for which data are available (2002), by family income fifths. The third panel simply combines the values in the first two panels.

The panel showing husbands' work hours exhibits relatively little variance. From the second quintile on up, these husbands tend to work more than full-time, full-year (which is defined as 52 weeks times 40 hours, or 2,080 hours), thus there is little room for them to expand work hours. (This is known as a "ceiling effect" since the variable under analysis—annual hours—is constrained by the available time in the day.) One interesting finding, discussed in more detail below, is the consistent decline in hours across income quintiles between 2000 and 2002.

TABLE 1.26 Annual hours worked by husbands and wives, age 25-54, with children

	1979	1989	2000	2002	1979-89	1989-2000	1979-2000	2000-02
Husbands								
Bottom fifth	1,722	1,722	1,827	1,732	0.0 %	6.1%	6.1%	-5.2%
Second fifth	2,069	2,137	2,117	2,070	3.3	-0.9	2.3	-2.2
Middle fifth	2,150	2,198	2,212	2,181	2.2	0.7	2.9	-1.4
Fourth fifth	2,194	2,257	2,291	2,241	2.9	1.5	4.4	-2.2
Top fifth	2,314	2,387	2,379	2,332	3.2	-0.3	2.8	-2.0
Wives								
Bottom fifth	523	712	842	758	36.2%	18.3%	61.1%	-9.9%
Second fifth	741	1,042	1,256	1,206	40.7	20.4	69.5	-3.9
Middle fifth	919	1,236	1,420	1,385	34.5	14.8	54.5	-2.5
Fourth fifth	1,109	1,363	1,475	1,439	22.9	8.3	33.1	-2.5
Top fifth	1,071	1,310	1,401	1,385	22.4	6.9	30.8	-1.1
Combined								
Bottom fifth	2,245	2,434	2,669	2,490	8.4%	9.7%	18.9%	-6.7%
Second fifth	2,810	3,179	3,372	3,276	13.2	6.1	20.0	-2.9
Middle fifth	3,069	3,434	3,632	3,566	11.9	5.8	18.4	-1.8
Fourth fifth	3,303	3,620	3,766	3,680	9.6	4.0	14.0	-2.3
Top fifth	3,384	3,697	3,780	3,717	9.2	2.2	11.7	-1.7

Addendum: Wives' extra work hours, 1979-2000

	Added wives' hours	Expressed as full-time weeks
Bottom fifth	319	8.0
Second fifth	515	12.9
Middle fifth	501	12.5
Fourth fifth	367	9.2
Top fifth	330	8.3

Source: Authors' analysis of March CPS data.

Wives, on the other hand, show marked increases in work hours, particularly over the 1980s, but in the 1990s as well. Low- and moderate-income wives (in the first two quintiles) increased their hours of work by between 60% and 70% between 1979 and 2000, while middle-income wives increased their hours by about half. Higher-income wives started from a significantly higher base and their hours grew less in percentage terms. They, too, however, increased their hours by about one-third over the 1980s and 1990s combined.

The addendum to the table gives a sense of how much more time these working wives spent in the paid labor market by income fifth. Moderate- and

FIGURE 1T Annual work hours, middle-income wives, age 25-54, with children, 1979-2002

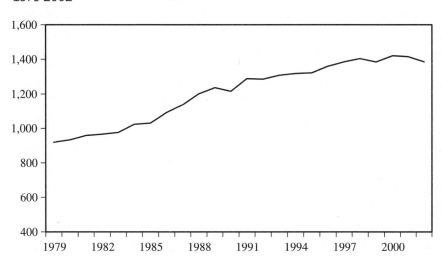

Source: Authors' analysis of March CPS data.

middle-income wives added more than three months to their time spent at work during the period between 1979 and 2000, while wives from low- and high-income families added over two months. These data provide some sense of why balancing work and family can present a challenge to these families with children.

While Table 1.26 shows hours of work during peak years, **Figure 1T** shows the trajectory of hours for middle-income wives by year from 1979 to 2002. Though the pace of hours growth was clearly faster over the 1980s, the increase in work by these wives has been fairly steady, at least until the late 1990s, when hours flattened. The 2.5% decline since 2000 is attributable to the weak labor market over that period. As the last column of the previous table revealed, hours losses were inversely related to income over this period (i.e., lower-income families experienced greater hours reductions).

The importance of wives' labor market contribution to family income is evident in **Table 1.27**. This table shows the average income of these married-couple families, again by income quintile. Real family income grew for each quintile between 1979 and 2000, with generally stronger income growth in the 1990s relative to the 1980s. The pattern of expanding income inequality, with much larger income growth at the top, can be clearly seen here as well.

TABLE 1.27 Average income by quintile, married-couple families with children and wives' contribution to income growth, 2002 dollars

	First fifth	Second fifth	Middle fifth	Fourth fifth	Top fifth
1979	$24,389	$43,541	$56,612	$72,171	$118,134
1989	23,951	45,036	61,362	81,263	142,219
2000	26,221	50,473	70,220	94,651	192,517
2002	24,537	48,848	69,082	93,457	184,746
1979-89	-1.8%	3.4%	8.4%	12.6%	20.4%
1989-2000	9.5	12.1	14.4	16.5	35.4
2000-02	-6.4	-3.2	-1.6	-1.3	-4.0
1979-2000	7.5	15.9	24.0	31.1	63.0
Percent change in income without wives' earnings, 1979-2000	-13.9%	-4.6%	5.1%	14.7%	51.5%
Contribution of wives, 1979-2000	21.4%	20.5%	19.0%	16.4%	11.5%

Source: Authors' analysis of March CPS data.

The question, however, is what role did wives' contributions to family income play in these income trends? The answer can be gleaned by examining family income growth without wives' earnings. As the second row from the bottom reveals, family income would have fallen steeply—by 13.9%—in the lowest quintile, and by 4.6% in the second quintile, had wives not contributed. Instead of increasing by 24% between 1979 and 2000, middle-income married-couple families with children would have seen an increase in their average income of only 5.1%.

The difference between the actual and simulated income results give the percent contribution by wives, shown in the last row of Table 1.27. For the bottom 60%, wives' contributions raised family income in each quintil by about one-fifth. Note that wives' contributions added less to family income at the top of the income scale, a result which suggests that wives' earnings had an equalizing effect on family income growth over this period. That is, in the absence of wives' extra earnings, the income distribution of these families would have been even more unequal than was actually the case.

Table 1.28 looks at wives' annual earnings (inflation-adjusted) over the 1979-2002 period and decomposes the growth therein into the part attributable to more annual hours and higher hourly wages. The growth in annual hours is

TABLE 1.28 Annual hours, wages, and earnings for prime-age wives with children, 1979-2002

	Bottom fifth	Second fifth	Middle fifth	Fourth fifth	Top fifth
Annual earnings					
(2002 dollars)					
1979	$3,264	$6,226	$9,312	$13,169	$16,361
2000	7,701	14,797	20,411	26,891	38,718
2002	7,073	14,024	20,484	26,137	39,251
Annual hours					
1979	523	741	919	1109	1071
2000	842	1256	1420	1475	1401
2002	758	1206	1385	1439	1385
Hourly wages					
1979	$6.25	$8.40	$10.13	$11.88	$15.28
2000	9.15	11.79	14.37	18.23	27.64
2002	9.33	11.63	14.79	18.16	28.34
Growth in annual earnings,					
1979-2000	85.8%	86.6%	78.5%	71.4%	86.1%
Due to more annual hours	47.7	52.7	43.5	28.6	26.9
More wives working	16.7	25.2	19.2	11.9	12.4
More weeks per year	22.1	20.3	16.1	10.7	7.7
More hours per week	8.9	7.3	8.2	6.0	6.7
Due to higher wages	38.1%	33.8%	35.0%	42.8%	59.3%
Growth in annual earnings,					
2000-02	-8.5%	-5.4%	0.4%	-2.8%	1.4%
Due to fewer annual hours	-10.5	-4.0	-2.5	-2.5	-1.1
Fewer wives working	-9.9	-2.2	-2.6	-1.8	-0.8
More or fewer weeks per year	1.3	0.2	0.5	-0.1	0.1
Fewer hours per week	-1.8	-2.0	-0.3	-0.6	-0.4
Due to higher or lower wages	2.0%	-1.3%	2.8%	-0.4%	2.5%

Note: Changes are in logs and thus do not match up exactly with the percent changes in earlier tables.

Source: Authors' analysis of March CPS data.

then further broken into the part due to more wives working, more weeks worked per year, and more hours worked per week.

Real annual earnings growth was quite strong for each fifth between 1979 and 2000, with gains close to or above 80% for each quintile except the fourth (71.4%). While hourly wage gains explained most of the earnings growth for the top two quintiles, for those in the bottom 60%, more annual hours worked was a bigger factor. For example, among families in the second fifth, increased hours of work explained 52.7% of their 86.6% gain in annual earnings. Of that increase in annual hours, about half came from more wives in the workforce, slightly less than half from more weeks per year, and the remainder from more hours worked per week. Clearly, more work and the higher wages of wives have been a key determinant of family income growth over the last few decades.

Further insight into this observation comes from the most recent trends in work and income over the recession and jobless recovery. Table 1.22 showed the decline in both husbands' and wives' hours, with wives' hours in the lowest quintile down 9.9% between 2000 and 2002, or 84 hours. Table 1.23 showed that these losses led to a 6.4% income decline in just two years for this bottom group, reversing most of the 7.5% gain made in over the full 1979-2000 period.

The bottom panel of Table 1.24 shows that real annual earnings fell 8.5% for wives in the lowest income fifth and by 5.4% for wives in the second fifth. Note that the decline in wives' hours is largely explained by higher unemployment (fewer wives working) and less so by cutbacks in hours worked.

The significant income losses in Table 1.23 should discourage any notion that this was a particularly mild recession. From the perspective of prime-age, married-couple families with children, the recent recession led to significant losses of labor market opportunity and income. For many working families with children, economic well-being is closely linked to spending more hours in the labor market than in past generations.

Conclusion

Given the centrality of family income to a study of the economic well-being of working families, this analysis began with a tour through the most important income trends and debates. Critical findings were the significant slowing of real median family growth after 1973, the increase in income inequality that continued after that year, and the long-term increase in hours spent at work by married-couple families with children. These specific findings underscore the two main themes outlined at the beginning of this chapter: income class as a major determinant of the extent of income growth and the importance of labor market opportunity to raising or lowering living standards.

Most recently, a period of very fast and broadly shared income growth in the late 1990s came to an end with the recession that began in 2001. The gains from that income-growth period are unmistakable and historically important. Not only did middle-income families get ahead over those years, but least-advantaged families did best, as outlined in the figure on racial/ethnic income gaps, which narrowed significantly in the late 1990s. It is notable, however, that due to historically large gains in salary and income related to capital holdings, the share of income accruing of the top 1% soared to levels not seen since the late 1920s (Figure 1E).

The recession and jobless recovery halted these gains. Real median family income fell by over $1,300 between 2000 and 2002 (Table 1.1), and the loss of employment opportunities alone explains 80% of the decline in middle-class family incomes over these years (Table 1.2). Income at the top also took a big hit, as the bursting of a stock market bubble led to large losses in capital gains. Additionally, hours of work fell for married-couple families at all income levels, as did their real incomes.

As noted in the introduction, the labor market is once again adding jobs, yet significant imbalances remain. Unemployment is still well above the level that helped to drive broad-based income gains in the 1990s, and wage growth, the subject of the next chapter, has been stagnant at best for many working- and middle-class families. These factors have constrained income growth thus far in the recovery that began in 2001. Whether they persist will be a primary determinant of income growth moving forward.

CHAPTER 2 ————————————————————————————————

Wages: battered by labor slack

Because wages and salaries make up roughly three-fourths of total family income (the proportion is even higher among the broad middle class), wage trends are the driving force behind income growth and income inequality trends. This chapter examines and explains the trends in wage growth and wage inequality during the last few decades up through 2003, with a particular focus on the current business cycle, from 2000 to 2003, and the earlier cycles over the 1979-89 and 1989-2000 periods. More recent wage trends, through early 2004, are examined in the Introduction.

The wage story of the last few years is mixed. The strong wage growth of the late 1990s continued into 2002, despite rising unemployment from 2000 to 2002. However, the high and continuous labor slack of the early 2000s eventually knocked down wage growth and reestablished a growing wage inequality not seen since the early 1990s.

The wage story of the past quarter century has three predominant themes. First, an era of stagnant and falling wages gave way to one of strong wage growth. Wages were stagnant overall and median wages fell from the early 1970s to 1995. After 1995, wages changed course, rising strongly in response to persistent low unemployment and the faster productivity growth relative to the 1973-95 period. Second, the pattern of wage growth shifted. In the 1980s wage inequality widened dramatically and, coupled with stagnant average wages, brought about widespread erosion of real wages. Wage inequality continued its growth in the 1990s but took a different shape: the wage gap between top and middle earners continued to widen, but the gap between middle and low earners narrowed; since 1999, however, the gap between the latter groups has held steady rather than narrow further. A third theme is the critical role played by rising unemployment in raising wage inequality and the role played by low unemployment in boosting wage growth overall, but particularly at the bottom. Understanding and explaining these trends is the task of this chapter.

The trends in average wage growth—the slowdown in the 1970s and the pick-up in the mid-1990s through the early 2000s—can be attributed to corresponding changes in productivity growth. Productivity accelerated in the mid-1990s, and its growth continued into the current recession, leading to historically high growth in average wages. But as Chapter 1 showed, income shifted from labor to capital during 1995-2000 (except the last few years), and the shift intensified from 2000 to 2003. As a result, the benefits of faster productivity growth went disproportionately to capital.

Explaining the shifts in wage inequality requires attention to several factors that affect low-, middle-, and high-wage workers differently. The experience of the late 1990s is a reminder of the great extent to which a low unemployment rate benefits workers, especially low-wage earners. Correspondingly, the high levels of unemployment in the early and mid-1980s and in recent years disempowered wage earners and provided the context in which other forces—specifically, a weakening of labor market institutions and globalization—could drive up wage inequality. Significant shifts in the labor market, such as the severe drop in the minimum wage and deunionization, can explain one-third of the growing wage inequality. Similarly, the increasing globalization of the economy—immigration, trade, and capital mobility—and the employment shift toward lower-paying service industries (such as retail trade) and away from manufacturing can explain, in combination, another third of the total growth in wage inequality. Macroeconomic factors also played an important role: high unemployment in the early 1980s greatly increased wage inequality, the low unemployment of the late 1990s reduced it, and high unemployment in recent years has renewed it.

The shape of wage inequality shifted in the late 1980s as the gap at the bottom—i.e., the 50/10 gap between middle-wage workers at the 50th percentile and low-wage workers at the 10th—began to shrink. However, over the last few years, this progress against wage inequality at the bottom has been halted among men and wage inequality among women has resumed its growth. This reversal is partially the effect of the rise in unemployment and partially a result of the continued drop in the real value of the minimum wage. The greatest increase in wage inequality at the bottom occurred among women and corresponded to the fall in the minimum wage over the 1980s, the high unemployment of the early 1980s, and the expansion of low-wage retail jobs. The positive trend in the wage gap over the 1990s owes much to increases in the minimum wage, low unemployment, and the slight, relative contraction in low-paying retail jobs in the late 1990s. The wage gap at the top—the 90/50 gap between high- and middle-wage earners—continued its steady growth in the 1990s and early 2000s but at a slightly slower pace than in the 1980s. The continuing influence of globalization, deunionization, and the shift to lower-paying service industries ("industry shifts") can explain the continued growth of wage inequality at the top.

There is a popular notion that the growth of wage inequality reflects primarily a technology-driven increase in demand for "educated" or "skilled" workers. Yet economists have found that the overall impact of technology on the wage and employment structure was no greater in the 1980s or 1990s than in the 1970s. Moreover, skill demand and technology have little relationship to the growth of wage inequality within the same group (i.e., workers with similar levels of experience and education), and this within-group inequality was responsible for half of the overall growth of wage inequality in the 1980s and 1990s. Technology has been and continues to be an important force, but there was no "technology shock" in the 1980s or 1990s and no ensuing demand for "skill" that was not satisfied by the continuing expansion of the educational attainment of the workforce.

The conventional story about technology leading to increased demand for skills and the erosion of wages among the less skilled does not readily explain the pattern of growth in wage inequality. In particular, the late 1990s are seen as a period of rapid technological change, yet during that period wage inequality diminished at the bottom. Similarly, education differentials grew slowly during most of the 1990s and declined in the early 2000s, a trend incompatible with rapid technological change driving up demand for skills. The decline in the wage payoff for experience in the later 1990s also runs counter to the technology story. Moreover, it is the growth of wage inequality among workers of similar education and experience not easily linked to technology that has accounted for all of the wage inequality growth since 1995.

Despite strong wage improvements starting in 1995, it was not until 1997 that the wage level for middle-wage workers (the median hourly wage) jumped above its 1979 level. The median *male* wage in 2000 was still below its 1979 level. Yet productivity was 44.5% higher in 2000 than in 1979. One reason for this divergence is increased corporate profitability (discussed in Chapter 1), which drove a wedge between productivity and compensation growth.

Another noteworthy trend is the decline in benefits in the late 1990s. Although health insurance coverage increased after falling for more than a decade, employer costs for insurance dropped in recent years. Employer pension contributions also fell. Since 2000 benefits have grown, fueled by rising health care costs.

As the wage of the typical worker fell in the early 1990s and rose in the latter 1990s, executive pay soared. From 1989 to 2000, the wage of the median chief executive officer grew 79.0%, and average compensation grew 342%. In 1965 CEOs made 26 times more than a typical worker; by 1989 the ratio had risen to 72-to-1, and by 2000 it was 310-to-1. This level of executive pay is a distinctly American phenomenon: U.S. CEOs make about three times as much as their counterparts abroad.

The turnaround of the late 1990s was a boon for workers' wages and incomes, but will those trends continue? Fortunately, productivity growth continued strongly through the recession that started in 2001, but persistent high unemployment has knocked down wage growth, particularly at the low end. A more rapid shift to more-skilled jobs than has already occurred seems unlikely, but continuing pressures from globalization and deunionization, higher unemployment, and a continuing fall in the real value of the minimum wage could weaken wages and exacerbate inequality. The renewed across-the-board widening of wage inequality will likely continue, especially if higher unemployment persists.

The chapter's wage analysis proceeds as follows. The first half of the chapter documents changes in the various dimensions of the wage structure, i.e., changes in average wages and compensation and changes by occupation, gender, wage level, education level, age, and race and ethnicity. These shifts in the various dimensions of wage inequality are then assessed and explained by focusing on particular factors such as unemployment, industry shifts, deunionization, the value of the minimum wage, globalization and immigration, and technology.

Contrasting work hours and hourly wage growth

To understand changes in wage trends, it is important to distinguish between trends in annual, weekly, and hourly wages. Trends in annual wages, for instance, are driven by changes in both hourly wages and the amount of time spent working (weeks worked per year and hours worked per week). Likewise, weekly wage trends reflect changes in hourly pay and weekly hours. In this chapter we focus on the hourly pay levels of the workforce and its sub-groups so that we can distinguish changes in earnings resulting from more (or less) pay rather than more (or less) work. Also, the hourly wage can be said to represent the "true" price of labor (exclusive of benefits, which we analyze separately). Moreover, changes in the distribution of annual earnings have been predominantly driven by changes in the distribution of hourly wages and not by changes in work time. Chapter 3 goes on to address employment, unem-

TABLE 2.1 Trends in average wages and average hours, 1967-2002 (2003 dollars)

Year	Productivity per hour (1992=100)	Wage levels			Hours worked		
		Annual wages	Weekly wages	Hourly wages	Annual hours	Weeks per year	Hours per week
1967	65.6	$24,025	$551.60	$14.02	1,716	43.5	39.3
1973	76.3	27,945	643.31	16.67	1,679	43.4	38.6
1979	81.9	28,152	642.00	16.53	1,703	43.8	38.8
1989	94.1	30,814	678.95	17.28	1,783	45.4	39.3
1995	102.7	31,698	689.95	17.35	1,827	45.9	39.8
2000	116.1	35,657	759.52	19.00	1,876	46.9	40.0
2001	118.3	36,051	770.91	19.38	1,860	46.8	39.8
2002	124.7	35,424	757.84	19.13	1,851	46.7	39.6
*Annual growth rate**							
1967-73	2.5%	2.5%	2.6%	2.9%	-0.4%	0.0%	-0.3%
1973-79	1.2	0.1	0.0	-0.1	0.2	0.2	0.1
1979-89	1.4	0.9	0.6	0.4	0.5	0.3	0.1
1989-2000	1.9	1.3	1.0	0.9	0.5	0.3	0.2
1989-95	1.5	0.5	0.3	0.1	0.4	0.2	0.2
1995-2000	2.5	2.4	1.9	1.8	0.5	0.4	0.1
2000-02	3.6	-0.3	-0.1	0.3	-0.7	-0.2	-0.5

* Log growth rates.

Sources: Authors' analysis of CPS data and Murphy and Welch (1989). For detailed information on table sources, see Table Notes.

ployment, underemployment, and other issues related to changes in work time and opportunities.

Table 2.1 illustrates the importance of distinguishing between annual, weekly, and hourly wage trends. Over the 2000-02 period (2002 is the latest year of data we have in this series), annual wages declined. However, hourly wages continued to grow in inflation-adjusted terms, though slower than in the late 1990s. The reason for this disparity was the recession-induced decline in annual work hours, driven by a shorter workweek and fewer weeks worked per year. In contrast, the annual wage and salary of the average worker in inflation-adjusted terms grew substantially faster than the average hourly wage in each of the last two decades because of a rise in work hours. Thus, hourly wages grew 0.4% each year over the 1979-89 period and 0.9% over the 1989-2000 period. Yet annual wages grew at 0.9% and 1.3%, reflecting the hourly wage growth and the 0.5% growth in annual hours worked. The most remarkable story in Table 2.1, however, is the sharp acceleration in hourly wage growth (to 1.8%) in the 1995-2000 period, a sharp departure from the measly 0.1% growth of the earlier part of the business cycle from 1989 to 1995 and the slow growth (0.4%) of the prior business cycle of 1979-89. Unfortunately, this strong hourly wage growth subsided in the early 2000s, a victim of the recession. Slower wage growth and a 0.7% decline in annual hours led to falling annual wages from 2000 to 2002.

Not surprisingly, trends in family income correspond to the shift from strong annual wage growth in the late 1990s and the decline thereafter. For instance, the strong pickup in wage growth in the late 1990s, along with an even stronger pickup of wage growth at the bottom end of the wage scale (detailed below), is the main factor behind the widespread improvements in family income in the late 1990s, discussed in Chapter 1, and the reductions in poverty, discussed in Chapter 5. Similarly, the fall in annual wages and reduced work hours led to falling family incomes and higher poverty in recent years.

Faster productivity growth is the main reason for the faster wage growth in the late 1990s and the continued, though subdued, wage growth during the recession. Productivity growth in 1996 and later years (2.5% annual growth from 1995 to 2000) was substantially higher than the productivity growth earlier in the business cycle (1.5% in 1989-95) or in the two prior business cycles (roughly 1.2% to 1.4%). Thus, productivity growth was 1% faster each year in the late 1990s than in the prior 22 years and comparable to the growth of the late 1960s (2.5% from 1967 to 1973). Productivity growth during the recession was very high, at 3.6% annual growth, reflecting the major cost restructuring and failure to add employment even as the economy began expanding.

There are two parts to an explanation for the faster wage growth in the late 1990s: first, persistent low unemployment enabled workers to attain a rising wage (through better jobs, better pay offers for new jobs, and greater bargaining power) that more closely reflected productivity growth; second, productivity growth accelerated (which itself requires an explanation, not discussed here). When the low unemployment of the late 1990s yielded to recessionary labor slack, the strong hourly wage growth was ratcheted down but remained positive (rather than falling in real terms) because of strong productivity growth.

Over the 1979-2000 period annual hours of work grew. Whether this long-term trend continues will be known only when the economy reaches lower levels of employment and workers' ability to work is less constrained. The growth in work hours in terms of families, rather than individuals, is discussed in Chapter 1.

Contrasting compensation and wage growth

A worker's pay—his or her total compensation—is made up of both non-wage payments, referred to as fringe benefits, and wages. This section examines the growth of compensation using the only two available data series and finds that, in the 1980s, hourly compensation grew at the same pace as wages. In the 1990s, however, hourly compensation grew more slowly than wages because, although wages grew, benefits grew only half as fast. The fast growth in benefits in recent years has led compensation growth to exceed that of wages, while over the long term, such as from 1979 to 2002, wages have grown somewhat faster than compensation. One implication of compensation and wages growing roughly in tandem is that analyses (such as the one below) that focus on wage trends are using an appropriate proxy for compensation. However, analyses of wage growth sometimes overstate the corresponding growth of compensation, as in the late 1990s, and sometimes understate compensation growth, as in recent years.

Table 2.2 examines the wage and compensation data that are part of the National Income and Product Accounts (NIPA), the Commerce Department's effort to measure the size of the national economy, termed the gross domestic product. Compensation levels exceed wage levels because they include employer payments for health insurance, pensions, and payroll taxes (primarily payments toward Social Security and unemployment insurance).

Benefits grew much faster than wages from the 1940s to the 1970s. For instance, over the 1948-73 period real benefits grew 7.3% annually, while wages grew at a 2.6% pace. Yet total compensation (wages and benefits) grew at relatively the same rate as wages, 3.0% versus 2.6% per year. This apparent contradiction is readily explained: non-wage compensation in 1948 totaled just 5.1% of total compensation. Thus, even a faster growth of a small part of compensation (benefits) did not lead to growth in total compensation much greater than that of wages.

Another way of portraying the limited role of benefits growth is to note that 1.0% annual growth in hourly benefits over the 1979-89 period translated (in 2002 dollars) to growth of $0.04 per year, boosting benefits from $3.62 an hour in 1979 to $3.99 in 1989.

Over the 1989-2000 period, benefits grew just 0.7% per year. In contrast, the annual growth in average hourly wages accelerated to 1.8% per year. Consequently, the benefits share of compensation fell sharply, from 18.4% to 16.6%, and compensation grew more slowly than wages (1.6% versus 1.8%). In contrast, over the 2000-02 period compensation grew 1.4% annually, faster than the 0.9% annual growth in wages because of the rapid 3.6% annual growth in benefits.

TABLE 2.2 Growth of average hourly wages, benefits, and compensation, 1948-2002 (2002 dollars)

Year	Wages and salaries	Benefits*	Total compensation	Benefit share of compensation
*Hourly pay***				
1948	$8.52	$0.46	$8.98	5.1%
1967	14.02	1.76	15.78	11.1
1973	16.21	2.67	18.89	14.2
1979	16.40	3.62	20.01	18.1
1989	17.72	3.99	21.71	18.4
1995	18.67	4.21	22.88	18.4
2000	21.58	4.30	25.88	16.6
2002	21.98	4.62	26.60	17.4
Annual dollar change				
1948-73	$0.31	$0.09	$0.40	
1973-79	0.03	0.16	0.19	
1979-89	0.13	0.04	0.17	
1989-2000	0.35	0.03	0.38	
1989-95	0.16	0.04	0.20	
1995-2000	0.58	0.02	0.60	
2000-2002	0.20	0.16	0.36	
Annual percent change				
1948-73	2.6%	7.3%	3.0%	
1973-79	0.2	5.2	1.0	
1979-89	0.8	1.0	0.8	
1989-2000	1.8	0.7	1.6	
1989-95	0.9	0.9	0.9	
1995-2000	2.9	0.4	2.5	
2000-2002	0.9	3.6	1.4	

*   Includes payroll taxes, health, pension, and other non-wage benefits.
** Deflated by personal consumption expenditures (PCE) index for all items, except health, which is deflated by PCE medical index.

Source: Authors' analysis of BEA NIPA data.

The data in **Table 2.3** take a different look at the role of benefit growth in driving total compensation growth. These data are drawn from the Bureau of Labor Statistics' Employment Cost Index (ECI) program, which provides the value of wages and employer-provided benefits for each year since 1987. These ECI data show that benefits, defined as pension, insurance (health and life), and payroll taxes dropped sharply in the late 1990s. The ECI data suggest a

TABLE 2.3 Growth in private-sector average hourly wages, benefits, and compensation, 1987-2003 (2003 dollars)

Year*	Wages and salaries	Benefits**	Total compensation	Benefit share of compensation
Hourly pay***				
1987	$17.37	$4.18	$21.54	19.4%
1989	17.03	4.17	21.20	19.7
1995	16.67	4.09	20.76	19.7
2000	17.66	3.79	21.45	17.7
2003	18.29	4.08	22.37	18.2
Annual dollar change				
1989-2000	$0.06	-$0.03	$0.02	
1989-95	-0.06	-0.01	-0.07	
1995-2000	0.20	-0.06	0.14	
2000-03	0.21	0.10	0.31	
Annual percent change				
1989-2000	0.3%	-0.9%	0.1%	
1989-95	-0.4	-0.3	-0.4	
1995-2000	1.2	-1.5	0.7	
2000-03	1.2	2.5	1.4	

* Data are for March.

** Includes payroll taxes, health, pension, and other non-wage benefits.

*** Deflated by CPI for all items except health, which is deflated by CPI medical care index.

Source: Authors' analysis of BLS ECI levels data.

sizable acceleration in benefits growth—2.5% annually—over the 2000-03 period. These data suggest that compensation growth closely paralleled wage growth over these years. These numbers vary from the ones presented earlier because they describe only the private sector (government employment is excluded), and the definition of "hours worked" is different. We return to a discussion of benefit growth below when we examine specific benefits, such as health insurance and pensions.

Although studies of labor market trends should examine both wages and benefits, those that focus on long-term wage trends alone (usually because of a lack of benefits data) are nevertheless appropriate. Taking account of payroll taxes or pension and insurance costs (including both health and life insurance), given their small size and slow growth, would not substantively alter the picture emerging from analyses of the last few decades that use (as we do) the conventional government wage data frequently employed to track labor market trends.

Wages by occupation

We now turn to the pattern of growth or decline in wages for the various segments of the workforce since 1973. Again, there are at least two distinct "wage regimes" over the last 30 years, one from 1973-95 that consisted of stagnant average wage growth and real wage reductions for the vast majority, and one from 1995 to the present that consists of faster real wage growth in the late 1990s and slowing growth in the recessionary conditions of the early 2000s. In general, the workers who experienced the greatest fall in real wages in the 1973-95 period were likely to be men, workers who initially had lower wages, workers without a college degree, blue-collar or service workers, or younger workers. In the early 1990s, however, wages also stagnated among male white-collar and college-educated workers. In the late 1990s real wages grew most rapidly among low-wage workers, the very highest-paid workers, and younger workers. The recession of the early 2000s knocked down wage growth, although the highest-wage earners fared best.

The data in **Table 2.4** and **Figure 2A** show wage trends for the 80% of the workforce who are production and non-supervisory workers. This category includes factory workers, construction workers, and a wide variety of service-sector workers ranging from restaurant and clerical workers to nurses and teachers; it leaves out higher-paid managers and supervisors. From 2000 to 2003 the hourly wage of production/non-supervisory workers grew 0.9% per year, though in the last year (2002-03) it didn't grow at all (see Figure 2A). The momentum of the strong wage growth of the late 1990s was offset by the recession, but it took a few years for the recession's impact to be felt; this delay reflects the fact that macroeconomic conditions affect the labor market with a long lag. Still, the 0.9% growth over the 2000-03 period is substantially less than the 1.4% growth over the 1995-2000 period.

As we have seen earlier, the differences in trends between the early and latter part of the 1989-2000 period are striking: hourly wages fell 0.1% a year from 1989 to 1995 and then grew 1.4% a year from 1995 to 2000, a turnaround of 1.3 percentage points. Over the longer term, from 1979 to 2003, wages are up only slightly, from $14.86 in 1979 to $15.35 in 2000, a growth of just 0.1% per year. Figure 2A also tracks an estimate of the hourly compensation of production/non-supervisory workers; with the exception of the 1970s, when compensation grew far faster than wages as wages stagnated (see the divergence between the two lines arising in the 1970s), compensation and wage growth show similar trends.

The trend in weekly earnings corresponds closely to that of hourly earnings, with a decline in the 1980s and early 1990s and a shift to strong positive growth after 1995. The fall in weekly hours in 2000 and after caused weekly

TABLE 2.4 Hourly and weekly earnings of private production and nonsupervisory workers,* 1947-2003 (2003 dollars)

Year	Real average hourly earnings	Real average weekly earnings
1947	$8.47	$340.01
1967	13.30	504.10
1973	14.85	547.82
1979	14.86	529.05
1982	14.34	497.67
1989	14.04	484.31
1995	13.95	478.84
2000	14.95	513.11
2003	15.35	519.56
	Annual growth rate	
Business cycles		
1947-67	2.3%	2.0%
1967-73	1.8	1.4
1973-79	0.0	-0.6
1979-89	-0.6	-0.9
1989-2000	0.6	0.5
1989-95	-0.1	-0.2
1995-2000	1.4	1.4
2000-03	0.9	0.4
1979-2003	0.1	-0.1

* Production and nonsupervisory workers account for more than 80% of wage and salary employment.

Source: Authors' analysis.

wage growth to be 0.5% less than hourly wage growth, 0.4% versus 0.9%, during 2000-03. Still, the weekly earnings of production and non-supervisory workers in 2003 were $519.56 per week (in 2003 dollars), about $10.00 less than in 1979 and still below the $547.82 level of 1973.

Table 2.5 presents wage trends by occupation since 2000 (because of a coding change, comparable data before 2000 are not available). As seen earlier with other data, inflation-adjusted hourly wages rose over the 2000-03 period by 3.8%. However, real wage growth declined to just 0.3% from 2002 to 2003, far less than the 1.5% and 1.9% growth of the two prior years. This wage slow-down reflects the momentum of the late-1990s wage growth continuing into

FIGURE 2A Hourly wage and compensation growth for production/ nonsupervisory workers, 1959-2003

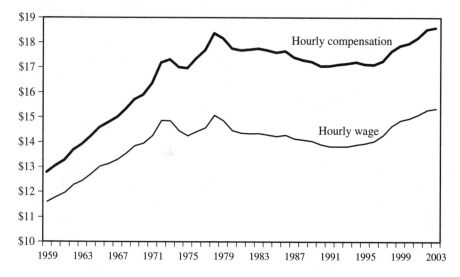

Source: Authors' analysis. For detailed information on figure sources, see Figure Notes.

2001, then slowing as a result of the persistent labor slump in 2002 and 2003. Real wages fell in four of the 10 occupations in 2003, including three lowest-paying occupations that make up 36.6% of the workforce. In contrast, management, business, and financial occupations experienced 2.1% real wage growth in 2003. This pattern of wage growth is consistent with high unemployment affecting low-wage workers more than high-wage workers.

Wage trends by wage level

For any given trend in *average* wages, particular groups of workers will experience different outcomes if wage inequality changes, as it has throughout the last 25 years: it grew pervasively in the 1980s, and grew at the top and fell or was stable at the bottom through most of the 1990s and early 2000s. Wage trends can be described by examining groups of workers by occupation, education level, and so on, but doing so omits the impact of changes such as increasing inequality within occupation or education groups. The advantage of an analysis of wage trends by wage level or percentile (the 60th percentile, for instance, is the wage at which a worker earners more than 60% of all earners but less

TABLE 2.5 Changes in hourly wages by occupation, 2000-03 (2003 dollars)

Occupation	Employment share 2003	Hourly wage 2000	2001	2002	2003	Percent change 2000-01	2001-02	2002-03	2000-03
All	100.0%	$16.52	$16.83	$17.09	$17.15	1.9%	1.5%	0.3%	3.8%
Construction and extraction	5.9	15.78	15.75	15.93	15.96	-0.2	1.1	0.2	1.1
Farming, fishing, and forestry	0.6	9.00	9.19	9.53	9.66	2.1	3.7	1.4	7.3
Installation, maintenance, and repair	3.7	16.60	16.57	16.81	16.74	-0.2	1.4	-0.4	0.8
Management, business, and financial	14.5	24.71	25.01	25.68	26.22	1.2	2.7	2.1	6.1
Office and administrative support	13.9	13.33	13.53	13.81	13.66	1.5	2.1	-1.1	2.4
Production	7.1	13.28	13.54	13.77	13.63	2.0	1.7	-1.1	2.6
Professional and related	20.7	22.04	22.11	22.52	22.58	0.4	1.8	0.3	2.5
Sales and related	11.9	15.26	15.99	16.00	16.10	4.8	0.1	0.6	5.5
Service	15.6	10.43	10.73	10.70	10.54	2.9	-0.3	-1.5	1.1
Transportation and material moving	6.2	13.12	13.37	13.52	13.67	1.9	1.1	1.1	4.2

Source: Authors' analysis of CPS data.

121

TABLE 2.6 Wages for all workers by wage percentile, 1973-2003 (2003 dollars)

Year	\multicolumn{10}{c}{Wage by percentile*}									
	10	20	30	40	50	60	70	80	90	95
Real hourly wage										
1973	$6.55	$7.91	$9.40	$10.93	$12.53	$14.38	$16.70	$19.09	$23.99	$30.10
1979	6.94	7.91	9.29	10.93	12.36	14.33	16.94	19.74	24.14	29.48
1989	5.96	7.42	8.90	10.63	12.36	14.44	17.18	20.53	25.94	31.88
1995	6.07	7.42	8.86	10.43	12.14	14.37	17.13	20.73	26.79	33.60
2000	6.74	8.30	9.69	11.21	13.07	15.47	18.34	22.28	29.13	37.15
2003	7.00	8.46	10.00	11.75	13.62	15.90	18.94	23.14	30.71	38.64
Dollar change										
1973-79	$0.38	$0.00	-$0.11	$0.00	-$0.17	-$0.04	$0.24	$0.65	$0.15	-$0.62
1979-89	-0.98	-0.49	-0.39	-0.29	0.00	0.10	0.24	0.80	1.79	2.40
1989-2000	0.78	0.88	0.79	0.57	0.71	1.03	1.16	1.75	3.19	5.27
1989-95	0.11	0.00	-0.04	-0.21	-0.22	-0.07	-0.05	0.20	0.86	1.72
1995-2000	0.67	0.88	0.83	0.78	0.93	1.10	1.21	1.55	2.33	3.55
2000-03	0.26	0.16	0.30	0.55	0.55	0.43	0.60	0.86	1.58	1.49
1979-2003	0.06	0.55	0.71	0.83	1.26	1.57	2.00	3.40	6.57	9.16
Percent change										
1973-79	5.9%	0.0%	-1.1%	0.0%	-1.4%	-0.3%	1.4%	3.4%	0.6%	-2.0%
1979-89	-14.1	-6.2	-4.2	-2.7	0.0	0.7	1.4	4.0	7.4	8.1
1989-2000	13.1	11.8	8.9	5.4	5.8	7.1	6.8	8.5	12.3	16.5
1989-95	1.8	-0.1	-0.4	-1.9	-1.8	-0.5	-0.3	1.0	3.3	5.4
1995-2000	11.1	11.9	9.4	7.5	7.7	7.7	7.1	7.5	8.7	10.6
2000-03	3.8	2.0	3.1	4.9	4.2	2.8	3.3	3.8	5.4	4.0
1979-2003	0.9	7.0	7.6	7.6	10.2	10.9	11.8	17.2	27.2	31.1

* The Xth percentile wage is the wage at which X% of the wage earners earn less and (100-X)% earn more.

Source: Authors' analysis.

than 40% of all earners), as in **Table 2.6**, is that it captures all of the changes in the wage structure.

Table 2.6 provides data on wage trends for workers at different percentiles (or levels) in the wage distribution, thus allowing an examination of wage growth for low-, middle-, and high-wage earners. The data are presented for the cyclical peak years 1973, 1979, 1989, and 2000, and for the most recent year for which we have a complete year of data, 2003, as well as for 1995-2000 (so we can examine the character of the rebound in wage growth over this period). Wage growth slowed between the 1995-2000 boom and the early 2000s recessionary period, though wage growth has remained better than that of the 1979-95 period of stagnant wages. Wages grew strongly across the board from 1995 to 2000, rising at least 7% at every wage level. Remarkably, the fastest growth was at the two lowest wage levels (10th and 20th), where wage growth was at least 11%. However, workers with the very highest wages, at the 95th percentile, saw almost comparable wage growth of 10.6%.

The deterioration in real wages from 1979 to 1995 was both broad and uneven. Wages were stagnant or fell for the bottom 70% of wage earners over the 1979-95 period, and grew modestly for higher-wage workers—just 0.5% at the 80th percentile and 1.0 to 1.25% annually at the 90th and 95th percentiles.

Starting in the early 1990s low-wage workers experienced either more or comparable wage growth to that of middle-wage workers, so that the expanding wage gap between the middle and bottom lessened and then stabilized. Increases in the minimum wage and the drop in unemployment in the late 1990s can explain this trend.

This overall picture, however, masks different outcomes for men and women. Among men over the 2000-03 period, wages grew just 1-2% for the bottom 50%, roughly 3% for 60th to the 90th groups, and 5.4% for the highest wage earners (**Table 2.7**). Thus, the wage gap between the top and the middle continued to grow. This trend contrasts with the strong broad-based wage growth of the latter 1990s, when low-wage workers fared better than middle-wage workers. However, the highest-wage workers—at the 90th and 95th percentiles—clearly fared better than other male workers, except those at the very bottom. Over the preceding 1979-95 period, the wage declines were substantial, exceeding 10%, for instance, for the median male worker (Table 2.7 and **Figure 2B**). In the middle, for instance, the median male hourly wage fell 7.0% between 1979 and 1989, while low-wage men lost 10.6%. In the early 1990s, across-the-board wage declines of roughly 3-4% affected the bottom 70% of male earners. Even high-wage men at the 90th percentile, who earned about $28 per hour in 1979, did well only in relative terms, since their wage was only about 6% higher in 1995 than in 1979.

As with the overall trend, the pattern of male wage deterioration shifted between the 1980s and the early 1990s. In the 1980s, wages fell most at the lower levels, while in the 1990s wages eroded in the middle and at the bottom. Thus, the wage gap between middle- and low-wage men was stable in the early 1990s, although the gap between high-wage men (at the 90th percentile) and middle- and low-wage men continued to grow.

Over the longer term (1979-2003), the 95th percentile male wage grew faster than any other, at 29.5%, while wages at the middle and lower end fell. The median male wage in 2003, for instance, was still 3.3% below its 1979 level.

In the 2000-03 period, wages grew more among women than men; they rose fairly uniformly about 4-6% for the bottom 90% of women (**Table 2.8**).

TABLE 2.7 Wages for male workers by wage percentile, 1973-2003 (2003 dollars)

Year	Wage by percentile*									
	10	20	30	40	50	60	70	80	90	95
Real hourly wage										
1973	$7.73	$9.93	$11.70	$13.41	$15.20	$17.23	$18.97	$21.83	$27.80	$33.51
1979	7.63	9.70	11.67	13.59	15.55	17.66	19.81	23.00	28.01	33.58
1989	6.82	8.55	10.49	12.42	14.46	17.02	19.68	23.06	28.89	35.86
1995	6.58	8.31	9.88	11.88	13.93	16.28	19.13	22.87	29.82	37.29
2000	7.33	8.99	10.74	12.73	14.89	17.32	20.39	24.73	32.95	41.26
2003	7.46	9.22	10.90	12.84	15.04	17.79	20.99	25.50	34.05	43.48
Dollar change										
1973-79	-$0.10	-$0.22	-$0.02	$0.18	$0.34	$0.42	$0.84	$1.18	$0.21	$0.08
1979-89	-0.81	-1.16	-1.19	-1.16	-1.09	-0.64	-0.13	0.06	0.88	2.28
1989-2000	0.51	0.44	0.25	0.31	0.43	0.30	0.71	1.68	4.07	5.40
1989-95	-0.24	-0.23	-0.61	-0.54	-0.53	-0.74	-0.55	-0.19	0.93	1.43
1995-2000	0.75	0.68	0.86	0.85	0.96	1.04	1.26	1.86	3.13	3.97
2000-03	0.13	0.23	0.15	0.11	0.15	0.47	0.61	0.77	1.10	2.22
1979-2003	-0.17	-0.48	-0.78	-0.75	-0.51	0.13	1.19	2.50	6.04	9.90
Percent change										
1973-79	-1.3%	-2.2%	-0.2%	1.3%	2.3%	2.5%	4.4%	5.4%	0.7%	0.2%
1979-89	-10.6	-11.9	-10.2	-8.6	-7.0	-3.6	-0.7	0.2	3.1	6.8
1989-2000	7.4	5.2	2.4	2.5	3.0	1.8	3.6	7.3	14.1	15.0
1989-95	-3.6	-2.7	-5.8	-4.3	-3.6	-4.3	-2.8	-0.8	3.2	4.0
1995-2000	11.4	8.1	8.7	7.1	6.9	6.4	6.6	8.1	10.5	10.6
2000-03	1.8	2.6	1.4	0.8	1.0	2.7	3.0	3.1	3.3	5.4
1979-2003	-2.2	-5.0	-6.7	-5.5	-3.3	0.7	6.0	10.9	21.6	29.5

* The Xth percentile wage is the wage at which X% of the wage earners earn less and (100-X)% earn more.

Source: Authors' analysis.

The highest wage women, those at the 95th percentile, enjoyed 7.1% wage growth in this period.

As with men, women's wages rose strongly across the board in the 1995-2000 period. It is remarkable that this wage growth was fairly even among all women, from about 8.5% to 10.5%. But the recessionary conditions of the early 2000s knocked down wage growth for women, as it did for men.

The most persistent wage growth between 1979 and 1995 was among the highest-wage women (Table 2.8 and **Figure 2C**). For instance, wages grew 19.7% for women at the 90th percentile from 1979 to 1989 and another 7.5% over 1989-95. In contrast, low-wage women saw their wages fall in the 1980s; the lowest paid at the 10th percentile experienced a decline of 16.2%. Middle-

FIGURE 2B Change in real hourly wages for men by wage percentile, 1973-2003

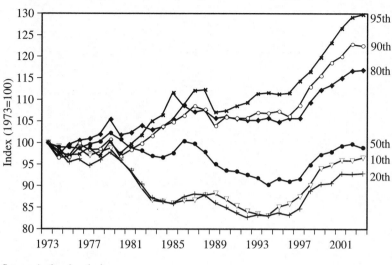

Source: Authors' analysis.

wage women saw 8.5% wage growth over that same period. In the early 1990s women's wages at the 40th percentile and above grew more slowly than in the 1980s, with the wages in the middle dropping to a stagnant 1.2% growth. A very positive development of the early 1990s was the fact that wages for 10th percentile women rose, a marked contrast to the sharp decline in the 1980s. As we will discuss below, minimum wage trends—falling in real value in the 1980s and rising in the 1990s—can explain this pattern.

As with men, the fastest wage growth by far among women was at the highest level—the 95th percentile—where wages grew 58.2% from 1979 to 2003. This is more than double the wage growth for the median woman, 25.0%, over the same period.

Shifts in low-wage jobs

Another useful way of characterizing changes in the wage structure is to examine the trend in the proportion of workers earning low, middle, and high wages. These trends are presented in **Table 2.9** for all workers and for men and women. The workforce is divided into six wage groups based on multiples of the "poverty-level wage," or the hourly wage that a full-time, year-round worker must earn to sustain a family of four at the poverty threshold, which was $9.04 in

TABLE 2.8 Wages for female workers by wage percentile, 1973-03 (2003 dollars)

Year	\multicolumn{10}{c}{Wage by percentile*}									
	10	20	30	40	50	60	70	80	90	95
Real hourly wage										
1973	$5.44	$6.77	$7.61	$8.51	$9.60	$10.80	$12.17	$14.03	$17.35	$20.50
1979	6.62	7.17	7.79	8.68	9.74	11.07	12.34	14.35	17.86	21.11
1989	5.55	6.84	7.91	9.09	10.57	12.07	14.22	17.03	21.38	25.79
1995	5.80	6.92	8.09	9.31	10.69	12.32	14.63	17.88	22.98	28.56
2000	6.40	7.62	8.78	10.17	11.61	13.42	15.90	19.31	25.38	31.18
2003	6.67	7.94	9.22	10.56	12.18	14.29	16.87	20.20	26.61	33.40
Dollar change										
1973-79	$1.17	$0.40	$0.17	$0.17	$0.15	$0.27	$0.17	$0.32	$0.51	$0.61
1979-89	-1.07	-0.33	0.13	0.41	0.82	1.00	1.88	2.68	3.52	4.68
1989-2000	0.86	0.79	0.87	1.08	1.04	1.35	1.68	2.28	4.00	5.39
1989-95	0.26	0.09	0.18	0.22	0.12	0.24	0.42	0.85	1.60	2.77
1995-2000	0.60	0.70	0.69	0.86	0.92	1.10	1.27	1.43	2.40	2.62
2000-03	0.27	0.32	0.44	0.39	0.57	0.87	0.97	0.88	1.23	2.22
1979-2003	0.05	0.77	1.43	1.88	2.44	3.21	4.54	5.85	8.75	12.29
Percent change										
1973-79	21.5%	5.9%	2.2%	2.0%	1.5%	2.5%	1.4%	2.3%	2.9%	3.0%
1979-89	-16.2	-4.7	1.6	4.7	8.5	9.0	15.2	18.7	19.7	22.2
1989-2000	15.4	11.5	11.0	11.9	9.9	11.2	11.8	13.4	18.7	20.9
1989-95	4.6	1.3	2.3	2.4	1.2	2.0	2.9	5.0	7.5	10.7
1995-2000	10.3	10.1	8.5	9.3	8.6	9.0	8.7	8.0	10.5	9.2
2000-03	4.2	4.2	5.0	3.8	4.9	6.5	6.1	4.6	4.9	7.1
1979-2003	0.8	10.7	18.4	21.6	25.0	29.0	36.8	40.8	49.0	58.2

* The Xth percentile wage is the wage at which X% of the wage earners earn less and (100-X)% earn more.

Source: Authors' analysis.

2003 (in 2003 dollars). Thus, workers are assigned to a wage group according to the degree to which they earned more (or less) than poverty-level wages.

Women are much more likely to earn low wages than men. In 2003, 29.4% of women earned poverty-level wages or less, significantly more than the share of men (19.6%). Women are also much less likely to earn very high wages. In 2003 only 9.4% of women, but 17.5% of men, earned at least three times the poverty-level wage.

In the 1989-2000 period the share of workers earning poverty-level wages fell, from 30.5% to 25.1%. This reversed the trend of the 1980s toward more poverty-level wage jobs. Progress toward reducing low-earning jobs continued over the 2000-03 period, excepting the last year (see **Figures 2D** and **2E**). This trend corresponds with the general finding of positive wage trends from the

FIGURE 2C Change in real hourly wages for women by wage percentile, 1973-2003

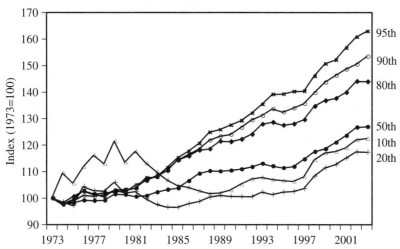

Source: Authors' analysis.

late 1990s spilling over into the first few years of the recession, followed by higher unemployment negatively impacting wages in 2002.

As Figures 2D and 2E show, the erosion of poverty-level wage jobs in the 1990s came in the latter part of the decade, which saw falling unemployment and broad-based real wage growth. The turnaround toward more poverty-level jobs in 2003 thus represents a reversal of a seven-year trend.

As with other dimensions of the wage structure, we see a sharp change in the trend before and after 1995. The share of workers earning at least 25% below the poverty-level wage (labeled "0-75") expanded significantly between 1979 and 1989, from 4.9% to 13.9% of the workforce. The total group earning poverty-level wages rose from 27.1% in 1979 to 30.5% in 1989. Thus, over the 1979-89 period there was not only a sizable growth (3.3% of the workforce) in the proportion of workers earning poverty-level wages, but also a shift within this group to those earning very low wages.

The share of workers earning poverty-level wages continued to expand, though more slowly, in the 1989-95 period, but then, not surprisingly given wage trends at the bottom, contracted in the 1995-2000 period (Figure 2D). The result was a fall in the poverty-wage employment share to 25.1% in 2000, down 5.4 percentage points from 1989 and the lowest level since 1973. Those earning very low wages still represented 9.8% of the workforce in 2000, 4.9% more than in 1979.

TABLE 2.9 Distribution of total employment by wage level, 1973-2003

	Share of employment by wage multiple of poverty wage*							
	Poverty-level wages:							
Year	0-75	75-100	Total**	100-125	125-200	200-300	300+	Total
All								
1973	11.7%	18.2%	29.9%	13.8%	35.0%	14.9%	6.4%	100%
1979	4.9	22.2	27.1	14.2	33.0	18.5	7.1	100
1989	13.9	16.5	30.5	12.6	30.9	17.2	8.9	100
2000	9.8	15.3	25.1	15.5	28.4	19.1	11.9	100
2003	8.2	16.1	24.3	13.8	29.5	18.8	13.6	100
Change								
1979-89	9.0%	-5.7%	3.3%	-1.6%	-2.1%	-1.4%	1.8%	
1989-2000	-4.1	-1.3	-5.3	2.8	-2.4	1.9	3.0	
2000-03	-1.7	0.9	-0.8	-1.7	1.1	-0.3	1.7	
Men								
1973	5.6%	11.9%	17.4%	11.2%	40.2%	21.5%	9.7%	100%
1979	2.8	12.9	15.7	10.8	35.5	26.8	11.2	100
1989	9.5	13.2	22.7	10.7	31.8	21.7	13.1	100
2000	7.3	12.4	19.6	13.7	28.6	22.3	15.7	100
2003	6.1	13.6	19.6	12.5	29.5	20.9	17.5	100
Change								
1979-89	6.7%	0.3%	7.0%	-0.1%	-3.7%	-5.1%	1.9%	
1989-2000	-2.2	-0.8	-3.0	3.0	-3.2	0.6	2.7	
2000-03	-1.2	1.2	0.0	-1.2	0.8	-1.4	1.8	
Women								
1973	20.5%	27.5%	48.0%	17.6%	27.5%	5.4%	1.6%	100%
1979	7.8	34.4	42.1	18.6	29.8	7.7	1.8	100
1989	19.0	20.3	39.2	14.8	29.8	12.0	4.2	100
2000	12.7	18.4	31.1	17.4	28.2	15.5	7.7	100
2003	10.4	18.9	29.4	15.2	29.6	16.5	9.4	100
Change								
1979-89	11.2%	-14.1%	-2.9%	-3.8%	0.1%	4.3%	2.4%	
1989-2000	-6.3	-1.8	-8.1	2.6	-1.6	3.6	3.5	
2000-03	-2.2	0.5	-1.7	-2.2	1.4	0.9	1.6	

* The wage ranges are equivalent in 2003 dollars to: $6.78 and below (0-75), $6.78-$9.04 (75-100), $9.04-$11.30 (100-125), $11.30-$18.08 (125-200), $18.18-$27.12 (200-300), and $27.12 and above (300+).
** Combines lowest two categories and represents the share of wage earners earning poverty-level wages.

Source: Authors' analysis.

FIGURE 2D Share of workers earning poverty-level wages by gender, 1973-2003

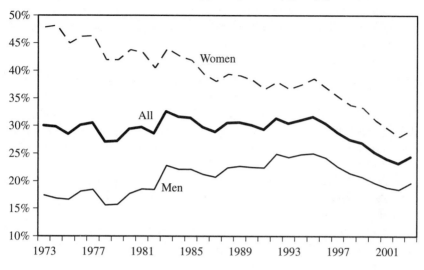

Source: Authors' analysis.

FIGURE 2E Share of workers earning poverty-level wages by race/ethnicity, 1973-2003

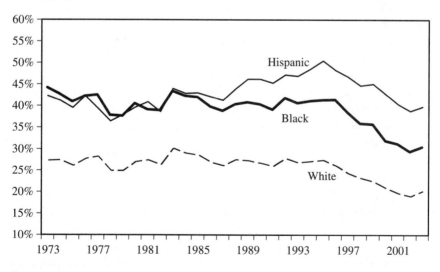

Source: Authors' analysis.

The real wage growth at the bottom of the wage scale in the latter 1990s thus rapidly diminished the share of workers earning poverty-level wages and offset the growth in poverty-wage shares over the 1979-95 period. However, a large share of the workforce, roughly a fourth, still earns poverty-level wages.

Over the 1979-89 period, the entire wage structure shifted downward, with proportionately fewer workers in the middle- and high-wage groups in 1989 than in 1979. The only exception is the modest expansion of the share of the workforce at the very highest earnings level (exceeding three times the poverty-level wage). In the 1989-2000 period there was a larger shift to the two highest-wage categories and a shift upward into lower-middle-wage jobs paying $9.04 to $11.30.

Overall trends in the share of workers earning poverty-level wages are primarily driven by trends among women, since women are disproportionately the ones earning these low wages. The share of women earning poverty-level wages declined modestly during the 2000-03 period, from 31.1% to 29.4%; all of the drop took place by 2002 and was slightly reversed in 2003 (Figure 2D). In the 1989-2000 period, the very bottom of the wage structure shrank as the proportion of women earning poverty-level wages, including the share earning very low wages, diminished. At the same time, the top two wage categories grew. The improvements, as Figure 2D shows, accelerated in the 1995-2000 period. Among women workers, 11.2% shifted into the very-low-wage category during the 1979-89 period, while at the same time the two highest-wage groups grew by 6.7 percentage points. The shift downward among women appears to be an enlargement of the workforce earning very low wages, even though the proportion earning poverty-level wages overall fell from 42.1% to 39.2%. Among men, the overall changes in the wage structure between 1979 and 1989 meant proportionately fewer middle-wage workers and more low-wage workers, with little growth in the share of very high earners. For instance, 7.0% of the male workforce shifted into the group earning less than the poverty-level wage, and the proportion of men in the other wage groups (except the highest) contracted. Over the 1989-2000 period the share of men earning poverty-level wages declined, by 3.2%. Regardless of the recent trends, the share of poverty-level earners among men was 19.6% in 2003, still 3.9% more than in 1979.

Tables 2.10, 2.11, and **2.12** (and Figure 2E) present an analysis similar to the one in Table 2.9 for white, black, and Hispanic employment. The proportion of minority workers earning low wages is substantial—30.4% of black workers and 39.8% of Hispanic workers in 2003. Minority women are even more likely to be low earners—33.9% of black women and 45.8% of Hispanic women in 2003. The wage structure for each race/gender group has shifted over the last few decades.

TABLE 2.10   Distribution of white employment by wage level, 1973-2003

| | Share of employment by wage multiple of poverty wage* | | | | | | | |
| | Poverty-level wages: | | | | | | | |
Year	0-75	75-100	Total**	100-125	125-200	200-300	300+	Total
All								
1973	10.3%	17.1%	27.5%	13.6%	35.8%	16.1%	7.1%	100%
1979	4.5	20.6	25.1	13.9	33.5	19.6	7.9	100
1989	12.3	15.1	27.5	12.3	31.6	18.5	10.1	100
2000	8.0	13.0	21.1	14.4	29.4	21.2	13.9	100
2003	7.0	13.4	20.4	12.5	30.3	20.9	15.9	100
Change								
1979-89	7.8%	-5.4%	2.4%	-1.5%	-1.9%	-1.1%	2.2%	
1989-2000	-4.3	-2.1	-6.4	2.1	-2.2	2.7	3.9	
2000-03	-1.1	0.4	-0.6	-1.9	0.9	-0.4	2.0	
Men								
1973	4.6%	10.3%	14.9%	10.7%	40.4%	23.1%	10.8%	100%
1979	2.4	11.0	13.4	10.0	35.7	28.4	12.4	100
1989	7.7	11.2	18.9	10.1	32.3	23.7	15.0	100
2000	5.4	9.6	15.0	11.7	29.3	25.2	18.8	100
2003	4.8	10.3	15.1	10.6	29.7	23.6	21.0	100
Change								
1979-89	5.3%	0.2%	5.5%	0.0%	-3.4%	-4.7%	2.6%	
1989-2000	-2.3	-1.6	-3.9	1.6	-3.0	1.5	3.7	
2000-03	-0.6	0.7	0.1	-1.1	0.3	-1.6	2.2	
Women								
1973	18.9%	27.2%	46.1%	17.9%	28.9%	5.6%	1.6%	100%
1979	7.4	33.2	40.6	18.9	30.7	8.0	1.9	100
1989	17.6	19.5	37.1	14.9	30.8	12.7	4.5	100
2000	10.9	16.7	27.6	17.3	29.5	16.9	8.7	100
2003	9.3	16.7	26.0	14.5	30.9	18.0	10.6	100
Change								
1979-89	10.2%	-13.6%	-3.4%	-4.1%	0.2%	4.7%	2.6%	
1989-2000	-6.7	-2.9	-9.5	2.4	-1.4	4.2	4.2	
2000-03	-1.6	0.0	-1.6	-2.8	1.4	1.1	1.9	

*   The wage ranges are equivalent in 2003 dollars to: $6.78 and below (0-75), $6.78-$9.04 (75-100), $9.04-$11.30 (100-125), $11.30-$18.08 (125-200), $18.18-$27.12 (200-300), and $27.12 and above (300+).
**   Combines lowest two categories and represents the share of wage earners earning poverty-level wages.

Source: Authors' analysis.

TABLE 2.11 Distribution of black employment by wage level, 1973-2003

| | Share of employment by wage multiple of poverty wage* | | | | | | | |
| | Poverty-level wages: | | | | | | | |
Year	0-75	75-100	Total**	100-125	125-200	200-300	300+	Total
All								
1973	20.2%	23.9%	44.1%	14.2%	31.1%	8.1%	2.4%	100%
1979	7.3	30.2	37.5	15.6	31.0	13.0	3.0	100
1989	19.8	20.9	40.7	14.6	28.3	12.6	3.8	100
2000	12.3	19.5	31.8	18.9	28.8	15.0	5.5	100
2003	10.1	20.3	30.4	17.1	30.3	15.2	7.0	100
Change								
1979-89	12.6%	-9.4%	3.2%	-1.0%	-2.7%	-0.4%	0.9%	
1989-2000	-7.5	-1.3	-8.9	4.3	0.5	2.4	1.7	
2000-03	-2.2	0.8	-1.4	-1.8	1.5	0.2	1.5	
Men								
1973	11.8%	20.2%	31.9%	13.4%	40.3%	11.4%	3.0%	100%
1979	4.9	22.3	27.2	14.6	35.2	18.5	4.5	100
1989	15.5	19.8	35.3	14.2	30.4	15.4	4.7	100
2000	10.0	16.3	26.3	19.4	30.5	17.2	6.6	100
2003	7.6	18.6	26.2	17.0	32.5	16.6	7.6	100
Change								
1979-89	10.6%	-2.5%	8.1%	-0.4%	-4.8%	-3.1%	0.2%	
1989-2000	-5.4	-3.5	-8.9	5.2	0.0	1.8	1.9	
2000-03	-2.4	2.3	-0.1	-2.4	2.0	-0.6	1.1	
Women								
1973	30.1%	28.1%	58.2%	15.2%	20.5%	4.4%	1.7%	100%
1979	9.8	38.7	48.5	16.6	26.5	7.1	1.4	100
1989	24.0	21.8	45.9	14.9	26.2	10.0	3.0	100
2000	14.3	22.2	36.5	18.4	27.3	13.2	4.6	100
2003	12.2	21.7	33.9	17.1	28.5	14.1	6.4	100
Change								
1979-89	14.2%	-16.9%	-2.7%	-1.6%	-0.2%	2.9%	1.7%	
1989-2000	-9.8	0.4	-9.4	3.5	1.1	3.3	1.6	
2000-03	-2.1	-0.5	-2.6	-1.3	1.1	0.9	1.8	

* The wage ranges are equivalent in 2003 dollars to: $6.78 and below (0-75), $6.78-$9.04 (75-100), $9.04-$11.30 (100-125), $11.30-$18.08 (125-200), $18.18-$27.12 (200-300), and $27.12 and above (300+).

** Combines lowest two categories and represents the share of wage earners earning poverty-level wages.

Source: Authors' analysis.

TABLE 2.12 Distribution of Hispanic employment by wage level, 1973-2003

	Share of employment by wage multiple of poverty wage*							
	Poverty-level wages:							
Year	0-75	75-100	Total**	100-125	125-200	200-300	300+	Total
All								
1973	16.8%	25.4%	42.3%	17.4%	30.4%	7.7%	2.1%	100%
1979	6.4	31.5	37.9	16.4	30.0	12.7	3.0	100
1989	21.8	24.4	46.2	13.0	27.2	10.0	3.6	100
2000	17.8	24.9	42.7	19.2	23.3	10.4	4.5	100
2003	12.8	26.9	39.8	18.1	26.0	10.8	5.3	100
Change								
1979-89	15.4%	-7.1%	8.3%	-3.4%	-2.8%	-2.7%	0.6%	
1989-2000	-4.0	0.5	-3.5	6.2	-3.9	0.4	0.9	
2000-03	-4.9	2.0	-2.9	-1.1	2.7	0.4	0.9	
Men								
1973	10.6%	21.0%	31.7%	16.7%	38.0%	10.6%	2.9%	100%
1979	4.3	22.8	27.1	15.9	35.0	17.8	4.1	100
1989	18.1	23.0	41.1	12.9	29.0	12.5	4.5	100
2000	14.5	23.7	38.2	20.2	24.6	11.9	5.2	100
2003	10.6	25.2	35.7	18.5	27.8	11.8	6.2	100
Change								
1979-89	13.8%	0.1%	14.0%	-3.0%	-6.1%	-5.3%	0.4%	
1989-2000	-3.6	0.7	-2.9	7.2	-4.4	-0.6	0.7	
2000-03	-3.9	1.5	-2.4	-1.7	3.2	0.0	0.9	
Women								
1973	27.6%	33.0%	60.6%	18.7%	17.2%	2.8%	0.7%	100%
1979	9.6	44.8	54.5	17.3	22.2	4.8	1.2	100
1989	27.2	26.6	53.8	13.2	24.6	6.3	2.1	100
2000	22.6	26.7	49.3	17.8	21.3	8.2	3.4	100
2003	16.2	29.6	45.8	17.5	23.3	9.3	4.1	100
Change								
1979-89	17.6%	-18.3%	-0.7%	-4.1%	2.4%	1.5%	0.9%	
1989-2000	-4.6	0.1	-4.4	4.6	-3.3	1.9	1.2	
2000-03	-6.4	2.8	-3.6	-0.2	2.0	1.1	0.7	

* The wage ranges are equivalent in 2003 dollars to: $6.78 and below (0-75), $6.78-$9.04 (75-100), $9.04-$11.30 (100-125), $11.30-$18.08 (125-200), $18.18-$27.12 (200-300), and $27.12 and above (300+).

** Combines lowest two categories and represents the share of wage earners earning poverty-level wages.

Source: Authors' analysis.

Table 2.10 shows the shift downward in the wage structure for whites in the 1979-89 period. In the 1989-2000 period, however, whites moved from poverty-level to low- to middle-wage jobs and into very-high-wage jobs. By 2000, the poverty-wage share among white workers had fallen to 21.1%, 4.0% below its 1979 level, all due to progress in the late 1990s. Over the entire period from 1979 to 2000, however, white workers shifted toward both the very bottom—the lowest earners—and the very top. The white male and white female wage structures have moved in different directions. In the 1980s, white women shifted substantially into the lowest and highest earnings groups. In contrast, the share of white men eroded in the middle-wage range in the 1980s, grew in the very-high-wage category, and shifted (although less than for women) to the very bottom. Similarly, the improvements in the 1990s were far greater for white women than for white men. Over the longer term, in fact, white women have seen their share of poverty-level earners decline remarkably, from 46.1% in 1973 to 27.6% in 2000. The share of high and very high earners also grew strongly among white women. In the 2000-03 period white women shifted up the wage scale, with fewer at low earnings and more in the higher-earning categories. White men, however, did not see any decline in poverty-level earnings over the 2000-03 period, but did see some shift to higher-paying jobs.

Blacks (Table 2.11) in the 1980s saw a dramatic downward shift out of middle-wage employment into both very-low-wage employment and higher-wage employment. The shift out of poverty-level jobs in the 1990s reversed the 1980s expansion of very low earners. By 2000, the share of poverty-wage earners among black men, 26.3%, was about the same as in 1979 but was at a historic low of 36.5% among women. Still, though, in 2000, 31.8% of black workers were in jobs paying less than poverty-level wages. The post-1979 trends, despite the improvement in the late 1990s, have left black men with fewer middle-wage jobs and more very-low-earning jobs, with some black men earning very high wages. Among black women, the share of very low-earners grew (from 9.8% in 1979 to 14.3% in 2000), but otherwise they saw a general movement up the wage structure. In the recent 2000-03 period, the jobs of black men and women were generally upgraded in the wage structure.

Since 1979, despite the improvements in the late 1990s, the Hispanic wage structure has generally shifted downward, for both men and women, with modest growth in the highest-wage jobs (Table 2.12). These trends could be due to a change in the composition of the Hispanic workforce—a larger share of immigrants—as well as a shift in the overall job structure, but unfortunately, we cannot distinguish between the two factors in this analysis. Both Hispanic women and men shifted in large numbers into the lowest-wage jobs between 1979 and 1989, and saw modest improvement over the 1990s. The growth in the percentage of Hispanic males earning poverty-level wages was substantial, up from 27.1% in 1979 to 38.2% in 2000. Roughly half (49.3%) of Hispanic women earned poverty-level wages in 2000, a decline from the 54.5% who did so in 1979. Among Hispanic men the share holding jobs over 125% of the poverty wage declined after 1979. In contrast, Hispanic women improved their share of the three highest wage categories since 1979. Both Hispanic men and women saw their jobs shifted to higher-wage categories in the 2000-03 period.

Trends in benefit growth and inequality

The analysis on the preceding pages shows that real wages declined for a wide array of workers over both the 1980s and the early 1990s, and then rose strongly after 1995 and continued growing after 2000. Also, total compensation, the real value of both wages and fringe benefits, grew at the same pace as wages over the 1979-95 period. Benefits grew faster than wages during much of that time, but since they make up a small (15-20%) share of compensation, their growth did not generate fast compensation growth overall. Benefits also grew faster than wages after 2000, thereby lifting compensation growth. Fast growth in health care costs was a major cause of benefit growth after 2000. In this section, we explore these issues further and examine changes in benefits by type of benefit and changes in health and pension coverage for different groups of workers. This analysis allows an examination of the growing inequality of benefits. We are not able to examine the benefit of stock options, because there are no comprehensive historical data on the extent and quality of stock option programs. What evidence is available suggests that stock options are mostly provided to top managerial workers (only 1.7% of all private-sector workers and 4.6% of executives had them in 1999).

Table 2.13 provides a breakdown of growth in non-wage compensation, or benefits, using the two available data series (the "aggregates" appear already in Tables 2.2 and 2.3). The NIPA data provide a long-term perspective. In the 1948-73 and 1973-79 periods, the average inflation-adjusted value of non-wage compensation (or benefits), including employer-provided health insurance, pension plans, and payroll taxes, grew by $0.09 and $0.16 each year, respectively, translating into annual growth rates of 7.3% and 5.2%. In contrast, total benefits grew just $0.04 per year over the 1979-89 period and an even lower $0.03 from 1989 to 2000, translating into annual growth rates of 1.0% in 1979-89 and 0.7% in 1989-2000. The ECI data, based on a survey of employers, show a decline of benefits, from $4.26 starting in 1992 to $3.79 in 2000. Both surveys show strong benefits growth since 2000, driven by greater costs for health insurance.

TABLE 2.13 Growth of specific fringe benefits, 1948-2003

Year	Voluntary benefits			Payroll taxes	Total benefits and non-wage compensation
	Pension	Health*	Subtotal		
BEA NIPA**					
(2002 dollars)					
1948	$0.13	$0.09	$0.22	$0.24	$0.46
1973	0.83	0.81	1.64	1.03	2.67
1979	1.18	1.16	2.34	1.28	3.62
1989	1.05	1.37	2.42	1.57	3.99
1995	1.07	1.47	2.54	1.67	4.21
2000	0.99	1.58	2.57	1.73	4.30
2002	1.05	1.74	2.79	1.83	4.62
Annual dollar change					
1948-73	$0.03	$0.03	$0.06	$0.03	$0.09
1973-79	0.06	0.06	0.12	0.04	0.16
1979-89	-0.01	0.02	0.01	0.03	0.04
1989-2000	0.00	0.02	0.01	0.01	0.03
1989-95	0.00	0.02	0.02	0.02	0.04
1995-2000	-0.02	0.02	0.01	0.01	0.02
2000-02	0.03	0.08	0.11	0.05	0.16
Annual percent change					
1948-73	7.8%	9.0%	8.3%	6.1%	7.3%
1973-79	6.0	6.2	6.1	3.6	5.2
1979-89	-1.2	1.7	0.4	2.1	1.0
1989-2000	-0.5	1.3	0.5	0.9	0.7
1989-95	0.4	1.1	0.8	1.1	0.9
1995-2000	-1.5	1.5	0.3	0.7	0.4
2000-02	2.8	4.9	4.1	2.8	3.6
BLS ECI levels***					
(2003 dollars)					
1987	$0.75	$1.66	$2.41	$1.77	$4.18
1989	0.61	1.72	2.33	1.84	4.17
1992	0.59	1.77	2.36	1.90	4.26
1995	0.63	1.55	2.18	1.92	4.09
2000	0.64	1.36	1.99	1.80	3.79
2003	0.67	1.52	2.19	1.89	4.08
Annual dollar change					
1989-2000	$0.00	-$0.03	-$0.03	$0.00	-$0.03
1989-95	0.00	-0.03	-0.03	0.01	-0.01
1995-2000	0.00	-0.04	-0.04	-0.02	-0.06
2000-03	0.01	0.05	0.07	0.03	0.10
Annual percent change					
1989-2000	0.4%	-2.1%	-1.4%	-0.2%	-0.9%
1989-95	0.5	-1.7	-1.1	0.6	-0.3
1995-2000	0.3	-2.6	-1.7	-1.3	-1.5
2000-03	1.8	3.8	3.2	1.7	2.5

*   Deflated by medical care price index.
**   National Income and Product Accounts (NIPA).
***   Employment cost index (ECI) levels data for March of each year.

Source: Authors' analysis of BLS and BEA data.

The data in Table 2.13 reflect "average" benefit costs. Given the rapid growth of wage inequality in recent years, it should not be surprising to find a growing inequality of benefits. **Tables 2.14** and **2.15** examine changes in health and pension insurance coverage for different demographic groups between 1979 and 2003. The share of workers covered by employer-provided health care plans dropped a steep 11.6 percentage points, from 69.0% in 1979 to 56.4%, in 2003 (Table 2.14). As **Figure 2F** shows, health care coverage eroded in the 1990s until 1993-94 and then started growing, another reflection of improved pay in the late 1990s. Still, health insurance coverage in 2000 was below its 1989 level (58.9% versus 61.5%) and far below 1979. Unfortunately, there are no data available to show the degree to which the quality of coverage has changed, i.e., whether health plans are more inclusive or more restricted.

Over the 1979-2003 period, health care coverage has declined twice as much among men (down 15.7 percentage points) than women (down 7.1 percentage points), and more among whites (9.9 percentage points) than among blacks (8.8 percentage points); Hispanics, though, suffered a large drop—21.1 percentage points. The pattern in the erosion of health insurance coverage by wage level shows a growth in inequality in the 1980s, with greater erosion the lower the wage. In the 1990s, however, there were modest extensions of coverage for the bottom 20%, while erosion continued for middle- and high-wage workers. Health insurance coverage eroded for all wage groups in the 2000-03 period. Consequently, over the longer period, 1979-2003, health insurance coverage declined sizably, and comparably, across the wage spectrum. Along education lines, however, there has been a growing inequality: employer-provided health insurance coverage fell 16.0 percentage points among high school graduates but by a lesser, though large, 9.2 percentage points among college graduates.

Pension plan coverage (Table 2.15) declined as quickly as health care coverage in the 1980s: it dropped from 50.6% in 1979 to 43.7% in 1989. This decline is one of the reasons for the lessening of pension costs for employers over that period. In the 1989-95 period, however, pension coverage expanded slightly to 45.8%. By 2000, however, coverage had grown to 48.3%, just 2.3% shy of 1979's level. Pension coverage receded, however, in the 2000-03 recession, so that overall pension coverage was only 45.9%, 4.7 percentage points less than the 50.6% coverage of 1979. This means that less than half the workforce is covered by employer-provided pensions.

Over the 1979-2003 period, lower pension coverage occurred primarily among men, for whom it fell from 56.9% to 47.2%. Women's pension coverage, on the other hand, rose slightly, from 41.3% to 44.3%, with setbacks in the 1980s and early 2000s. By 2003, women workers were less likely (44.3% versus 47.2%) than men to be covered by an employer's pension plan. Both black

TABLE 2.14 Change in private-sector employer-provided health insurance coverage, 1979-2003

Group*	Health insurance coverage (%)					Percentage-point change			
	1979	1989	1995	2000	2003	1979-89	1989-2000	2000-03	1979-2003
All workers	69.0%	61.5%	58.5%	58.9%	56.4%	-7.4	-2.7	-2.5	-12.6
Gender									
Men	75.4%	66.8%	62.6%	63.2%	59.7%	-8.7	-3.6	-3.4	-15.7
Women	59.4	54.9	53.3	53.6	52.3	-4.5	-1.3	-1.3	-7.1
Race									
White	70.3%	64.0%	61.7%	62.7%	60.3%	-6.3	-1.2	-2.4	-9.9
Black	63.1	56.3	53.0	55.4	54.3	-6.8	-0.9	-1.1	-8.8
Hispanic	60.4	46.0	42.1	41.8	39.3	-14.3	-4.3	2.5	-21.1
Education									
High school	69.6%	61.2%	56.3%	56.2%	53.6%	-8.4	-5.0	-2.6	-16.0
College	79.6	75.0	72.1	71.3	70.4	-4.6	-3.8	-0.9	-9.3
Wage fifth									
Lowest	37.9%	26.4%	26.0%	27.4%	24.9%	-11.5	1.0	-2.5	-13.0
Second	60.5	51.7	49.5	50.9	46.9	-8.8	-0.8	-4.0	-13.6
Middle	74.7	67.5	62.9	63.9	62.0	-7.2	-3.6	-1.9	-12.7
Fourth	83.5	78.0	74.0	73.7	71.1	-5.5	-4.3	-2.5	-12.3
Top	89.5	84.7	81.5	79.9	77.8	-4.7	-4.8	-2.1	-11.7

* Private-sector wage and salary workers age 18-64, who worked at least 20 hours per week and 26 weeks per year.

Source: Authors' analysis.

TABLE 2.15 Change in private-sector employer-provided pension coverage, 1979-2003

Group*	Pension coverage (%)					Percentage-point change			
	1979	1989	1995	2000	2003	1979-89	1989-2000	2000-03	1979-2003
All Workers	50.6%	43.7%	45.8%	48.3%	45.9%	-7.0	4.6	-2.4	-4.7
Gender									
Men	56.9%	46.9%	48.6%	50.3%	47.2%	-10.1	3.4	-3.1	-9.7
Women	41.3	39.6	42.5	45.8	44.3	-1.7	6.2	-1.5	3.0
Race									
White	52.2%	46.1%	49.5%	53.7%	51.1%	-6.1	7.6	-2.6	-1.1
Black	45.8	40.7	42.6	41.3	40.9	-5.1	0.7	-0.4	-4.9
Hispanic	38.2	26.3	24.7	27.5	25.8	-11.9	1.2	-1.7	-12.4
Education									
High school	51.2%	42.9%	43.2%	43.8%	40.9%	-8.3	0.9	-2.9	-10.3
College	61.0	55.4	58.8	63.7	60.2	-5.6	8.3	-3.5	-0.8
Wage fifth									
Lowest	18.4%	12.7%	13.7%	16.3%	14.6%	-5.7	3.6	-1.7	-3.8
Second	36.8	29.0	32.0	35.8	31.7	-7.7	6.8	-4.2	-5.1
Middle	52.3	44.5	47.0	50.9	48.6	-7.8	6.4	-2.3	-3.7
Fourth	68.4	60.0	63.2	64.8	62.2	-8.3	4.8	-2.6	-6.1
Top	78.5	72.8	74.8	74.8	73.3	-5.8	2.1	-1.5	-5.2

* Private-sector wage and salary workers age 18-64, who worked at least 20 hours per week and 26 weeks per year.

Source: Authors' analysis of March CPS data.

139

FIGURE 2F Private-sector employer-provided health insurance coverage by race/ethnicity, 1979-2002

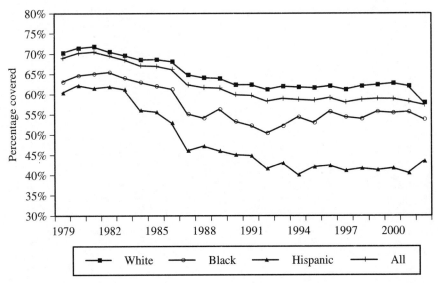

Source: Authors' analysis.

and white workers saw pension coverage erode in the 1980s, but Hispanics experienced a large decline—an 11.9 percentage-point drop from 1979 to 1989. In the late 1990s, however, whites expanded their pension coverage and attained a level of 53.7%, 1.5 percentage points above the 1979 level of 52.2%. Hispanics also increased their share in the 1990s but still had coverage—27.5% in 2000—far below the 1979 level. Black workers saw a modest 0.7 percentage-point increase in coverage in the 1990s. Surprisingly, black workers saw pension coverage erode during the late 1990s recovery. Pension coverage eroded dramatically among all racial/ethnic groups over the 1979-2003 period: down 1.1 percentage points among whites, 4.9 percentage points among blacks, and 12.4 percentage points among Hispanics.

The pattern of decline in pension coverage by wage level shows coverage dropping relatively evenly across wage groups in the 1980s and broadening across the board in the 1990s, with coverage expanding the most in the middle. Nevertheless, lower-wage workers are unlikely to have jobs with employer-provided pension plans (14.6% were covered in 2003), and less than half of middle-wage workers have pension coverage. Over the entire 1979-2003 period, pension coverage eroded the most among higher-wage workers. It should be noted that there was little coverage for low-wage workers to lose—just 18.4% for the lowest fifth and 36.8% for the second-lowest fifth in 1979. In 2003, the highest-wage workers were nearly five times as likely to have pension coverage as low-wage workers (73.3% versus 14.6%). Changes in pension coverage by education show a growing inequality: over the 1979-2003 period pension coverage fell 10.3 percentage points among high school graduates but only 0.8 percentage points among college graduates.

The widening coverage of employer-provided pension plans in the 1990s was most likely due to the expansion of 401(k) and other defined-contribution pension plans. These plans differ from defined-benefit plans, which are generally considered the best plans from a workers' perspective because they guarantee a worker a fixed payment in retirement based on pre-retirement wages and years of service regardless of stock market performance. Yet, as shown in **Figure 2G**, a larger share of workers are now covered by defined-contribution plans, in which employers make contributions (to which employees often can add) each year. With this type of plan, a worker's retirement income depends on his or her success in investing these funds, and investment risks are borne by the employee rather than the employer. Therefore, the shift from traditional defined-benefit plans to defined-contribution plans represents an erosion of pension quality. Chapter 4 provides further discussion of pensions and retirement assets and income.

Explaining wage inequality

In this section we shift the discussion from a descriptive presentation of wage and benefit trends overall and for sub-groups to an examination of explanations for the pattern of recent wage growth. It is important to understand the average performance of wage growth and why particular groups fared well or poorly compared to others.

The data presented up to this point have shown the stagnation of wages and overall compensation between 1973 and 1995 and strong wage growth in the late 1990s. The momentum of the strong wage growth from the latter 1990s carried into the first few years of the early 2000s recession and prolonged labor slump, with wages starting to falter in 2002. **Table 2.16** presents indicators of a variety of dimensions (excluding race and gender differentials) of the wage structure that have grown more unequal over the 1973-2003 period. Any explanation of growing wage inequality must be able to explain the movement of these indicators. (These inequality indicators are computed from our analysis of the Current Population Survey (CPS) outgoing rotation group (ORG) data series. These trends, however, parallel those in the other major data series, the March CPS.)

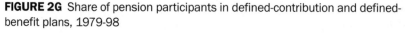

FIGURE 2G Share of pension participants in defined-contribution and defined-benefit plans, 1979-98

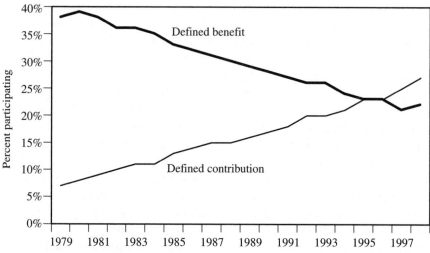

Source: U.S. Department of Labor (2001).

The top section of Table 2.16 shows the trends, by gender, in the 90/10 wage differential and its two components, the 90/50 and 50/10 wage differential (whose annual values are shown in **Figures 2H** and **2I**), over the 1973-2003 period. These differentials reflect the growth in overall wage inequality. The 90/10 wage gap, for instance, shows the degree to which 90th percentile workers—"high-wage" workers who earn more than 90% but less than 10% of the workforce—fared better than "low-wage" workers, who earn at the 10th percentile. The 90/50 wage gap shows how high earners fared relative to middle earners, and the 50/10 wage gap shows how middle earners fared relative to low earners.

Wage inequalities have been growing continuously since 1979, although the pattern differs across time periods. For instance, among both men and women the shape of growing inequality differed in the 1980s (through about 1987-88) and thereafter. Over the 1979-89 period (as we saw above in the analysis of wage deciles in Tables 2.6 through 2.8), there was a dramatic across-the-board widening of the wage structure, with the top pulling away from the middle and the middle pulling away from the bottom. In the late 1980s, however, the wage inequality in the bottom half of the wage structure, as reflected in the 50/10 differential, began shrinking and continued to shrink through 1999,

TABLE 2.16 Dimensions of wage inequality, 1973-2003

	Log wage differentials						Percentage-point change			
	1973	1979	1989	1995	2000	2003	1973-79	1979-89	1989-2000	2000-03
Total wage inquality										
90/10										
Men	128.0%	130.0%	144.3%	151.1%	150.3%	151.8%	2.0	14.3	6.0	1.5
Women	115.9	103.2	134.9	137.6	137.7	138.4	-12.7	31.8	2.8	0.7
90/50										
Men	60.3%	58.8%	69.2%	76.1%	79.5%	81.7%	-1.5	10.4	10.2	2.3
Women	59.2	60.6	70.5	76.5	78.2	78.2	1.4	9.9	7.7	0.0
50/10										
Men	67.6%	71.1%	75.1%	75.0%	70.8%	70.1%	3.5	3.9	-4.2	-0.8
Women	56.7	42.5	64.4	61.1	59.5	60.2	-14.2	21.9	-4.9	0.7
Between group inequality*										
College/H.S.										
Men	25.3%	20.1%	33.9%	37.1%	42.0%	41.5%	-5.2	13.9	8.1	-0.5
Women	37.7	26.5	41.0	46.7	47.9	46.1	-11.2	14.5	6.9	-1.8
H.S./Less than H.S.										
Men	22.3%	22.0%	22.1%	26.5%	26.0%	24.5%	-0.3	0.1	3.9	-1.4
Women	26.2	21.3	26.4	29.8	29.5	27.1	-4.9	5.1	3.0	-2.4
*Experience** Middle/young*										
Men	22.0%	21.5%	25.7%	27.0%	22.9%	25.2%	-0.5	4.1	-2.8	2.4
Women	8.0	9.5	17.8	21.8	18.4	20.5	1.5	8.3	0.6	2.1
Old/middle										
Men	3.4%	8.2%	12.4%	12.7%	8.8%	7.6%	4.7	4.3	-3.6	-1.3
Women	-2.0	0.4	2.1	5.4	4.6	5.3	2.4	1.7	2.5	0.7
Within group inequality**										
Men	42.3%	42.8%	46.7%	47.8%	48.1%	48.9%	1.4%	9.0%	3.0%	2.4%
Women	41.8	40.2	44.7	46.7	45.8	47.3	-3.8	11.4	2.4	1.4

*   Differentials based on a simple human capital regression of log wages on four education categorical variables, age as a quartic, race, marital status, region, and ethnicity (Hispanic).

**   Age differentials between 25- and 35-year-olds and 35- and 50-year-olds.

***   Mean square error from same regressions used to estimate experience and education differentials. Changes measured as percent change.

Source: Authors' analysis.

FIGURE 2H   Men's wage inequality, 1973-2003

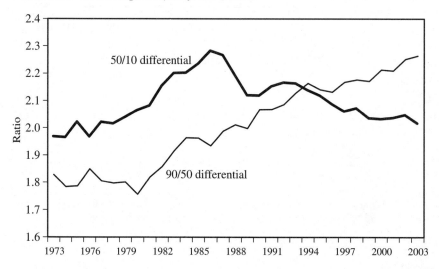

Source: Authors' analysis.

FIGURE 2I   Women's wage inequality, 1973-2003

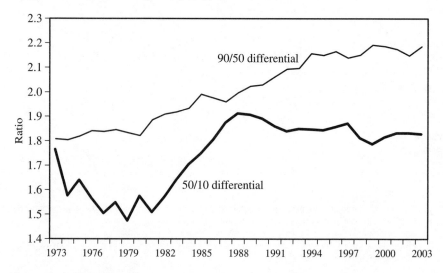

Source: Authors' analysis.

FIGURE 2J   95/50 percentile wage inequality, 1973-2003

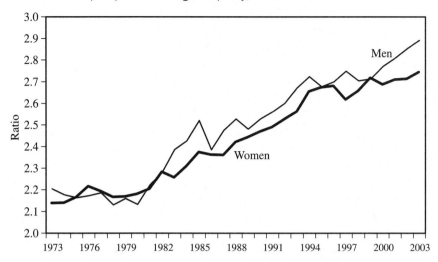

Source: Authors' analysis.

then stabilized among men and rose a bit among women. On the other hand, the 90/50 differential continued to widen in the 1990s and early 2000s, as it had done in the 1980s (the growth of the 90/50 wage gap slowed somewhat among women starting in the mid-1990s). This widening of the top is even stronger in the 95/50 differential, shown **Figure 2J.** (The 95th percentile is the highest wage we feel can be tracked in our data with technical precision). These disparate trends between high- versus middle-wage growth and middle- versus low-wage growth should motivate explanations that focus on how causal factors affect particular portions of the wage structure—top, middle, or bottom—rather than on how causal factors affect inequality generally.

The trends in the later years, 2000-03, may signal a return to the 1980s pattern of an across-the-board widening of wage inequality. The 50/10 wage gap started growing again among women after 1999 and stopped falling among men (except in 2003). At the top, the wage gap (95/50 or 90/50) spiked upward sharply among men and grew moderately among women. Overall wage inequality, measured by the 90/10 ratio, grew among men and women over the 2000-03 period at about three-fourths the pace of the 1990s and far faster than in the late 1990s.

Among men, wage inequality grew dramatically at the top and bottom in the 1979-89 period, and the growth in the 90/50 differential continued as quickly through the 1989-2000 period (Table 2.16 and Figure 2H). Specifically, the 90/50 wage gap grew roughly 10 (log) percentage points in both periods. As discussed above, the character of this growing male wage inequality shifted in the most recent period. In the 1980s the separation between both the top and the middle and the middle and the bottom grew (seen in the 50/10 differential). However, in the 1989-2000 period, all of the growing wage inequality was generated by a divergence between the top and everyone else: the 90/50 differential grew while the 50/10 differential actually fell. The drop in the 50/10 wage gap among men actually began in 1986 (Figure 2H). After 2000, the 90/50 wage gap continued to grow, and the 50/10 wage gap decline slightly (though all from the 2002-03 period).

Among women, the wage inequality trends across time periods correspond to those of men. The 90/10 ratio dropped significantly between 1973 and the late 1970s, primarily because of the strong equalization in the 50/10 wage gap. In the 1980s, however, the 50/10 wage gap grew tremendously (up 21.9 percentage points) reversing the 1970s compression and increasing the gap another 8 percentage points over 1973. One conclusion that can be reached about women's wage inequality is that it has been driven much more by what happened at the bottom—the 10th percentile—than was the change for men. This is likely due to the importance of the legal minimum wage to low-wage women, as we will discuss in a later section. Among women, the growth of the 90/50 differential was comparable to that of men in the 1980s but somewhat less in the 1990s. As with men, the 50/10 wage gap declined in the 1990s (Figure 2I shows the drop starting in about 1987). As mentioned above, the wage gap at the bottom among women started rising again after 1999.

The 95/50 wage gap among women followed approximately the same track as for men (Figure 2J). Wage inequality between the very top earners and those in the middle has been growing strongly, and steadily, since about 1980, confirming the continuous widening of wages at the top over the last two decades. The only exception is the flattening of the 95/50 gap among women since 1999.

Analysts decompose, or break down, growing wage inequality into two types of inequality—"between-group" and "within group." The former is illustrated in Table 2.16 in two ways: the growing wage differentials between groups of workers defined either by their education levels or by their labor market experience. The "college wage premium"—the wage gap between college and high school graduates—fell in the 1970s among both men and women but exploded in the 1980s, growing about 14 percentage points for each. Growth then slowed after 1989. The pattern of growth of this key education differential in the 1990s, however, differed between men and women (see **Figure 2K**). Among men there was only modest growth in the education premium in the early

FIGURE 2K College/high school wage premium, 1973-2003

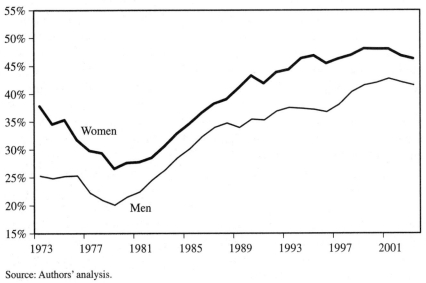

Source: Authors' analysis.

1990s—year-by-year trends (discussed below) show it to be relatively flat between 1987 and 1996—but it grew strongly thereafter. Thus, the 1990s growth
in the male education premium primarily occurred in the last few years. Among
women, however, the college wage premium grew steadily but modestly in the
early 1990s and then evened out starting around 1995. The college wage premium among both men and women remained fairly flat in the late 1990s and
declined a bit in the early 2000s.

Table 2.16 also presents the trends in another education differential—between those completing high school and those without high school degrees;
this differential would be expected to affect the wage distribution in the bottom
half, as about 10% of the workforce has less than a high school education, and
high school graduates make up about a third of the workforce (see discussion
of Tables 2.17 through 2.19). In 1973 as in 2003, those with a high school
degree earned about 25% more than those without a degree. This wage differential has been fairly stable among men over the last 30 years, suggesting that
education differentials have not been a driving force behind the changes in the
50/10 wage gap (up in the 1980s and declining thereafter). Among women, the
wage gap between middle- and low-wage workers is far higher in 2003 than in
1973, yet the high school/less than high school differential is roughly the same.

This suggests that changing wage differentials at the bottom among women have had only a weak relationship to changing education differentials.

Experience, or age, is another way of categorizing "skill." The growth of experience differentials reflect the wage gap between older and middle-age and younger workers. The wage gap between middle-age and younger workers grew in the 1980s but not in the 1990s, particularly because the 1995-2000 wage boom, characterized by relatively faster wage growth among younger workers, markedly reduced this differential. The wage gap between older and middle-age women workers grew over the 1973-95 period and was relatively flat thereafter; it grew as well for men until 1995, and then declined by 2000 with a bump up in the early 2000s.

Within-group wage inequality—wage dispersion among workers with comparable education and experience—has been a major dimension of growing wage inequality. Unfortunately, most discussions of wage inequality focus exclusively on the between-group dimensions of wage inequality discussed above, even though within-group wage inequality is by far the most important dimension of wage inequality's growth. The growth of within-group wage inequality is presented in the last section of Table 2.16, with changes measured in percent. These data show that within-group inequality grew slightly among men in the 1970s and 1990s but grew strongly, by 9.0%, over the 1980s. Among women, within-group inequality fell in the 1970s, grew by 11.4% in the 1980s, and then grew a modest 2.4% in the 1990s. However, within-group wage inequality fell among women in the 1995-2000 period, while rising slightly among men. Growth in within-group wage inequality returned in the 2000-03 period among both men and women.

This measure of within-group wage inequality is a "summary measure" describing changes across the entire wage distribution. Unfortunately, such a measure does not help us understand changes in particular measures of wage inequality, such as the 90/50 and 50/10 differentials presented in Table 2.16. This shortcoming is particularly troublesome for an analysis of the 1989-2000 period in which inequalities were expanding at the top (i.e., the 90/50) but shrinking at the bottom (i.e., the 50/10). A summary measure of inequality by definition reflects the net effect of the two disparate shifts in wage inequality in the 1990s, and explains the small change of within-group wage inequality from 1989 to 2000.

Since changes in within-group wage inequality have been a significant factor in various periods, it is important to be able to explain and interpret these trends. In a later section, we show that about half of the growth of wage inequality since 1979 has been from growing within-group wage inequality. Unfortunately, the interpretation of growing wage inequality among workers with similar "human capital" has not been the subject of much research. Some analysts suggest it reflects growing premiums for skills that are not captured by traditional human capital measures available in government surveys. Others suggest that changing "wage norms," employer practices, and institutions are responsible.

We now turn to a more detailed examination of between-group wage differentials such as education, experience, and race/ethnicity as well as an examination of within-group wage inequality.

Productivity and the compensation/productivity gap

The most commonly mentioned reason for the wage stagnation of the 1970s and 1980s is slow productivity growth (i.e., changes in output per hour worked) since 1973. Productivity grew about 1.5% annually over the entire 1973-95 period, slower than over the pre-1973 period (see Table 2.1). The latter period has thus been marked by a "productivity slowdown."

Slow productivity growth was a major problem in this period, but it provides only a partial explanation for the slow average wage trends because productivity grew significantly more than wages or compensation. At the same time, the pickup of productivity growth after 1995 provides a major explanation for the much stronger real wage growth in recent years. In both time periods (1973-95 and 1995-2003), however, productivity growth far outpaced that of compensation.

The relationship between hourly productivity and compensation growth is portrayed in **Figure 2L**, which shows the growth of each relative to 1973 (i.e., each is indexed so that 1973 equals 100). As the figure illustrates, productivity grew 72% from 1973 to 2003, enough to generate broadly shared growth in living standards and wages. There are two important gaps displayed in Figure 2L. First, the growth in average compensation lagged behind productivity growth. Second, median hourly compensation grew far less than average compensation, reflecting growing wage and benefit inequality. Thus, there have been two wedges between the typical median workers' compensation and overall productivity growth: one is that workers, on average, have not seen their pay keep up with productivity (partly reflecting the shift from wage to capital income described in Chapter 1), and the other is that median workers have not enjoyed growth in compensation as fast as that of as higher-wage workers (reflecting growing wage and benefit inequality).

There are several possible interpretations of the gap between average compensation and productivity. One is that prices for national output have grown more slowly than prices for consumer purchases. Therefore, the same growth

FIGURE 2L Productivity and hourly compensation growth, 1973-2003

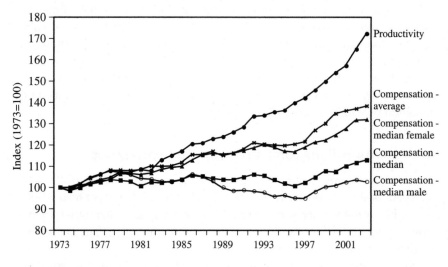

Source: Authors' analysis.

in nominal, or current dollar, wages and output yields faster growth in real (inflation-adjusted) output (which is adjusted for changes in the prices of investment goods, exports, and consumer purchases) than in real wages (adjusted for changes in consumer purchases only). That is, workers have suffered worsening "terms of trade," in which the prices of things they buy (i.e., consumer goods) have risen faster than the items they produce (consumer goods but also capital goods). Thus, if workers consumed microprocessors and machine tools as well as groceries, their real wage growth would have been better.

This terms-of-trade scenario is actually more of a description than an explanation. A growing gap between output and consumer prices has not been a persistent characteristic of the U.S. economy, and the emergence of this gap requires an exploration of what economic forces are driving it. Once the causes of the price gap are known (not simply accounted for) it can be interpreted. In the meantime, there are two ways to look at the divergence of compensation and productivity created by the terms-of-trade shift of prices. One is to note that, regardless of cause, the implication is that the "average" worker is not benefiting fully from productivity growth. Another is to note that the price divergence does not simply reflect a redistribution from labor to capital; the gap between compensation and productivity growth reflects, at least in part, differences in price trends rather than a larger share of productivity growth going to capital incomes.

This leaves open the question of whether wages are being squeezed by higher profits. In other words, has the growth in rates of profit (defined broadly as profits and interest per dollar of assets) meant that wages have grown less than they would have otherwise? As discussed in Chapter 1, the share of income going to capital has grown significantly, driven by a large increase in "profitability," or the return to capital per dollar of plant and equipment. Labor's share of corporate-sector income has dropped correspondingly, thus providing evidence of a redistribution of wages to capital incomes. As discussed in Chapter 1, had growth in profitability been more modest up to the 1996-2000 period, hourly compensation would have been 5.3% higher in 2000.

Rising education/wage differentials

Changes in the economic returns to education affect the structure of wages by changing the wage gaps between different educational groups. The growth in "education/wage differentials" has led to greater wage inequality in the 1980s and 1990s (see Table 2.16 and Figure 2K) and helps explain the relatively faster wage growth among high-wage workers. This section examines wage trends among workers at different levels of education and begins the discussion, carried on through the remainder of the chapter, of the causes of rising education/wage differentials.

Table 2.17 presents the wage trends and employment shares (percentage of the workforce) for workers at various education levels over the 1973-2003 period. It is common to point out that the wages of "more-educated" workers have grown faster than the wages of "less-educated" workers since 1979, with the real wages of less-educated workers falling sharply (or rising more slowly in the 1995-2000 period). This pattern of wage growth is sometimes described in terms of a rising differential, or "premium," between the wages of the college-educated and high-school-educated workforces (as shown earlier in Table 2.16).

The usual terminology of the less educated and more educated is misleading. Given that workers with some college education (from one to three years) also experienced falling real wages (down 4.1% from 1979 to 1995), it is apparent that the "less-educated" group whose wages fell includes everyone with less than a four-year college degree, a group that comprises nearly three-fourths of the workforce. Moreover, it is notable that the "college-educated" group consists of two groups: one, with just four years of college, enjoyed a modest 8.5% wage gain over the 1979-95 period, while the other, the more-educated ("advanced degree") but smaller group (8.8% of the workforce in 2000), enjoyed 17.2% wage growth.

TABLE 2.17 Real hourly wage for all by education, 1973-2003 (2003 dollars)

Year	Less than high school	High school	Some college	College	Advanced degree
Hourly wage					
1973	$11.83	$13.56	$14.60	$19.77	$23.90
1979	12.07	13.55	14.48	18.99	23.19
1989	10.38	12.65	14.20	19.91	25.68
1995	9.39	12.42	13.89	20.61	27.19
2000	9.76	13.13	14.93	22.93	29.00
2001	9.87	13.31	15.17	23.42	29.21
2002	10.04	13.51	15.25	23.46	29.94
2003	10.12	13.57	15.23	23.44	29.58
Annualized percentage change					
1973-79	0.3%	0.0%	-0.1%	-0.7%	-0.5%
1979-89	-1.5	-0.7	-0.2	0.5	1.0
1989-2000	-0.6	0.3	0.5	1.3	1.1
1989-95	-1.6	-0.3	-0.4	0.6	1.0
1995-2000	0.8	1.1	1.5	2.2	1.3
1979-2000	-1.0	-0.1	0.1	0.9	1.1
2000-03	1.2	1.1	0.7	0.7	0.7
Share of employment					
1973	28.5%	38.3%	18.5%	10.1%	4.5%
1979	20.1	38.5	22.8	12.7	6.0
1989	13.7	36.9	26.0	15.6	7.9
1995	10.8	33.3	30.5	17.3	8.0
2000	11.1	31.8	29.6	18.8	8.8
2003	10.6	30.6	29.7	19.7	9.4

Source: Authors' analysis.

Table 2.17 also shows, however, that the strong real wage growth of the 1995-2000 period was evident among all education groups, with the fastest wage growth among the college-educated workers. Real wages grew for all education groups even after the 1990s boom ended, continuing through to 2002. However, the higher unemployment in this period led to slow-growing or falling wages from 2002 to 2003. (An analysis of trends in the last few years is presented in the Introduction.)

The increased wage differential between college-educated and other workers is frequently ascribed to a relative increase in employer demand for workers with greater skills and education. This interpretation follows from the fact that the wages of college-educated workers increased relative to others despite an increase in their relative supply, from 12.7% of the workforce in 1979 to 18.8% in 2000. That is, given the increased supply of college-educated workers, the fact that their relative wages went up implies a strong growth in employer demand for more-educated workers, presumably reflecting technological and other workplace trends.

Yet an increased relative demand for educated workers is only a partial explanation, especially if ascribed to a benign process of technology or other factors leading to a higher value for education, thus bidding up the wages of more-educated workers. Note, for instance, that the primary reason for an increased wage gap between college-educated and other workers is the precipitous decline of wages among the non-college-educated workforce in the 1979-95 period and not any strong growth in the college wage. Moreover, as discussed below, there are many important factors (that may not reflect changes in the relative demand for skill), such as high unemployment, the shift to low-wage industries, deunionization, a falling minimum wage, and import competition, that can also lead to a wage gap between workers with more and less education. Below, we argue that technological change has not been the driving force behind growing wage inequality.

Tables 2.18 and **2.19** present trends in wage and employment shares for each education group for men and women. Among men, the wages of non-college-educated workers fell steadily from 1979 to 1995. The decline in wages was sizable even among men with "some college"—8.0% from 1979 to 1995. The wage of the average high-school-educated male fell more, 14.1%, from 1979 to 1995, while the wages of those without a high school degree fell 25.8%. By contrast, the wages of male college graduates actually rose just 2.9% from 1979 to 1989 and an additional 1.4% over the 1989-95 period. Year-by-year data show male college wages in the 1979-95 period peaked in 1987. The period from 1995 to 2000 was one of strong real wage growth among men in every education category, although stronger for the higher-education groups. Real wages continued to grow from 2000 to 2002 but then were either flat or falling from 2002 to 2003. We interpret this as momentum from the 1990s eventually being knocked down by high and sustained unemployment.

This 1979-95 pattern of modestly growing wages for college-educated males and declining wages for non-college-educated males meant a rise in the relative wage, or wage premium for male college graduates in this period. As shown in Table 2.16, the estimated college/high school wage premium (where experience, race, and other characteristics are controlled for) grew from 20.1% in 1979 to 33.9% in 1989 and to 42.0% in 2000. As Figure 2K shows, however, there was a flattening of the male college/high school premium over the 1988-

TABLE 2.18 Real hourly wage for men by education, 1973-2003 (2003 dollars)

Year	Less than high school	High school	Some college	College	Advanced degree
Hourly wage					
1973	$13.83	$16.39	$16.76	$22.62	$25.12
1979	13.93	16.32	16.98	22.19	25.24
1989	11.76	14.68	16.19	22.84	28.40
1995	10.34	14.01	15.63	23.18	30.15
2000	10.72	14.83	16.91	26.04	32.53
2001	10.69	14.91	17.12	26.66	32.59
2002	10.99	15.08	17.05	26.68	33.67
2003	11.04	15.07	17.03	26.63	33.31
Annualized percentage change					
1973-79	0.1%	-0.1%	0.2%	-0.3%	0.1%
1979-89	-1.7	-1.1	-0.5	0.3	1.2
1989-2000	-0.8	0.1	0.4	1.2	1.2
1989-95	-2.1	-0.8	-0.6	0.2	1.0
1995-2000	0.7	1.1	1.6	2.4	1.5
1979-2000	-1.2	-0.5	0.0	0.8	1.2
2000-03	1.0	0.5	0.2	0.8	0.8
Share of employment					
1973	30.6%	34.4%	19.2%	10.3%	5.4%
1979	22.3	35.0	22.4	13.2	7.1
1989	15.9	35.2	24.4	15.7	8.8
1995	12.6	33.2	28.3	17.3	8.6
2000	13.1	32.0	27.5	18.4	9.1
2003	12.5	32.6	27.6	18.3	9.0

Source: Authors' analysis.

95 period, particularly in the early 1990s. Since there has not been an accelera-tion of the supply of college-educated men (as shown in a later section), this implies, within a conventional demand-supply framework, that growth in the relative demand for college workers slowed in that period. From 1995 to 1999, however, this key education differential among men grew modestly. The col-lege wage premium was flat or falling after 1999.

A somewhat different pattern has prevailed among women (Table 2.19). In the 1979-89 and 1989-95 periods wages were stagnant among high-school-educated women but fell significantly among those without a high school de-

TABLE 2.19 Real hourly wage for women, by education, 1973-2003 (2003 dollars)

Year	Less than high school	High school	Some college	College	Advanced degree
Hourly wage					
1973	$8.34	$10.32	$11.15	$15.45	$20.46
1979	8.94	10.60	11.38	14.41	18.46
1989	8.16	10.56	12.23	16.55	21.57
1995	7.88	10.67	12.23	17.78	23.41
2000	8.22	11.26	13.07	19.68	24.83
2001	8.53	11.53	13.34	20.02	25.29
2002	8.49	11.76	13.56	20.19	25.64
2003	8.57	11.87	13.60	20.19	25.47
Annualized percentage change					
1973-79	1.2%	0.4%	0.3%	-1.1%	-1.7%
1979-89	-0.9	0.0	0.7	1.4	1.6
1989-2000	0.1	0.6	0.6	1.6	1.3
1989-95	-0.6	0.2	0.0	1.2	1.4
1995-2000	0.9	1.1	1.3	2.0	1.2
1979-2000	-0.4	0.3	0.7	1.5	1.4
2000-03	1.4	1.8	1.3	0.9	0.9
Share of employment					
1973	25.6%	44.0%	17.5%	9.9%	3.1%
1979	17.2	43.0	23.4	12.0	4.4
1989	11.2	38.8	27.8	15.4	6.8
1995	8.8	33.6	32.8	17.4	7.4
2000	8.9	31.7	31.9	19.2	8.4
2003	8.2	29.8	32.4	20.3	9.3

Source: Authors' analysis.

gree (11.9%). Women with some college saw wage gains in the 1980s (unlike their male counterparts), but not in the early 1990s. College-educated women saw strong wage growth throughout the 1979-95 period (23.4% overall). This pattern of wage growth resulted in growth of the college/high school wage differential comparable to that of men (Table 2.16), from 26.5% in 1979 to 41.0% in 1989 and to 46.7% in 1995 (the increase up to 1995 being more than among men). Thus, the education/wage gap grew more among women as among men in the 1979-95 period but the relative losers—non-college-educated women—saw stagnant, not declining wages.

Wage growth was strong over the 1995-2000 period among women at all education levels. As with men, wage growth was strongest among those with a college degree, and wages for women continued to grow from 2000 to 2002, reflecting the momentum of the late 1990s. However, wage growth from 2002-03 flattened considerably.

Even though the wages of college-educated women have grown rapidly since 1979, a female college graduate in 2003 still earned $6.44, or 24%, less than a male college graduate in 2003.

Table 2.20 shows a breakdown of the workforce in 2003 by the highest degree attained. Some 29.1% of the workforce had at least a four-year college degree (19.7% have no more than a college degree and 9.4% also have a graduate or professional degree). Correspondingly, 70.9% of the workforce has less than a college degree, with 10.6% never completing high school; 30.6% completing high school; another 20.4% having attended college but earning no degree beyond high school; and an additional 9.3% holding associate degrees. These data reinforce the earlier discussion that the wage reductions experienced by the "less educated" (frequently defined by economists as those without a college degree) between 1979 and 1995 affected a very large share of the workforce. It is also interesting to note that the group of workers with more than a high school degree but less than a four-year college degree now make up a group equivalent in size (29.7%) to that of high school graduates (30.6%).

Young workers' wages

Young workers' prospects seem to be an apt barometer of the strength of the labor market—when the labor market is strong for workers the prospects for young workers are very strong, and when the labor market is weak their prospects are very weak. For instance, the most dramatic erosion of wages over the 1973-1995 period was among young workers. However, young workers also experienced the fastest wage growth over the 1995-2000 period. As a result, there have been significant changes—up and down—in the wage differentials between younger and older workers, as shown earlier in Table 2.16.

Table 2.21 presents trends in wages for entry-level (one to five years of experience) high school and college graduates. Since the wages of both younger and non-college-educated workers fell most rapidly in the 1979-95 period, it should not be surprising that entry-level wages for men and women high school graduates in 2003 were still below their levels in 1979 or 1973. For instance, the entry-level hourly wage of a young male high school graduate in 1995 was 24.8% less than that for the equivalent worker in 1979, a drop of $3.15 per

TABLE 2.20 Educational attainment of the labor force, 2003

Highest degree attained	Percentage of workforce		
	All	Men	Women
Less than high school	10.6%	12.8%	8.2%
High school/GED	30.6	31.3	29.8
Some college	20.4	19.3	21.7
Assoc. college	9.3	8.0	10.7
College B.A.	19.7	19.2	20.3
Advanced degree*	9.4	9.5	9.3
Total	100.0	100.0	100.0
Memo			
High school or less	41.2%	44.1%	38.0%
Less than B.A. degree	70.9	71.3	70.4
College B.A. or more	29.1	28.7	29.6
Advanced degree	9.4	9.5	9.3

* Includes law degrees, Ph.D.s, M.B.A.s, and similar degrees.

Source: Authors' analysis.

hour. Among women, the entry-level high school wage fell 13.3% in this period. Entry-level wages for high school graduates rebounded strongly after 1995, growing over 9% among both men and women. However, wage growth was stunted during the 2000-03 period of high unemployment. The dramatic decline in entry-level wages among high school graduates and their recent recovery is illustrated in **Figure 2M**.

Entry-level wages among male college graduates were stagnant over the 1973-89 period and fell 7.3% from 1989 to 1995, as illustrated in **Figure 2N**. Thus, new male college graduates earned $0.75 less per hour in 1995 than their counterparts did in 1973. A decline in entry-level wages of college graduates also took place among women in the early 1990s, when the wage fell 2.1%. Wages for young college graduates grew very strongly—20.9% among men and 11.7% among women—during the 1995-2000 wage boom. This solid wage growth boosted entry-level male college graduates to a wage 12.1% higher than in 1989, offsetting the early 1990s decline; young women college graduates attained wages in 2000 that were 9.3% higher than in 1989. This astounding growth of wages for young college graduates continued in 2001 (see Figure 2N), but the economic downturn drove down young college wages in 2002 and 2003. Consequently, entry-level college wages

TABLE 2.21 Hourly wages of entry-level and experienced workers by education, 1973-2003 (2003 dollars)

Education/experience	Hourly wage						Percent change				
	1973	1979	1989	1995	2000	2003	1973-79	1979-89	1989-2000	1995-2000	2000-03
High school											
Men											
Entry*	$12.61	$12.71	$10.30	$9.56	$10.46	$10.50	0.8%	-19.0%	1.5%	9.3%	0.4%
34-40	18.03	18.20	15.92	15.27	15.90	15.98	1.0	-12.5	-0.2	4.1	0.5
49-55	19.00	19.41	17.96	17.25	17.07	17.11	2.2	-7.5	-4.9	-1.0	0.2
Women											
Entry*	$9.24	$9.39	$8.42	$8.14	$8.94	$8.94	1.7%	-10.3%	6.1%	9.8%	0.0%
34-40	10.60	10.97	11.04	11.18	11.85	12.18	3.5	0.6	7.3	6.1	2.7
49-55	11.05	11.29	11.62	11.72	12.46	12.99	2.2	2.9	7.2	6.3	4.3
College											
Men											
Entry**	$16.73	$16.75	$17.23	$15.98	$19.32	$18.64	0.2%	2.8%	12.1%	20.9%	-3.5%
34-40	26.99	26.03	25.49	26.12	28.93	30.58	-3.6	-2.1	13.5	10.8	5.7
49-55	27.82	28.86	28.66	28.96	29.80	30.26	3.7	-0.7	4.0	2.9	1.6
Women											
Entry**	$14.02	$13.25	$15.00	$14.68	$16.40	$16.20	-5.5%	13.2%	9.3%	11.7%	-1.2%
34-40	16.72	15.19	17.32	19.52	21.31	22.72	-9.2	14.0	23.1	9.2	6.6
49-55	15.95	15.37	16.81	19.70	20.56	20.99	-3.7	9.4	22.3	4.4	2.1

* Entry-level wage measured as wage of those from 19 to 25 years of age.
** Entry-level wage measured as wage of those from 23 to 29 years of age.

Source: Authors' analysis.

FIGURE 2M Entry-level wages of male and female high school graduates, 1973-2003

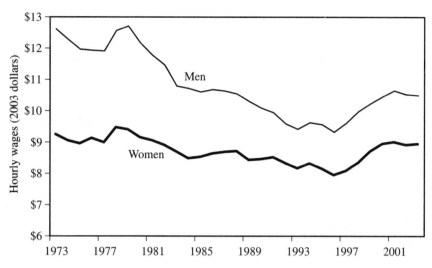

Source: Authors' analysis.

FIGURE 2N Entry-level wages of male and female college graduates, 1973-2003

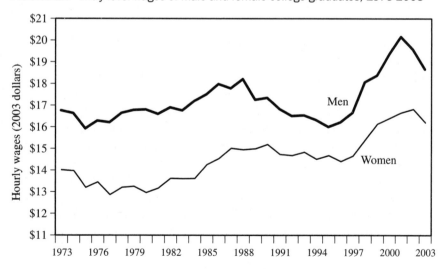

Source: Authors' analysis.

FIGURE 20 Health and pension coverage for recent high school graduates, 1979-2002

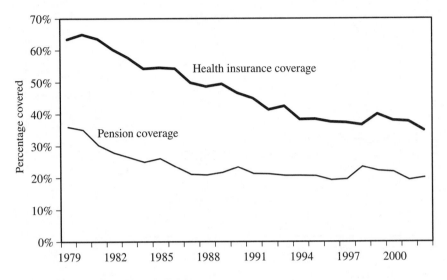

Source: Authors' analysis of March CPS data.

fell among both men (down 3.5%) and women (down 1.2%) over the 2000-03 period.

The erosion of job quality for young workers can also be seen in the lower likelihood of their receiving employer-provided health insurance or pensions. **Figures 2O** and **2P** show the rate of employer-provided health insurance and pension coverage in entry-level jobs for, respectively, high school graduates and college graduates. Employer-provided health insurance among recent high school graduates in their entry-level jobs fell from 63.3% in 1979 to roughly half that level, 34.7%, in 2002 (the latest data). Pension coverage fell over this period as well, from the low level of 36.0% in 1979 to an even lower 20.1% in 2002.

Among recent college graduates, health insurance coverage fell, but not as drastically as among recent high school graduates: health insurance coverage was 77.7% in 1979 and fell to 67.9% in 2002, including a sharp drop from 1999 to 2002 of 4.6 percentage points. Pension coverage among young college graduates fell from 1979 to the late 1980s and then regained its earlier level by 1998. This follows the overall pattern of pension coverage discussed above. However, pension coverage for young college graduates fell over the 1999-2002 period by 3.7 percentage points.

FIGURE 2P Health and pension coverage for recent college graduates, 1979-2002

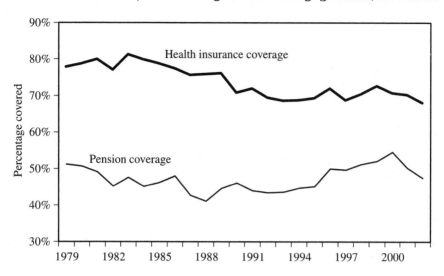

Source: Authors' analysis of March CPS data.

The growth of within-group wage inequality

The data presented so far illustrate the various dimensions of wage inequality. The "between-group" inequality for workers by both education and experience (or age) can be characterized as a growth in differentials in education and experience, which are sometimes labeled as an increase in the "returns to education and experience" or as a shift in the rewards or price of "skill." We now examine in greater depth the growth of "within-group" wage inequality, the inequality among workers with similar education and experience.

This growth in within-group wage inequality was shown earlier in Table 2.16. The analysis in **Table 2.22** illustrates the growth of this type of inequality by presenting wage trends of high-, middle-, and low-wage workers among high school and college graduates. In other words, the data track the wages of 90th, 50th (median), and 10th percentile high-school-educated and college-educated workers by gender and show a growing wage gap among college graduates and high school graduates.

Because of rising within-group inequality, the wage growth of the median or "typical" worker within each group has been less than that of the "average" worker. For instance, the wage of the median male high school graduate fell

TABLE 2.22 Hourly wages by decile within education groups, 1973-2003 (2003 dollars)

Education/wage decile	Hourly wage						Percent change					
	1973	1979	1989	1995	2000	2003	1973-79	1979-89	1989-2000	1995-2000	2000-03	1973-2003
High school												
Men												
Low*	$8.57	$7.95	$6.88	$6.68	$7.30	$7.44	-7.2%	-13.5%	6.1%	9.3%	1.8%	-13.2%
Median	15.46	15.17	13.36	12.33	12.97	13.16	-1.9	-11.9	-2.9	5.2	1.4	-14.9
High	25.26	24.76	23.55	22.67	23.76	24.71	-2.0	-4.9	0.9	4.8	4.0	-2.2
Women												
Low	$5.81	$6.64	$5.47	$5.70	$6.25	$6.34	14.3%	-17.7%	14.4%	9.7%	1.3%	9.1%
Median	9.60	9.39	9.45	9.31	9.96	10.28	-2.1	0.6	5.5	7.0	3.1	7.1
High	15.88	16.03	17.02	17.20	17.88	18.86	1.0	6.2	5.1	4.0	5.5	18.8
College												
Men												
Low	$10.59	$10.26	$9.76	$9.33	$10.65	$10.14	-3.1%	-5.0%	9.1%	14.1%	-4.7%	-4.2%
Median	19.88	19.35	20.23	19.98	22.01	22.68	-2.7	4.5	8.8	10.2	3.0	14.1
High	37.07	35.55	36.67	39.03	42.68	45.30	-4.1	3.2	16.4	9.3	6.1	22.2
Women												
Low	$8.14	$7.38	$7.69	$7.85	$8.70	$9.00	-9.4%	4.3%	13.1%	10.8%	3.4%	10.5%
Median	14.07	12.80	14.87	15.82	17.12	17.66	-9.0	16.1	15.2	8.2	3.1	25.5
High	22.22	21.76	25.89	29.35	32.82	33.52	-2.1	19.0	26.8	11.8	2.1	50.8

* Low, median, and high earners refer to, respectively, the 10th, 50th, and 90th percentile wage.

Source: Authors' analysis.

14.9% over the 1973-2003 period, compared to the 8.1% wage drop of the "average" male high school graduate (Table 2.18). Similarly, the wage growth of male college graduates in the 1973-2003 period was 17.7% at the average (Table 2.18) but only 14.1% at the median (Table 2.22)

The growing disparity of wages within groups is amply demonstrated in Table 2.22. While the high (90th percentile) wage among female college graduates grew 50.8% from 1973 to 2003, the low (10th percentile) wage in this group rose 10.5%, a 40 percentage-point disparity. Similarly, wage trends at the top of the college male wage ladder (22.2% growth) and the bottom (a 4.2% decline) diverged dramatically over the 1973-2003 period.

The question remains, however, as to how much the growth in overall wage inequality in particular time periods has been driven by changes in between-group versus within-group wage inequality. It would also be useful to know the role of the growth of between- and within-group inequality on growing wage inequality at the top (the 90/50 differential) versus the bottom (the 50/10 differential), but measurement techniques for answering this question are not readily available.

Table 2.23 presents the trends in overall wage inequality, as measured by the standard deviation of log hourly wages, and the trends in within-group wage inequality. These measures allow an examination of how much of the change in overall wage inequality in particular periods was due to changes in within-group wage inequality and between-group wage inequality (primarily changes in the differentials for education and experience).

The data in Table 2.23 indicate that roughly 60% of the growth of wage inequality since 1979 has been driven by the growth of within-group wage inequality. Among women, for instance, overall wage inequality grew 0.12 over the 1979-2003 period, of which 0.071 was due to the growth of within-group wage inequality. Similarly, 0.061 of the 0.097 increase in overall male wage inequality over the 1979-2003 period was due to growing within-group inequality.

Wage inequality over the 1995-2000 period was essentially unchanged among men and declined among women, the latter a result of a decline in within-group wage inequality. Thus, Table 2.23 makes clear that any explanation of growing wage inequality must go beyond explaining changes in skill, education, experience, or other wage differentials and be able to explain growing inequalities within each of these categories.

It is also noteworthy that between-group wage inequality did not rise in the 1995-2000 technology-related productivity and wage boom, nor did it rise during the fast productivity period from 2000 to 2003. This finding is inconsistent with a story that technology has generated greater wage inequalities by ex-

TABLE 2.23 Decomposition of total and within-group wage inequality, 1973-2003

Year	Women				Men			
	Overall wage inequality* (1)	Between-group inequality** (2)	Within-group inequality*** (3)	Contribution of within-group inequality (3)/(1)	Overall wage inequality* (1)	Between-group inequality** (2)	Within-group inequality*** (3)	Contribution of within-group inequality (3)/(1)
1973	0.478	0.061	0.418	—	0.506	0.083	0.423	—
1979	0.446	0.044	0.402	—	0.506	0.078	0.428	—
1989	0.529	0.082	0.447	—	0.579	0.112	0.467	—
1995	0.562	0.095	0.467	—	0.595	0.118	0.478	—
2000	0.552	0.094	0.458	—	0.595	0.114	0.481	—
2003	0.566	0.093	0.473	—	0.603	0.114	0.489	—
Change								
1973-79	-0.033	-0.017	-0.016	49.1%	0.000	-0.005	0.006	n.a.****
1979-89	0.083	0.038	0.046	54.7	0.073	0.034	0.038	52.8%
1989-2000	0.023	0.012	0.011	46.6	0.016	0.002	0.014	86.3
1989-95	0.033	0.013	0.019	59.5	0.016	0.006	0.011	65.5
1995-2000	-0.009	-0.001	-0.009	91.8	0.000	-0.003	0.003	n.a.****
2000-03	0.014	-0.001	0.015	109.2	0.008	0.000	0.008	97.8
1979-2003	0.120	0.049	0.071	59.4%	0.097	0.037	0.061	62.2%
1973-2003	0.088	0.032	0.055	63.2	0.098	0.031	0.066	67.9

*   Measured as standard deviation of log wages.

**   Measured as mean square error from a standard (log) wage regression.

***   Reflects changes in education, experience, race/ethnicity, marital status, and regional differentials.

****   n.a. indicates "not applicable" because denominator is zero or too small.

Source: Authors' analysis.

panding skill differentials—primarily by education and experience. These data show that, while it is true that the college/high school wage differential grew in the 1995-99 period, experience differentials fell and education differentials between high-school-educated workers and workers without a high school education were stable (see Table 2.16). From 1995 to 2003 the growth of wage inequality has essentially been due to the growth of within-group inequalities.

Wage growth by race and ethnicity

Race and ethnicity have long played an important role in shaping employment opportunities and labor market outcomes. **Tables 2.24** and **2.25** present the wage trends by gender for two indicators of the wage structure (the median wage and the high school wage) for four populations: white, black, Hispanic, and Asian. (A finer breakdown of groups was not possible in the 1990s because of sample size limitations and, for the same reason, the trends for the 1980s are not available. Also, note that our definitions of race/ethnicity categories exclude Hispanics from the white, black, and Asian groups.)

The male median wage trends show that all groups experienced declining wages during the 1989-95 period, followed by strong wage growth between 1995 and 2000 (Table 2.24). With the strong wage growth after 1995, the median male wage among each group other than Hispanics returned to and exceeded its 1989, pre-recession level. A similar pattern is evident among high-school-educated male workers: wages declined significantly over the 1989-95 period, then grew in 1995-2000. Again, Hispanics were the exception, falling short of having wages in 2000 greater than in 1989. Wages grew for every race/ethnic group among men, at the median and among high school graduates, over the 2000-03 period.

Wage trends among women correspond to those of men except for slightly faster wage growth. For instance, the median or typical white, black, Hispanic, or Asian woman worker lost ground or had modest wage growth in 1989-95 but recovered strongly during 1995-2000. By 2000, women's median wages were at least 10% above their 1989 levels for whites, blacks and Asians, but were just 4.2% improved among Hispanics. Wage growth among high-school-educated women showed a similar pattern. As with men, women's wages for each race/ethnic group continued to grow through the 2000-03 period.

The gender wage gap

As discussed in several earlier sections, women's wages have generally fared better than men's over the last few decades. For instance, in 1973 the ratio of the median woman's wage to the male median wage was 63.1% but rose to

TABLE 2.24 Hourly wage growth among men by race/ethnicity, 1989-2003 (2003 dollars)

	Hourly wage				Percent changes			
	1989	1995	2000	2003	1989-2000	1989-95	1995-2000	2000-03
Medians								
White	$15.55	$14.96	$16.28	$16.82	4.7%	-3.8%	8.8%	3.3%
Black	11.25	10.93	11.90	12.23	5.8	-2.8	8.9	2.7
Hispanic	10.46	9.53	10.44	10.67	-0.1	-8.9	9.6	2.1
Asian	14.53	14.40	16.18	17.55	11.4	-0.9	12.4	8.4
By education								
*High school**								
White	$15.27	$14.65	$15.69	$16.49	2.8%	-4.0%	7.1%	5.1%
Black	12.20	11.72	12.56	13.63	3.0	-3.9	7.2	8.5
Hispanic	12.65	12.09	12.54	13.60	-0.9	-4.4	3.7	8.4
Asian	13.35	13.04	13.87	15.21	3.9	-2.3	6.4	9.7

*Average wage.

Source: Authors' analysis.

81.0% by 2003 (see **Table 2.26** and **Figure 2Q**). The rapid closing of the gender gap occurred between 1979 and 1995, primarily as the result of a fall in the male median wage and the modest growth of the female median wage. The gender wage gaps at other points in the wage distribution—e.g., the 20th and the 90th percentiles—have a similar trend.

Unfortunately, there is no research that explains these trends or examines how changes in skills, the gender composition of work, and other factors have contributed to the closing and then flattening of the gender gap.

Unemployment and wage growth

One category of factors shaping wage growth can be labeled "macroeconomic." These factors reflect the overall health of the economy and determine whether it is producing less than it has the capacity to do, as indicated by high unemployment and excess production capacity. Generally, "slack" in the economy is driven by monetary policy (the growth of the money supply, interest rates), fiscal policy (the size of the government surplus/deficits, with increasing deficits adding to demand and thereby lessening slack), and the U.S. international position (trade deficits, the flow of investment dollars abroad or from abroad to the United States). Factors that affect growth include those that limit or generate slack but also those that shape productive potential, such as public and

TABLE 2.25 Hourly wage growth among women by race/ethnicity, 1989-2003 (2003 dollars)

	Hourly wage				Percent changes			
	1989	1995	2000	2003	1989-2000	1989-95	1995-2000	2000-03
Medians								
White	$10.89	$11.15	$12.20	$12.94	12.1%	2.4%	9.5%	6.0%
Black	9.70	9.59	10.67	11.14	10.0	-1.1	11.2	4.4
Hispanic	8.65	8.48	9.02	9.75	4.2	-2.0	6.4	8.1
Asian	11.27	11.47	13.01	13.33	15.4	1.8	13.4	2.4
By education								
*High school**								
White	$10.72	$10.90	$11.53	$12.73	7.6%	1.6%	5.8%	10.3%
Black	9.89	9.84	10.59	11.49	7.1	-0.5	7.7	8.5
Hispanic	9.95	10.02	10.43	11.38	4.8	0.8	4.0	9.1
Asian	10.20	10.32	11.09	11.67	8.7	1.1	7.5	5.2

*Average wage.

Source: Authors' analysis.

TABLE 2.26 Gender wage ratio, 1973-2003

	Median wage		Ratio:
	Women	Men	Women/Men
1973	$9.60	$15.20	63.1%
1979	9.74	15.55	62.7
1989	10.57	14.46	73.1
1995	10.69	13.93	76.7
2000	11.61	14.89	78.0
2003	12.18	15.04	81.0

Source: Authors' analysis.

private investment, technological change, workforce skills, and work organization (how factors of production are combined).

Macroeconomic conditions greatly affect wage growth and wage inequality. The issue of productivity and wage growth was discussed in an earlier section, so here we focus on macroeconomic factors. The burdens of an underperforming economy and high employment are not equally shared; lower- and middle-income families are more likely to experience unemployment,

FIGURE 2Q Gender wage ratio by percentile, 1973-2003

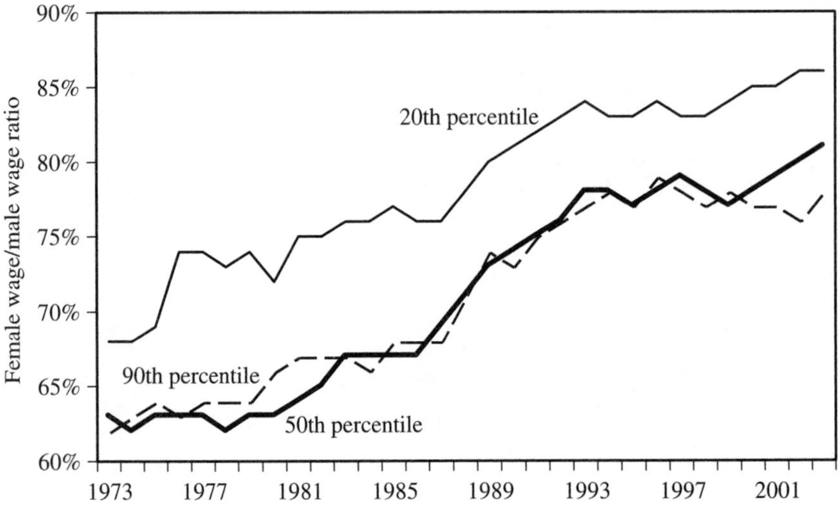

Source: Authors' analysis.

underemployment, and slower wage growth because of a weak economy (see Chapter 3 for a discussion of unemployment and family income). For many years, until recently, white-collar workers and high-wage workers were relatively unaffected by unemployment and recessions. Not surprisingly, therefore, high unemployment is a factor that widens wage and income inequality.

There are a number of mechanisms through which high unemployment affects wages and, especially, affects them differently for different groups of workers. The wages of groups that have lower wages, less education or skill, and less power in the labor market are generally more adversely affected by high unemployment. In other words, those already disadvantaged in the labor market become even more disadvantaged in a recession or in a weak economy. Conversely, as unemployment falls in a recovery and stays low, the greatest benefit accrues to those with the least power in the labor market—non-college-educated, blue-collar, minority, and low-wage workers. How does this happen?

First, these groups experience the greatest unemployment growth in a downturn and the greatest fall in unemployment in a recovery. This greater-than-average drop in unemployment reflects higher demand for these workers and consequently provides them with greater leverage with employers, generating higher wages. Second, as unemployment drops, more opportunities arise for upward mobility for these workers, as they switch jobs either to a new employer or within the same firm. Third, unions are able to bargain higher wages when unemployment is low. Fourth, there is an important interaction between macroeconomic conditions and the impact of other institutional and structural factors. For instance, the early 1980s saw a surge of imports and a growing trade deficit, a decline in manufacturing, a weakening of unions, and a large erosion of the minimum wage that coincided with (and in some cases, such as the trade and manufacturing problems, partly caused) the rising unemployment at that time. The impact of these factors on wage inequality was probably greater because of high unemployment. So, for example, the impact of trade on wages (discussed below) was greater because the recession had already induced a scarcity of good jobs.

Estimates of the effect on wages of increases in unemployment in the 1979-85 period and decreases in unemployment in the 1995-2000 period are presented in **Table 2.27**. These estimates focus on the effect of unemployment trends on the 10th, 50th, and 90th percentile wages and the 90/50 and 50/10 wage ratios for each gender.

Figure 2R shows the course of unemployment in these two periods—the sharp rise in unemployment in the early 1980s and the persistent drop in unemployment to roughly 4% in the late 1990s. During the 1980s recession wage inequality rose sharply, both at the top (the 90/50 ratio) and the bottom (the 50/10 ratio), with low-wage women being most adversely affected. Correspondingly, during the 1995-2000 boom the 50/10 wage ratios became smaller among both men and women while the 90/50 ratio continued to grow.

How much of these shifts in wage inequality are due to unemployment trends? Table 2.27 presents the results of simulations that estimate the effect of unemployment trends during the 1979-85 and 1995-2000 periods on the wages in the final year of each period—1985 and 2000, respectively. For instance, the early 1980s recession lowered the wages (relative to what they otherwise would have been) of workers at the 10th percentile in 1985 by 15.2% among men and 17.2% among women. The drop in unemployment in the 1995-2000 period raised wages for low-wage (10th percentile) men and women by 10.2% and 7.0%, respectively. Unemployment had a sizable but lesser effect on the wages of middle- and high-wage workers; surprisingly, unemployment seems to affect middle- and high-wage workers to the same extent—about an 8-9% reduction in the 1980s and a 3-4% improvement in the late 1990s. Thus, unemployment did not greatly affect the 90/50 wage ratio, which grew in both periods. However, the very large impact of unemployment on the wages at the bottom led to large changes in the 50/10 wage ratio—a roughly 5 percentage-point reduction in the late 1990s and a 6.6 percentage-point increase for men and a 10.5 percentage-point increase for women in the early 1980s. Consequently,

TABLE 2.27 Impact of rising and falling unemployment on wage levels and wage ratios, 1979-2000

| | 1979-85 | | 1995-2000 | |
	Men	Women	Men	Women
Actual changes				
Unemployment rate	1.4	1.4	-1.6	-1.6
50/10 (log)	9.6	17.0	-3.9	-1.8
90/50 (log)	8.7	8.0	3.8	1.1
Simulated effect of change in unemployment on:				
Hourly wages				
10th percentile	-15.2%	-17.2%	10.2%	7.0%
50th percentile	-9.4	-8.0	4.1	2.3
90th percentile	-8.9	-8.3	3.1	3.7
Wage ratios (log)				
50/10	6.6	10.5	-5.7	-4.5
90/50	0.6	-0.3	-0.9	1.4
Unemployment contribution to change				
50/10 (log)	68%	62%	145%	257%
90/50 (log)	6	-4	-25	131

Source: Authors' analysis.

the higher unemployment in the early 1980s can account for over 60% of the growth in the 50/10 wage ratio in that period. Moreover, lower unemployment can account for more than all of the diminution of wage inequality at the bottom in the late 1990s, indicating that unemployment offset other factors (such as immigration, trade, and so on, as discussed below) that otherwise would have generated growth in wage inequality.

The higher unemployment and overall labor slack in the early 2000s (documented in Chapter 3) clearly took their toll on wage growth and exacerbated wage inequality. Simulations, comparable to those presented in Table 2.27, show that the yearly growth of real median wages was slowed by 1.5% among men and 1.0% among women. The persistently high unemployment had an even greater effect on the wage growth of low-wage (10th percentile) workers, knocking growth of their wages down 2.2% and 1.5% per year, respectively, among

FIGURE 2R Unemployment, 1973-2003

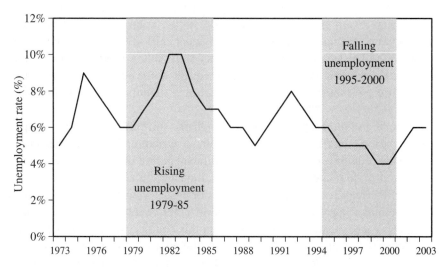

Source: Bureau of Labor Statistics.

men and women. As a result, wage inequality was higher at the bottom—as reflected in the 50/10 wage gap—than it would have been if low unemployment had been maintained: the 50/10 wage gap would have fallen slightly among women (0.7 percentage points) rather than risen slightly and fallen much faster among men (2.5 percentage points) than the slight fall (by 0.7 percentage points) that actually occurred. Since wage growth for high-wage workers was affected to the same extent as those of middle-wage workers, higher unemployment did not fuel the continuing growth of the wage gap at the top.

The shift to low-paying industries

One causal factor that is frequently considered in any analysis of growing inequality is a changing mix of industries in the economy. Such changes include the continued shift from goods-producing to service-producing industries. The significance for the labor market results from the consequent shift in the mix of employment among industries, which matters because some industries pay more than others for workers of comparable skill.

These industry employment shifts are a consequence of trade deficits and deindustrialization as well as patterns of productivity growth across industries.

(Industries facing the same growth in demand for their goods and services will generate more jobs the slower their productivity growth.) This section examines the significant erosion of wages and compensation for non-college-educated workers that resulted from an employment shift to low-paying industries in the 1980s. The smaller impact of industry shifts in the 1990s among women is one of the reasons that low-wage women saw some economic gains in the 1990s. Adverse industry shifts, led by declining manufacturing employment, resumed in the early 2000s.

Despite a common perception, this industry-shift effect is not the simple consequence of some natural evolution from an agricultural to a manufacturing to a service economy. For one thing, a significant part of the shrinkage of manufacturing is trade related. More important, industry shifts would not provide a downward pressure on wages if service-sector wages were more closely aligned with manufacturing wages, as is the case in other countries. Moreover, since health coverage, vacations, and pensions in this country are related to the specific job or sector in which a worker is employed, the industry distribution of employment matters more in the United States than in other countries. An alternative institutional arrangement found in other advanced countries sets health, pensions, vacation, and other benefits through legislation in a universal manner regardless of sector or firm. Therefore, the downward pressure of industry shifts on pay can be said, in part, to be the consequence of the absence of institutional structures that lessen inter-industry pay differences.

Trends in employment growth by major industry sector and the annual compensation and "college intensity" (the share of workers with a college degree) in 2003 of each sector are presented in **Table 2.28**. Over the 2000 to 2003 period payroll employment fell by 1,855,000 (a drop explored in great detail in Chapter 3). More than all of the job loss was in manufacturing (down 2,738,000), but jobs also declined in highly paid industries like information and professional and business services that had grown rapidly in the 1989-2000 period. Thus, industry shifts in the current business cycle have put downward pressure on compensation levels.

The 1979-89 period also saw significant downward pressure on pay due to industry shifts. The 18.1 million (net) jobs created between 1979 and 1989 involved a loss of manufacturing (1.4 million) and mining (258,000) jobs and an increase (19.0 million) in the service-producing sector. The largest amount of job growth (13.9 million) occurred in the two lowest-paying service-sector industries—retail trade and services (business, personnel, and health). In fact, these two industries accounted for 77% of all the net new jobs over the 1979-89 period.

The shift toward low-paying industries continued in the 1990s, although at a much slower pace. Low-wage retail jobs played a smaller role in overall job

TABLE 2.28 Employment growth and compensation by sector, 1979-2003

Industry sector	Employment (thousands)				Job growth			Industry share of job change			Annual compensation* 2002	Percent college graduates
	1979	1989	2000	2003	1979-89	1989-00	2000-03	1979-89	1989-00	2000-03		
Goods producing	24,997	24,045	24,649	21,817	-952	604	-2,832	-5.3%	2.5%	-152.7%	$54,391	18.7%
Mining	1,008	750	599	571	-258	-151	-28	-1.4	-0.6	-1.5	74,425	9.7
Construction	4,562	5,309	6,787	6,722	747	1,478	-65	4.1	6.2	-3.5	48,966	22.3
Manufacturing	19,426	17,985	17,263	14,525	-1,441	-722	-2,738	-8.0	-3.0	-147.6	56,154	23.3
Durable goods	12,220	11,004	10,876	8,970	-1,216	-128	-1,906	-6.7	-0.5	-102.7	59,298	23.3
Nondurable goods	7,206	6,981	6,388	5,555	-225	-593	-833	-1.2	-2.5	-44.9	50,977	20.8
Service producing	64,935	83,969	107,136	108,114	19,034	23,167	978	105.3%	97.5%	52.7%	$45,413	17.5%
Trans., utilities	3,637	4,118	5,012	4,758	481	894	-254	2.7	3.8	-13.7	54,277	26.4
Wholesale	4,485	5,284	5,933	5,606	798	650	-328	4.4	2.7	-17.7	61,061	16.0
Retail	10,180	13,108	15,280	14,912	2,928	2,172	-368	16.2	9.1	-19.9	31,005	
Information	2,375	2,622	3,631	3,198	247	1,009	-433	1.4	4.2	-23.3	71,279	39.9
Fin., ins., real est.	4,843	6,562	7,687	7,974	1,719	1,125	287	9.5	4.7	15.5	68,831	38.1
Services	23,347	34,349	48,805	50,092	11,002	14,456	1,287	60.8	60.8	69.4	41,275	35.7
Prof., business	7,312	10,555	16,666	15,997	3,243	6,111	-669	17.9	25.7		55,288	40.5
Edu., health	6,767	10,616	15,109	16,577	3,849	4,493	1,468	21.3	18.9		42,537	46.0
Government	16,068	17,927	20,790	21,575	1,859	2,863	785	10.3	12.0	42.3	56,886	38.9
Federal	2,894	3,136	2,865	2,756	242	-271	-109	1.3	-1.1	-5.9	77,076	n.a.
State and local	13,174	14,791	17,925	18,819	1,617	3,134	894	8.9	13.2	48.2	51,465	n.a.
Total	89,932	108,014	131,787	129,932	18,082	23,773	-1,855	100.0%	100.0%	100.0%	$48,784	29.1%

* Per full-time equivalent.

Source: Authors' analysis.

173

creation, contributing 9.1% of the new jobs, but the services industry (primarily health and temporary services) continued to play an important role, supplying 60.8% of the net new jobs. Together, these low-wage industries accounted for 69.9% of all new jobs in 1989-2000. Manufacturing job loss was only about half as great in the 1990s as in the 1980s, and higher-wage industries such as construction and transportation/communications expanded more in the 1990s than in the 1980s. Thus, industry shifts were less adverse in the 1990s.

The extent of the industry shifts is more evident in an analysis of changes in the shares of the workforce in various sectors (**Table 2.29**). Several high-wage sectors, such as construction, transportation, wholesale, communications, and government, increased employment in the 1980s but ended up providing a smaller or similar share of overall employment over time. A lower share of employment in these high-wage sectors puts downward pressure on wages. Overall, the share of the workforce in low-paying services and in retail trade was 6.6 percentage points higher in 1989 than in 1979. The parallel trend was the roughly 7 percentage-point drop in the share of the workforce in high-paying industries, such as manufacturing, construction, mining, government, transportation, and utilities.

The data in Table 2.29 illustrate the different, and less adverse, shifts in industry employment in the 1990s relative to the 1980s. Although durable manufacturing's share of employment declined in the 1990s (by 1.9 percentage points), this was less than the decline of the 1980s (3.4 percentage points). The low-wage retail trade sector expanded by 0.8 percentage points in the 1980s but shrank in the 1990s. Similarly, higher-wage sectors such as construction and transportation/utilities expanded or were stable in the 1990s but contracted in the 1980s. In general, high-wage sectors fared better in terms of employment growth in the 1990s than the 1980s. Correspondingly, the 1990s contraction of retail trade, by far the lowest-wage sector, helped wages grow. Thus, one reason that median wages eroded less and low wages did better in the early 1990s than in the 1980s might be related to this different pattern of industry employment growth.

In the period from 2000 to 2003 the only private-sector industry with above-average compensation to expand employment share was the finance, insurance, and real estate industry. Government, based on growth of state and local government employment, also expanded employment relative to other industries. Nearly all of the well-paying sectors lost employment share in recent years: manufacturing (down 1.9 percentage points); information (down 0.3); transportation, utilities, and wholesale trade (together down 0.3); and professional/business services, the highest-paid part of services (down 0.3).

TABLE 2.29 Employment growth by sector, 1979-2003

Industry sector	Employment shares				Percentage-point change		
	1979	1989	2000	2003	1979-89	1989-2000	2000-03
Goods producing	27.8%	22.3%	18.7%	16.8%	-5.5	-3.6	-1.9
Mining	1.1	0.7	0.5	0.4	-0.4	-0.2	0.0
Construction	5.1	4.9	5.2	5.2	-0.2	0.2	0.0
Manufacturing	21.6	16.7	13.1	11.2	-5.0	-3.6	-1.9
Durable goods	13.6	10.2	8.3	6.9	-3.4	-1.9	-1.3
Nondurable goods	8.0	6.5	4.8	4.3	-1.5	-1.6	-0.6
Service producing	72.2%	77.7%	81.3%	83.2%	5.5	3.6	1.9
Trans., utilities	4.0	3.8	3.8	3.7	-0.2	0.0	-0.1
Wholesale trade	5.0	4.9	4.5	4.3	-0.1	-0.4	-0.2
Retail trade	11.3	12.1	11.6	11.5	0.8	-0.5	-0.1
Information	2.6	2.4	2.8	2.5	-0.2	0.3	-0.3
Fin., ins., real est.	5.4	6.1	5.8	6.1	0.7	-0.2	0.3
Services	26.0	31.8	37.0	38.6	5.8	5.2	1.5
Prof., business	8.1	9.8	12.6	12.3	1.6	2.9	-0.3
Edu., health	7.5	9.8	11.5	12.8	2.3	1.6	1.3
Government	17.9	16.6	15.8	16.6	-1.3	-0.8	0.8
Federal	3.2	2.9	2.2	2.1	-0.3	-0.7	-0.1
State and local	14.6	13.7	13.6	14.5	-1.0	-0.1	0.9
Total	100.0%	100.0%	100.0%	100.0%			

Source: Authors' analysis.

Table 2.30, which presents an analysis of the impact of the shift in the industry mix of employment on the growth of the college/high school wage premium, provides some systematic evidence of how industry shifts affect the growth of wage inequality, at least on this one wage premium. Industry shifts affect the education premium because some industries are more likely to employ college graduates; if these industries expand more quickly they raise the demand of college-educated workers. This analysis uses wage data on individuals to determine the growth of the college/high school wage premium when one does and does not control for industry shifts—the "constant" and "actual" under "industry composition." Comparing the growth of the education premium in the first two columns provides information on the impact of changes in the industry composition of employment, or industry shifts. This analysis suggests that the employment shift to low-wage industries accounted for almost 20% of the growth of education premiums over the 1979-89 period among men and women. Among men, for instance, the college/high school wage premium grew 13.9 percentage points from 1979 to 1989, but would have grown by 11.4 percentage points had industry composition not changed. Therefore, 2.5 percentage points of the 13.9 percentage-point growth, equivalent to 18% of the total growth in the college/high school differential in the 1980s, can be accounted for by industry shifts.

Among men, the industry shift effect was smaller in 1989-99 (we use 1999 rather then 2000 as the breakpoint because a shift in industry definitions make the data between 1999 and 2000 not comparable) than in 1979-89, 1.5% versus 2.5%, and was especially slow during the 1995-99 period. Among women, industry shifts actually reduced inequality in the 1990s due to the trends over the 1995-2000 boom. Thus, the industry shift effect went from inducing a 2.7% increase in the college wage premium in the 1980s to reducing this premium by 0.7% in the 1990s, a 3.4% turnaround in trend. It is likely that this reversal is due to the corresponding reversal of retail trade employment (which disproportionately comprises women) in the 1990s—its employment share contracted rather than expanded, as it had in the 1980s. On the other hand, industry shifts remained a persistent factor in the 1990s, causing rising wage inequality among men.

Interestingly, industry shifts in the 2000-03 period did not raise demands for college graduates or lead to rising wage inequality among men. On the contrary, industry shifts lowered the college/high school wage premium by 0.3 percentage points, explaining more than half of the overall decline of 0.5 percentage points. The erosion of jobs in the information sector is probably the cause of this lessened demand for education. Among women, the industry shift in recent years raised the demand for college graduates and helped to slow

TABLE 2.30 The effect of industry shifts on the growth of the college/high school wage differential, 1973-2003

| | College/high school wage differential | | Industry shift: | |
| | Industry composition: | | | |
	Actual*	Constant**	Effect	Share***
Men				
1973	25.3%	30.3%		
1979	20.1	24.8		
1989	33.9	36.2		
1995	37.1	38.3		
1999	41.5	42.3		
2000	42.0	41.7		
2003	41.5	41.5		
Change				
1979-89	13.9%	11.4%	2.5%	18.0%
1989-99	7.6	6.1	1.5	19.9
1989-95	3.2	2.1	1.1	33.6
1995-99	4.4	4.0	0.4	9.9
2000-03	-0.5	-0.2	-0.3	59.4
Women				
1973	37.7%	35.2%		
1979	26.5	25.2		
1989	41.0	37.1		
1995	46.7	42.1		
1999	47.9	44.7		
2000	47.9	45.4		
2003	46.1	43.5		
Change				
1979-89	14.5%	11.9%	2.7%	18.4%
1989-99	6.9	7.6	-0.7	-9.9
1989-95	5.7	5.1	0.7	11.5
1995-99	1.2	2.6	-1.3	-109.7
2000-03	-1.8	-1.9	0.2	-8.6

* Estimated with controls for experience as a quartic, marital status, race, and four regions.
** Adds 12 industry controls to the regression reported in first column, thereby holding industry "constant."
*** Share of the rise in "actual" that is explained by industry shifts, calculated from the difference between "actual" and "constant" relative to "actual."

Source: Authors' analysis.

slightly the decline in the college wage premium, from 1.9 to 1.8 percentage points. This reverses the pattern from the late 1990s, when industry shifts were equalizing among women.

Trade and wages

The process of globalization since the 1980s has been an important factor in both slowing the growth rate of average wages and reducing the wage levels of workers with less than a college degree. In more recent years trade and globalization have begun to affect white-collar and college-educated workers to a great extent as well. The increase in international trade and investment flows affects wages through several channels. First, increases in imports of finished manufactured goods, especially from countries where workers earn only a fraction of what U.S. workers earn, reduces manufacturing employment in the United States. While increases in exports create employment opportunities for some domestic workers, imports mean job losses for many others. Large, chronic trade deficits over the last 17 years suggest that the jobs lost to import competition have outnumbered the jobs gained from increasing exports. Given that export industries tend to be less labor intensive than import-competing industries, even growth in "balanced trade" (where exports and imports both increase by the same dollar amount) would lead to a decline in manufacturing jobs.

Second, imports of intermediate manufactured goods (used as inputs in the production of final goods) also help to lower domestic manufacturing employment, especially for production workers and others with less than a college education. The expansion of export platforms in low-wage countries has induced many U.S. manufacturing firms to purchase part of their production processes from low-wage countries. Since firms generally find it most profitable to purchase the most labor-intensive processes, the increase in intermediate inputs from abroad has hit non-college-educated production workers hardest. The growth in imports of intermediate inputs is shown in **Figure 2S** from 1979 to 2000 (the latest data) (Bivens 2004). For all of manufacturing, the share of intermediate inputs into the production process that were imported rose from 7.7% in 1979 to 14.1% in 2000. In transportation equipment, the imported intermediate inputs share rose from 10.7% in 1979 to 17.8% by 2000.

Third, low wages and greater world capacity for producing manufactured goods can lower the prices of many international goods. Since workers' pay is tied to the value of the goods they produce, lower prices from international competition, despite possible lower inflation, can lead to a reduction in the earnings of U.S. workers, even if imports themselves do not increase.

FIGURE 2S   Share of intermediate inputs supplied by imports, 1979-2000

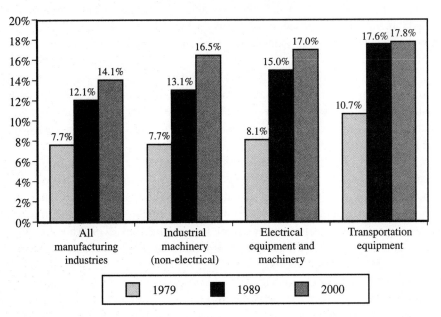

Source: Bivens (2004).

Fourth, in many cases the mere threat of direct foreign competition or of the relocation of part or all of a production facility can lead workers to grant wage concessions to their employers.

Fifth, the very large increases in direct investment (i.e., plant and equipment) flows to other countries have meant reduced investment in the domestic manufacturing base and significant growth in the foreign manufacturing capacity capable of competing directly with U.S.-based manufacturers.

Sixth, the effects of globalization go beyond those workers exposed directly to foreign competition. As trade drives workers out of manufacturing and into lower-paying service jobs, not only do their own wages fall, but the new supply of workers to the service sector (from displaced workers plus young workers not able to find manufacturing jobs) also helps to lower the wages of those already employed in service jobs.

Last, trade in services has recently gained prominence as call center operations, computer programming, doctor support services (reading X-rays, for instance), and other white-collar services have been transferred or purchased abroad, sometimes to countries with far lower wages than the United States (most notably India and China). Less is known about this recent phenomenon, sometimes called "offshoring," but it seems to be a mechanism through which globalization is now adversely affecting white-collar jobs and wages (and will increasingly continue to do so).

This section briefly examines the role of international trade and investment in recent changes in the U.S. wage structure. Since even the preceding list of channels through which globalization affects wages is not complete and not yet quantified, this analysis *understates* the impact of globalization on wages in the 1980s and 1990s.

Table 2.31 provides information on the growth of the manufacturing trade deficit (the excess of imports over exports) from 1979 to 2000 by region and type of industry—industries that heavily use unskilled labor, skilled labor, or capital. The trade deficit grew to $368.4 billion in 2000 (and has grown further since), whereas U.S. manufacturing trade was balanced in 1979. This growing trade deficit reflects the fast growth of imports in the 1980s and 1990s and the much slower growth of exports.

The sizable deterioration in the U.S. trade balance over the 1980s was driven in large part by trade with Asian developing countries (Singapore, Taiwan, Korea, and Hong Kong), China, and Japan. However, the deficit with other advanced (and higher-wage) countries also grew (see the line for the OECD, which includes the advanced countries, including Japan, and some middle-income countries such as Mexico and Korea).

Much of the growth in the trade deficit from 1989 to 2000 came from China and Mexico trade—$105.5 billion of the $249.6 billion growth—and another chunk from trade with Japan—$31.5 billion. Trade with lower-wage countries was responsible for the majority of the growth in the trade deficit (see the non-OECD line and add Mexico). In the 1990s, the trade deficit grew more quickly and grew more rapidly with lower-wage countries. This pattern would suggest a greater impact of trade on the wage structure in the 1990s than in the 1980s.

Table 2.31 also provides a breakdown of the manufacturing trade deficit by the skill-intensity and capital-intensity of the product. In fact, deficits have grown in each of the three product types, both skilled-intensive and unskilled-intensive as well as capital-intensive products.

These data suggest not only a large increase in the trade deficit but a growing exposure of a broad range of industries to foreign competition from the most advanced countries and from lower-wage developing countries. This growth in the trade deficit and increased global competition can, and would be expected to, adversely affect the wages of non-college-educated workers relative

TABLE 2.31 Net trade in U.S. manufactures by factor intensity and trading partner, 1979-2000 (millions of U.S. dollars)

Country/region	Skilled-intensive			Unskilled-intensive			Capital-intensive			Total		
	1979	1989	2000	1979	1989	2000	1979	1989	2000	1979	1989	2000
OECD	$10,400	-$11,412	-$43,225	-$14,261	-$32,582	-$51,040	-$9,183	-$51,061	-$121,985	-$13,044	-$95,056	-$216,250
Latin America	5,756	6,136	16,961	-3,512	-5,339	-15,978	4,038	2,272	7,392	6,282	3,069	8,376
Asia - 4 Tigers*	-418	-11,959	-22,110	-7,611	-23,481	-16,435	812	1,416	-1,368	-7,216	-34,024	-39,913
Japan	-5,700	-32,500	-47,800	-3,750	-4,250	-4,910	-9,300	-29,000	-44,600	-18,750	-65,750	-97,310
Mexico	2,320	180	-16,000	-210	-740	-5,460	1,800	1,220	-6,000	3,910	660	-27,460
China	242	-238	-32,100	-177	-6,760	-47,100	24	285	-4,930	89	-6,713	-84,130
Non-OECD	17,400	5,122	-37,175	-9,839	-38,218	-115,960	9,506	9,361	985	17,067	-23,734	-152,150
World	27,800	-6,290	-80,400	-24,100	-70,800	-167,000	323	-41,700	-121,000	4,023	-118,790	-368,400

* Singapore, Taiwan, South Korea, and Hong Kong

Source: Bivens (2004) update of Cline (1997) using data from Feenstra (2002) and the University of California-Davis Center for International Data.

to others. In fact, any potential gains from trade would be created precisely through such a mechanism—a redeployment of workers and capital into more highly skilled or capital-intensive industries, a movement that lessens the need for non-college-educated workers. The offshoring trend is a mechanism whereby workers with high levels of education are being replaced, but this is still a smaller phenomenon than the more usual trade impact on middle- and low-wage workers.

We now turn to an examination of the types of jobs that were lost as the trade deficit grew, as job losses in import-sensitive industries exceeded job gains in export industries. In periods of low unemployment, it may be the case that a trade deficit does not cause actual job loss because workers displaced by rising imports have found employment in non-traded sectors such as services. Nevertheless, even with low unemployment a trade deficit will affect the composition of jobs (less manufacturing, more services), thereby affecting wage inequality. In this light, **Table 2.32** indicates how trade flows affect the composition of employment by wage level and education relative to a situation in which the ratios of imports and exports to output remained at 1979 levels. Specifically, Table 2.32 shows the number of jobs lost because of the growing trade deficit in recent time periods and the share of jobs lost in particular education and wage categories. This analysis relies on information on the types of jobs in each industry and the changes in the trade deficit by industry. By using an input-output model, the analysis can examine how jobs across the economy are affected, including jobs that feed into other industries (e.g., showing how steel workers are affected by fewer car sales).

In the 1980s, 87.8% of the 1,766,000 trade-related job losses were jobs held by non-college-educated workers. In contrast, 73.0% of all jobs were held by workers without college degrees. Therefore, trade disproportionately impacted the non-college-educated workforce. Moreover, workers with less education credentials were generally more intensely affected by trade; those without high school degrees were disproportionately affected relative to those with high school degrees, and those with no college were affected more than those with some college. Likewise, trade-deficit-related job losses in the 1980s fell disproportionately on the lowest-wage workers and lower-middle-wage workers. The 51.7% of the workforce in the two lowest pay categories suffered 65.0% of the trade-related job losses. Consequently, non-college-educated and middle- and lower-wage workers disproportionately bore the costs and pressures of trade deficits and global competition, at least in the 1980s.

Interestingly, trade-related job losses were more evenly spread across wage and education levels in the 1990s and early 2000s than in the 1980s. After 1994, about 23% of the trade-related job losses were borne by college gradu-

TABLE 2.32 Trade-deficit-induced job loss by wage and education level, 1979-2002

Job characteristic	Share of total employment, 2000	1979-89	1989-94	1994-2000	2000-02
Trade-deficit related job loss (thousands)					
Education level					
College graduate*		-215	-31	-695	-210
Non-college		-1,551	-356	-2,350	-670
Some college		-403	-55	-845	-246
High school (HS)		-653	-148	-1,106	-306
Less than HS		-495	-153	-399	-118
*Wage level**					
Highest wage		-163	-34	-422	-126
High wage		-186	-27	-389	-117
Upper-middle		-269	-36	-712	-217
Lower-middle		-478	-96	-796	-222
Lowest-wage		-670	-194	-726	-197
Total		-1,766	-387	-3,044	-879
Trade-deficit related job loss (share of total)					
Education level					
College graduate*	27.1%	12.2%	8.0%	22.8%	23.9%
Non-college	73.0	87.8	92.0	77.2	76.2
Some college	29.0	22.8	14.2	27.8	28.0
High school (HS)	31.4	37.0	38.2	36.3	34.8
Less than HS	12.6	28.0	39.5	13.1	13.4
*Wage level**					
Highest wage	13.3%	9.2%	8.8%	13.8%	14.4%
High wage	12.4	10.5	7.0	12.8	13.3
Upper-middle	22.7	15.2	9.3	23.4	24.6
Lower-middle	27.7	27.1	24.8	26.1	25.3
Lowest-wage	23.9	37.9	50.1	23.8	22.4
Total	100.0%	100.0%	100.0%	100.0%	100.0%

*   Four years of college or more.

**   Corresponding to jobs that paid in the following wage percentiles in 1979: 90-100, 75-89, 50-74, 21-49, 0-20.

Source: Scott et al. (1997), Tables 1 and 2 and EPI analysis of U.S. Bureau of the Census and BLS Data in Bivens (2004).

ates, a share not much below their 27.1% share of the workforce. Likewise, trade cost high-wage jobs after 1994 roughly in proportion to their presence in the workforce (see the two highest wage categories contributing 13% or 14% of the losses, comparable to their workforce share). This pattern suggests that, though trade deficits grew larger in the 1990s, their effect may have been more evenly spread over the workforce; thus, trade may have had a lesser effect on inequality between education or wage-level groups than in the 1980s (creating a more broad-based loss of worker bargaining power in the economy). This analysis probably overstates the adverse trade impact on the higher wage and education groups because one of its underlying assumptions is that when an industry loses jobs it does so proportionately across types of jobs (e.g., a 10% loss of jobs means 10% fewer jobs in each category within the industry). Since the response to lost export opportunities or displacements from greater imports has almost surely fallen disproportionately on the non-college-educated workforce of each industry (rather than the white-collar or technical workers), this analysis understates the degree to which trade and globalization affect non-college-educated workers relative to those with college degrees. Nevertheless, this analysis does show that the industries adversely affected recently by trade are higher-paying and employ more college-educated workers than the trade-impacted industries of the 1980s.

Taken together, Tables 2.31 and 2.32 suggest that trade, particularly with low-wage developing countries, accelerated the long-term decline in manufacturing employment. The data also suggest that the fall in employment opportunities was especially severe for non-college-educated manufacturing production workers in the 1980s, with broader but more even impacts in the 1990s. Since production (and white-collar) workers in manufacturing earn, on average, substantially more than workers with similar skills in non-manufacturing jobs, these trade-induced job losses contributed directly to the deterioration in the wage structure, particularly for middle-wage and lower-wage workers. Since millions of trade-displaced workers sought jobs in non-manufacturing sectors, trade also worked to depress wages of comparable workers employed outside manufacturing. The result is to weaken the wages of middle- and low-wage workers relative to those of high-earning workers.

Little concrete evidence is available on the other channels discussed at the beginning of this section—the "threat effect" of imports and plant relocation on U.S. manufacturing wages and the reality of large-scale international direct investment flows. Nevertheless, these effects are likely to be as large as or larger than those that are more readily quantifiable.

In the early 2000s globalization's adverse impacts seemed to be moving far upscale, affecting so-called knowledge workers such as computer programmers, scientists, and doctors, as work previously done in the United States was located in or relocated to other countries. This phenomenon of offshoring high-tech, white-collar work is noteworthy because those workers affected, especially computer-related professionals, were frequently discussed as the winners in the globalization process. If the jobs of such highly educated workers are now at risk in the global economy, it makes one wonder which jobs cannot be moved offshore. Two factors seem to have made offshoring of white-collar work a potentially significant phenomenon. One is that technology, particularly fast Internet and other communications technology, makes coordination and transmission of work worldwide much easier. A second factor is what could be called a "supply shock," or the availability of millions of highly educated workers in places such as China, India, Eastern Europe, Russia, and elsewehere who are willing to do the work for a lower wage than U.S. workers.

Hard data that could inform us of the extent of offshoring and how much more to expect in the future are not available because our data systems are not well suited to measuring trade in services (including that which is transferred over the Internet) as opposed to goods. Even if the current level of offshoring is modest, the high public profile of this practice and the statements from firms of their intentions to deepen their offshoring is sufficient to depress wage expectations in the relevant labor markets.

Outsourcing also emerged as a concern for many workers at a time when the labor market for college-educated workers, especially new college graduates, was faring poorly. As discussed above, wages for entry-level college graduates fell in the early 2000s. The review of unemployment and employment trends in Chapter 3 shows that the college graduate unemployment rate increased more in this than in earlier recessions and that the employment rates of college graduates declined in recent years, a highly unusual development. The data in the next chapter also points to high unemployment among software programmers and engineers. In this light, offshoring is affecting a group that has already been experiencing unusual labor market distress.

There is some evidence to suggest that the increased global sourcing of software work is not just a future possibility but an ongoing development. **Figure 2T** examines trends in information technology (IT) software *employment* relative to *demand* for IT software. Some analysts have pointed to the bursting of the IT investment bubble as a major source of the labor market distress for IT professionals; however, the burst bubble has not been the sole source of IT labor market woes.

While the lesser investment in IT software following the bursting of the IT investment bubble surely led to declining IT employment, by early 2004 real (inflation-adjusted) spending on IT software had actually exceeded its 2000 peak. Yet, employment in IT software industries remains well below its peak level. One interpretation is that this employment gap is due to the movement of IT software work offshore. The experiences of the United States and India offer some persuasive, though indirect, evidence.

FIGURE 2T Employment in IT software industries and software investment, 1994-2004

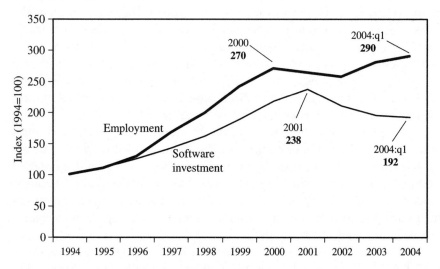

Source: Bivens and Price (2004).

Software employment can be examined by measuring employment in software-producing *industries* or in software *occupations*. Software-producing industries (software publishing, custom software, and computer systems design) employ many people who actually work in non-computer occupations, like sales or accounting. On the other hand, software occupations (e.g., programmers and software engineers) are also found in a range of other industries, such as finance, manufacturing, and professional services.

Domestic software-related jobs, however measured, have declined significantly in recent years (**Figure 2U**). Employment in software-producing industries declined by 128,000 (10%) between 2000 and 2004, while jobs in software occupations shrank by 154,000 (5%) from 2000 to 2002 (the last year for which data are available).

The story in India is quite different. India's industry association of software and related companies (NASSCOM) published an analysis of recent trends indicating that the professional jobs in India's software export sector rose by 150,000 from 1999 to 2003. Given that 67.7% of its software exports go to the United States, this growth implies that Indian software jobs servicing the U.S. market have increased by roughly 100,000 over the last four years. The

FIGURE 2U Change in software-related jobs since 2000

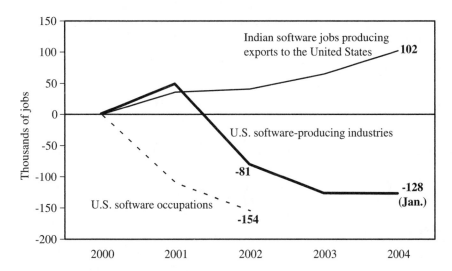

Sources: EPI calculations of data from the Bureau of Labor Statistics and the National Association of
Software and Service Companies (India); Bivens and Price (2004).

NASSCOM report also indicates that its two largest customers abroad are in
the banking, financial services, and insurance industry (39% of exports) and in
the manufacturing industry (12%). Both industries have traditionally employed
people to produce software in-house. Increased movement of work overseas
that had been formerly performed in-house at these companies may explain
why U.S. jobs fell by 154,000 in software *occupations* but by only 81,000 in
software-producing *industries* between 2000 and 2002.

Another aspect of globalization is immigration. The percentage of immigrants in the labor force declined in the United States over the first half of the
last century but began to grow in the 1960s and started to grow faster in the
1980s, as seen in **Table 2.33** (which shows the immigrant share of the workforce
in each of four education categories from 1960 through 2000). Holding all else
constant, a rise in immigration increases the available labor supply in the United
States and thus tends to reduce wages. If one workforce group—say, those
without a high school degree—experiences the largest growth in immigration,
then that group will have wage growth inferior to (or real wage declines greater
than) that of other less-affected groups. The largest share of immigrants is among
the least educated, those without a high school degree (20.8% of young high

TABLE 2.33 Changes in immigration by education, 1960-2000

Education/ years of experience	Share of male labor force foreign-born					Change	
	1960	1970	1980	1990	2000	1980-90	1990-2000
High school dropouts							
1-5	2.6%	3.9%	8.5%	18.4%	20.8%	9.9%	2.4%
21-25	4.4	6.0	12.5	28.5	40.5	16.0	12.0
High school							
1-5	1.2%	2.1%	3.2%	8.0%	12.3%	4.8%	4.3%
21-25	3.0	3.2	4.8	7.6	9.4	2.8	1.8
Some college							
1-5	2.3%	3.5%	5.2%	6.6%	9.7%	1.4%	3.1%
21-25	3.0	3.2	4.8	7.6	9.4	2.8	1.8
College graduate							
1-5	3.4%	4.1%	5.0%	9.0%	12.4%	4.0%	3.4%
21-25	6.4	5.6	8.5	10.2	11.5	1.7	1.3

Source: Authors analysis of Borjas (2003).

school dropouts in 2000 and 40.5% of those with 21 to 25 years of experience). However, the share of immigrants is slightly higher in the college-educated labor force than in the high school and "some college" categories. Likewise, the greatest growth of immigration appears among those without a high school degree, while the share among those with a high school education, some college, or a college degree rose fairly evenly and consistently. Recall that those without a high school degree made up only 12% of the workforce in 2000, so this large impact of immigration was intensely focused on a small group at the bottom of the education ladder. On the other hand, immigration and its increase have been broadly felt by all of the other education groups, including those with a college degree. These numbers suggest that immigrants compete disproportionately with the least-skilled U.S. workers and therefore have generated pressure to lower wages for those without a high school degree, particularly since the end of the 1970s.On the other hand, immigration has probably not been associated with growing wage inequality between high- and middle-wage earners.

Given this downward pressure on the wages of low-wage workers from increased immigration, it is surprising that wages at the bottom did better in the 1990s than in the 1980s and that the 50/10 wage gap has been stable or declin-

FIGURE 2V   Union membership in the United States, 1973-2003

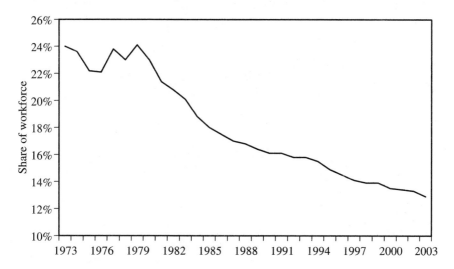

Source: Hirsch and Macpherson (1997) and the Bureau of Labor Statistics.

ing since the late 1980s. However, two increases in the minimum wage and many years of persistent low unemployment in the 1990s may have offset the impact of immigration. In the early 2000s there was no low unemployment or minimum wage increases to boost low wages, and the 50/10 wage gap stopped its strong decent and instead grew slightly among women and fell a small bit among men. Immigration may be asserting an adverse impact under these conditions.

The union dimension

The percentage of the workforce represented by unions was stable in the 1970s but fell rapidly in the 1980s and continued to fall in the 1990s and the early 2000s, as shown in **Figure 2V**. This falling rate of unionization has lowered wages, not only because some workers no longer receive the higher union wage but also because there is less pressure on non-union employers to raise wages (a "spillover" or "threat effect" of unionism). There are also reasons to believe that union bargaining power has weakened, adding a qualitative shift to the quantitative decline. This erosion of bargaining power is partially related to a harsher economic context for unions because

TABLE 2.34 Union wage and benefit premium, 2003 (2003 dollars)

	Hourly pay			
	Wages	Insurance	Pension	Compensation
All workers				
Union	$23.25	$2.99	$1.73	$30.68
Non-union	17.66	1.34	0.54	21.36
Union premium				
Dollars	$5.59	$1.65	$1.19	$9.32
Percent	31.7%	123.1%	220.4%	43.6%
Blue collar				
Union	$22.74	$3.16	$1.95	$30.76
Non-union	14.49	1.31	0.39	18.11
Union premium				
Dollars	$8.25	$1.85	$1.56	$12.65
Percent	56.9%	141.2%	400.0%	69.9%

Source: Authors' analysis of BLS data.

of trade pressures, the shift to services, and ongoing technological change. However, analysts have also pointed to other factors, such as employer militancy and changes in the application and administration of labor law, that have helped to weaken unions.

Table 2.34 shows the union wage premium—the degree to which union wages exceed non-union wages—by type of pay (benefits or wages) for all workers and for blue-collar workers in 2003. The union premium is larger for total compensation (43.6%) than for wages alone (31.7%), reflecting the fact that unionized workers are provided insurance and pension benefits that are more than double those of non-union workers. For blue-collar workers (where the comparison is more of an "apples to apples" one), the union premium in insurance and benefits is even larger: union blue-collar workers receive 141.2% and 400.0% more in health and pension benefits, respectively, than do their non-union counterparts.

Table 2.35, using a different data source and methodology, presents another set of estimates of the union wage premium. Specifically, the premium is computed so as to reflect differences in hourly wages between union and non-union workers who are otherwise comparable in experience, education, region, industry, occupation, and marital status. This methodology yields a lower but

TABLE 2.35 Union wage premium by demographic group, 2003

Demographic group	Percent union*	Union premium**	
		Dollars	Percent
Total	14.3%	$1.63	15.5%
Men	15.6	2.33	18.7
Women	12.9	1.07	11.6
Whites	14.2%	$1.38	13.8%
Men	15.9	2.17	17.3
Women	12.4	0.72	9.1
Blacks	18.2%	$2.56	20.9%
Men	19.9	3.13	23.8
Women	16.8	2.05	18.2
Hispanics	11.9%	$2.92	23.2%
Men	12.1	3.44	25.5
Women	11.6	2.25	19.5
Asians	12.8%	$1.11	12.4%
Men	12.6	1.52	13.9
Women	13.1	1.22	12.3

*   Union member or covered by a collective bargaining agreement.
** Regression-adjusted union premium advantage controlling for experience, education,
     region, industry, occupation, and marital status.

Source: Authors' analysis.

still sizable union premium of 15.5% overall—18.7% for men and 11.6% for women. There are sizable differences in union wage premiums across demographic groups, with blacks and Hispanics having union premiums of 20.9% and 23.2%, respectively, far higher than the 13.8% union premium for whites. Consequently, unions raise the wages of minorities more than whites (the wage effect of unionism on a group is calculated as the unionism rate times the union premium), helping to close racial/ethnic wage gaps. Hispanic and black men tend to reap the greatest wage advantage from unionism, though minority women have significantly higher union premiums than their white counterparts. Unionized Asians have a wage premium close to that of whites, with men and women having a similar premium.

Table 2.36 provides information on the union premium for various non-wage dimensions of compensation related to health insurance, pensions, and

TABLE 2.36 Union premiums for health, retirement, and paid leave

Benefit	Union	Nonunion	Difference Unadjusted	Adjusted*	Union premium
Health insurance					
Percent covered	83.5%	62.0%	21.5%	17.5%	28.2%
Employer share (%)					
Single	88.3%	81.8%	6.5%	9.1%	11.1%
Family	76.3%	64.9%	11.4%	10.1%	15.6%
Deductible ($)	$200	$300	-$100	-$54	-18.0%
Retiree health coverage	76.6%	59.8%	16.7%	14.6%	24.4%
Pension					
Percent covered	71.9%	43.8%	28.1%	23.6%	53.9%
Employer costs (per hour)					
Defined benefit	—	—	—	$0.39	36.1%
Defined contribution	—	—	—	-$0.11	-17.7%
Time off					
Vacation weeks	2.98	2.35	0.63	—	26.6%
Paid holiday/vacation (hours)	—	—	—	22.2	14.3%

* Adjusted for establishment size, occupation, industry, and other factors.

Source: Buchmueller, DiNardo, and Valletta (2001) and Mishel et al. (2003).

paid time off. The first two columns present the characteristics of compensation in union and non-union settings. The difference between the union and non-union compensation packages are presented in two ways, unadjusted (simply the difference between the first two columns) and adjusted (for differences in characteristics other than union status such as industry, occupation, and establishment size). The last column presents the union premium, the percentage difference between union and non-union compensation, calculated using the "adjusted" difference.

These data show that a union premium exists in every dimension of the compensation package. Unionized workers are 28.2% more likely to be covered by employer-provided health insurance. Unionized employers also provide better health insurance, paying an 11.1% higher share of single-worker coverage and a 15.6% higher share of family coverage. Moreover, deductibles are $54, or 18.0%, less for union workers. Finally, union workers are 24.4% more likely to receive health insurance coverage in their retirement.

TABLE 2.37 Union impact on paid leave, pension, and health benefits

	Paid leave	Pension and retirement	Health insurance
Union impact on benefit incidence	3.2%	22.5%	18.3%
Union impact on benefit cost per hour			
Total impact	11.4%	56.0%	77.4%
From greater incidence	3.4%	28.4%	24.7%
From better benefit	8.0%	27.7%	52.7%

Source: Pierce (1999b, Tables 4, 5, and 6).

Similarly, 71.9% of union workers have employer-provided pensions, compared to only 43.8% of non-union workers. Thus, union workers are 53.9% more likely to have pension coverage. Union employers spend 36.1% more on defined-benefit plans but 17.7% less on defined-contribution plans. As defined-benefit plans are preferable, as discussed earlier, these data indicate that union workers are more likely to have the better form of pension plans.

Union workers also get more paid time off. Their three weeks of vacation amount to about three days (0.63 weeks) more than non-union workers receive. Including both vacations and holidays, union workers enjoy 14.3% more paid time off.

Table 2.37 provides a more refined analysis of the union wage premium by comparing the employer costs in unionized settings to non-union settings in comparable occupations and establishments (factories or offices). Specifically, the estimated union premium controls for the sector (public or private) in which the establishment is located, the establishment's size, full-time or part-time status of its employees, and its detailed industry and region. Unionized workers are 18.3% more likely to have health insurance, 22.5% more likely to have pension coverage, and 3.2% more likely to have paid leave. Unionized employers pay more for these benefits because the benefits they provide are better than non-union employers and because unionized employers are more likely to provide these benefits. For instance, unionized employers pay 77.4% more in health insurance costs per hour, 24.7% more because of the greater incidence and 52.7% because of the better benefit.

This analysis also shows that unionized employers pay 56.0% more per hour for pension plans, 28.4% from a greater incidence of providing pensions, and 27.7% from providing better pensions. Similarly, unionized workers have

TABLE 2.38 Effect of deunionization on male wage differentials, 1978-97

Effect of union decline on wages

	Percent union			Union wage premium*			Union effect**		
	1978	1989	1997	1978	1989	1997	1978	1989	1997
By occupation									
White collar	14.7%	12.1%	10.4%	1.1%	-0.3%	2.2%	0.2%	0.0%	0.2%
Blue collar	43.1	28.9	23.6	26.6	23.3	22.2	11.5	6.7	5.3
Difference	-28.4	-16.7	-13.2	-25.6	-23.6	-20.1	-11.3	-6.8	-5.0
By education									
College	14.3%	11.9%	11.6%	6.3%	4.2%	5.1%	0.9%	0.5%	0.6%
High school	37.9	25.5	20.8	21.7	21.5	20.8	8.2	5.5	4.3
Difference	-23.6	-13.6	-9.2	-15.3	-17.3	-15.8	-7.3	-5.0	-3.8

Contribution of union decline on wage differentials

	Change in wage differential***			Change in union effect			Contribution of lower union effect		
Differential	1978-89	1989-97	1978-97	1978-89	1989-97	1978-97	1978-89	1989-97	1978-97
White collar/ blue collar	9.3%	2.4%	11.6%	4.6%	1.7%	6.3%	49.2%	74.3%	54.3%
College/ high school	13.4	2.3	15.8	2.3	1.2	3.5	17.2	52.8	22.5

*   Estimated with a simple human capital model plus industry and occupation controls.
**   Calculated as the product of percent union and the union wage premium.
*** Estimated with a simple human capital model.

Source: Authors' update of Freeman (1991).

11.4% greater costs for their paid leave, mostly because of the more extensive paid leave (the 8.0% "better benefit" effect).

The effect of the erosion of unionization on the wages of a segment of the workforce depends on the degree to which deunionization has taken place and the degree to which the union wage premium among that segment of the workforce has declined. **Table 2.38** shows both the degree to which unionization and the union wage premium have declined by occupation and education level over the 1978-97 period (1979 data were not available). These data, which are for men only, are used to calculate the effect of weakened unions (less representation and a weaker wage effect) over the 1978-97 period on the wages of particular groups and the effect of deunionization on occupation and education wage differentials.

Union representation fell dramatically among blue-collar and high-school-educated male workers from 1978 to 1997. Among the high-school-graduate workforce, unionization fell from 37.9% in 1978 to 20.8% in 1997, almost by half. This decline obviously weakened the effect of unions on the wages of both union and non-union high-school-educated workers. Because unionized high school graduates earned about 21% more than equivalent non-union workers (a premium that did not change over the 1978-97 period), unionization raised the wage of the average high school graduate by 8.2% in 1978 (the "union effect"). Unions had a 0.9% impact on male college graduate wages in 1978, leaving the net effect of unions to narrow the college/high school gap by 7.3 percentage points in that year. The decline in union representation from 1978 to 1997, however, reduced the union effect for high school male workers to 4.3% in 1997 while hardly affecting college graduates; thus, unions closed the college/high school wage gap by only 3.8 percentage points in 1997. The lessened ability of unions to narrow this wage gap (from a 7.3% to a 3.8% narrowing effect) contributed to a 3.5 percentage-point rise in the college/high school wage differential, an amount equal to 22.5% of the total rise in this wage gap.

The weakening of unionism's wage impact had an even larger effect on blue-collar workers and on the wage gap between blue-collar and white-collar workers. The 43.1% unionization rate among blue-collar workers in 1978 and their 26.6% union wage premium boosted blue-collar wages by 11.5%, thereby closing the blue-collar/white-collar wage gap by 11.3 percentage points in that year. The union impact on this differential declined as unionization and the union wage premium declined, such that unionism reduced the blue-collar/white-collar differential by 5.0 rather than 11.3 percentage points in 1997, a 6.3 percentage-point weakening. This lessened effect of unionism can account for about half (54.3%) of the 11.6 percentage-point growth of the blue-collar/white-collar wage gap over the 1978-97 period.

Unions reduce wage inequalities because they raise wages more at the bottom and in the middle of the wage scale than at the top. Lower-wage, middle-wage, blue-collar, and high-school-educated workers are also more likely than high-wage, white-collar, and college-educated workers to be represented by unions (see **Table 2.39**). These two factors—the greater union representation and the larger union wage impact for low- and mid-wage workers—are key to unionization's role as a major factor in reducing wage inequalities.

The larger union wage premium for those with low wages, in lower-paid occupations, and with less education, is shown in Table 2.39. For instance, the union wage premium for blue-collar workers in 1997, 23.3%, was far larger than the 2.2% union wage premium for white-collar workers. Likewise, the 1997 union wage premium for high school graduates, 20.8%, was much higher

TABLE 2.39 Union wage premium for subgroups

Demographic group	Union wage premiums	Percent union	Source
Occupation			
White collar (1997)	2.2%	11.6%	Mishel et al. (2003, Table 2.3a)
Blue collar (1997)	23.3	20.8	Mishel et al. (2003, Table 2.3a)
Education			
College (1997)	5.1%	10.4%	Mishel et al. (2003, Table 2.3a)
High school (1997)	20.8	23.6	
All (1992, 1993, 1996)	24.5	n.a.	Gundersen (2003, Table 5.1 and Appendix C)
High school or less	35.5	n.a.	
Wage distribution (1989)			Card (1991)
Lowest fifth	27.9%	23.5%	
Second fifth	16.2	30.3	
Middle fifth	18.0	33.1	
Fourth fifth	0.9	24.7	
Top fifth	10.5	17.7	

than the 5.1% premium for college graduates. The union wage premium for those with a high school degree or less at 35.5% is significantly greater than the 24.5% premium for all workers.

Table 2.39 presents a comprehensive picture of the impact of unions on employees by showing the union wage premiums by the wage distribution. The sample is split into five equal groups of workers from the lowest-wage to the highest-wage workers. The union wage premium was far greater among low-wage workers (27.9%) than among middle-wage (18.0%) or the highest-wage workers (10.5%). The table also shows the greater unionization rates in the middle of the wage distribution and greater unionization at the bottom than the top.

There are several ways that unionization's impact on wages goes beyond the workers covered by collective bargaining to affect non-union wages and labor practices. For example, in industries and occupations where a strong core of workplaces are unionized, non-union employers will frequently meet union standards or, at least, improve their compensation and labor practices beyond what they would have provided if there were no union presence. This dynamic is sometimes called the "union threat effect," the degree to which non-union workers get paid more because their employers are trying to forestall unionization.

TABLE 2.40 Illustration of impact of unions on average wages of high school graduates

	Share of workforce	Union wage impact	Union contribution to higher average wage
Nonunion	75%	5.0%	3.8%
Union	25	20.0	5.0
Total	100	8.8	8.8

Source: Authors' analysis.

There is a more general mechanism (without any specific "threat") in which unions have affected non-union pay and practices: unions have set norms and established practices that become more generalized throughout the economy, thereby improving pay and working conditions for the entire workforce. This has been especially true for the 75% of workers who are not college educated. Many fringe benefits, such as pensions and health insurance, were first provided in the union sector and then became more generalized—though, as we have seen, not universal. Union grievance procedures, which provide due process in the workplace, have been mimicked in many non-union workplaces. Union wage-setting, which has gained exposure through media coverage, has frequently established standards of what workers generally, including many non-union workers, expect from their employers. Until the mid-1980s, in fact, many sectors of the economy followed the patterns set in collective bargaining agreements. As unions have weakened, especially in the manufacturing sector, their ability to set broader patterns has diminished. However, unions remain a source of innovation in work practices (e.g., training, worker participation) and in benefits (e.g., child care, work-time flexibility, sick leave).

The impact of unions on wage dynamics and the overall wage structure is not easily measurable. The only dimension that has been subject to quantification is the threat effect. The union effect on total non-union wages is nearly comparable to the effect of unions on total union wages. **Table 2.40** illustrates the union impact on union, non-union, and average wages among workers with a high school education. In this illustration, for high school workers in a 25% unionized industry, the threat effect raises the average non-union wage by 5.0%, thereby lifting the average wage by 3.8%. Assuming that unions have raised the wages of union workers by 20%, the average high school wage would be raised by 5% (25% of 20%). The total effect of unions on the average high school wage in this example is an 8.8% wage increase, 3.8 percentage points of which are due to the higher wages earned by non-union workers and 5.0 percentage points of which are due to the union wage premium enjoyed by non-unionized workers.

Two conclusions can be reached based on these studies. First, unions have a positive impact on the wages of non-union workers in industries and markets in which unions have a strong presence. Second, because the non-union sector is large, the union effect on the overall aggregate wage comes almost as much from the impact of unions on non-union workers as on union workers.

The decline of union coverage and power affects men more than women and adversely affects middle-wage men more than lower-wage men. Consequently, deunionization has its greatest impact on the growth of the 90/50 wage gap among men. In this light, it is not surprising that the period of rapid decline of union coverage from 1979 to 1984 (during a deep recession, and at a time that the manufacturing sector was battered by the trade deficit) was also one where the male 90/50 wage gap grew the most. Recall from Table 2.38 that male blue-collar unionization fell from 43.1% in 1978 to just 28.9% in 1989, contributing to the rapid growth of male wage inequality in the 1980s. The decline of unionization in the 1990s put continued downward pressure on middle-wage men and contributed to the continued growth of the 90/50 wage gap.

An eroded minimum wage

The real value of the minimum wage has fallen considerably since its high point in the late 1960s (**Figure 2W**). The decline was particularly steep and steady between 1979 and 1989, when inflation whittled it down from $6.81 to $4.80 (in 2003 dollars), a fall of 29.5% (**Table 2.41**). Despite the legislated increases in the minimum wage in 1990 and 1991 and again in 1996 and 1997, the value of the minimum wage in 2003 was still 22.9% less than in 1967. The increases in the 1990s raised its 2000 value 14.7% over 1989.

Another way to illustrate the historically low level of the current minimum wage is to examine the ratio of the minimum wage to the average workers' wage (as measured by the average hourly earnings of production/non-supervisory workers), as shown in **Figure 2X**. In 2003, the minimum wage was worth just 34% of what an average worker earned per hour. This ratio was at its lowest point in 40 years. In contrast, the ratio of the minimum wage to the average wage was about 50% in the late 1960s, about 45% in the mid-1970s and about 40% in the early 1990s. This analysis shows that the earnings of low-wage workers have fallen seriously behind those of average workers.

It has been argued that the minimum wage primarily affects teenagers and others with no family responsibilities. **Table 2.42** examines the demographic composition of the workforce that benefited from the 1996-97 increases in the mini-

FIGURE 2W   Real value of the minimum wage, 1960-2005*

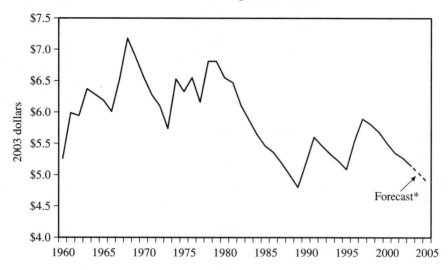

* Calculated using the CBO's consumer price index forecast, and assuming no legislative increases.

Source: Authors' analysis.

FIGURE 2X   Minimum wage as percentage of average hourly earnings, 1964-2003

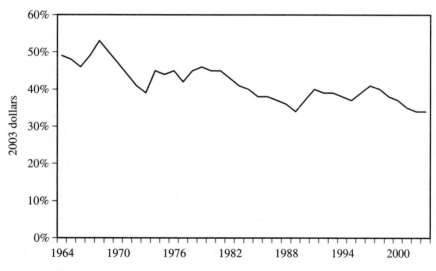

Source: Authors' analysis.

TABLE 2.41 Value of the minimum wage, 1960-2003

	Minimum wage	
Year	Current dollars	2003 dollars
1960	$1.00	$5.38
1967	1.40	6.68
1973	1.60	5.87
1979	2.90	6.81
1989	3.35	4.80
1990	3.80	5.18
1991	4.25	5.60
1996	4.75	5.54
1997	5.15	5.89
2000	5.15	5.50
2003	5.15	5.15
Period averages		
1960s	$1.29	$6.41
1970s	2.07	6.50
1980s	3.33	5.65
1990s	4.53	5.48
1979-2003	3.99	5.61
Percent change		
1979-89		-29.5%
1989-2000		14.7
2000-03		-6.4
1967-2003		-22.9

Source: Authors' analysis.

mum wage. In fact, only 28.6% of the affected 9.9 million minimum wage workers were teenagers, suggesting that many minimum wage workers have important economic responsibilities. The information at the bottom of the table shows that minimum wage earners contribute 54% of their family's weekly earnings. Although the majority work part time (less than 35 hours weekly), 46.0% worked full time and another 33.3% worked more than 20 hours each week. While minorities are disproportionately represented among minimum wage workers, almost two-thirds are white. These workers also tend to be women (58.2% of the total). Table 2.42 also shows that minimum wage and other low-wage workers are heavily concentrated in the retail trade industry but are underrepresented in manufacturing industries and among unionized employers.

TABLE 2.42 Characteristics of minimum wage and other workers, October 1995-September 1996

Characteristic	Workers directly affected by new minimum ($4.25-$5.14)	Other low-wage workers ($5.15-$6.14)	Workers above minimum wage ($6.15+)	All workers
Average wage	$4.73	$5.72	$14.64	$12.73
Employment	9,886,158	9,610,926	89,079,931	110,999,085
Share of total	8.9%	8.7%	80.3%	100.0%
Demographics				
Male	41.8%	41.9%	54.9%	52.3%
16-19	13.7	8.1	1.0	2.9
20+	28.2	33.8	53.9	49.4
Female	58.2	58.1	45.1	47.7
16-19	14.9	7.9	0.7	2.8
20+	43.2	50.2	44.0	44.9
White	62.8	67.7	77.9	75.4
Male	24.6	26.2	42.8	39.4
Female	38.2	41.5	35.1	36.0
Black	16.1	13.8	10.4	11.3
Male	6.4	5.5	5.1	5.3
Female	9.8	8.3	5.3	6.0
Hispanic	17.5	14.8	7.9	9.5
Male	9.3	8.6	4.9	5.7
Female	8.2	6.2	3.0	3.8
Teens (16-19)	28.6%	16.0%	1.7%	5.6%
Work hours				
Full time (35+)	46.0%	62.7%	87.7%	81.1%
Part time				
20-34 hours	33.3%	25.4%	9.0%	13.0%
1-19 hours	20.7	11.9	3.3	5.9
Industry				
Manufacturing	8.8%	12.7%	19.7%	17.8%
Retail trade	42.6	35.8	12.2	17.3
Union*				
Union	4.4%	6.3%	19.1%	16.4%
Non-union	95.6	93.7	80.9	83.6

Share of weekly earnings contributed by minimum wage workers, 1997

	Average	Median
All families with affected worker	54%	41%
Excluding one-person families	44	27

* Includes both union members and non-members covered by union contracts.

Source: Bernstein and Schmitt (1998).

An analysis of only those earning between the old and the new minimum wage would be too narrow, since a higher minimum wage affects workers who earn more than but close to the minimum; they will receive increases when the minimum wage rises. For these reasons, Table 2.42 also presents the demographic breakdown of those workers who earned within a dollar of the new minimum wage level ($5.15-$6.14) at that time, a group labeled "other low-wage workers." This more broadly defined minimum wage workforce includes an additional 9.6 million workers, or an additional 8.7% of the total workforce. Thus, any significant change in the minimum wage would affect a substantial group, as much as 18% of the workforce. The demographic breakdown of these other low-wage workers is more inclusive of full-time and adult workers but has proportionately fewer minority workers compared to the group of directly affected minimum wage earners.

Table 2.43 assesses the impact of the lowering of the real value of the minimum wage on key wage differentials. The analysis is limited to women, who are affected most by the minimum wage. As the bottom of Table 2.43 shows, 20.1% of women workers in 1989 earned less than the real 1979 value of the minimum wage; in other words, they were directly affected by its erosion in value after 1979. Women without a high school degree were hit hardest, with 43.4% and 53.7% earning below the 1979 minimum wage level in 1989 and 1997, respectively.

The analysis in Table 2.43 of the impact of a lower minimum wage on the wage structure is based on a simple simulation. Data on individual workers' wages in recent years are used to construct what the wage structure would have been in 1989 and 1997 if the 1979 minimum wage (again, inflation adjusted) had prevailed. Drawing on these simulated counterfactuals, the analysis compares the actual growth in wage differentials to the growth that would have occurred if the 1979 minimum wage had been maintained. The difference between "actual" and "simulated" is a measure of the impact of the lowering of the real value of the minimum wage on particular wage differentials.

The minimum wage most affects women at the 10th percentile and women with the least education, so it should not be surprising that wage differentials between middle- and low-wage women (the 50/10 differential) and college/less-than-high-school wage differentials are greatly affected by a decline in the minimum wage. For instance, the 50/10 differentials (in logs, which approximate percentage differences) would have grown from 0.39 in 1979 to only 0.41, rather than to 0.64, in 1989 had the minimum wage been maintained. Thus, 0.23 of the 0.26 rise in the 50/10 differential in the 1980s among women, or 91.1% of the rise, can be attributed to the declining real value of the minimum wage. Similarly, the devaluing of the minimum wage can explain 44.2% of the

TABLE 2.43 Impact of lower minimum wage on key wage differentials among women, 1979-97

Wage differential	Actual wage differentials			Simulated wage differentials at 1979 minimum wage		1979-89				1979-97			
						Change in wage differential			Minimum wage effect	Change in wage differential			Minimum wage effect
	1979	1989	1997	1989	1997	Actual	Simulated	Difference		Actual	Simulated	Difference	
Wage ratios (logs)													
50/10	0.39	0.64	0.63	0.41	0.41	0.26	0.02	0.23	91.1%	0.24	0.02	0.21	89.5%
90/10	1.00	1.35	1.39	1.12	1.18	0.35	0.12	0.23	66.4%	0.39	0.18	0.21	54.3%
Education differentials													
College/high school	0.31	0.46	0.51	0.42	0.48	0.15	0.11	0.04	28.1%	0.20	0.17	0.03	15.8%
College/less than high school	0.49	0.69	0.75	0.60	0.67	0.20	0.11	0.09	44.2%	0.26	0.18	0.08	29.4%
Addendum: Percent earning less than 1979 minimum													
Less than high school	43.4%	53.7%											
High school	23.6	26.2											
College	6.1	7.0											
All	20.1	21.5											

Source: Authors' analysis.

TABLE 2.44 Distribution of minimum wage gains and income shares by fifth for various household types

Income fifth	Share of gain from increase	Share of income	Average income
Prime-age working households,* 1997			
Lowest	35.3%	5.4%	$15,728
Second	22.8	11.0	32,547
Middle	15.2	15.9	47,699
Fourth	14.5	22.3	66,104
Highest	12.2	45.3	134,128
All prime-age households (including non-working), 1997			
Lowest	28.0%	3.8%	$10,518
Second	22.8	9.8	26,965
Middle	20.2	15.6	42,848
Fourth	15.8	22.7	62,502
Highest	13.3	48.0	131,991

* Prime-age households are headed by a person age 25-54. One-person households are included. The top panel excludes households with no earners.

Source: Bernstein and Schmitt (1997).

growth in the college/less-than-high-school wage gap among women in the 1980s. A lower minimum wage also greatly affected the college/high school wage gap, explaining 28.1% of its growth in the 1980s. This analysis confirms the importance of the erosion of a key labor market institution, the minimum wage, on the growth of women's wage inequality at the bottom of the wage scale.

Because there is substantial evidence (with some controversy, of course) that a moderately higher minimum wage does not significantly lower employment (or reduce it at all), there has been an increased focus on which groups of low-wage workers benefit from a higher minimum wage. In other words, because a higher minimum may not have much of an effect on efficiency or output, the merit of such a policy will depend greatly on its fairness.

Table 2.44 presents a computation of which families benefited from the higher minimum wage legislated over the 1996-97 period. The analysis calculates the annual gain to each worker based on the amount of his or her wage increase (i.e., based on the distance to the new minimum) and annual hours worked. Given this information, it is possible to calculate the share of the aggregate wage gain generated from the higher minimum wage that accrues to each household income fifth. As shown in Table 2.44, 35.3% of the gains generated by the higher minimum wage were received by the poorest 20% of working households; 58.1% of the gains were received by the poorest 40%.

Minimum wage increases generate the most help to those with the least income and the least help to those with the most income. For instance, as Table 2.44 also shows, the poorest fifth of working households had 5.4% of all income but received 35.3% of the gains from the higher minimum wage. In contrast, the best-off families received 45.3% of all income but received only 12.2% of the benefits of the higher minimum wage. The results are comparable when the analysis is repeated for all households, including those with no workers.

What happens to the minimum wage level strongly affects the wage gains of low-wage workers, particularly low-wage women whose wage is essentially set by the legislated minimum. Thus, the erosion of the minimum wage's value led to a precipitous drop in the wages of low-wage women in the 1980s and to a large increase in the 50/10 wage gap. The level of women's low wages (i.e., the 10th percentile) stabilized in the late 1980s when the wage level descended to its lowest possible level (at which employers could still hire) and as unemployment dropped. Thereafter, the 50/10 gap was flat or declined as unemployment fell to low levels in the late 1990s and as two increases in the minimum wage were implemented. Between 1999 and 2001, as the value of the minimum wage eroded and unemployment rose, the wages of low-wage women once again weakened and the 50/10 wage gap grew.

The technology story of wage inequality

Technological change can affect the wage structure by displacing some types of workers and by increasing demand for others. Given the seemingly rapid diffusion of microelectronic technologies in recent years, many analysts have considered technological change a major factor in the recent increase in wage inequality. Unfortunately, because it is difficult to measure the extent of technological change and its overall character (whether it requires less skill from workers or more, and by how much), it is difficult to identify the role of technological change on recent wage trends. More than a few analysts, in fact, have simply assumed that whatever portion of wage inequality is unexplained by measurable factors can be considered to be the consequence of technological change. This type of analysis, however, only puts a name to our ignorance.

It is easy to understand why people might consider technology to be a major factor in explaining recent wage and employment trends. We are often told that the pace of change in the workplace is accelerating, and there is a widespread visibility of automation and robotics; computers and microelectronics provide a visible dimension evident in workplaces such as offices not usually affected by technology. Perhaps even more important is that technology has provided advances in products used by consumers, including home computers, CD players, VCRs, microwaves, electronic games, advanced televisions, cell phones, and so on. Equally visible is the use of the Internet among both consumers and business people. Given these advances, it is not surprising that many non-economists readily accept that technology is transforming the wage structure. It needs to be noted, however, that technological advances in consumer products are not related to changes in labor market outcomes—it is the way goods and services are produced and changes in the relative demand for different types of workers that affect wage trends. Since many high-tech products are made with low-tech methods, there is no close correspondence between advanced consumer products and an increased need for skilled workers. Similarly, ordering a book over the Internet rather than at a downtown bookstore does not necessarily change the types of jobs available in the economy—truckers, warehouse workers, and so on still do the work of getting the book to the buyer.

The economic intuition for a large role for technology in the growth of wage inequality is that the growth of wage inequality and the employment shift to more-educated workers has occurred within industries and has not been caused primarily by shifts across industries (i.e., more service jobs, fewer manufacturing jobs). Research has also shown that technological change has traditionally been associated with an increased demand for more-educated or "skilled" workers. As we have noted, the wage premium for "more-educated" workers, exemplified by college graduates, has risen over the last two decades. This pattern of change suggests, to some analysts, an increase in what is called "skill-biased technological change" that is thought to be generating greater wage inequality.

Because wages have risen the most for groups whose supply expanded the fastest (e.g., college graduates), most economists have concluded that non-supply factors (i.e., shifts in demand or institutional factors, such as those discussed in earlier sections) are the driving force behind growing wage inequality. These economists reason that those groups with the relatively fastest growth in supply would be expected to see their wages depressed relative to other groups unless there were other factors working strongly in their favor, such as rapid expansion in demand. Rapid technological change favoring more-educated groups could logically explain demand-side shifts leading to wider wage differences.

There are many reasons to be skeptical of a technology-led increase in demand for "skill" as an explanation for growing wage inequality. Unfortunately, the "skills/technology" hypothesis frequently is presented as if evidence that technological change is associated with a greater need for skills or education is sufficient to show that technological change has led to the growth in wage inequality since 1979. This is not the case, since the impact of technology must have "accelerated" in order to explain why wage inequality started to grow in the 1980s and 1990s and did not grow in the prior decades. For instance, it is generally true that investment and technological change are associated with the need for more workforce skill and education—but this was true for the entire 20th century, and it therefore does not explain why wage inequality began to grow two decades ago. Moreover, the skills and education level (and quality) of the workforce have been continually improving. Thus, the issue is whether technology's impact on skill demand was significantly greater in the 1980s and 1990s than in earlier periods.

The skills/technology story is also, unfortunately, frequently presented as a single-cause explanation of the growth in wage inequality. On this account, however, it fails to explain the pattern and timing of the growth in wage inequality over the last two decades. Specifically, there seems to be no consistent technology explanation for the relationship over time between productivity (presumably technologically driven) and wage inequality; the shifts over time in the various dimensions of wage inequality—within-group wage inequality, education differentials, and experience differentials; or the shifts in wage inequality at various parts of the wage structure, such as between the 90th and 50th or 50th and 10th percentiles. We now turn to an exploration of the various patterns documented earlier in this chapter and whether a technology story can explain them.

First consider the correspondence, or lack thereof, between productivity growth and wage inequality. It is plausible to assume that technological change that is radically shifting the demand for skills in the workplace would also raise productivity growth. Yet the greatest period of rising wage inequality, the early and mid-1980s, was a period in which productivity growth (measured as multifactor or labor productivity growth) was no faster than in the "stagnant" 1970s. Overall, wage inequality continued to grow through the mid-1990s, but productivity continued its slow pace. However, when productivity accelerated after 1995, there was no accompanying growth of wage inequality, and between-group wage inequality (mainly wage differences by education and experience) actually fell (see Table 2.23). Fast, if not faster, productivity growth continued into the 2000-03 business cycle, but there was still no growth in between-group wage inequality. Perhaps a process began in the 1979-95 period that led to a radical restructuring of skill demand and that ultimately led to the post-1995 productivity growth, but we are not aware of any such explanation.

Second, as we discussed above, there are two dimensions of wage inequality—the between-group wage differentials, such as those relating to education and experience, and the within-group wage inequality that occurs among workers of similar education and experience—and the technology story does not readily fit either pattern. The growth of within-group inequality, which accounts for more than half the growth of overall wage inequality over the 1980s and 1990s, may be related to technological change if it is interpreted as a reflection of growing economic returns to worker skills (motivation, aptitudes for math, etc.) that are not easily measured. However, there are no signs that the growth of within-group wage inequality has been fastest in those industries where the use of technology grew the most. It is also unclear why the economic returns for measurable skills (e.g., education) and unmeasured skills (e.g., motivation) should not grow in tandem. In fact, between-group and within-group inequality have failed to move together in the various sub-periods since 1973.

The timing of the growth of within-group wage inequality does not easily correspond to a technology story. For instance, consider what happened during the 1995-2000 period associated with a technology-led productivity boom: within-group wage inequality actually declined among women and was essentially flat among men. In the early 1990s, the so-called early stages of the new economy, within-group wage inequality grew moderately, whereas it grew rapidly in the low-productivity 1980s. Within-group wage inequality did, however, start growing again as productivity accelerated further after 2000. All in all, changes in within-group wage inequality do not seem to mirror the periods of rapid productivity growth or technological change.

Nor does the pattern of growth of education and experience differentials correspond easily to a technology story. Before reviewing these patterns, however, it is worth noting that these skill differentials are affected by much more than technology. For instance, we have shown in earlier sections that changes in labor market institutions such as the minimum wage and unionization are responsible for some of the rise in education wage differentials. Other factors, such as trade and industry shifts, also affect education and other skill differentials, and so, of course, there is not a complete correspondence of technology with skill differentials.

Again, the timing of change in skill differentials does not easily match the simple technology story. The education differential pattern most in conflict with a technology story is the one between high school graduates and those without a high school degree. This wage gap (Table 2.16) rose modestly over the entire 1973-95 period. Thus, if those without a high school degree can be considered "unskilled," then the wage structure has not shifted much against these unskilled workers, even during the 1995-2000 technology-led boom. It is apparent, therefore, that shifts in education differentials do not drive the changes in wage inequality at the bottom, since the 50/10 wage gap rose markedly in the 1980s and has fallen since, all while the education gap at the bottom was relatively stable.

The change in the college wage premium does not easily conform to a technology story either. For instance, the college/high-school wage gap (see Table 2.16 and Figure 2K) grew most rapidly in the early 1980s but then about half as fast in the 1989-2000 period, when technological change is thought to have been more rapid. This differential has even fallen since 2000 among men, while the overall wage inequality at the top—the 90/50 differential—grew, suggesting no connection between the education gap and rising education differentials. Among women, the college wage premium grew between 1979 and 1995, but rose hardly at all after 1995, when technology might have been expected to have its greatest impact. Moreover, the college wage premium among women fell after 2003 and, although the wage gap at the top did not rise, the fall in the college premium did not lead to a lessened 90/50 wage gap.

The wage gap by age—experience differentials—is frequently considered a skill gap driven by technological change. And it is true that experience and education differentials both grew in the 1980s, giving the impression they both were affected by a common factor, such as technology. Among men, experience differentials grew only modestly in the early 1990s, as did the college wage premium, but they *fell* after 1995 as the college premium grew faster (Table 2.16). The consequence is that overall between-group inequality was stable or falling in the 1995-2000 period—a pattern true among both men and women. How can technology be driving wage inequality when between-group wage inequality (the dimension of inequality most closely corresponding to technology-related skill) was flat or down during the 1995-2000 technology-led boom?

The experience since the mid- to late 1980s does not accord with the conventional technology story, whose imagery is of computer-driven technology bidding up the wages of more-skilled and more-educated workers, leaving behind a small group of unskilled workers with inadequate abilities. The facts are hard to reconcile with the notion that technological change grew as fast or faster in the 1990s, especially in the later 1990s, than in earlier periods. If technology were adverse for unskilled or less-educated workers, then we would expect a continued expansion of the wage differential between middle-wage and low-wage workers (the 50/10 differential). Yet, the 50/10 differential has been stable or declining among both men and women from 1986 or 1987 to 2003. Instead, we are seeing the top earners steadily pulling away from nearly all other earners—reflected in the 90/50 or 95/50 wage gap. Therefore, there seem to be factors driving a wedge between the top 10% and everyone else, rather than a skill-biased technological change aiding the vast majority but leaving a small group of unskilled workers behind. Further confirmation of the breadth of those left behind is that wages were stable or in decline for the bottom 80% of men and the bottom 70% of women over the 1989-95 period, and wages fell for the entire non-college-educated workforce (roughly 73% of workers).

Finally, the notion that technology has been bidding up the wages of the skilled relative to the unskilled does not accord with many of the basic facts presented earlier. Or, it holds true in a relative but not an absolute sense. The wages of skilled men, defined as white-collar, college-educated, or 90th percentile workers, were flat or in decline from the mid-1980s to the mid-1990s. As described in Chapter 3, white-collar men were increasingly becoming displaced and beset by employment problems in the early 1990s. High-wage women have continued to see their wages grow, but is it likely that technology is primarily affecting skilled women but not skilled men? The dramatic fall of entry-level wages for all college graduates in the early 1990s, for both men and women, reinforces this point. The most recent technological developments may even be undercutting the wages of white-collar technical workers, as we saw in our earlier discussion of offshoring.

Table 2.45 presents data on trends from 1984 to 1997 in the use of computers at work both overall and by gender, race, age, and education. These data facilitate a test of a common version of the technology story of wage inequity: the increased use of computers at work by some groups (e.g., the college-educated) has led them to be more skilled and productive relative to other groups (e.g., the non-college-educated), thereby enlarging the wage gap between these groups. Table 2.45 allows us to compare the change in wage gaps by education, gender, race, and age to see whether they correspond to changes in the intensity of computer use. The data reveal that trends in computer use are generally poor predictors of wage trends.

The use of computers at work doubled from 1984 to 1997, rising from 24.5% to 49.9% of the workforce. Computer use grew more rapidly (looking annually) in the 1984-89 period than in the 1989-97 period. The faster pace of technological change in the 1980s corresponds to the faster growth of wage inequality in that period compared to the 1990s.

Table 2.45 also shows that computer use is greater among those with more education. However, the relative use of computers did not change much, with high-school-educated workers half as likely to use computers as college graduates in both 1984 and in 1997 (47.7 % and 48.1%, respectively). Of course, this pattern does not accord with the trends in the college/high school wage premium, which rose a great deal in the 1980s and rose modestly in the 1990s. Among women, the relative rate of computer use between high school and

TABLE 2.45 Use of computers at work, 1984-97

	1984	1989	1993	1997
All workers	24.5%	36.8%	46.0%	49.9%
By education				
Less than high school	4.8%	7.4%	8.9%	11.3%
High school	19.8	29.2	34.0	36.1
Some college	31.9	46.4	53.5	56.3
College or more	41.5	57.9	69.1	75.2
Ratio high school/college	47.7%	50.5%	49.1%	48.1%
Men	30.2	34.2	34.2	35.5
Women	69.4	69.3	66.9	62.7
By gender				
Men	21.1%	31.6%	40.3%	44.1%
Women	29.0	43.2	52.7	56.7
Ratio male/female	73.0%	73.2%	76.5%	77.8%
By race				
Whites	25.3%	37.9%	47.3%	51.3%
Blacks	18.2	27.2	36.2	39.9
Other	23.7	36.0	42.3	48.2
Ratio black/white	72.1%	71.7%	76.7%	77.7%
By age				
Under 30	24.7%	34.9%	41.4%	44.5%
30-39	29.5	42.0	50.5	53.8
40-49	24.6	40.6	51.3	54.9
50 and older	17.6	27.6	38.6	45.3

Note: Entries display percentage of employed individuals who answer that they "directly use a computer at work."

Source: Card and DiNardo (2002).

college graduates fell from 69.4% in 1984 to 62.7% in 1997, moving opposite to the upward shift in the college wage premium among women.

Women use computers at work more than men, a fact that does not, of course, accord with the higher level of men's wages. This gender computer gap, however, closed modestly in the 1990s, as use of computers by men grew more rapidly. The opposite occurred with wages, however, with women's wages faring better than men's (Table 2.26). Likewise, the black/white gap in computer use narrowed in the 1990s, yet the racial wage gap changed little (Table 2.24 and 2.25). So neither gender nor racial wage gaps correspond well to technology intensity trends.

The change in computer use by age in the 1980s does accord with changes in the wage gap by age (or by experience—see Table 2.16). For instance, in the 1984-89 period computer use rose more among those in their thirties or forties than for younger workers, a time when younger workers also fared worse in wage growth. Nevertheless, the far-better wage growth by younger rather than older workers in the 1990s is not associated with any catch-up in computer use—in fact, they fell further behind. Thus, computer use trends do not help much in understanding changes in the wage gaps by age.

It may be the case that there was a large increase in overall computer use at work that corresponds to the growth of overall wage inequality in the 1980s. However, when one examines what happened for particular subgroups by gender, education, race, or age, there does not seem to be any strong link between the increase in computer use and the growth of the associated dimensions of wage inequality.

Executive pay soars

Another cause of greater wage inequality has been the enormous pay increases received by chief executive officers (CEOs) and the spillover effects (the pay of other executives and managers rising in tandem with CEO pay) of these increases. These large pay raises go far beyond those received by other white-collar workers.

The 1980s and 1990s have been prosperous times for top U.S. executives. **Table 2.46** presents the trends in CEO pay over the 1989-2003 period. For instance, the median wage (cash payments including bonuses of CEOs) grew 79.0% from 1989 to 2000, far exceeding the growth in any other occupation. In contrast, the median hourly wage for all workers grew just 5.8% from 1989 to 2000 (Table 2.6). CEO wages grew 14.6% from 2000 to 2003, while the median wage grew only 4.2%. CEO wage increases were probably larger if measured as averages rather than at the median (as Table 2.46 does).

The growth in CEO pay can also be measured by including all of the components of direct compensation: salaries, bonuses, incentive awards, stock options exercised, stock granted, and so on. By this measure, the full compensation of CEOs increased more than threefold over the 1989-2000 period, growing 342% from 1989 to 2000. CEO compensation peaked, however, in 2000 and declined 36.0% by 2003, reflecting the fall in stock values and the value of stock options available to CEOs. This decline affected only the very highest

TABLE 2.46 Executive annual pay, 1989-2003 (2003 dollars)

Pay category and percentile	Thousands of dollars					1992-2003		Percent change		
	1989	1992	1995	2000	2003	($000)	Percent	1989-2000	1995-2000	2000-03
*Realized direct compensation**										
25th percentile	n.a.	$1,235	$1,455	$1,707	$2,073	$838	67.9%	n.a.	17%	21.5%
Median	n.a.	1,991	2,388	3,101	3,600	1,609	80.8	n.a.	30	16.1
75th percentile	n.a.	3,797	4,284	7,638	7,938	4,141	109.1	n.a.	78	3.9
Average	$2,531	4,483	3,575	11,194	7,161	2,678	59.8	342%	213	-36.0
*Cash compensation***										
Index, 1989 = 100										
Median	$100.0	$105.9	$129.6	$179.0	$205.1	n.a.	93.7%	79.0%	38.1%	14.6%

* Sum of salary, bonus, gains from options exercised, value of restricted stock at grant, and other long-term incentive award payments.
** Salary and cash bonuses.

Source: Authors' analysis of *Wall Street Journal*/Mercer Survey (2004).

FIGURE 2Y Ratio of CEO to average worker pay, 1965-2003

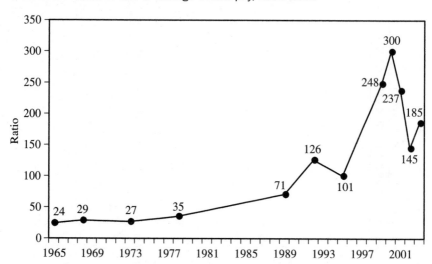

Source: Authors' analysis of *Wall Street Journal* and William M. Mercer (2004).

paid CEOs, as those at the median and the 25th and 75th percentiles saw increases (16.1% at the median). Still, over the period from 1992 (the first year of data for all but the average CEO) to 2003 CEOs saw sizable pay increases, with the median CEO getting an 80.8% raise.

The increased divergence between the growth of CEO pay and an average worker's pay is captured in the growth of the ratio of CEO to worker pay, shown in **Figure 2Y**. In 1965, U.S. CEOs in major companies earned 24 times more than an average worker; this ratio grew to 35 in 1978 and to 71 in 1989. The ratio surged in the 1990s and hit 300 at the end of the recovery in 2000. In other words, in 2000, a CEO earned more in one workday (there are 260 in a year) than what an average worker earned in 52 weeks. In 1965, by contrast, it took a CEO two weeks to earn a worker's annual pay. The ratio of CEO to worker compensation tumbled from 2000 to 2002 as CEO compensation fell. The ratio rose to 185 in 2003, a lower ratio than at the 2000 peak (300) but still far higher than the pay gap between CEOs and average workers that prevailed in the mid-1960s (24)or late 1970s (35).

Not only are U.S. executives paid far better than U.S. workers, they also earn substantially more than CEOs in other advanced countries. **Table 2.47** presents CEO pay in 13 other countries in 1988 and 2003 and an index (in the

TABLE 2.47 CEO pay in advanced countries, 1988-2003 (2003 dollars)

Country	CEO compensation				Foreign pay relative to U.S. pay, 2003 (U.S. = 100)	
	Thousands of dollars		Percent change 1988-2003	Ratio of CEO to worker pay, 2003*	CEO	Worker
	1988	2003				
Australia	$170,336	$694,638	308%	22.1	31%	62%
Belgium	361,591	697,030	93	16.0	31	85
Canada	398,946	889,898	123	24.5	40	71
France	381,015	735,363	93	17.2	33	83
Germany	388,486	954,726	146	21.3	42	88
Italy	322,743	841,520	161	23.7	37	69
Japan	473,655	456,937	-4	9.5	20	94
Netherlands	373,545	675,062	81	18.3	30	72
New Zealand		449,414		19.5	20	45
Spain	331,708	620,080	87	21.8	28	56
Sweden	221,138	700,290	217	17.6	31	78
Switzerland	481,125	1,190,567	147	19.8	53	118
United Kingdom	427,335	830,223	94	27.9	37	58
United States	**759,043**	**2,249,080**	196	**44.0**	**100**	**100**
Non-U.S. average	$360,969	$748,904	129%	19.9	33%	75%

* Ratio of CEO compensation to the compensation of manufacturing production workers.

Source: Authors' analysis of Towers Perrin (1988 and 2003).

last two columns) that sets U.S. compensation equal to 100 (any index value less than 100 implies that that country's CEOs earn less than U.S. CEOs). The index shows that U.S. CEOs earn three times the average of the 13 other advanced countries for which there are comparable data (note the non-U.S. average of 33%). In fact, there is only one country, Switzerland, whose CEOs are paid even as much as 50% that of U.S. CEOs. This international pattern does not hold true for the pay of manufacturing workers, for whom an index is also presented in Table 2.47. Workers in other advanced countries earn 75% of what U.S. workers earn. Not surprisingly, the ratio of CEO to worker pay was far larger in the United States in 2003 than in other countries, 44.0 versus 19.9. (Note that these cross-country comparisons employ different data, and definitions, than those used for historical U.S. trends in Table 2.46 and Figure 2Y and therefore yield a different CEO/worker pay ratio.) Last, Table 2.47 shows that CEO pay in other countries has tended to grow rapidly over the 1988-2003 period, but in all but two countries (Sweden and Australia) CEO pay has not grown as rapidly as the 196% growth in the U.S. (the non-U.S. average was a 129% growth in CEO pay).

Jobs of the future

This section presents an analysis of the pay levels and education requirements of the jobs that are projected by the Bureau of Labor Statistics to be created over the next 10 years. Some analysts examine which occupations are expected to grow at the fastest (and slowest) rates, while others examine which occupations will create the most (or least) absolute number of jobs. Our purpose here is to assess whether the types of jobs that are expected to be created will significantly change the wages that workers earn or significantly raise the quality of work or the skill/education requirements needed to fill tomorrow's jobs. This exercise requires an analysis of how the composition of jobs will change, i.e., which occupations will expand or contract their share of overall employment.

Table 2.48 presents such an analysis of the 725 occupations for which the Bureau of Labor Statistics provides projections from 2002 to 2012. Through a shift-share analysis (weighting each occupation's characteristic, such as wage level, by its share of total employment) we show what the characteristics of jobs are in 2002 and what they would be in 2012 if the projections are realized.

There are a few drawbacks to this analysis. One is that it does not take into account how the jobs of a particular occupation will change over the next 10 years (for example, will the education requirements of a bank teller grow?). In other words, the changing "content" of particular jobs will be a major determi-

TABLE 2.48 Changes in pay and education requirements, 2002-12

| Year | Median annual wage | Percent of employment with: | | | |
		High school or less	Some college	College or higher	Total
2002	$33,017	44.3%	28.8%	26.9%	100.0%
2012*	33,360	43.4	28.7	27.9	100.0
Change, 2002-12	1.0%	-0.9%	0.0%	0.9%	

* Based on a shift-share analysis of changes in employment across 725 occupations.

Source: Authors' analysis of BLS employment projections, Hecker (2004).

nant of future skill requirements. Second, we have no point of historical comparison (for lack of data availability owing to changing occupational definitions) for judging whether what's expected in the future is fast or slow relative to the past. However, there is still much to learn from how occupational composition shifts will affect the job and wage structure.

Table 2.48 shows that employment will be shifting to occupations with higher median annual wages, but the effect will be to raise annual wages by 1% over 10 years (or 0.1% per year). This is not a large change compared to the real wage growth that occurs each year or to the composition effects evaluated in earlier years (using a different occupation coding system). The jobs of the future will require greater education credentials but not to any great extent. In 2002, according to these data, the occupational composition of jobs requires that 26.9% of the workforce have a college degree or more. This share will rise by one percentage point to 27.9% by 2012. The jobs will entail no need to expand the share of the workforce with only some college, a group roughly the same size as the college-educated workforce required. The demand for workers with a high school degree or less will fall slightly, from 44.3% to 43.4% over the 2002-12 period.

These projections show that there will continue to be an occupational upgrading in the future whereby the jobs created will be in occupations with somewhat higher wages and educational requirements. This type of trend has been evident over the last century, and the developments in the future do not appear to be extraordinary in any sense. Whether workers earn substantially more in the future than now will primarily be determined by how much earnings in particular occupations rise rather than by any change in the occupational composition of jobs.

Conclusion

The wage structure has changed dramatically over the last two decades or so. From 1979 to 1995, the real hourly wages of most workers fell, with non-college-educated workers, especially new entrants to the labor force, experiencing the greatest wage decline. Given that over 70% of the workforce has not earned a four-year college degree, the wage erosion of high school graduates (whose wages fell somewhat less than those of high school dropouts but somewhat more than those of workers with some college) meant that the vast majority of men and many women were working at far lower wages in 1995 than their counterparts did a generation earlier. In the early 1990s, wages were falling or stagnant, even among college graduates and white-collar workers, especially men. New college graduates in the mid-1990s earned less than their counterparts did in the late 1980s.

Starting in 1995, however, there was a very different, and far better, wage performance as real wages grew rapidly for nearly all segments of the workforce. Wage growth at the bottom, in particular, was strong, and wage inequality at the bottom declined, as it has since the late 1980s. Faster productivity growth, persistent low unemployment, and increases in the minimum wage were responsible for this turnaround.

The recent recession and ensuing jobless recovery challenged these positive trends. As the Introduction shows, wage growth lessened as unemployment grew. Moreover, wage inequality has been broadening since 2000, with the wage gap at the top expanding and the wage gap at the bottom among women rising for the first time in over 10 years.

CHAPTER 3 ——————————————————————————————

Jobs: persistent jobless recovery
follows 2001 recession

As discussed in Chapter 2, the 2001 recession reversed important wage trends that accompanied the tight labor market of the 1990s. The focus of this chapter is on jobs, with an emphasis on the effects of the 2001 recession and the subsequent recovery.

The 1990s expansion improved the economic prospects of American workers, and in 2000 (the last full year of that business cycle), unemployment averaged 4.0%, a 31-year low. During this time employment opportunities expanded considerably, especially for traditionally disadvantaged groups, including women, African Americans, and Hispanics. Overall, low unemployment strengthened workers' bargaining power as employers competed for workers. This demand in turn spurred strong wage and income gains over the latter half of the 1990s economic boom. Today, a tight labor market is needed to recoup the gains that working Americans experienced in the 1990s economy.

March 2001 marked the official beginning of the last recession, a time of higher unemployment and labor slackness that resulted in a substantial amount of underutilized labor. While the unemployment rate was low relative to past recessions, the rate continued to increase two years after the recovery began. Moreover, during the recovery the labor force grew more slowly than in past recoveries and employment rates fell. Had the employment rate remained stable, the actual unemployment rate would have been 7.2%, rather than 5.6% in June 2004.

The lack of job creation in this latest recovery has been unprecedented, which is why the recovery was deemed a "jobless" one. A jobless recovery occurs when an economy begins to expand (as defined by the National Bureau of Economic Research) but businesses continue to shed jobs. As of this writing, in summer 2004, the employment level was 1.2 million jobs below the March 2001 peak level—an unparalleled occurrence this far into a recovery.

As is usual in a downturn, the 2001 recession disproportionately affected minority workers and workers with less education. In 2001, African Americans had an unemployment rate of 8.7%, versus the overall average of 4.8%. However, it adversely affected other groups usually thought to have some protection against recessions. For example, the employment-to-population ratio for young college graduates hit a 30-year low during the recovery. The recession and its aftermath affected a broadly diverse contingent of workers: young and old, the less educated to the highly educated, and laborers and professionals. The nation lost manufacturing jobs for a record 41 consecutive months, and significant job loss occurred in other sectors such as information technology. The stock market bubble burst in 2000, leaving many white-collar workers unemployed. In addition, technological advancements coupled with a supply shock of skilled labor from global markets has brought the practice of "offshoring" jobs to the forefront of economic discourse.

The lack of job creation affected long-term unemployment (defined as unemployment for 27 or more weeks) and the average duration of unemployment spells. The share of long-term unemployed as a percent of total employment was 22.1% in 2003 (unemployment was 6.1%), the highest rate in two decades. Short- and long-term unemployment increased substantially for higher-educated and older, more experienced workers. In relative terms, long-term unemployment rates increased severely, not just for those in manufacturing but also for workers in industries such as professional and business services and information. The mean duration of unemployment (in weeks) also revealed a disturbing upward trend; it was approximately 12 weeks at the beginning of the recession and continued to climb throughout the recession and into 2004. Since November 2003 it has hovered around 20 weeks (a 20-year high), even though the unemployment rate has fallen somewhat to 5.6% or 5.7%.

Unemployment

The unemployment rate rose not only through the recession year of 2001, but it also continued to increase two years thereafter, peaking at 6.3% in June 2003. The annual unemployment rate increased from 4.0% in 2000 to 6.0% in 2003 (**Figure 3A** and **Table 3.1**). In June 2004, the most recent data available as of this writing, unemployment was 5.6%, the same as it was at the beginning of the recovery.

The separate unemployment rates for men, women, whites, African Americans, and Hispanics shown in Table 3.1, were all lower in 2000 than they were

FIGURE 3A Unemployment rate and its trend, 1948-2003

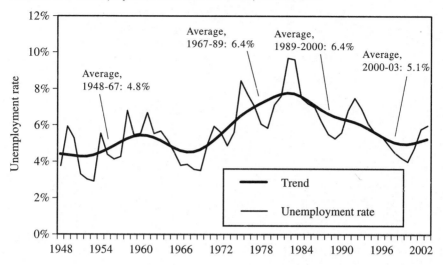

Source: Authors' analysis of BLS (2002a) data. For detailed information on figure sources, see Figure Notes.

during any peak year since the early 1970s. During three months of 2000 (March, April, and September), near the peak of the business cycle, the unemployment rate for African Americans fell to 7.3%, the lowest since the Bureau of Labor Statistics began tabulating unemployment separately by race in 1972. Even so, in 2000, as has historically been the case, the unemployment rate for African Americans (7.6%) remained more than double that of whites (3.5%). However, African Americans were again experiencing annual double-digit unemployment in 2003 (after annual rates of 7.6% and 8.7% in 2000 and 2001, respectively), and in June 2004 the unemployment rate for African Americans was still twice that of whites.

Unemployment rates for Hispanic workers tend to lie between those for whites and African Americans. The peak-to-peak average for Hispanics was 10.3% from 1979 to 1989, and in the last business cycle the average fell to 8.6%. The rates for Asians (for whom the government started tracking unemployment rates in 2000) are just about the same as for whites.

During the 1947-79 period, women workers generally had unemployment rates substantially higher than the rate for males. However, in 2001 and 2003 the unemployment rate for men surpassed that of women. As of June 2004 the unemployment rates of men and women were the same (5.6%).

TABLE 3.1 Unemployment rates, 1947-2003

Business cycle peaks	Total	Men	Women	White	African American	Hispanic*	Asian
1947	3.9	4.0	3.7	n.a.	n.a.	n.a.	n.a.
1967	3.8	3.1	5.2	4.3	n.a.	n.a.	n.a.
1973	4.9	4.2	6.0	5.1	9.4	7.5	n.a.
1979	5.8	5.1	6.8	6.2	12.3	8.3	n.a.
1989	5.3	5.2	5.4	4.9	11.4	8.0	n.a.
2000	4.0	3.9	4.1	3.5	7.6	5.7	3.6
2001**	4.8	4.8	4.7	4.2	8.7	6.6	4.5
2003***	6.0	6.3	5.7	5.2	10.8	7.7	6.0
2004****	5.5	5.6	5.6	4.8	10.9	6.8	n.a.
Annual averages							
1947-67	4.7	4.5	5.3	n.a.	n.a.	n.a.	n.a.
1967-73	4.6	4.0	5.7	5.8	n.a.	7.5	n.a.
1973-79	6.5	5.8	7.5	6.8	12.5	9.5	n.a.
1979-89	7.1	7.0	7.3	5.5	14.7	10.3	n.a.
1989-2000	5.6	5.6	5.5	4.2	10.8	8.6	n.a.

* Hispanic category includes blacks and whites.
** Recession year.
*** Most recent annual data.
**** 2004 uses seasonally adjusted monthly data for June, the latest available data.

Source: Authors' analysis of BLS (2004c) data.

Unemployment and the earnings distribution

The solid compensation and benefit gains experienced by workers in the 1990s were a result of the tight labor market and low unemployment rates. The consequence of the prolonged weak labor market between 2001 and 2003 was a decrease in hours worked, and slower hourly wage growth (see Chapter 2). Hence, high unemployment affects not only those who lose their jobs or cannot find work, but it also affects those who remain employed. A prolonged period of labor slack, as the United States has recently experienced, will lower family incomes. Since in a recession unemployment (usually) rises more for minorities and for low- and middle-wage workers compared to higher-wage and white-collar workers, it may not be surprising that high unemployment exacerbates inequalities in family income. Likewise, strong recoveries tend to lessen family income inequalities.

Figure 3B illustrates this point by showing estimates of the gains in income attributable to lower unemployment in the late 1990s. The figure charts income gains by fifth due to unemployment's fall from 5.6% to 4.0% between 1995 and 2000. Lower-income families gained the most percentage-wise, although they gained the least in terms of actual dollars, since their incomes start off at a lower level.

Data on unemployment generally show that disadvantaged groups experience the most gains from a recovery and the greatest losses during a recession. The prolonged economic recovery into the late 1990s, which brought steep declines in unemployment, disproportionately benefited the bottom 60% of families; the recession, in turn, disproportionately affected those same families. **Table 3.2** shows how changes in the unemployment rate affect earnings and income across the income distribution by estimating the effect of a 1% increase in unemployment on the annual earnings and income in each income fifth (estimated over the 1973-2000 period). The last column shows the effect of a 1% increase in the unemployment rate on the "average" family: among all persons, annual earnings decrease $512 (in 2000 dollars), about 1.4% of the corresponding family's total earnings, and annual family income decreases by $517, about 1.2% of family income. (Family income includes government cash assistance, such as unemployment compensation and welfare payments.) Higher unemployment hurts low-income families the most: families in the lowest fifth experience a 4.1% decrease in earnings with a 1% increase in unemployment, whereas families in the highest fifth experience only a 0.9% decrease. The effects on family income are more evenly distributed: families in the bottom fifth experience a 1.8% decrease in average family income, while those in the top fifth experience a 1.0% decrease.

The 5.6% unemployment rate experienced as of this writing is 1.6 percentage points higher that the annual unemployment rate of 4.0% in 2000. According

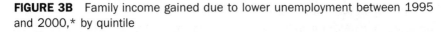

FIGURE 3B Family income gained due to lower unemployment between 1995 and 2000,* by quintile

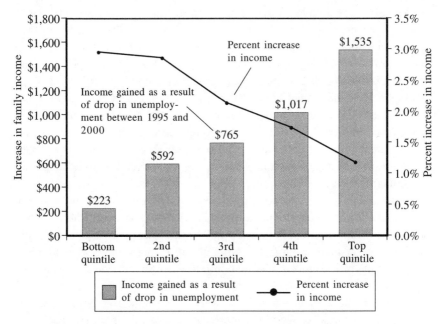

* The unemployment rate during this period fell from 5.6% to 4.0%.

Source: Bartik (2002).

to the estimates in Table 3.2, a rise of this magnitude is associated with a 2.2% decline in family income for a middle-class family (1.6 times 1.4) and a 2.9% family income decline for the poorest fifth of families. The next section will address the uniqueness of the severe and sustained jobless recovery that followed the 2001 recession and how it has affected various facets of the economy.

The prolonged weak recovery

The official recession lasted from March 2001 (peak) until November 2001 (trough), or eight months. The average length of contractions since 1945 is 10.2 months, though the last two contractions were both eight months in length. During the 2001 recession the economy lost 1.6 million nonfarm payroll jobs (see **Figure 3C**). A severe "jobless" recovery, during which an additional 1.1 million jobs were lost, followed the recession and lasted 21 months (November

TABLE 3.2 Effect of a 1% higher unemployment rate on mean annual earnings, mean annual income, and share of total family income, by family income quintile, 1973 to 2000 (in 2000 dollars)

	Lowest fifth	Second fifth	Middle fifth	Fourth fifth	Highest fifth	All families
Family earnings						
Average family earnings	$2,659	$13,235	$27,992	$46,874	$90,573	$36,266
Earnings decline	-$108	-$437	-$501	-$698	-$815	-$512
(Standard error)	(47)	(53)	(68)	(78)	(173)	(59)
Implied percentage effect	-4.1%	-3.3%	-1.8%	-1.5%	-0.9%	-1.4%
Family income						
Average family income	$7,590	$20,563	$34,722	$52,855	$100,587	$43,263
Family income decline	-$140	-$370	-$478	-$636	-$959	-$517
(Standard error)	(24)	(49)	(59)	(74)	(180)	(62)
Implied percentage effect	-1.8%	-1.8%	-1.4%	-1.2%	-1.0%	-1.2%

Source: Bartik (2002).

FIGURE 3C Employment: 2001 recession and recovery

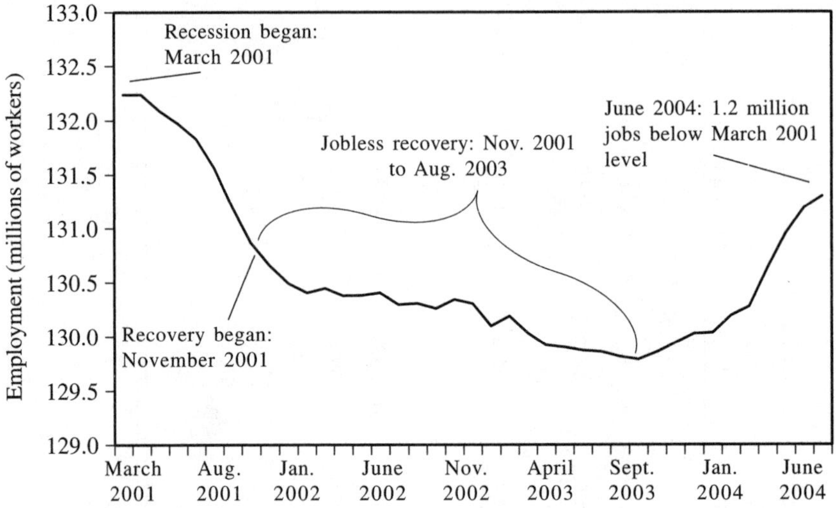

Source: Authors' analysis of BLS (2004d) data.

2001 until August 2003). In June 2004 (the most recent data available) the economy was still down 1.2 million jobs from the March 2001 peak. The downturn of the early 2000s did not drive unemployment to the heights attained in earlier post-war recoveries—the highest recorded was the 10.8% rate of November and December 1982. There are three reasons why the level of unemployment has not been an accurate reflection of the degree of labor market slack in recent years. First, because the unemployment rate was at a very low 4.0% in 2000, a sizable rise in unemployment did not generate a historically high unemployment rate. Second, rather than remain unemployed, millions of workers dropped out of the labor force. Third, as described above, employment continued to erode for nearly two years after the official recovery began. This chapter will address each of these points in detail.

Figure 3D illustrates the percent change in employment 39 months after the business cycle peaks for post-WWII recessions. The most recent 39-month post-peak period is measured from March 2001 to June 2004. This pictorial comparison allows us to contrast the 2001 recession and the subsequent employment trends with those of past business cycles over a similar period.

Prior to the last two recessions, an expanding economy was accompanied by employment growth. Understanding the jobless nature of this recovery is

FIGURE 3D   Percent change in employment 39 months after business cycle peak

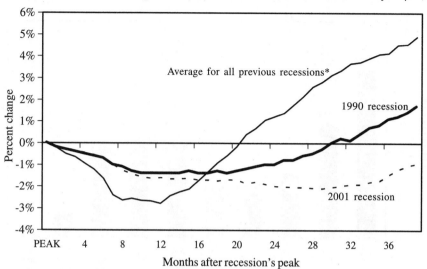

*1945 to 1981: 1980, 1990, and 2001 recessions not included.

Source: Authors' analysis of BLS (2004d) data.

important for appreciating the extent of labor slack, and economic vulnerability at this point, in spite of a low unemployment rate relative to that of the 1980s and early 1990s. Moreover, future jobless recoveries are a real possibility.

Figure 3D shows that, on average, job losses in past recessions (1945 to 1981, excluding the 1980 dip from the 1980 and 1981 "double dip" recession) were much deeper than in the last two recessions, but job growth regained and surpassed prior peak employment much faster—in approximately 20 months. The jobless recovery that followed the 1990 recession was not as deep as the current recovery, nor as prolonged. The downturn in jobs through the 2001 recession and jobless recovery that followed was the longest sustained labor slump since 1939.

The focus of Figure 3D is the change in employment from business cycle peaks—which included the recession, as well as, the recovery—to 39 months out. **Figure 3E** measures changes in employment from the trough of a business cycle to 31 months out. The trough of the 2001 recession (November) to the most recent data (June 2004) is 31 months. This analysis enables us to isolate recoveries from recessions for comparison purposes.

FIGURE 3E Change in private-sector employment 31 months after recovery began

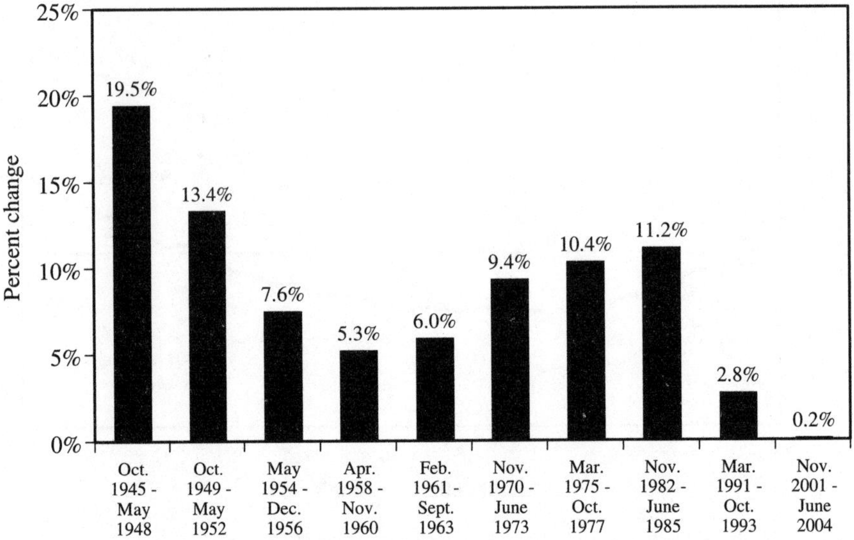

Source: Authors' analysis of BLS (2004c) data.

Figure 3E shows a stark contrast in employment growth for the most recent recovery compared to nine other recoveries. At just 0.2%, the employment change from the 2001 trough to the most recent date was far below that of all other recoveries since 1945. On average, the previous nine recoveries saw a 9.5% rise in employment this far out from the trough. Even the jobless recovery that followed the 1990 recession had a 2.8% increase in employment 31 months out.

Figure 3F, which shows the trajectory of gross job gains and gross job losses from the second quarter of 1990 to the third quarter of 2003, provides a look at another dimension of job growth over the last two jobless recoveries. The area between the two lines represents net job gains or losses. When job gains are above job losses there is a net gain, and vice versa. The figure illustrates that the 2001 jobless recovery is plagued not by increasing job losses but by a persistent failure to produce gross job gains. As expected, during each recession job losses outweighed job gains, and a net loss of jobs resulted. During the 1990 recession/recovery, job losses lasted five quarters, were slightly positive one quarter, and then negative for another quarter. A long stretch of net

FIGURE 3F   Gross job gains and losses (quarterly data, 1990q2 to 2003q3)

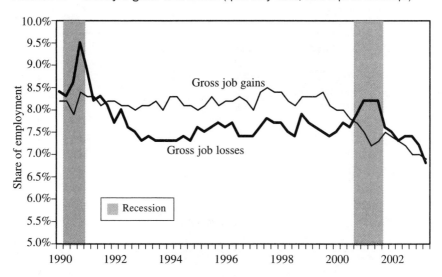

Source: Authors' analysis of BLS (2004F) data and Faberman (2004).

gains occurred between first-quarter 1992 and first-quarter 2001. On average, net job gains were about 0.6% or 614,000 jobs per quarter during this period. The 2001 recession/recovery produced net job losses for six quarters, then a zero gain for one quarter, followed by three more quarters of net job losses. The most recent data (third-quarter 2003) showed a small net job gain—only because gross job losses fell more steeply than gross job gains.

For both of the jobless recoveries job losses started to slow, somewhat dramatically, around the end of the recessions. The most striking contrast between these two recessions was that, in the 1990 recession, job gains ticked down to a low of 7.9% in fourth-quarter1990 but jumped up to 8.4% the next quarter. From fourth-quarter 1999 job gains fell precipitously through third-quarter 2001, when they fell to 7.2%, rebounded for two quarters (to 7.5%), then continued their decline through third-quarter 2003, when they reached a low of 6.9%. Therefore, the two jobless recoveries are similar in that job losses slowed quickly and considerably after each recession. But following the 1990 recession, job gains were quickly back on track and held steady within a short period of time. In contrast, job gains started to slip in fourth-quarter 1999 and continued to trend downward over the recession and the ensuing recovery.

FIGURE 3G Percent change in employment by industry 10 quarters after business cycle trough

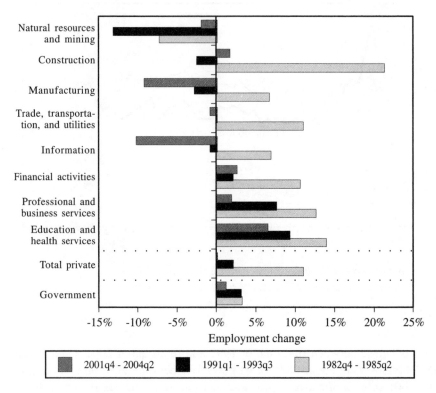

Source: Authors' analysis of BLS (2004d).

Figure 3G gives some insight into where jobs have been gained or lost by industry. This figure tracks the percent change in employment 10 quarters after the last three business cycle troughs. This time frame is used to examine the state of the current recovery compared to two prior recoveries—10 quarters examines the 2001 recovery up until the latest data available.

The recovery following the 1982 recession saw an 11% increase in employment (for the private sector) 10 quarters after the end of the recession. Every industrial sector had positive job growth, except the relatively small sector of natural resources and mining. The 1991 jobless recovery had a 2% change in employment in the private sector and a 3% increase in the public sector. More traditionally hard-hit sectors, such as construction and manufacturing, were still lacking employment growth 10 quarters out from the recession.

The current recovery had little employment growth in the private sector (0.2%) or in the public sector (1.1%). The manufacturing sector, along with the information, mining, and utilities sectors, still had significant employment declines 10 quarters out from the trough of the recession.

Unemployment

The most notable point regarding annual unemployment rates is that they rose not only through the recessionary year, but that they continued to increase two years thereafter. The overall unemployment rate, as is evident in Table 3.1, can provide an incomplete picture in terms of demographics—some groups fare much better than others. **Table 3.3**, which shows annual unemployment rates from 2000 to 2003 broken down by gender, education, and race, further explores the demographic breakdown of changes in unemployment in the current business cycle.

Unemployment rates for those with at least a high school degree are below the overall average for all demographic groups except for African Americans. Only African Americans with college degrees had unemployment rates below overall averages for these four years. In 2003, the unemployment rate of African American college graduates (4.5%) was the same as whites with some college (4.5%) and just below that of whites with a high school degree (4.8%).

Tables 3.4 and **3.5** present percentage-point changes in unemployment rates by gender and race for the current and previous business cycles (the 1980 dip is again excluded from this analysis). Table 3.4 shows the change in unemployment 13 quarters out from business cycle peaks. (We have chosen 13 quarters because that is the length of time from the last peak to this writing.) Hence, this table includes recessions and recoveries. Interestingly, 13 quarters out from the last five peaks unemployment was still higher than the peak level, except for the 1981 recession. However, focusing on recoveries (Table 3.5) tells a different story. By this measure, overall unemployment rates decreased 10 quarters from the trough for all the recoveries except the last two, where percentage-point changes were 0.2 and zero. All demographic groups (except Hispanics in the latest recovery) experienced percentage-point increases in unemployment.

Figure 3H shows that the percentage-point increases in unemployment by education level were more evenly shared in the latest recovery than in the early 1990s. In the 1990s recovery the unemployment rate for those without a high school degree had risen 2.5 percentage points, far more than the 1.8 percentage-point rise in the current recovery. However, unemployment rose more in this recovery than the last one for those with a high school degree or some college.

TABLE 3.3 Unemployment rates by gender, race, and educational status (persons 25 years or older)

Educational status	2000	2001	2002	2003	2000 to 2001	2001 to 2003	2002 to 2003	2000 to 2003
					Percentage-point change			
Total								
Less than high school	6.3%	7.2%	8.4%	8.8%	0.9	1.6	0.4	2.5
High school	3.4	4.2	5.3	5.5	0.8	1.3	0.2	2.1
Some college	2.9	3.5	4.8	5.2	0.6	1.7	0.4	2.3
College graduates	1.7	2.3	2.9	3.1	0.6	0.8	0.2	1.4
Men								
Less than high school	5.4%	6.4%	7.8%	8.2%	1.0	1.8	0.4	2.8
High school	3.4	4.3	5.4	5.7	0.9	1.4	0.3	2.3
Some college	2.7	3.4	4.7	5.4	0.7	2.0	0.7	2.7
College graduates	1.5	2.2	3.0	3.2	0.7	1.0	0.2	1.7
Women								
Less than high school	7.8%	8.6%	9.5%	9.8%	0.8	1.2	0.3	2.0
High school	3.5	4.0	5.1	5.2	0.5	1.2	0.1	1.7
Some college	3.0	3.6	4.9	4.9	0.6	1.3	0.0	1.9
College graduates	1.8	2.3	2.8	2.9	0.5	0.6	0.1	1.1
White								
Less than high school	5.6%	6.5%	7.6%	7.8%	0.9	1.3	0.2	2.2
High school	2.9	3.6	4.6	4.8	0.7	1.2	0.2	1.9
Some college	2.6	3.2	4.4	4.5	0.6	1.3	0.1	1.9
College graduates	1.6	2.1	2.7	2.8	0.5	0.7	0.1	1.2
African American								
Less than high school	10.7%	11.8%	13.3%	13.9%	1.1	2.1	0.6	3.2
High school	6.4	7.4	8.8	9.3	1.0	1.9	0.5	2.9
Some college	4.2	5.1	6.9	8.6	0.9	3.5	1.7	4.4
College graduates	2.5	2.7	4.2	4.5	0.2	1.8	0.3	2.0
Hispanic								
Less than high school	6.2%	7.4%	7.7%	8.2%	1.2	0.8	0.5	2.0
High school	3.9	4.5	5.9	5.9	0.6	1.4	0.0	2.0
Some college	3.3	3.8	5.7	5.8	0.5	2.0	0.1	2.5
College graduates	2.2	3.6	3.4	4.1	1.4	0.5	0.7	1.9
Overall unemployment rate (25 years or older)	3.0%	3.7%	4.6%	4.8%	0.7	1.1	0.2	1.8

Source: Authors' analysis of BLS (2004c) data.

TABLE 3.4 Change in unemployment rates 13 quarters after business cycle peak

	Percentage-point change in unemployment 13 quarters after business cycle peak				
	1969q4-1973q1	1973q4-1977q1	1981q3-1984q4	1990q3-1993q4	2001q1-2004q2
Total	1.4	2.7	-0.1	0.9	1.4
Men	1.4	2.7	0.0	1.0	1.4
Women	1.4	2.7	-0.3	0.9	1.2
White	1.2	2.5	-0.1	1.0	1.3
Men	1.2	2.4	0.0	1.0	1.4
Women	1.1	2.5	-0.3	0.9	1.1
African American	n.a.	4.9	-0.5	0.4	1.9
Men	n.a.	5.3	-0.5	0.4	1.7
Women	n.a.	4.4	-0.6	0.2	2.1
Hispanic*	n.a.	3.3	0.5	2.7	1.0

* Seasonally adjusted data unavailable for Hispanics by gender.

Source: Author's analysis of BLS (2004c) data.

TABLE 3.5 Change in unemployment rates 10 quarters after business cycle trough

	Percentage-point change in unemployment 10 quarters after business cycle trough				
	1970q4-1973q2	1975q1-1977q3	1982q4-1985q2	1991q1-1993q3	2001q4-2004q2
Total	-0.9	-1.3	-3.4	0.2	0.0
Men	-0.9	-1.5	-4.0	0.2	0.0
Women	-0.7	-1.2	-2.7	0.2	0.0
White	-1.0	-1.5	-3.2	0.2	0.1
Men	-1.1	-1.6	-3.6	0.1	0.1
Women	-0.9	-1.4	-2.5	0.2	0.0
African American	n.a.	0.0	-5.5	0.3	0.1
Men	n.a.	-0.1	-7.2	0.5	0.2
Women	n.a.	0.0	-3.8	0.1	0.1
Hispanic*	n.a.	-1.8	-4.8	0.9	-0.4

* Seasonally adjusted data unavailable for Hispanics by gender.

Source: Author's analysis of BLS (2004c).

FIGURE 3H Percentage-point change in unemployment 13 quarters after peak for the two most recent recessions, by educational status

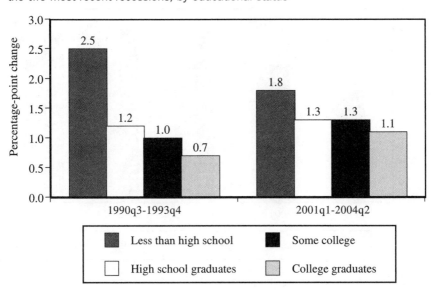

Source: Authors' analysis of BLS (2004c) data.

Especially notable is the significant rise in the unemployment rate among college graduates in this recovery, up 1.1 percentage points versus 0.7 percentage points in the 1990s recovery.

Unemployment by occupation

Another unusual dimension of the current business cycle is the increased unemployment faced by white-collar workers, at least relative to their historical experience. **Figure 3I** shows unemployment rates for major occupational categories from the 2000 peak to the recession year of 2001, annually for two subsequent years, and for the first half of 2004. For all five time periods, white-collar workers fared better than blue-collar and services workers. In 2000, unemployment was the same for blue-collar and service workers, but since then blue-collar workers had higher unemployment rates than services workers, a reflection of the fact that the economy lost manufacturing jobs for 41 consecutive months from August 2001 to January 2004. Unemployment among white-collar workers increased from 2000 to 2002. Unemployment in the service sector increased from 5.2% to 7.1% from 2000 to 2003. From the 2000 peak through the first half of 2004,

FIGURE 3I   Unemployment by selected occupational classifications, 2000-04*

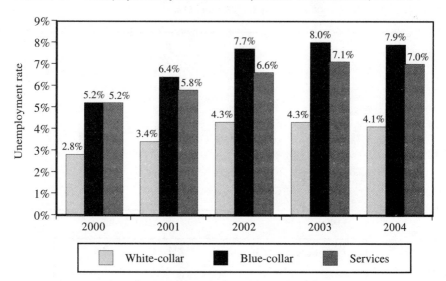

* Quarterly data used for 2004. See Figure Notes.
Source: Authors' analysis of BLS (2004c) data.

there have been significant increases in unemployment across occupational classifications.

The technology bubble burst in 2000, which adversely affected the information and technology sectors. **Figure 3J** shows unemployment rates for all workers, computer programmers, and software engineers from the 2000 peak to the first half of 2004. At the end of the 1990s boom unemployment was extremely low for information technology occupations (2.0% for programmers and 1.7% for software engineers)—far below the 4.0% total unemployment rate. For the past three years, unemployment rates climbed for computer programmers, rising to 7.6% in 2004. Unemployment increased for software engineers from 1.7% in 2000 to 5.2% in 2003, but fell to 3.1% in the first half of 2004.

Even though unemployment disproportionately affects lower-educated and blue-collar workers, during the latest recession and recovery many educated white-collar workers found it difficult to hold on to their jobs. Just as workers in the manufacturing industry found it difficult to keep their jobs in the face of global competition, so now do white-collar workers, whose employers face escalating global competition for a cheaper and highly educated workforce.

FIGURE 3J   Unemployment by information technology occupations, 2000-04*

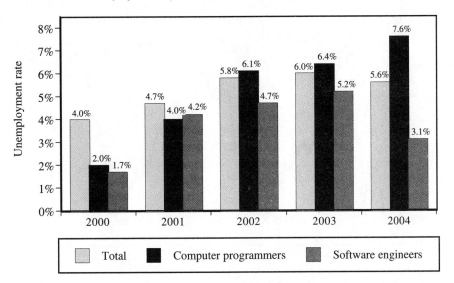

* Quarterly data used for 2004. See Figure Notes.

Source: Authors' analysis of BLS (2004c) data and unpublished data from BLS.

Long-term unemployment

Another important aspect of unemployment is the length of unemployment spells (i.e., the number of weeks spent looking for work). Given the lack of job creation (see Figure 3F) it is not surprising that the length of unemployment spells has increased. The increase in long-term unemployment and average spells of unemployment accompanied by levels of unemployment that were previously considered modest is another indication that the unemployment rate has not been an adequate measure of labor slack in the current business cycle. The relationship between the unemployment rate and mean duration of unemployment is shown in **Figure 3K**. In general, the mean duration of unemployment is higher the higher the unemployment rate. A problematic trend that has accompanied the current weak recovery was a dramatic increase in the mean duration of unemployment since the end of the 2001 recession. Since that time, unemployment fluctuated between 5.6% and 6.3%, but the mean duration of unemployment trended significantly upward and hovered around 20 weeks since November 2003, even as the unemployment rate held steady at 5.6-5.7%.

FIGURE 3K   Mean duration of unemployment in weeks, 1979-2004

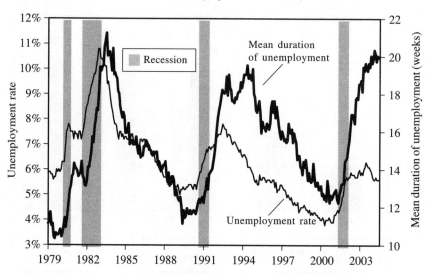

Source: Authors' analysis of BLS (2004c) data.

The latest data available show that the mean duration of unemployment was 19.9 weeks in June 2004, close to the recent high of 20.3 weeks reached in February 2004. That level was the highest since July 1983, when the mean duration of unemployment was 21.2 weeks and the unemployment rate was 9.4%. By contrast, June 2004's duration of 19.9 weeks was associated with a 5.6% unemployment rate. The high duration of unemployment with such a relatively low unemployment rate reflects the difficulty facing unemployed workers in finding employment and indicates that the labor market continued to have significant slack long after the 2001 recession/recovery.

The mean duration of unemployment is closely linked to another important aspect of unemployment—long-term unemployment. Long-term unemployment—when unemployed workers have been seeking work for six months or more—is the most severe form of joblessness. The consequences of extended periods of joblessness are significant: the long-term unemployed often face financial, personal, and health care hardships as well as the loss of unemployment insurance benefits. **Figure 3L** compares long-term unemployment as a share of total unemployment with the unemployment rate. Here, another troublesome trend emerges. As of 2003, the share of long-term unemployment was 22.1% of all unemployment, the second highest share of long-term unemployment on

FIGURE 3L Long-term unemployment* as a share of total unemployment compared to the unemployment rate, 1963-2003

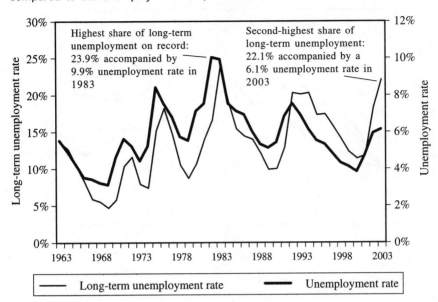

* Long-term unemployment defined as job seekers going without work for 27 or more weeks.
Source: Authors' analysis of BLS (2004c) data.

record. The highest share occurred in 1983 (23.9%) when the unemployment rate was 9.9%, far higher than it is now.

Long-term unemployment is a serious issue in any recovery, but it is a consequence of a jobless recovery. **Figure 3M** plots the share of long-term unemployment 31 months out from the end of the four most recent recessions (excluding the 1980 dip). One month after the 1975 recession the share of long-term unemployment was 11.9%; at the same point after the 1982 recession it was 23.1%. Although the starting points for these two series were very different, 31 months out they were similar—13.5% and 15.3%, respectively.

The trend in the share of long-term unemployment was much different for the last two recoveries. This trend is driven by the declines in gross job gains illustrated in Figure 3F. At the official end of the last two recessions the shares of long-term unemployment were relatively low. However, shares continued to trend upward 31 months out, to 20.4% after the 1991 recession and 21.6% after the downturn in 2001.

FIGURE 3M Long-term unemployment 31 months from the start of the recovery

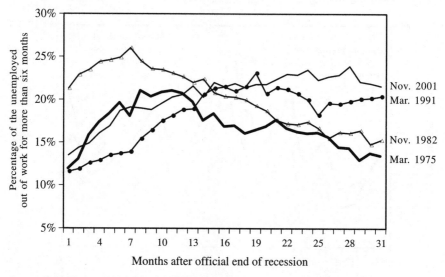

Source: Authors' analysis of BLS (2004c) data.

Just as unemployment is distributed unevenly by demographic characteristics, such as educational attainment or race, so is long-term unemployment. **Table 3.6** shows the levels and shares of unemployment and long-term unemployment by educational attainment in the peak year of 2000, the recessionary year of 2001, and the most period with available data, 2003. This analysis examines what has happened from the latest peak, through the recession and up to the most recent data available.

Both unemployment and long-term unemployment continued to increase two years after the 2001 recession. However, the shares of unemployment and long-term unemployment shifted dramatically over this period. **Figure 3N** gives the percentage-point change in the shares of unemployment and long-term unemployment by educational attainment from 2000 to 2003. Although workers with at most a high school degree disproportionately experience unemployment, Figure 3N shows that their actual shares of unemployment and long-term unemployment fell between 2000 and 2003. At the same time, the shares of unemployment and long-term unemployment for those with some college and a bachelor's degree or more increased significantly. These data again indicate the broad-based nature of the most recent recession/recovery.

TABLE 3.6 Unemployment and long-term unemployment by education, 2000, 2001, and 2003

	Number of unemployed	Number of long-term unemployed	Share of total unemployed	Share of long-term unemployed
Total 2000	5,691,886	649,119	100.0%	100.0%
High school or less	3,744,026	420,002	65.8%	64.7%
Some college	1,259,936	136,698	22.1	21.1
Bachelor's degree or more	687,924	92,418	12.1	14.2
Total 2001	6,800,531	800,995	100.0%	100.0%
High school or less	4,299,968	504,958	63.2%	63.0%
Some college	1,551,411	172,356	22.8	21.5
Bachelor's degree or more	949,152	123,681	14.0	15.4
Total 2003	8,774,065	1,935,814	100.0%	100.0%
High school or less	5,236,971	1,075,552	59.7%	55.6%
Some college	2,194,688	491,146	25.0	25.4
Bachelor's degree or more	1,342,406	369,115	15.3	19.1

Source: Allegretto and Stettner (2004).

FIGURE 3N   Percentage-point change in share of unemployment and
long-term unemployment by education, 2000-03

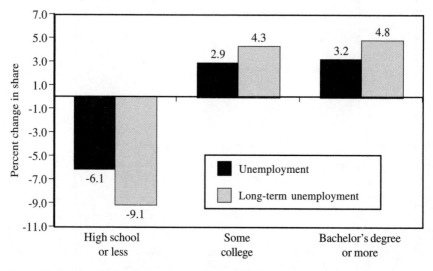

Source: Authors' analysis of Allegretto and Stettner (2004).

Table 3.7 shows long-term unemployment growth by several demographic
categories and occupational and industrial breakdowns from 2000 to 2003. The
increases across the board are significant. Overall, long-term unemployment
increased 198.2% in this period. Those with a bachelor's degree or more experienced a remarkable 299.4% increase. The industry breakdown again illustrates the broad based nature of the prolonged weak recovery. The increase in
long-term unemployment in the manufacturing sector, 259.0%, was less than
the increases for the information sector (353.6%) or the professional and business services (285.3%).

Underemployment and the missing labor force
Overall unemployment and long-term unemployment capture important features of labor market difficulties. However, those statistics may fall short in
explaining the severity of downturns and weak labor markets and the extent of
the underutilization of labor. Forever lost is the output from underutilized human resources, and the economic impact is far-reaching. Unemployment data
include only workers who report that they are willing and able to work and have
looked for work in the last four weeks; the data overlook workers who are not

TABLE 3.7 Long-term unemployment growth, 2000-03

	2000 totals	2003 totals	Percent change 2000-03
All groups	649,119	1,935,814	198.2%
Education			
High school degree or less	420,002	1,075,552	156.1%
Some college	136,698	491,146	259.3
Bachelor's degree or more	92,418	369,115	299.4
Age			
16-24	153,219	374,065	144.1%
25-44	280,085	876,362	212.9
45+	215,815	685,387	217.6
Occupation			
Construction and extraction	46,147	130,774	183.4%
Management, business, financial	47,090	192,369	308.5
Office and administrative support	91,804	261,922	185.3
Production	81,647	224,619	175.1
Professional and related	53,922	236,800	339.2
Sales and related	59,549	197,196	231.1
Service	127,746	295,175	131.1
Transportation and material moving	58,728	163,637	176.6
Industry			
Construction	51,605	149,895	190.5%
Educational and health services	66,542	173,562	160.8
Financial activities	32,875	91,028	176.9
Information	17,990	81,601	353.6
Leisure and hospitality	72,058	172,042	138.8
Manufacturing	102,311	367,323	259.0
Professional and business services	72,103	277,844	285.3
Transportation and utilities	28,848	75,716	162.5
Wholesale and retail trade	83,486	268,470	221.6
Gender			
Women	287,558	801,811	178.8%
Men	361,561	1,134,002	213.6
Race			
African American	181,407	475,229	162.0%
Hispanic	116,054	235,402	102.8
White	309,100	1,063,284	244.0
Other	42,557	161,898	280.4

Source: Allegretto and Stettner (2004).

TABLE 3.8 Underemployment, 2001 recession to current period

	Peak to trough of 2001		Current month	Monthly percent change	
	March 2001	November 2001	June 2004	Peak to trough	Trough to current month
Underemployment					
Unemployed	6,187	8,078	8,248	3.4%	0.1%
Discouraged*	288	289	442	0.0	1.4
Other marginally attached*	719	866	884	2.3	0.1
Involuntary part time	3,309	4,328	4,566	3.4	0.2
Total underemployed	10,503	13,560	14,139	3.2%	0.1%
Civilian labor force (in thousands)	143,873	144,254	147,279	0.0%	0.1%
				Percentage-point change	
Underemployment rate	7.3%	9.4%	9.6%	2.1	0.2
Unemployment rate	4.3	5.6	5.6	1.3	0.0

* Marginally attached workers are those who currently are neither working nor looking for work, but who indicate that they want and are available for a job and have looked for work in the last 12 months. Discouraged workers are the subset of the marginally attached who have given a job-market-related reason for not currently looking for a job.

Source: Authors' analysis of BLS (2004c).

fully employed or who would like to be employed but are not actively seeking a job. A broader measure of "underemployment" in the economy is presented in **Table 3.8**. This alternative measure includes unemployed workers as well as: (1) those working part time but who want to work full time ("involuntary" part-timers); (2) those who want to work but have been discouraged from searching by their lack of success ("discouraged" workers); and (3) others who are neither working nor seeking work at the moment but who indicate that they want and are available to work and have looked for a job in the last 12 months. (The second and third categories together are described as "marginally attached" workers.) Table 3.8 tracks underemployment rates from the beginning of the recession (March 2001) through the business cycle trough (November 2001) to the most recent data available (June 2004). All of the sub-categories that make up underemployment had increases from March to November 2001 and from November 2001 to June 2004.

FIGURE 3O   Monthly underemployment and unemployment rates

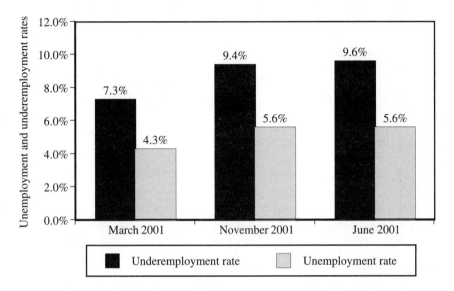

Source: Authors' analysis of BLS (2004c) data.

Table 3.8 along with **Figure 3O** shows that the latest unemployment rate (5.6%) is the same as it was at the end of the 2001 recession/start of the recovery. The underemployment rate, however, was 7.3% in March 2001 increased to 9.4% at the end of the recession, and increased further to 9.6% in June 2004. In other words, underemployment has actually grown during the recovery.

An extremely important dimension of the current business cycle has been a fall in labor force participation unseen in earlier downturns and recoveries. Those who have failed to enter the labor force or have dropped out of it represent a considerable amount of labor market slack. **Figure 3P** shows the recent drop in the labor force participation rate, i.e., all persons classified as employed or unemployed as a percent of the civilian non-institutionalized population. **Figures 3Q** and **3R** break down labor force participation rates by gender and ethnicity from 1973 to 2003. Historically, the male labor force participation rate has been trending downward, while women's rates have trended upward. Also, among males the labor force participation rate for Hispanics was higher than that of whites and African Americans, but among women the rate for African Americans was higher than that of whites and Hispanics.

FIGURE 3P   Annual labor force participation rate, 1973-2003

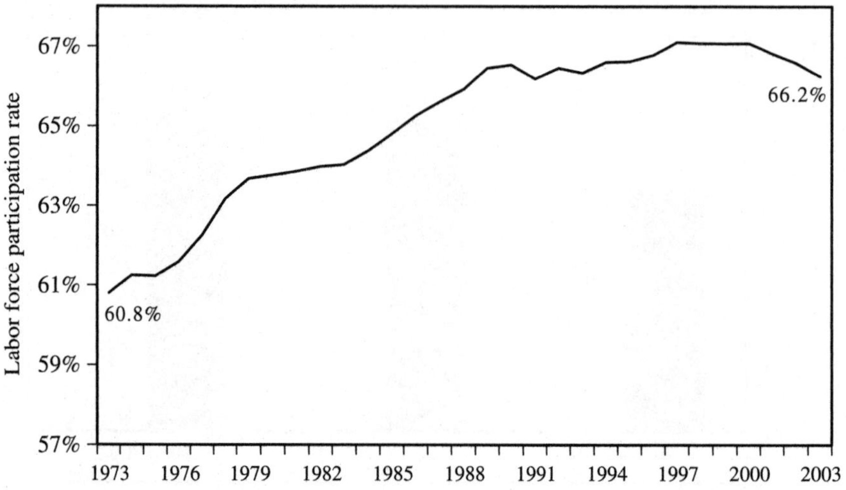

Source: Authors' analysis of BLS (2004c) data.

The labor force participation rate was 66.8% in 2001, and it was 67.0% at the business cycle peak in March. By 2003 it had declined to 66.2%. This may seem like a small change, but an erosion of 0.8% of the labor force is large relative to the rise of unemployment. Moreover, we would have expected labor force participation to have continued to rise, so the actual erosion understates the falloff in participation. **Figure 3S** shows the effects of lower labor force participation rates on the size of the civilian labor force and the size of the "missing labor force"— those who were not but could have been expected to participate in the workforce. The estimated labor force is constructed by holding the labor force participation rate constant at the March 2001 rate of 67.0%. Therefore, this figure shows that, had the labor force participation rate not fallen from its March 2001 level, the economy would have had 2.5 million more people in the labor force in June 2004.

These additional 2.5 million workers and job seekers would have had a considerable effect on the official unemployment rate. **Figure 3T** takes this scenario into account by assuming that the individuals who make up the missing labor force wanted jobs but were not able to find unemployment and were therefore counted as unemployed. In this scenario the unemployment rate would have been 1.6% higher in June 2004, or 7.2%, a rate that better reflects the slack in the labor market at that time.

FIGURE 3Q Labor force participation rates for men by race/ethnicity, 1973-2003

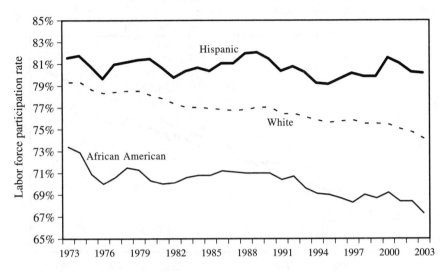

Source: Authors' analysis of BLS (2004c) data.

FIGURE 3R Labor force participation rates for women by race/ethnicity, 1973-2003

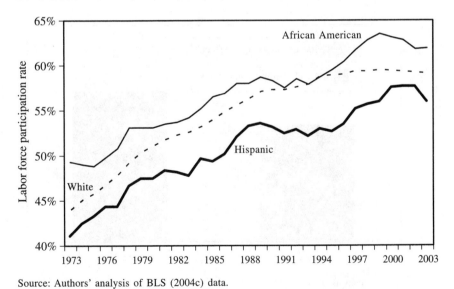

Source: Authors' analysis of BLS (2004c) data.

FIGURE 3S Effects of lower labor force participation rates on the size of the civilian labor force, 1998-2004

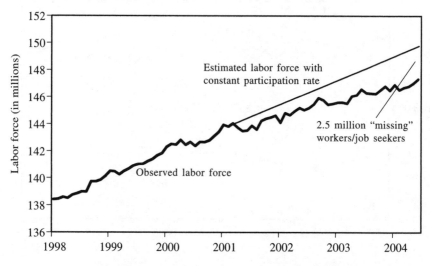

Source: Authors' analysis of BLS (2004c) data.

FIGURE 3T Missing labor force and its effect on the unemployment rate

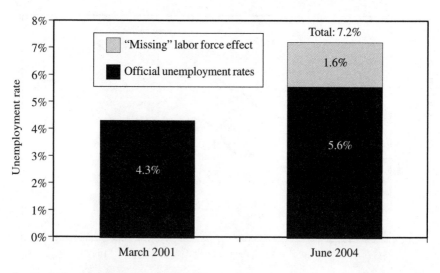

Source: Authors' analysis of BLS (2004c) data.

Employment

Though employment rates (the share of the population with a job) tend to get less attention than unemployment rates, they can be informative in a period like the current one, when pervasive labor market weakness is leading many potential workers to give up their job search. Since they are not seeking work, such persons will not be counted among the unemployed, but they will show up in lower employment rates. When this occurs, employment rates arguably provide a better indicator of the extent of job market opportunity than do unemployment rates.

Rising employment rates generally indicate rising opportunities, as, for example, was the case for women in the post-war period. Rising employment rates mean that more people are able to find work and opportunities are plentiful. Alternatively, falling employment rates indicate a weak business cycle.

Table 3.9 shows the share of the working-age population employed in selected years from 1973 to 2003. Employment rates vary considerably by gender and race. In 2003, for example, men had much higher employment rates (71.7%) than women (57.5%). Among men, Hispanics had the highest employment rate (78.6%), followed by whites (72.5%), with African Americans trailing considerably (64.1%). Among women, however, African Americans had the highest employment rate (58.6%), followed by whites (57.3%), and Hispanics (53.6%).

Trends in employment rates also differ across demographic groups. Employment rates for men fell between 1973 and 2003 across all racial and ethnic groups, with the largest declines in the years 1973-79 and 1979-89. In the 1990s, however, the long-term decline in male employment rates decelerated noticeably. The share fell slightly for men (0.3 percentage points), even though percentage-point changes for whites, African Americans, and Hispanics all increased; this apparent discrepancy is explained by the fact that Asians are not included in the numbers prior to 2000 but are included thereafter. From the 2000 peak year to 2003 employment rates have fallen—especially for men (2.5 percentage points) but less so for women (0.9 percentage points).

Tables 3.10 and **3.11** analyze the change in employment rates for the last five recessions (not including the first dip of the 1980-1981 "double dip" recession) using two different time periods. Table 3.10 shows employment changes 13 quarters out from the last five business cycle peaks (a time frame that enables us to analyze the full current business cycle using the most recent data available). This analysis combines recessionary quarters with recovery quarters. For each of the five time periods, men's employment rates decreased 13 quarters out from the peaks, and women's employment rates increased in all but the last recession. The current business cycle stands out as having a large erosion in the

TABLE 3.9 Employment rates, 1973-2003

						Percentage-point change				
	1973	1979	1989	2000	2003	1973-2003	1973-79	1979-89	1989-2000	2000-03
All (age 16 and over)	57.8%	59.9%	63.0%	64.4%	62.3%	4.5	2.1	3.1	1.4	-2.1
Adults (age 20 and over)										
Men	78.6%	76.5%	74.5%	74.2%	71.7%	-6.9	-2.1	-2.0	-0.3	-2.5
White	79.2	77.3	74.5	74.9	72.5	-6.7	-1.9	-2.8	0.4	-2.4
African American	73.7	69.1	67.0	67.7	64.1	-9.6	-4.6	-2.1	0.7	-3.6
Hispanic	81.3	80.3	79.4	81.7	78.6	-2.7	-1.0	-1.0	2.3	-3.1
Women	42.2%	47.7%	54.9%	58.4%	57.5%	15.3	5.5	7.2	3.5	-0.9
White	41.6	47.3	54.9	58.0	57.3	15.7	5.7	7.6	3.1	-0.7
African American	47.2	49.3	54.6	61.3	58.6	11.4	2.1	5.3	6.7	-2.7
Hispanic	38.3	43.7	50.5	55.8	53.6	15.2	5.3	6.9	5.3	-2.3

Source: Authors' analysis of BLS (2004c) data.

TABLE 3.10 Change in employment rates over recession and recovery

	Percentage-point change in employment rate 13 quarters after business cycle peak				
	1969q4 - 1973q1	1973q4 - 1977q1	1981q3 - 1984q4	1990q3 - 1993q4	2001q1 - 2004q2
Total	-0.7	-1.0	0.8	-0.8	-2.1
Men	-2.0	-3.6	-0.3	-1.8	-2.6
Women	0.3	1.3	1.9	0.1	-1.6
White	-0.3	-0.6	0.7	-0.8	-1.9
Men	-1.5	-3.1	-0.4	-1.7	-2.5
Women	0.7	1.6	1.8	0.2	-1.3
African American	n.a.	-3.8	2.5	-0.8	-3.4
Men	n.a.	-6.4	1.7	-2.6	-3.8
Women	n.a.	-1.6	3.1	0.6	-3.1
Hispanic*	n.a.	-1.0	1.1	-2.8	-1.7

* Seasonally adjusted data not available for Hispanics by gender.

Source: Author's analysis of BLS (2004c) data.

TABLE 3.11 Change in employment rates for economic recoveries

| | Percentage-point change in employment rate 10 quarters after business cycle trough | | | | |
	1970q4- 1973q2	1975q1- 1977q3	1982q4- 1985q2	1991q1- 1993q3	2001q4- 2004q2
Total	0.9	1.8	2.7	-0.1	-0.8
Men	0.1	0.6	2.7	-0.7	-1.1
Women	1.6	2.8	2.7	0.4	-0.5
White	1.1	1.9	2.5	0.0	-0.7
Men	0.4	0.8	2.5	-0.6	-1.0
Women	1.7	2.9	2.5	0.5	-0.4
African American	n.a.	0.6	4.6	-0.5	-1.5
Men	n.a.	-0.7	4.9	-1.4	-2.1
Women	n.a.	1.8	4.3	0.1	-1.0
Hispanic*	n.a.	0.7	3.6	-1.0	-0.4

* Seasonally adjusted data unavailable for Hispanics by gender.

Source: Author's analysis of BLS (2004c) data.

employment rate among women and a larger employment rate decline overall and among men (except in the mid-1970s) than in earlier business cycles. This is important evidence that the current downturn was in no way mild when it came to the loss of job opportunities.

Table 3.11 repeats this analysis but only for recovery periods. The time frame is 10 quarters out from the start of the five most recent recoveries. For the 1970, 1975, and 1982 recoveries employment rates, 10 quarters out, increased overall, by gender, and by race, except among African American men during the 1975 recovery. The 1982 recovery saw large increases in employment rates for all groups—especially for African Americans. However, for the most recent two jobless recoveries, African American men were particularly hard hit, with employment rates falling by 1.4 and 2.1 percentage-points 10 quarters after the 1991 and 2001 recessions. The current recovery is the only one in which the employment rate for women fell. The employment rate fell more in this recovery among men, down 1.1 percentage points, than in the early 1990s recovery. In fact, employment rates have fallen more for every demographic group (by gender) in this recovery than in any other recent recovery, with Hispanics the only exception.

Figure 3U uses data from Table 3.11 to further illustrate how this last recovery differed significantly from the average of the four prior recoveries. This figure supports the claim that this recovery differs from prior recoveries because of the decline in employment rates.

Employment rates are further broken down by age groups and for college graduates in **Figures 3V** and **3W**. Figure 3V shows historical employment rates for young (20-24 years old), prime-age (25-54 years old), and older (55+ years old) workers. Since 1947 employment rates for young and prime-age workers steadily increased until 2000, when they were at their peaks—72.2% and 81.5%, respectively. Since 2000 the employment rates for these two age groups have fallen consistently. Conversely, employment rates for older workers trended downward between 1948 and 1993—42% to 28.1%—and they rose to 34.2% in 2003. There are several theories as to why rates for older workers have increased recently. First, most people get some portion of their health insurance coverage through their employers, and since health care costs have risen significantly, workers are working longer to cover them. Second, and related to the first theory, is the notion that Medicare is insufficient to cover health care costs. Third, people are working longer due to pension losses after the stock market crash.

Another indicator of the broad-based nature of the 2001 recession/recovery is evident in employment rates of college graduates. Figure 3W illustrates the employment rates of all college graduates (25+ years old) and young college

FIGURE 3U Change in employment rates during economic recoveries by gender and race

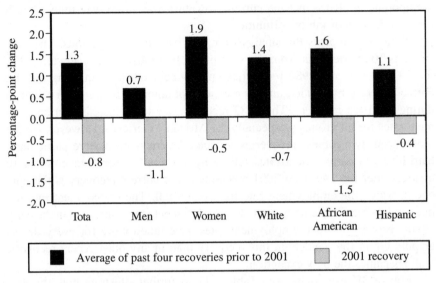

Source: Authors' analysis of BLS (2004c) data.

FIGURE 3V Annual employment rates by age group, 1948-2003

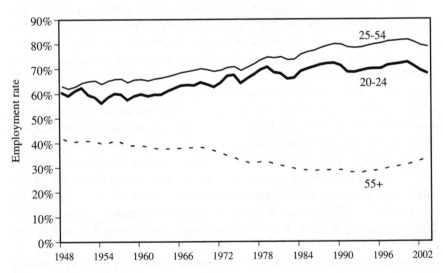

Source: Authors' analysis of BLS (2004c) data.

FIGURE 3W   Employment rates of college graduates by age group,
1979q1-2004q1

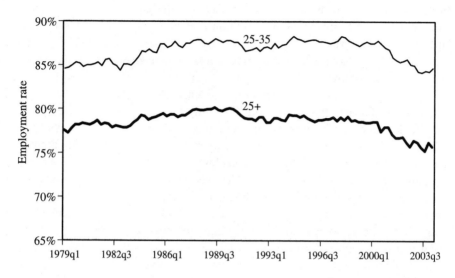

Source: Authors' analysis of BLS (2004c) data.

graduates (25-35 years old). In the first quarter of 1979, 77.5% of all college graduates were employed; this rate peaked at 80.1% in the second quarter of 1989. The employment rate was fairly level from 1991 until the technology bubble burst in the second quarter of 2000, when the rate fell sharply; it continued to fall throughout the 2001 recession and recovered to 75.2% in the third quarter of 2003. The rate was 75.7% in the first quarter of 2004, which is lower than 1979 rates, suggesting a unique and steep erosion of employment opportunities among college graduates in this business cycle. The employment rate of young college graduates was 84.6% in first-quarter 1979, and it peaked at 88.3% in fourth-quarter 1979. The rate also fell sharply at the time of the stock market crash of 2000. It trended downward to 84.2% in second-quarter 2003, also lower than the 1979 rate, and increased slightly to 84.7% in first-quarter 2004. The drop in employment opportunities among college graduates has fallen hardest on the younger group. While blue-collar workers continue to be hit hard by recessions, the last two downturns have reached white-collar workers as well, with the decline in employment particularly pronounced in the 2001 recession/recovery.

Nonstandard work

Broadly defined, nonstandard work consists of employment arrangements that are not regular, full-time work. This section analyzes several types of nonstandard work: regular part-time employment, self-employment, and what is called "just-in-time" employment. Just-in-time practices include temporary, part-time, and overtime employment.

On the supply side, many workers—students, older workers, workers with families—prefer jobs that offer more flexibility than the traditional 9-to-5 job. On the demand side, businesses hire contingent workers in several ways for a variety of reasons. Some put workers directly on their payrolls but assign them to an internal temporary worker pool. Others hire on-call workers and day laborers. Employers also use temporary help agencies and contracting firms to obtain workers on a temporary basis, sometimes for long periods. Some businesses hire independent contractors to perform work that would otherwise be done by direct-hire employees. The theory behind just-in-time employment is that firms adjust labor the way that they have adjusted inventory levels—cyclically with demand fluctuations. Retaining workers through economic downturns and hiring while testing the strength and sustainability of the upturns is now a cost that many employers are not willing or able to incur. Just-in-time employment practices allow employers to circumvent some of the costs and risks associated with hiring.

This section reports results from special analyses of nonstandard work arrangements, namely the Contingent Work Supplements to the Current Population Survey (the monthly government household survey that has provided much of the information on wages and employment presented in this book). These data allow an examination of the different types of nonstandard work, their prevalence, and their associated pay and working conditions. While the surveys provide a comprehensive look at nonstandard work arrangements from the mid-1990s to 2001, no comparable earlier surveys exist. After reviewing the most recent data, we will turn to other data that can give some indication of longer-term trends in the growth of nonstandard work arrangements. The second half of this section addresses a specific theme in nonstandard employment—just-in-time employment. Because just-in-time employment practices were a critical facet of this jobless recovery, it is important to understand the ramifications and uses of these practices.

Table 3.12 shows the distribution of employment by type of work arrangement. Men are more likely to be in standard employment than women: in 2001, 69.1% of women and 77.1% of men held regular full-time jobs (these figures exclude some self-employed workers). Among women, by far the largest nonstandard category was regular part-time work (19.7%), followed by independ

TABLE 3.12 Employed workers by work arrangement, 1995 and 2001 (February)

Work arrangement	Percentage of women employed		Percentage of men employed	
	1995	2001	1995	2001
Regular part time	21.3%	19.7%	7.1%	6.8%
Temporary help agency	1.1	1.1	0.8	0.7
On-call/day laborer	1.7	1.6	1.5	1.7
Self-employed	4.8	3.2	6.1	4.9
Independent contractor (wage & salary)	0.9	0.7	0.9	0.8
Independent contractor (self-employed)	3.7	4.1	7.3	6.7
Contract company	0.8	0.6	1.6	1.2
All nonstandard arrangements	34.3%	31.0%	25.3%	22.8%
Regular full time	25.3%	69.1%	74.7%	77.1%
All	100.0%	100.0%	100.0%	100.0%

Source: Kalleberg et al. (1997) and Wenger (2002).

dent contracting/self-employment (4.1%). Men in nonstandard employment are also more likely to be regular part-time workers (6.8%) or self-employed independent contractors (6.7%). The proportion of women and men in other categories of nonstandard employment are relatively similar, except that twice as many men work for a contract company (1.2% of men and 0.6% of women). During economic expansions, when unemployment falls, the proportion of workers in nonstandard arrangements also tends to fall, as workers find stable, full-time employment if they want it. This was true over the late 1990s: between 1995 and 2001, the percent of women employed in nonstandard work decreased by 3.3 percentage points, from 34.3% to 31.0%; among men it decreased by 2.5 percentage-points, from 25.3% to 22.8%.

One reason that more women are disproportionately employed in nonstandard work may be that they need greater flexibility in their work schedules; this may be especially true for single women raising children. With workers putting in more hours on the job, workplace flexibility has become increasingly important. Flexible workplaces offer an array of benefits to workers, such as allowing workers to telecommute, to work at home regularly or occasionally, to set their own hours (usually within boundaries established by the employer, including "core" hours when everyone must be at work), or to bank flextime (work longer one day in order to leave early the next).

FIGURE 3X Responsibility for determining own hours of work, by family type, 1998

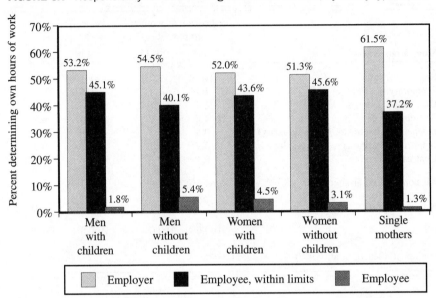

Note: Single mothers are a subcategory of women with children.

Source: McCrate (2002).

Workers with familial responsibilities are the ones who may need workplace flexibility, yet not only are flexible workplaces not generally established, but it is single mothers who are least likely to have control over their work hours—only 1.3% report that they have responsibility for determining their own work hours (**Figure 3X**). Men without children have the most flexibility—5.4%.

Workers who have been traditionally disadvantaged in the labor market are more likely to be in nonstandard employment (**Table 3.13**). In 2001, women made up less than half (46.9%) of the total workforce, but represented well over half (58.5%) of temporary workers. Women, however, were notably underrepresented (35.1%) among self-employed independent contractors, the category of nonstandard work that offers the highest pay and benefits as well as the greatest reported satisfaction rates (see Tables 3.14 and 3.16). African American and Hispanic workers and workers with less than a high school degree were overrepresented in the typically least remunerative kind of nonstandard arrangements—temp and on-call work—and underrepresented in independent contracting.

TABLE 3.13 Characteristics of nonstandard workers, 2001

Characteristic	Nonstandard work arrangement								Regular full time	All workers
	Regular part time	Temporary help agency	On-call/day laborer	Self-employed	Independent contractor (wage & salary)	Independent contractor (self-employed)	Contract company	All nonstandard arrangements		
Gender										
Women	71.8%	58.5%	45.0%	36.7%	41.7%	35.1%	30.5%	54.5%	44.2%	46.9%
Men	28.2	41.5	55.0	63.3	58.3	64.9	69.5	45.5	55.8	53.1
Race										
White	77.8%	52.8%	70.7%	87.2%	73.4%	81.9%	71.8%	78.5%	72.1%	73.8%
African American	9.3	24.5	11.8	2.8	11.0	6.3	9.9	8.4	11.7	10.8
Hispanic	9.2	17.8	14.5	5.5	10.9	7.1	12.6	9.0	11.6	10.9
Other	3.7	4.9	3.0	4.5	4.7	4.8	5.6	4.2	4.6	4.5
Education										
Less than high school	13.8%	14.8%	11.9%	6.6%	8.5%	8.7%	8.1%	11.2%	9.4%	9.9%
High school	27.1	30.8	28.7	29.5	27.7	30.6	26.9	28.4	31.7	30.8
Some college	40.2	36.9	36.9	27.8	24.3	27.7	29.8	34.6	28.6	30.2
Bachelor's degree	13.6	14.1	17.9	21.7	27.7	21.7	21.8	17.5	20.8	19.9
Graduate degree	5.3	3.4	4.6	14.4	11.8	11.2	13.4	8.3	9.6	9.2

Source: Wenger (2002).

TABLE 3.14 Hourly wages of nonstandard workers, compared to regular full-time workers by gender and work arrangement, 1999

Work arrangement	Women	Men
Controlling for personal characteristics		
Regular part time	-14.8%*	-24.9%*
Temporary help agency	-10.7*	-9.6
On-call/day laborer	-20.0*	-12.1*
Self-employed	-25.3*	-11.5*
Independent contractor (wage and salary)	0.3	2.1
Independent contractor (self-employed)	25.0*	13.6*
Contract company	5.9	16.2*
Controlling for personal and job characteristics		
Regular part time	-1.2%	-11.0%*
Temporary help agency	1.5	3.2
On-call/day laborer	-8.1*	-4.7
Self-employed	-7.2*	9.4*
Independent contractor (wage and salary)	14.8*	10.7
Independent contractor (self-employed)	22.3*	7.0*
Contract company	8.6	14.9*

* Statistically significant at the .05 level.

Source: Wenger (2002).

Nonstandard workers generally earn less and receive fewer fringe benefits than workers with similar skills in regular full-time jobs, as shown in **Table 3.14**. For example, as illustrated in the top section, which controls for key worker characteristics such as the level of education and years of work experience, regular part-time women workers—who make up about one-fifth of the female workforce—earned, on average, 14.8% less than similar women in full-time employment; self-employed women earned 25.3% less. Men who regularly worked part time experienced a higher wage penalty, 24.9%, than did women. The gap between men and women who worked as temps and their regular full-time counterparts was about 10%. Not all nonstandard workers, however, earned less than regular full-timers. For example, women who were independent contractors/self-employed (3.9% of all women workers in 1999) earned 25.0% more than their full-time counterparts, and men working with contract companies (1.2% of all male workers in 1999) earned 16.2% more than comparable standard workers.

One reason that nonstandard wages are lower than those for regular full-time workers is that nonstandard workers tend to be concentrated in low-paying industries and occupations. The second section of the table shows results that control for both workers' personal characteristics and the characteristics of the jobs they performed. In this analysis, the wage "penalty" for working in nonstandard jobs was smaller than when we ignore job characteristics. In half the cases, nonstandard workers appear to earn more than do regular full-time workers with similar personal skills in the same kinds of jobs. This evidence supports the view that nonstandard workers tend to work in less-well-paid industries and occupations.

Nonstandard workers are not only often paid less, but they are less likely to receive benefits from their employers (**Table 3.15**). Compared to nonstandard workers, those in standard employment were more likely to have had health care through their employer and were more likely to have had health insurance overall. Among regular, full-time workers, 66.8% of women and 70.8% of men had employer-provided health insurance, compared to only 14.8% of women and 12.4% of men in nonstandard employment. Part-time workers—the largest share of nonstandard workers—were most likely to go without health insurance through their employer. A common argument is that nonstandard workers receive health insurance through their spouses, so that lack of employer-provided health insurance is not a significant problem. However, this argument is not consistent with the data. Nonstandard workers are less likely than regular, full-time workers to have *any* health insurance coverage: 89.6% of all women and 87.0% of all men in regular, full-time employment have health insurance, compared to 77.7% of women and 73.0% of men in nonstandard employment. This indicates that many nonstandard workers are not making up for lower employer-provided health insurance with spousal benefits. Nonstandard workers are also less likely to receive pensions through their employer or any other source. Among women, only 20.1% of nonstandard workers have pension coverage from their employer, compared to 66.5% among regular, full-time women workers.

Workers may appreciate the flexibility that nonstandard work arrangements provide, but a substantial share of these workers would prefer to have regular full-time employment (**Table 3.16**). In 2001, over half of women (56.3%) and two-fifths of men (43.7%) with temporary jobs said that they would rather have a standard job; similar levels of on-call workers also expressed that preference. Self-employed independent contractors, who generally enjoy pay and benefits comparable to standard workers, strongly prefer their nonstandard arrangements to standard work. As the economy improved between 1995 and 2001, the share

TABLE 3.15 Health and pension coverage by nonstandard work arrangement, 2001

	Share with health insurance				Share eligible for pension			
	Women		Men		Women		Men	
	Any coverage	Through own employer	Any coverage	Through own employer	Any coverage	Through own employer	Any coverage	Through own employer
All workers	86.0%	50.7%	83.8%	57.4%	59.3%	52.4%	61.5%	53.3%
All full-time workers	88.3%	61.9%	85.1%	61.7%	66.6%	61.4%	65.2%	56.7%
Regular full time	89.6	66.8	87.0	70.8	68.9	66.5	67.9	66.0
All nonstandard arrangements	77.7%	14.8%	73.0%	12.4%	37.7%	20.1%	39.6%	11.1%
Full-time and nonstandard								
Temporary help agency	49.9%	11.0%	43.0%	15.2%	24.9%	10.2%	23.0%	12.7%
On-call/day laborer	76.4	39.8	66.3	52.5	48.2	40.4	53.3	50.4
Self-employed	80.1	n.a.	83.0	n.a.	38.8	n.a.	57.0	n.a.
Independent contractor, WS*	65.4	17.6	67.5	25.8	36.7	15.8	37.5	18.7
Independent contractor, SE**	75.2	n.a.	72.5	n.a.	44.4	n.a.	44.5	n.a.
Contract company	88.8	54.9	83.3	59.4	68.7	64.0	63.3	53.2
All part-time workers	78.7%	16.2%	70.2%	13.6%	36.6%	23.2%	23.9%	14.0%
Regular part time	78.5	19.4	72.0	15.9	36.1	28.0	21.4	17.1
Part-time and nonstandard								
Temporary help agency	70.0%	0.9%	36.9%	0.0%	11.5%	3.3%	0.0%	0.0%
On-call/day laborer	69.9	10.6	60.8	12.0	33.6	18.7	25.5	14.4
Self-employed	88.0	n.a.	78.5	n.a.	42.7	n.a.	47.2	n.a.

(cont.)

TABLE 3.15 (cont.) Health and pension coverage by nonstandard work arrangement, 2001

	Share with health insurance				Share eligible for pension			
	Women		Men		Women		Men	
	Any coverage	Through own employer	Any coverage	Through own employer	Any coverage	Through own employer	Any coverage	Through own employer
Part-time and nonstandard (*cont.*)								
Independent contractor, WS*	77.8%	4.%7	64.5%	19.0%	28.0%	4.3%	40.1%	15.9%
Independent contractor, SE**	81.5	n.a.	61.4	n.a.	44.9	n.a.	34.0	n.a.
Contract company	80.5	12.7	82.0	19.0	28.3	17.1	26.1	9.6

* Wage and salary.
** Self-employed.

Source: Wenger (2002).

263

TABLE 3.16 Workers preferring standard employment by type of nonstandard work arrangement, 1995 and 2001

	Women			Men		
	1995	2001	Percentage-point change	1995	2001	Percentage-point change
Regular part time	24.9%	23.4%	-1.5	35.5%	17.4%	-18.1
Temporary help agency	66.4	56.3	-10.1	79.2	43.7	-35.5
On-call	59.4	55.1	-4.3	72.9	44.2	-28.7
Self-employed	10.8	7.3	-3.5	6.0	8.1	2.1
Independent contractor, WS*	23.9	22.8	-1.1	22.3	23.6	1.3
Independent contractor, SE**	9.2	7.7	-1.5	8.6	6.8	-1.8

* Wage and salary.
** Self-employed.

Source: Kalleberg et al. (1997) and Wenger (2002).

of workers in each category that prefers standard work declined, suggesting that many nonstandard workers unhappy with their arrangements were able to find full-time employment as jobs became more plentiful; at the same time, those left in nonstandard arrangements may have been those who most enjoyed the flexibility and other benefits their type of work provided. Another possible explanations for the decline in dissatisfaction with nonstandard arrangements is that the abundance of work near the end of the 1990s economic boom reduced the inherent uncertainty of nonstandard arrangements.

The most recent evidence on nonstandard work shows that such arrangements are widespread, varied, and generally substandard. Nonstandard work pays less, is much less likely to provide health or pension benefits, and, almost by definition, provides far less job security than regular full-time employment. Unfortunately, the kind of detailed survey that has allowed us to sketch the main features of nonstandard work in the mid-1990s does not exist for earlier periods. As a result, we have some difficulty gauging the growth in nonstandard work over the last two decades of substantial economic change. The following sections look at the data that do exist on the growth of several types of nonstandard work: regular part-time employment, self-employment, and just-in-time employment practices. The just-in-time section includes temporary employment, part-time employment (revisited in a historical perspective), and overtime.

Part-time work

The most pervasive form of nonstandard employment is part-time work. Many workers prefer a part-time schedule because it allows time to pursue education, family responsibilities, or more leisure. Nevertheless, part-timers generally have lower pay, less-skilled jobs, poor chances of promotion, less job security, inferior benefits (such as vacation, health insurance, and pension), and lower status overall within their places of employment. For these and other reasons, some part-timers would prefer to work full time. Even those who work part-time schedules by choice would prefer to receive the same compensation (hourly pay rate and prorated benefits) in exchange for performing work done by their full-time coworkers.

According to the data in **Table 3.17**, 17.2% of employees worked part time in 2003. Between 1973 and 1989, part-time work increased 1.6 percentage points, from 15.6% to 17.2% of all employees, and the increase resulted almost entirely from the rise in *involuntary* part-time work, which expanded 1.2 percentage points, from 2.9% to 4.1% of employment. By 1989, nearly one-fourth of all part-time workers were involuntary part-timers. The rise in part-time work over the 1970s and 1980s, therefore, did not reflect workers' preferences for shorter hours.

TABLE 3.17 Nonagricultural employment by full-time and part-time status, 1973-2003

Year	Total	Percent part time Involuntary	Voluntary	Percent full time	Total
1973	15.6%	2.9%	12.7%	84.4%	100.0%
1979	16.5	3.5	13.0	83.5	100.0
1989	17.2	4.1	13.1	82.8	100.0
2000	16.0	2.3	13.7	84.0	100.0
2003	17.2	3.4	13.8	82.8	100.0

* Data for 2003 not strictly comparable with earlier years because of survey changes. See Table Notes.

Source: Authors' analysis of BLS (2004c) data.

Part-time employment declined between 1989 and 2000 (the economic peak), from 17.2% to 16.0% of all workers, with the share of involuntary part-time employment falling even more (1.8 percentage points). As employment opportunities expanded during the 1990s, workers seeking full-time work were more able to find it, meaning that fewer part-time workers were involuntarily working less than full time. By 2000, the share of involuntary part-time workers was below its 1973 level. Between 1989 and 2000, voluntary part-time employment increased by 0.6 percentage-points, from 13.1% to 13.7%. This rise highlights the somewhat complicated nature of nonstandard employment: on the one hand, part-time workers are paid less than their similarly skilled full-time colleagues (as shown in Table 3.14), but, for many workers, nonstandard employment provides the flexibility that they need to balance work with their personal life. As unemployment fell during the late 1990s, voluntary part-time employment may have risen because employers, seeking to lure reticent workers into employment during a tight labor market, were more likely to offer nonstandard arrangements. Another reason may have been that the strong wage growth of the late 1990s softened the blow of the part-timers' wage penalty. Even so, after the 2001 recession, the incidence of part-time work increased from 16.0% to 17.2%, and the increase was driven overwhelmingly by increases in involuntary part-time employment. As Table 3.8 showed, the growth in involuntary part-time employment continued through 2001, and increased 3.2% monthly between March and November 2001. From the end of the 2001 recession until June 2004, involuntary part-time work increased 0.1% per month.

TABLE 3.18 Workers feeling overworked, 1997

Percent who have high levels of feeling overworked among:	
Part-time workers	19%
Full-time workers	37
Those working	
1-19 hours/week	6%
20-34 hours/week	23
35-49 hours/week	34
50+ hours/week	45
Those who work *the same or fewer* hours than they prefer	26%
Those who work *more* hours than they prefer	44

Source: Galinsky, Kim, and Bond (2001).

Many workers choose to work overtime or multiple jobs and appreciate the extra income that it brings. Increased hours of work incur costs, however, both to workers and to their families. The extent to which individuals feel "overworked" is reported in **Table 3.18**. At 45%, those who work the most (50-plus hours per week) are most likely to report feeling overworked; at 6%, those who work the least (1-19 hours per week) are least likely to report feeling overworked. Workers who are full time are more likely to report feeling overworked relative to part-timers. Not surprisingly, those working more hours than they prefer are more likely to report feeling overworked relative to those working the same or fewer hours than they prefer (44% versus 26%).

More employment, whether in the form of adding more family members to the labor market or increasing the hours of work for those already employed, adds to individual and family stress levels. Increasingly, workers must do "double duty" at work and at home. Benefit trends—in particular, paid time off and flexible workplaces—have failed to generate more time outside work over the past few decades. At the turn of the century, workers are less likely to have paid time off than they were 30 years ago.

The increase in temporary work (see Figure 3Y) and the decreased benefits and security of part-time work may make it necessary for workers to have more than one job. Additionally, workers may cope with declining or stagnant real wages and economic hardship by having several jobs. **Table 3.19** shows the historical trends for multiple jobholders. In 1973, 6.6% of men and just 2.7% of women held more than one job. By 2003, the rate fell to 5.1% for men and

TABLE 3.19 Multiple job holders, 1973-2003

Year	Number of multiple job holders* (thousands)			Multiple-job holding rate		
	All	Men	Women	All	Men	Women
1973	4,262	3,393	869	5.1%	6.6%	2.7%
1979	4,724	3,317	1,407	4.9	5.9	3.5
1989	7,225	4,115	3,109	6.2	6.4	5.9
2000	7,604	3,996	3,608	5.6	5.5	5.7
2001	7,357	3,834	3,523	5.4	5.2	5.5
2002	7,291	3,734	3,557	5.3	5.1	5.6
2003	7,315	3,716	3,599	5.3	5.1	5.6
	Percent change			*Percentage-point change*		
1973-79	10.8%	-2.2%	61.9%	-0.2	-0.7	0.8
1979-89	52.9	24.1	121.0	1.3	0.5	2.4
1989-2000	5.2	-2.9	16.1	-0.6	-0.9	-0.2
2000-03	-3.8	-7.0	-0.2	-0.3	-0.4	-0.1

* 2000 onward not directly comparable to earlier years due to population-weighting adjustments.

Source: Authors' analysis of BLS (1997 and 2004a) data.

increased to 5.6% for women. The level of female multiple job holding was less than that of men for all years until 2000, perhaps because women were more likely to be employed part time and because on average the wages of women are less than those for men. Since the 2001 recession, multiple job-holding rates remained constant. The jobless recovery may be partly responsible.

Self-employment
Another form of nonstandard work is self-employment, those whose primary job is working in their own business, farm, craft, or profession. In 1948, 12.0% of all workers were self-employed (**Table 3.20**); by 1967 only 7.3% of workers were self-employed. The lowest level of self-employment during a business cycle peak was in 1973 and in 2002 (6.7%). The rate jumped up to 6.9% in 2003, a move which may suggest that, for some workers, self-employment is a refuge against the inability to find regular employment. However, during peak years self-employment has remained fairly stable, which may indicate that people are more willing to step into entrepreneurship when the economy is healthy or when it is more likely a business will succeed. The data also show that men are consistently more likely to be self-employed than are women. Research sug-

TABLE 3.20 Self-employment, 1948-2003 (percentage of total employment by gender*)

Year	All	Men	Women
1948	12.0%	n.a.	n.a.
1967	7.3	n.a.	n.a.
1973	6.7	n.a.	n.a.
1979	7.1	8.8%	4.9%
1989	7.5	9.0	5.8
2000	6.8	7.8	5.8
2001	6.8	7.7	5.7
2002	6.7	7.6	5.6
2003**	6.9	8.0	5.7

*   Nonagricultural industries.

Source: Authors' analysis of BLS (2004c) data.

gests that one factor in the different rates of self-employment is that women often lack the kinds of access that men have to the capital and networks necessary to start and sustain small businesses.

Just-in-time employment

Two features of the last two recoveries make them unique. First, they have been jobless recoveries, the only two such recoveries the economy has experienced. Second, they saw a greater use of just-in-time employment practices, a form of hiring that is akin to inventory adjustment practices. Just-in-time employment allows employers to quickly adjust the size of their workforces to meet fluctuations in demand. Following the 2001 recession, when many firms successfully sought to raise their profit margins, employers valued the flexibility to cut labor costs when demand fell. Yet while such a strategy may raise profits, it prolongs the lack of job creation, and as such is likely one of the factors explaining the unusually weak recent trend in job gains as shown in Figure 3D. It also contributes to significant growth in jobs that, by dint of their less permanent status, create greater worker insecurity and lower job quality.

Temporary employment. **Table 3.21** reports the number of workers employed in personnel services industries, which included temporary help agencies, between 1973 and 2002. Unfortunately, the government did not gather

TABLE 3.21 Employment in personnel services industry, 1973-2002

Year	Number (thousands)			As share of total employment	As share of total personnel services	
	All	Men	Women		Men	Women
1973	247	118	128	0.3%	47.9%	52.1%
1979	508	210	298	0.6	41.4	58.6
1989	1,455	581	874	1.3	39.9	60.1
1992	1,629	676	954	1.5	41.5	58.5
1999	3,616	1,684	1,932	2.8	47.8	53.4
2000	3,883	1,855	2,028	2.9	47.8	52.2
2001	3,446	1,633	1,813	2.6	47.4	52.6
2002	3,169	1,515	1,654	2.4	47.8	52.2

Source: Authors' analysis of BLS (2004d) data.

data on temporary work before 1982, and even the data that the government has collected on a regular basis since 1982 are not directly comparable to the detailed information in Table 3.12 or Figure 3Y. All three data sources used either different methodologies or different coding classifications. Therefore, the information in Table 3.23 is used to illustrate the historical trend in this type of employment. In 1973 just 0.3% of workers were employed in the personnel services industry; by 2000 this percentage increased to 2.9%. Since the recession the percent has fallen to 2.4%.

Figure 3Y shows employment in the temporary help industry as a share of total employment. This data series started in 1990, and the share in the temporary help industry was 1.3%. Throughout the 1990s the share of temporary help employment grew—to 2.4% by 2000. After the stock bubble burst and throughout the recession this share fell precipitously to 2.0%. The temporary employment share fluctuated throughout 2003, as businesses perhaps tested the reliability and resiliency of the recovery. As of June 2004, the percentage of workers working in the temporary help industry rose to 2.2% as the economy picked up.

When the jobless recovery ended in August 2003 and jobs began to be created, the share of jobs in the temporary employment industry was about 2.0%. Remarkably, 13% of all jobs created since the jobless recovery ended are in the temporary employment industry. This is a significant increase in the use of temporary employees and corroborates the growth of just-in-time employment practices.

Historical part-time work. **Figure 3Z** illustrates part-time employment as a percent of all employment from January 1973 to June 2004. The gray areas represent recessions. Since 1973 part-time employment has trended upward, and increases were especially significant during recoveries. During the tight labor market of the mid-to-late 1990s, the share of part-time employment decreased considerably, a drop in part caused by the tight labor market and employers' need for full-time workers to meet increased demand. Since the 2001 recession, the share of part-time employment has trended upward with greater variability than at anytime in the last 30 years, reflecting the theory that businesses were testing the recovery waters while utilizing employment practices that enable them to adjust employment with modest costs and little commitment.

Overtime employment. The last aspect of just-in-time employment is the liberal use of overtime by employers. Employers have used overtime prior to hiring full-time workers on a more permanent basis while they gauge the strength and sustainability of a recovery. However, the use of overtime by firms now

271

FIGURE 3Y Employment in temporary help industry as share of total employment, 1990-2004

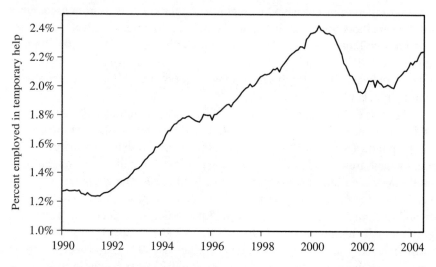

Source: Authors' analysis of BLS (2004d) data.

FIGURE 3Z Part-time employment as a percent of all employment

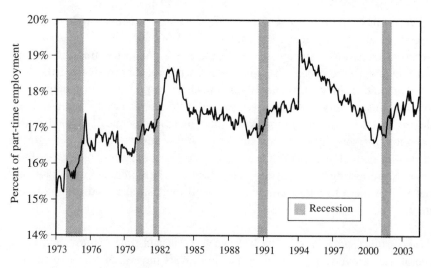

Source: Authors' analysis of BLS (2004c) data.

lasts longer into the recovery. **Figures 3AA** and **3BB** show three important characteristics of manufacturing: employment, overtime, and output.

These figures show that manufacturing employment and output were procyclical during the last two recessions, but, contrary to previous recoveries, employment at the beginning of the jobless recoveries was countercyclical to manufacturing output. Figure 3AA shows that at the end of the last two recessions—as manufacturing output was expanding (Figure 3BB)—employment continued to fall while average weekly overtime hours increased. Employment in manufacturing increased modestly in January 2004 although increases in manufacturing output started a significant upward trend in June 2003. These two figures are just one example of the use of overtime to meet increased demand at a time when employment was falling.

Effects of just-in-time employment. Firms are relying more on part-time and temporary workers and overtime from existing workers to meet the ebbs and flows of demand—practices that preclude the hiring of more permanent full-time workers. The increased reliance on just-in-time employment practices affects workers' perceptions, feelings of job security, and their ability to find stable employment. **Table 3.22** presents results on reported levels of job security from a nationally representative survey of workers in the peak years of 1978, 1989, 1996, 2000, and the most recent data available for 2002 (no survey data exist for 1979, the normal comparison year used throughout this chapter). Job security is defined as workers' ability to remain in an employment relationship for as long as their job performance is satisfactory. The share of workers who said they thought they were very or fairly likely to lose their jobs in the next 12 months was 8.0% in both 1978 and 1989 (despite a slight decline in the national unemployment rate between the two years). Between 1989 and 1996, however, the share of workers who thought they faced a significant chance of losing their jobs in the next year rose 3 percentage points to 11%. Perceived job security fell over the period even though the national unemployment rate was essentially identical in the two years (5.3% in 1989 compared to 5.4% in 1996). The same polling data also show a large drop between 1978 and 1996 in the share of workers who thought that they were not at all likely to lose their job in the next 12 months. In 1978, 71% of workers thought that they faced very little chance of losing their job; by 1996, the figure had fallen 11 percentage points to 60%. As before, most of the decline in perceived job security took place in the 1990s, with 9 percentage points of the decline occurring between 1989 and 1996, compared to only a 2 percentage-point drop between 1978 and 1989. The share of workers who felt they may lose their jobs rose sharply from the peak of the last business cycle (2000) until the most recent data available in 2002. In

FIGURE 3AA Employment and average weekly overtime hours in manufacturing

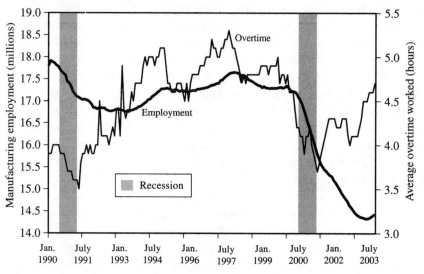

Source: Authors' analysis of BLS (2004d) data.

FIGURE 3BB Manufacturing output

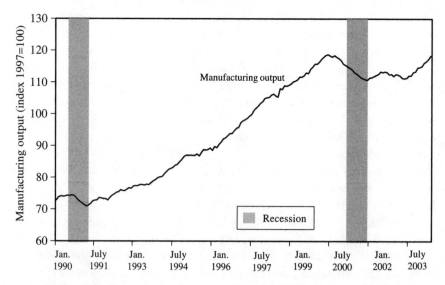

Source: Authors' analysis of the Federal Reserve Board of Governors (2004) data.

TABLE 3.22 Perceptions of job security, 1978-2002

Reason	1978*	1989	1996	1998	2000	2002	Percentage-point change		
							1978-89	1989-2002	2000-02
How likely to lose your job or be laid off in next 12 months?									
Very or fairly likely	8%	8%	11%	8%	8%	13%	0.0	5.0	5.0
Not at all likely	71	69	60	64	69	62	-2.0	-7.0	-7.0
How easy to find a job with another employer with about the same income and benefits?									
Not easy at all	38%	37%	39%	33%	29%	39%	-1.0	2.0	10.0
Very easy	28	34	27	30	37	24	6.0	-10.0	-13.0
Unemployment rate	6.1%	5.3%	5.4%	4.5%	4.0%	5.8%	-0.8	0.5	1.8

* No data available for 1979.

Source: GSS data provided by The Roper Center for Public Opinion Research (2004).

2000, only 8% of workers thought it likely they would lose their jobs. By 2002, this percentage increased by 4 percentage points to 13%.

As expected, workers also appear less optimistic about their employment prospects in the event that they do lose their jobs. During the boom of the late 1990s and into 2000, more workers felt they could find a job with another employer with about the same income and benefits. By 2002, after the prolonged weak recovery, those workers who said it was not easy at all to find comparable work increased 10 percentage points to 39%. At the same time, those who thought it was very easy to find similar work decreased from 37% in 2000 to just 24% in 2002.

The data on workers' perceptions show a high and growing level of job insecurity that is likely correlated with the increase in just-in-time employment practices.

Conclusion

September 2003 was the beginning of 10 straight months of positive job growth that signaled the end of a jobless recovery that lasted from November 2001 to August 2003. However, job creation exceeded 150,000—the number needed to keep up with the new entrants into the labor force—in only four of those months. Due to the recession and prolonged weak recovery, as discussed in Chapter 2, the strong wage growth that accompanied the tight labor market of the late 1990s eroded, and wages began to fall. Compensation, benefits, and general improvements for labor are contingent on a strong labor market with plenty of employment opportunities.

The labor market is beset with lingering uncertainty. Firms are uncertain if demand is solid and sustainable. They have delayed the hiring of full-time permanent workers and made use of just-in-time employment practices that played a large role in creating and sustaining the jobless recovery and that are now facilitating the relatively weak recovery. The offshoring of white-collar jobs is becoming more prevalent, and it will challenge white-collar labor in the same way that blue-collar workers have been challenged by manufacturers moving abroad.

As firms remain uncertain in their hiring, workers feel unsettled by the persistent shedding of jobs during the recovery and subsequent weak job growth. The once common practice of layoffs—with the promise of being called back as soon as the economy turned around—is no longer customary. The economy is facing structural shifts—i.e., increased globalization and technological advancements—as well as cyclical shifts—i.e., the stock market crash and a slack labor market—that are a continuing challenge to both employers and employees.

CHAPTER 4

Wealth: persistent inequality

The main focus of the preceding chapters has been the wages and incomes of American families. Like wages and incomes, wealth is a vital component of a family's standard of living. Over the long term, families try to accumulate wealth in order to finance education, purchase a house, start a small business, and fund retirement. In the short term, wealth—particularly financial assets such as checking account balances, stocks, and bonds—can help families cope with financial emergencies related to unemployment or illness. The level of wealth a family obtains determines how sufficiently it can smooth consumption when financial emergencies arise. Those families with little wealth can be financially devastated by any economic setback.

It is a challenge for middle- and lower-income families to accumulate ample wealth. Families that do not have sufficient wealth for short-term or long-term expenses accumulate debt or go without necessities during hard financial times. Some debt, such as a mortgage, can be considered good debt, but can be hard to acquire. Other types of debt, such as the use of high-interest-bearing credit cards, can be much more problematic—especially when balances accrue to meet day-to-day living expenses. This chapter will analyze how assets, liabilities, and debt are distributed across households.

Several key features about American wealth stand out. The wealthiest 1% of all households control just over 33% of national wealth, while the bottom 80% of households hold only 16%. Changes in the share of average wealth by wealth class show that wealth inequality is stark and that it has persisted over the last 20 years. The ownership of stocks is particularly unequal. The top 1% of stockowners hold close to half (44.9%) of all stocks, by value, while the bottom 80% of stockholders own just 5.8% of total stock holdings. The most recent government data show that only half of all house-holds hold stock in any form, including mutual funds and 401(k)-style pension plans. The same data reveal that 48% of households have no stock, while another 11.8% have less than $5,000 of stock. While this means that most Americans did not benefit from the stock market boom of the late 1990s, it also means that most have not been directly hurt by the crash of the stock market in 2000.

Total household net worth decreased by 13.1% after the bursting of the stock market bubble between 2000 and 2001. Stocks and mutual funds, a component of net worth, fell almost 19.6% between 2000 and 2001. Net worth continued to fall throughout the 2001 recession and into the weak recovery. The share in the distribution of net worth going to the top 20% increased slightly during the boom years, while it decreased slightly for the bottom 80% during this same time period.

Home ownership—the most important source of assets for most American families—continued the upward trend that started in 1994, especially among nonwhite households. Home ownership rates vary considerably by income and race. Only 50% of those in the bottom quarter of the income distribution own their homes, while 88% in the top quarter of the income distribution own homes. Blacks and Hispanics, while slowly increasing their home ownership rates, still lag behind whites. The overall unequal distribution of home ownership across racial and ethnic groups persists.

The 1990s boom left most Americans better prepared for retirement than before: for almost three out of four Americans, income from Social Security, pensions, and defined-contribution plans will replace at least half of their pre-retirement income. This was a marked improvement from 1998, when 42.5% could not expect to replace half of their current income in retirement, but just a bit better than the rate of 30.5% in 1989.

Household debt as a share of assets was 18% in 2003, on average. As expected, debt burdens continued to plague lower-income families disproportionately, although debt burdens for the typical household decreased slightly. By 2001, middle-income families had a slight increase in debt, but experienced larger increases in stocks, assets, and overall net worth. Conversely, the most recent government data showed that 16% of households in the $20,000 to $39,999 range had debt-service obligations that exceeded 40% of their income, while 11.7% of these households had at least one bill that was more than 60 days past due. Moreover, the official report of debt by the Federal Reserve Board has undoubtedly understated serious financial hardships—akin to debt—incurred by households with high levels of financial insecurity. These house-holds increasingly access loans and money through nontraditional or predatory

TABLE 4.1 Distribution of income and wealth, 2001

| | Distribution of: | | |
	Household income	Net worth	Net financial assets
All	100.0%	100.0%	100.0%
Top 1%	20.0	33.4	39.7
Next 9%	25.2	38.1	40.1
Bottom 90%	54.8	28.5	20.2

Source: Wolff (2004).
For detailed information on table sources, see Table Notes.

lending institutions such as pawn shops and check-cashing centers. Additionally, despite the robust state of the economy, personal bankruptcy rates reached all-time highs in 2001.

Net worth

The concept of wealth used in this chapter is net worth, or sum of all of a family's assets—real estate, checking and savings account balances, stock holdings, retirement funds (such as 401(k) plans and individual retirement accounts), and other assets—minus the sum of all of a family's liabilities—mortgages, credit-card debt, student loans, and other debts. Changes in household wealth levels occur through new investments, returns on existing investments, savings, or inheritances. Net worth excludes assets in defined-benefit contribution plans because workers do not legally own the assets held in these plans and thus do not necessarily benefit from improvements in the value of assets used to pay the defined benefit. (Their companies do benefit, however, because higher asset values lower the contributions companies have to pay to meet future defined benefits). Nor do workers suffer financially if the underlying assets under perform expectations. For similar reasons, this analysis also excludes Social Security and Medicare from the net worth calculations (although the section projecting retirement income does include expected income from Social Security).

A key feature of the wealth distribution is that it is much more unequal than the distribution of either wages or incomes. **Table 4.1** shows income and wealth data from the most recent Survey of Consumer Finances (SCF) conducted by the Federal Reserve Board. The first column shows that, in 2001 (the

TABLE 4.2 Growth of household wealth, 1949-2003

Type of wealth	Annual growth of net worth per household					
	1949-67	1967-73	1979-89	1989-2000	2000-03	2001-03
Total net worth*	2.3%	-0.8%	2.3%	4.4%	-6.4%	-2.9%
Net tangible assets**	2.7	-0.4	2.5	4.2	-3.9	-0.6
Net financial assets***	1.9	3.0	1.2	0.3	3.0	4.2
Financial assets:						
Stock	7.0%	-8.1%	4.0%	8.9%	-12.4%	-6.7%
Mutual funds	11.7	-8.7	19.9	14.4	-1.3	4.1
Stock and mutual funds	7.2	-8.1	5.6	10.2	-8.9	-3.2

*   Includes all households, personal trusts, and nonprofit organizations.
**   Consumer durables, housing, and land assets less home mortgages.
***   Financial assets less nonmortgage debt.

Source: Authors' analysis of Federal Reserve Board (2004a) and Bureau of Economic Analysis (2004).

latest year available), the 1% of households with the highest incomes received 20% of all income. In comparison, these households held 33.4% of all net worth. At the other end of the distribution, the 90% of households with the lowest incomes received 54.8% of all income but had only 28.5% of all net worth.

The beginning of the 21st century saw household net worth decline sharply. Household net worth fell 6.4% annually between 2000 and 2003. **Table 4.2** illustrates how this decrease occurred across all types of assets, except net financial assets. The decline in net worth was led by the rapid reduction in the value of stock (at an annual rate of -12.4%) and, to a lesser extent, mutual funds (at an annual rate of -1.3%). The stock market decline lasted from April 2000 until approximately October 2002, and the subsequent recovery into 2003 helped to dampen losses between 2001 and 2003.

This analysis of changes in the level and distribution of wealth is based on tabulations of the seven SCF surveys conducted between 1962 and 2001 (the latest year available). The distribution of household wealth by wealth class has not changed significantly since 1983. **Figure 4A** illustrates the fairly consistent, stark inequality that persisted even during the boom years of the late 1990s. The top 1% of wealth holders consistently owned well over 30% of all wealth from 1983 to 2001. The bottom 80% of wealth holders, without exception, held under 20% of all wealth. Those in the bottom 80% held 18.7% of all wealth in 1983, which decreased to 15.6% in 2001. The top 1% lost some share of wealth

FIGURE 4A Distribution of wealth by wealth class, 1983-2001

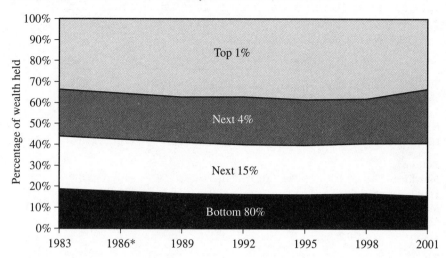

Source: Authors' analysis of Wolff (2004).

* For detailed information on figure sources, see Figure Notes.

to the next 4% across the 1989 to 2001 period, but the wealth holdings of the top 5% remained fairly consistent from 1983 to 2001.

Tables 4.3 and **4.4** provide a more detailed analysis of the distribution of wealth from 1962 to 2001. Table 4.3 shows that, in 2001, the top fifth of households held 84.4% of all wealth; the middle fifth held a mere 3.9% (its lowest share since 1962); and the bottom fifth actually had negative net worth—they owed 0.4% more than they owned. There were some shifts of wealth among the top fifth of wealth holders, but overall they gained a 0.9% share of wealth from 1989 to 2001, while the bottom four-fifths gave up that percentage.

The data in Table 4.4 illustrate how the absolute level of wealth changed over time for households at different points in the wealth distribution. From 1989 to 2001, the average wealth of the top 1% of households grew by $2.8 million, from $9.9 million in 1989 to $12.7 million in 2001 (a 2.1% annual increase). The average wealth of the middle 20% of households grew from $63,900 in 1989 to $75,000 in 2001 (a 1.3% annual increase). While the annualized growth increase of average wealth was 3.0% between 1989 and 2001, the growth for the top fifth was above average, while the growth for the bottom four-fifths was below average. Additionally, the poorest households, which had improved considerably from 1989 to 1998, still had, on average, negative net

TABLE 4.3 Changes in the distribution of wealth, 1962-2001

						Percentage-point change		
Wealth class	1962	1983	1989	1998	2001	1962-83	1989-98	1989-2001
Top fifth	81.0%	81.3%	83.5%	83.4%	84.4%	0.4	-0.1	0.9
Top 1%	33.4	33.8	37.4	38.1	33.4	0.3	0.7	-4.0
Next 4%	21.2	22.3	21.6	21.3	25.8	1.2	-0.2	4.2
Next 5%	12.4	12.1	11.6	11.5	12.3	-0.2	-0.1	0.7
Next 10%	14.0	13.1	13.0	12.5	12.9	-0.9	-0.5	-0.1
Bottom four-fifths	19.1%	18.7%	16.5%	16.6%	15.6%	-0.4	0.1	-0.9
Fourth	13.4	12.6	12.3	11.9	11.3	-0.8	-0.4	-1.0
Middle	5.4	5.2	4.8	4.5	3.9	-0.2	-0.3	-0.9
Second	1.0	1.2	0.8	0.8	0.7	0.2	-0.1	-0.1
Lowest	-0.7	-0.3	-1.5	-0.6	-0.4	0.4	0.9	1.1
Total	100.0%	100.0%	100.0%	100.0%	100.0%			

* Wealth defined as net worth (household assets minus debts).

Source: Wolff (2004).

worth (-$8,200 in 2001, up from -$20,000 in 1989). Across almost all levels of wealth, annualized wealth grew more rapidly in the 1989-2001 period than it did in the 1962-83 or 1989-98 periods.

A closer look at Table 4.4 reveals an increasing and persistent trend in the growth of inequality. The ratio of median to average wealth overtime has been decreasing, down from 0.27 in 1962 to 0.19 in 2001. This decrease occurred because average wealth was growing relatively faster than median wealth. The increase in average wealth was driven by those at the top of the wealth distribution who had commanded control over greater shares of wealth since 1962.

Inequality also increased among the very wealthy between 1983 and 2003. **Figure 4B** shows the minimum, average, and maximum levels of wealth of the members of the Forbes 400, an annual, unrepresentative but carefully constructed list of the 400 wealthiest people in the United States. The figure shows wealth holdings on a log scale, which compresses large differences and allows the three lines to fit on the same graph. The gap between the wealthiest and the least wealthy members of the Forbes 400 grew significantly in the late 1990s. As the stock market began to slide between 2000 and 2002, however, the net worth of the very rich fell, but it resumed its upward trend from 2002 to 2003.

TABLE 4.4   Change in average wealth by wealth class, 1962-2001 (thousands of 2001 dollars)

Wealth class	1962	1983	1989	1998	2001	Annualized growth 1962-83	1989-98	1989-2001
Top fifth	$638.2	$939.3	$1,105.1	$1,224.2	$1,604.7	1.8%	1.1%	3.1%
Top 1%	5,271.5	7,795.8	9,889.0	11,086.4	12,692.1	1.9	1.3	2.1
Next 4%	834.6	1,289.5	1,427.0	1,565.9	2,453.0	2.1	1.0	4.5
Next 5%	390.1	560.8	614.5	677.4	937.4	1.7	1.1	3.5
Next 10%	220.4	302.8	343.2	374.7	490.3	1.5	1.0	3.0
Bottom four-fifths	$37.5	$53.9	$54.5	$61.0	$74.0	1.7%	1.2%	2.5%
Fourth	105.7	145.2	163.0	175.3	215.3	1.5	0.8	2.3
Middle	42.8	60.3	63.9	66.3	75.0	1.6	0.4	1.3
Second	7.5	13.6	11.1	12.1	13.9	2.9	0.9	1.9
Lowest	-5.8	-3.5	-20.0	-9.6	-8.2	n.a.	n.a.	n.a.
Median	$42.2	$59.3	$63.5	$65.9	$73.5	1.6%	0.4%	1.2%
Average	157.7	231.0	264.6	293.6	380.1	1.8	1.2	3.0
Ratio: Median-to-average	0.27	0.26	0.24	0.22	0.19			

* Wealth defined as net worth (household assets minus debts).

Source: Wolff (2004).

The average net worth of the Forbes 400 in 2003 was below its peak level hit in 2000. Overall, these data suggest that inequality—as defined by the ratio of maximum to average wealth—among the very top holders of wealth (above the level captured by the SCF, which, by design, excludes members of the Forbes 400) grew rapidly throughout the 1990s, despite a slight reversal at the beginning of the 2000s.

Low net worth

Another important feature of the wealth distribution is the large share of households with low, zero, or negative net worth. Despite growth in income and wealth from 1989 to 2001, many households were left with little or no wealth. These households are extremely vulnerable to financial distress and insecurity. **Table 4.5** reports the share of all households with zero or negative net worth or net worth of less than $10,000. The overall share of households with low net worth

FIGURE 4B Annual net worth of "Forbes 400" wealthiest individuals

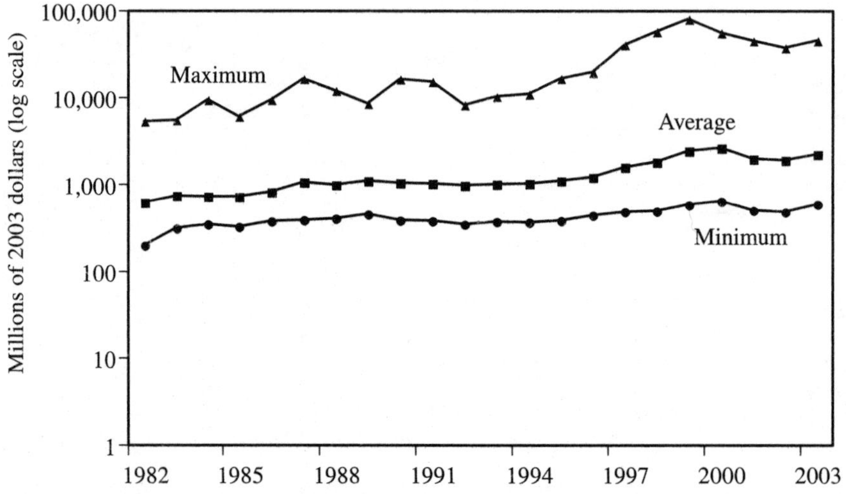

Source: Broom and Shay (2002) and Forbes (2004).

remained relatively constant over the 1990s and into the 2000s. In 2001, 17.6% of all households had a zero or negative net worth, while just over 30% had net worth of less than $10,000. In terms of race, the experience of black households differed significantly from that of white households, an aspect of wealth distribution that will be discussed in more detail in the following section. As **Table 4.6** shows, in 2001 more than twice as many black households (30.9%) as white households (13.1%) had zero or negative net worth.

The circumstances of black households improved substantially from 1989 to 1998, with a 13.3 percentage-point decline in households with zero or negative net wealth. However, black households had an increase in this statistic from 1998 to 2001, jumping from 27.4% in 1998 to 30.9% in 2001.

Racial divide

As suggested in the above analysis, an extremely important feature of wealth in America is that its distribution is profoundly unequal by race. Table 4.6 presents wealth data separately for blacks and whites. The first section shows average wealth by race. In 2001, the latest year available, the average black household had a net worth equal to about 14% of the average white household. Due to the fact that white wealth has grown faster than black wealth since 1992, this ratio has declined significantly.

TABLE 4.5 Households with low net wealth, 1962-2001 (percent of all households)

Net worth	1962	1983	1989	1998	2001	Percentage-point change		
						1962-83	1983-89	1989-2001
Zero or negative	23.6%	15.5%	17.9%	18.0%	17.6%	-5.6	2.5	-0.3
Less than $10,000*	34.3	29.7	31.8	30.3	30.1	-4.6	2.1	-1.7

* Constant 1998 dollars.

Source: Wolff (2004).

TABLE 4.6 Wealth* by race, 1983-2001 (thousands of 2001 dollars)

Race	1983	1989	1992	1995	1998	2001
Average wealth						
Black	$50.8	$53.5	$57.4	$47.4	$63.3	$66.3
White	269.9	319.3	309.0	281.6	348.7	465.8
Black-to-white ratio	18.8%	16.8%	18.6%	16.8%	18.2%	14.2%
Median wealth						
Black	$5.2	$2.4	$13.0	$8.5	$10.9	$10.7
White	77.7	92.3	77.4	70.9	88.7	106.4
Black-to-white ratio	6.7%	2.6%	16.8%	12.1%	12.2%	10.0%
Households with zero or negative net wealth						
Black	34.1%	40.7%	31.5%	31.3%	27.4%	30.9%
White	11.3	12.1	13.8	15.0	14.8	13.1
Black-to-white ratio	300.8	337.7	228.1	209.0	209.0	235.2
Average financial wealth						
Black	$25.6	$26.2	$32.7	$24.7	$40.8	$43.2
White	198.9	241.4	237.9	219.0	276.8	369.7
Black-to-white ratio	12.9%	10.9%	13.7%	11.3%	14.8%	11.7%
Median financial wealth						
Black	$0.0	$0.0	$0.2	$0.2	$1.3	$1.1
White	21.6	29.2	23.8	21.0	40.8	42.1
Black-to-white ratio	0.0%	0.0%	0.7%	1.1%	3.2%	2.6%

* Wealth defined as net worth (household assets minus debts).

Source: Wolff (2004).

The second section of Table 4.6 gives the median wealth holdings for blacks and whites. The most striking aspect of these data is the extremely low level of median wealth of black households. In 1998, the median black household had a net worth of $10,900, about 12% of the corresponding figure for whites. Since the median wealth of black families is so low, relatively small dollar movements have a large impact on the ratio of the black median to the white median. Perhaps surprisingly, the 10% figure in 2001 was below the 12% ratio in 1998, and significantly below the ratio of nearly 17% in 1992, suggesting that economic growth over the 1990s has done nothing to narrow the wealth gap between the two races. Black households were especially unlikely to hold financial assets such as stocks and bonds (government and corporate debt). In 2001, the average financial wealth of black households (as shown in Table 4.6, fourth section) was only about 12% of the average wealth for white households, a decrease from nearly 15% in 1998. The median financial wealth for blacks (as shown in the last section of Table 4.6) was just $1,100, less than 3% of the corresponding figure for whites. The unchanging distribution of wealth between blacks and whites is indicative of the lasting legacy of discrimination.

To summarize, the data on net worth reveal the highly unequal distribution of wealth by class, which is further exacerbated by race. A large share of the population has little or no net worth, while, over the last 40 years at least, the wealthiest 20% has consistently held over 80% of all wealth and the top 1% has controlled close to 40%. Wealth inequality increased sharply during the 1980s and showed no signs of improving over the new decade.

Assets

The preceding section summarized the overall distribution of net worth—the sum of each household's assets and liabilities. This section focuses on the first major component of net worth: assets. Households hold a variety of assets, from houses and boats to stocks and bonds. The distribution of assets among wealth classes, however, differs significantly by asset. Some assets, such as stocks and bonds, are highly concentrated; other assets, such as houses, are more widely held. The portfolio of wealth holdings varies with the amount of wealth. Wealthy households, for example, tend to have much of their wealth in stocks and bonds and other wealth-generating financial assets. Less affluent households typically hold most of their wealth in housing equity. **Table 4.7** shows the distribution of several types of household assets in 2001. The top 0.5% of stock-owning households held 25.6% of all stock, while the bottom 80% of households owned just 10.7%. By contrast, the top 0.5% of home-owning households held only 6.3% of total

TABLE 4.7 Distribution of asset ownership across households, 2001

Wealth class	Percentage of all holdings of each asset				
	Common stock excluding pensions*	All common stock**	Non-equity financial assets***	Housing equity	Net worth
Top 0.5%	34.8%	25.6%	37.4%	6.3%	24.1%
Next 0.5%	10.1	8.0	12.6	4.8	9.3
Next 4%	27.9	28.9	25.7	18.4	25.8
Next 5%	12.3	14.5	9.1	13.6	12.3
Next 10%	9.1	12.3	8.0	19.9	12.9
Bottom 80%	5.8	10.7	7.2	37.0	15.6
Total	100.0	100.0	100.0	100.0	100.0

*   Includes direct ownership of stock shares and indirect ownership through mutual funds and trusts.
**   Includes direct ownership of stock shares and indirect ownership through mutual funds, trusts, IRAs, Keogh plans, 401(k) plans, and other retirement accounts.
*** Includes direct ownership of financial securities and indirect ownership through mutual funds, trusts and retirement accounts, and net equity in unincorporated businesses.

Source: Wolff (2004).

housing equity, while the bottom 80% held 37%. While housing equity is unequally distributed, it is more equally distributed than stocks.

Stocks

While the 1990s witnessed a breathtaking run-up in the price of stocks, the beginning of the new decade saw a significant stock market collapse. As **Figure 4C** illustrates, the inflation-adjusted value of the Standard & Poor's 500 index of stocks increased 234% between 1990 and 2000, then fell 22% between 2000 and 2003. During the stock market boom, when discussions of its performance seemed ubiquitous in the national discourse, about half of all U.S. households had no stock holdings of any form, either direct (owning shares in a particular company) or indirect (owning shares through a mutual fund or through a 401(k)-style, defined-contribution pension plan). This fact contradicts the popular notion that the average household is greatly invested in the stock market. The reality is that the average household is not greatly affected by the volatility inherent in the stock market.

The most recent year of data available on the distribution of stock ownership is from 2001, which was a recessionary year (the recession was officially dated March 2001 to November 2001). Additionally, this time period was marred

FIGURE 4C   Growth of U.S. stock market, 1955-2003 (2003 dollars)

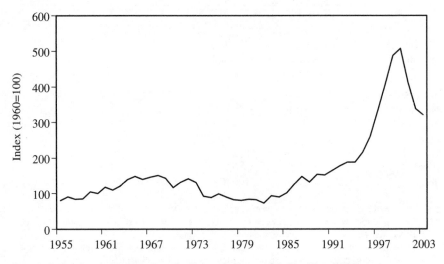

Source: Authors' analysis of data from the Economic Report of the President (2004).

TABLE 4.8   Share of households owning stock, 1989-2001

Stock holdings	1989	1992	1995	1998	2001
Any stock holdings					
Direct holdings	13.1%	14.8%	15.2%	19.2%	21.3%
Indirect holdings	24.7	28.4	30.2	43.4	47.7
Total	31.7	37.2	40.4	48.2	51.9
Stock holdings of $5,000 or more*					
Direct holdings	10.0%	11.4%	12.3%	13.6%	14.6%
Indirect holdings	16.9	21.5	22.7	32.2	36.8
Total	22.6	27.3	28.8	36.3	40.1

* Constant 1995 dollars.

Source: Wolff (2004).

by corporate scandal and corruption that facilitated the fall of the stock market.
Table 4.8 shows that 51.9% of households held stock of some kind in 2001,
which leaves almost half of households without any stock holdings. Only 40.1%
of Americans held stock worth more than $5,000.

TABLE 4.9 Average household assets and liabilities by wealth class (thousands of 2001 dollars)

Asset type	Top 1%	Next 9%	Next 10%	Next 20%	Middle 20%	Bottom 40%	Average
Stocks*							
1962	$2,617.4	$133.9	$14.9	$4.8	$1.2	$0.3	$41.6
1983	1,699.5	109.7	13.1	5.0	1.7	0.4	30.1
1989	1,282.8	141.0	27.6	9.7	4.0	0.7	31.7
1998	2,743.7	316.7	86.4	29.9	10.0	1.8	78.0
2001	3,568.4	512.3	131.9	41.3	12.0	1.8	106.3
All other assets							
1962	$2,847.4	$491.6	$233.6	$129.9	$70.3	$16.7	$142.0
1983	6,540.8	849.0	343.2	176.6	86.9	18.3	235.8
1989	9,090.9	933.3	368.9	201.5	96.8	21.0	279.3
1998	8,649.8	897.7	360.0	196.8	106.0	25.9	267.3
2001	9,449.5	1,221.1	438.4	234.6	113.5	26.6	328.3
Total debt							
1962	$193.3	$37.8	$28.0	$29.0	$28.7	$16.1	$25.9
1983	444.5	74.0	53.5	36.4	28.3	13.6	34.9
1989	484.7	98.7	53.3	48.2	37.0	26.1	46.3
1998	307.1	114.0	71.7	51.5	49.7	26.5	51.7
2001	325.8	122.3	79.9	60.5	50.5	25.5	54.5
Net worth							
1962	$5,271.5	$587.7	$220.4	$105.7	$42.8	$0.9	$157.7
1983	7,795.8	884.7	302.8	145.2	60.3	5.1	231.0
1989	9,889.0	975.6	343.2	163.0	63.9	-4.4	264.6
1998	11,086.4	1,100.3	374.7	175.3	66.3	1.2	293.6
2001	12,692.1	1,611.0	490.3	215.3	75.0	2.9	380.1

*All direct and indirect stock holdings.

Source: Wolff (2004).

The top segment of **Table 4.9** provides a more detailed description of the distribution of stock ownership by wealth class. In 2001, the wealthiest 1% of households owned an average of almost $3.6 million in stocks. The holdings of the next 9% of households averaged $512,300. By comparison, the average direct and indirect stock holdings of the middle 20% of households were small, at $12,000, and the average for the bottom 40% of households was just $1,800. Average assets for a middle-class household totaled $125,500 ($12,000 in stocks plus $113,500 in other assets in 2001). Fewer than 10% of all assets were in stock holdings for middle-class households.

FIGURE 4D Distribution of stock market holdings by wealth class, 2001

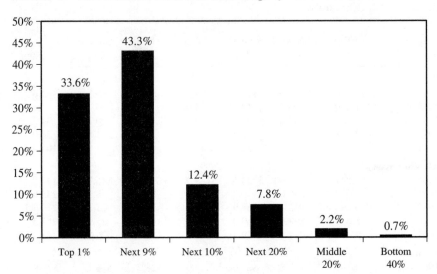

Source: Wolff (2004).

Although the value of stock holdings grew by an average of 36.3% between 1998 and 2001, this growth was not evenly distributed across wealth classes. Stock holding increased 30.1% and 61.8% for the top 1% and next 9%, respectively. The increases were well below average for the bottom 60% of households. The total value of stocks owned by the middle 20% of households, for example, grew only 20% between 1998 and 2001. There was no change in value for stocks held by the bottom 40%.

Figure 4D (derived from Table 4.9) presents the distribution of stock market holding by wealth class in 2001. The top 1% owned 33.6% of all stock market holdings, while the next 9% owned 43.3%. The bottom 90%, by far the largest wealth class by population, only owned 23.1% of all stock market holdings. **Figure 4E** (derived from Table 4.9) shows that the persistent and imbalanced distribution of stock market wealth by class continued throughout the 1990s boom years. Marginal gains were made in stock market wealth holding by the bottom 80% from 1989 to 2001. They held 9.8% of all stock market wealth in 1989, and this increased to 11.9% in 2001.

For further insight, **Figure 4F** (derived from Table 4.9) illustrates the distribution of the growth in stock market holdings, by wealth class, between 1989 and 2001. Almost a third (30.4%) of the growth over the period went to the wealthi-

FIGURE 4E Distribution of stock market wealth by wealth class, 1989-2001

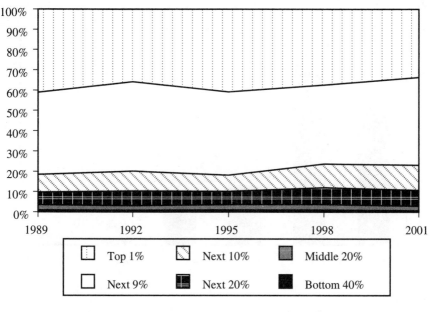

Source: Wolff (2004).

est 1% of households, while 44.5% of stock market growth went to the next 9% of households. The middle 20% of households received only 2.1% of the rise in the overall value of stock holdings over the period. There was almost no growth (0.6%) in stock market holdings for the bottom 40%. These figures illustrate that, even for middle- and lower-class households that held stock, growth in the value of stocks did little to increase the living standards of these households over the last decade.

Stocks are also highly concentrated by household income. **Table 4.10** reports the share of all stock owned by households at different income levels. In 2001, the 2.7% of all households with annual incomes of $250,000 or more owned 40.6% of all stocks (see the bottom section of Table 4.10). Households with annual incomes of $100,000 or more—about 14.0% of all households—controlled 68.6% of all stock. By contrast, the 27.7% of households with annual incomes in the $25,000-$49,999 range owned just 8.3% of all stocks by value. The concentration of stocks within upper income levels holds true even for stocks in pension plans, such as 401(k)s. The main difference between stock holdings in pension plans and other (direct) stock holdings is that pension assets are more evenly

FIGURE 4F Distribution of growth in stock market holdings by wealth class, 1989-2001

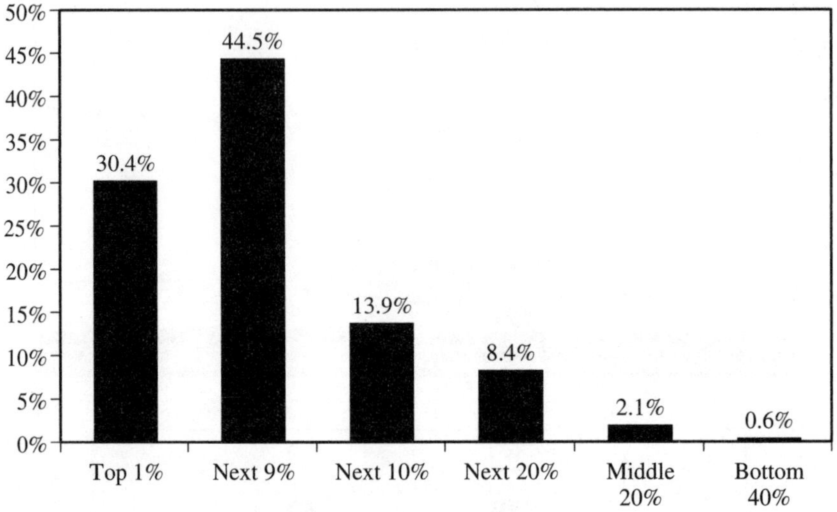

Source: Wolff (2004).

distributed *among high-income households*. While the highest-income group—households with an annual income above $250,000—controls 58.8% of all publicly traded stock, these high earners own 24.3% of stocks in pension plans, and households in the $100,000-$249,999 range own an even greater share (35.5%). At the same time, the bottom three-fourths of households—those with annual incomes of $49,999 or less—still held only 12.1% of all stocks in pension plans (and only 6.1% of publicly traded stock).

The high concentration of stock ownership means that the gains associated with the late 1990s stock boom were highly concentrated among those with the most wealth and income. Moreover, the losses from the bust years will also be concentrated among those with higher incomes.

Home ownership
Much attention is paid to the ups and downs of the stock market, despite the fact that housing equity is actually a far more important form of wealth for most households. The second section of Table 4.9, which shows the distribution of all non-stock assets by overall household wealth, makes this point indirectly. In 2001, the total value of all non-stock assets—comprised primarily of housing equity—

TABLE 4.10 Concentration of stock ownership by income level, 2001

Income level	Share of households	Percent who own	Percent of stocks owned	
			Shares	Cumulative
Publicly traded stock				
$250,000 or above	2.7%	72.7%	58.8%	58.8%
$100,000-249,999	11.3	52.1	20.0	78.8
$75,000-99,999	9.3	31.3	5.2	84.0
$50,000-74,999	17.5	25.3	9.8	93.8
$25,000-49,999	27.7	15.7	4.9	98.8
$15,000-24,999	14.8	7.9	0.9	99.7
Under $15,000	16.7	3.7	0.3	100.0
All	100.0	21.3	100.0	
Stocks in pension plans*				
$250,000 or above	2.7%	75.4%	24.3%	24.3%
$100,000-249,999	11.3	76.0	35.5	59.8
$75,000-99,999	9.3	70.8	12.9	72.7
$50,000-74,999	17.5	61.1	15.2	87.9
$25,000-49,999	27.7	36.3	10.0	97.9
$15,000-24,999	14.8	16.1	1.3	99.2
Under $15,000	16.7	6.5	0.8	100.0
All	100.0	41.4	100.0	
All stocks**				
$250,000 or above	2.7%	93.9%	40.6%	40.6%
$100,000-249,999	11.3	88.3	27.9	68.6
$75,000-99,999	9.3	79.8	8.9	77.4
$50,000-74,999	17.5	73.1	11.8	89.3
$25,000-49,999	27.7	49.2	8.3	97.6
$15,000-24,999	14.8	25.7	1.3	98.9
Under $15,000	16.7	11.0	1.1	100.0
All	100.0	51.9	100.0	

*   All defined-contribution stock plans including 401(k) plans.
**   All stock directly or indirectly held in mutual funds, IRAs, Keogh plans, and defined-contribution pension plans.

Source: Wolff (2004).

held by the middle 20% of households was $113,500, more than nine times larger than the average stock holdings for the same group ($12,000).

Census data graphed in **Figure 4G** indicate that, in 2003, over two-thirds of households owned their own homes. Home ownership rates fluctuated within a fairly narrow band—64% to 65%—between the early 1970s and the late 1980s.

FIGURE 4G Average home ownership rates, 1965-2003

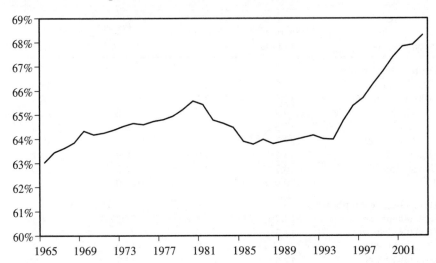

Source: Authors' analysis of U.S. Bureau of Census, Housing Vacancy Survey (2003).

However, ownership rates rose sharply and steadily from the early 1990s to 2003, when 68.3% of households were homeowners.

Table 4.11 presents data collected through the biennial American Housing Survey which show that home ownership rates vary considerably by race and income. Table 4.11 and **Figure 4H** show that, in 2003 (the most recent year for which data are available), white households were much more likely than black households to own their own homes (72.1% compared to 48.1%). Black households were slightly more likely than Hispanic households to own their own homes (48.1% compared to 46.7% in 2003). Even though a substantial racial divide exists for home ownership rates, all races and income levels have experienced increasing rates of home ownership over time, particularly minorities. Specifically, percentage-point increases in home ownership rates were higher for blacks (4.8) and Hispanics (7.0) than for whites (2.2) from 1989 to 2001.

Table 4.11 also shows that 88% of households in the top 25% of the income distribution were home owners, compared to just 50.9% of households in the bottom 25%. **Figure 4I** charts this information and illustrates that there is a lot of room for growth in home ownership rates for the bottom 50% of income groups.

TABLE 4.11 Home ownership rates by race and income

	Home ownership rate						Percentage-point change		
	1979	1989	1997	1999	2001	2003	1979-89	1989-2001	1999-2003
All	65.4%	64.0%	65.8%	66.8%	67.8%	68.3%	-1.4	3.8	1.5
White	68.4%	69.4%	72.5%	70.5%	71.6%	72.1%	1.0	2.2	1.6
Black*	44.4	42.9	45.2	46.3	47.7	48.1	-1.5	4.8	1.8
Hispanic	n.a.	40.3	42.8	45.5	47.3	46.7	n.a.	7.0	1.2
By income									
Top 25%	87.0%	84.5%	86.5%	87.4%	88.0%	n.a.	-2.5	3.5	0.6**
Next 25%	72.3	68.6	71.4	73.1	73.7	n.a.	-3.6	5.1	0.7**
Next 25%	56.2	56.3	57.5	57.8	59.4	n.a.	0.0	3.1	1.6**
Bottom 25%	46.2	46.4	48.0	49.4	50.9	n.a.	0.2	4.4	1.5**

* Black includes all nonwhite in 1979.
** Home ownership data by income only available through 2001.

Source: Authors' analysis of U.S. Bureau of Census (2003); U.S. Bureau of Census (1999); U.S. Bureau of Census (2004); and Economy.com (2004b).

FIGURE 4H Home ownership rates by race, 1989-2003

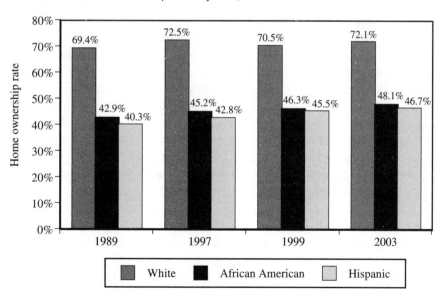

Source: Authors' analysis of U.S. Bureau of the Census (2003); U.S. Bureau of the Census (1999); U.S.Bureau of the Census (2004); and Economy.com (2004).

FIGURE 4I Average rate of home ownership by income, 2001

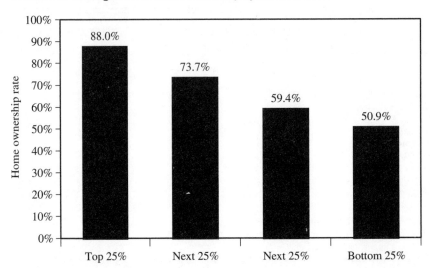

Source: Authors' analysis of U.S. Bureau of the Census (2004).

Retirement wealth and income adequacy

Over the 1990s, as net worth increased, more families became increasingly prepared for retirement. **Table 4.12** shows the proportion of households that met a common test of retirement income adequacy: the ability in retirement to replace half of current income, based on expected pension, Social Security benefits, and returns on personal savings. In 2001 (the latest year for which data are available), 28.1% of households headed by someone age 47 to 64 expected inadequate retirement income; this was a decrease of 14.4 percentage points since 1998 and a 2.4 percentage-point decrease since 1989. Stated differently, approximately 72% of households could expect to have retirement wealth of at least one-half of their current income in 2001.

Like many aspects of income and wealth, expected retirement adequacy was not uniformly distributed. African American or Hispanic households were more likely to have low incomes in retirement—40.0% will be unable to replace half of current income. Comparatively, 25.4% of white households were not expected to have adequate means in retirement. The percentage-point decreases over the 1989 to 2001 period were similar for blacks and whites. Having a college degree made little difference in expected retirement income—25.4% for households with a college degree or more were

TABLE 4.12   Retirement income adequacy, 1989-2001

| Group | Percent of households age 47-64 with expected retirement income less than one-half of current income | | | |
	1989	1998	2001	Percentage-point change, 1989-2001
All	30.5%	42.5%	28.1%	-2.3
By race/ethnicity*				
Non-Hispanic white	27.3%	40.3%	25.4%	-2.0
African American or Hispanic	42.1	52.7	40.0	-2.1
By education**				
Less than high school	39.2%	48.6%	29.2%	-10.0
High school degree	24.7	40.9	29.0	4.3
Some college	18.8	42.4	30.1	11.3
College degree or more	20.8	40.7	25.4	4.6
By family status				
Married couple	26.5%	37.3%	24.1%	-2.4
Single male	22.6	62.4	26.5	3.9
Single female	43.8	45.0	39.0	-4.8
By home owner status				
Owns a home	24.9%	39.5%	25.1%	0.2
Renter	49.8	52.8	40.1	-9.7

*   Asian and other races are excluded from the table because of small sample sizes.
**   Households are classified by the schooling level of the head of household.

Note: A 7% real return on assets is assumed for financial wealth and net worth. Households are classified by the age of the head of household. Retirement income is based on marketable wealth holdings and all expected pension and social security benefits.

Source: Wolff (2004).

expected to have a retirement income of less than half their current income, compared to around 29% or 30% for other education levels. However, retirement income adequacy improved the most, between 1989 and 2001, among households headed by someone with less than a high school degree (+10.0 percentage-point change). Curiously, households where the head had some college, but no degree, experienced an 11.3 percentage-point increase between 1989 and 2001 in the percentage that expected inadequate retirement income.

FIGURE 4J Change in mean retirement wealth by income class, age 47-55, 1989-2001

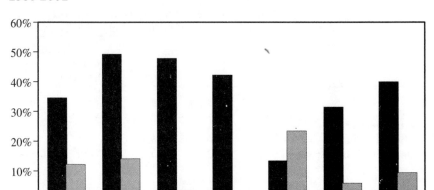

Source: Wolff (2004).

Family status is another important facet of expected retirement adequacy. Married couples and single female households experienced decreases in inadequate retirement preparedness, with drops of -2.4 and -4.8 percentage points, respectively. Households headed by single males had a 3.9 percentage-point increase in this measure.

Figure 4J illustrates changes in mean retirement wealth by income class over the late 1980s into the 2000s. All households saw significant increases in retirement wealth over the 1989 to 1998 time period. The change in mean retirement wealth for the shorter, but more recent period spanning 1998 to 2001 is mixed depending on income class. The cohort at the high end of income, those earning over $100,000, had gains of more than 10%, while those in the $75,000 to $99,000 income range had only slight gains in mean retirement wealth. The income cohort of $50,000 to $74,999, on average, lost retirement wealth from 1998 to 2001. The largest gain (almost 24%) was for those in the $35,000 to $49,999 income group, while those with incomes less than $35,000 also had very modest gains in mean retirement wealth.

TABLE 4.13 Household debt by type, 1949-2003

	As a share of disposable personal income				All debt as a share of all assets	Mortgage debt as a share of real estate assets
	All debt	Mortgage	Home equity loans*	Consumer credit		
1949	32.9%	19.6%	n.a.	10.2%	6.1%	15.0%
1967	69.1	42.5	n.a.	18.8	12.0	30.8
1973	66.9	39.6	n.a.	19.7	12.6	26.3
1979	73.2	46.1	n.a.	19.5	13.7	27.5
1989	86.4	57.1	n.a.	19.8	14.8	31.4
1995	94.3	62.4	6.2%	20.7	15.8	40.2
2000	106.8	70.3	9.2	22.7	15.4	40.2
2003	114.5	85.0	10.9	24.0	18.3	44.1
Annual percentage-point change						
1949-73	2.8	1.6	n.a.	0.8	0.5	1.1
1949-79	2.4	1.5	n.a.	0.6	0.5	0.9
1989-2000	1.8	1.2	n.a.	0.3	0.1	0.8
2000-03	2.6	4.9	0.6	0.4	1.0	1.3

* Data for 1989 refer to 1990.

Source: Authors' analysis of Federal Reserve Board (2004b) and Economagic (2004).

Liabilities

An examination of the other side of the balance sheet—liabilities—reveals the increase in household debt in 2003. As **Table 4.13** indicates, in 2003 the total value of all forms of outstanding household debt was 18.3% of all assets. Mortgage debt equaled 85% of total disposable income, and consumer credit debt (mostly credit-card debt) was almost one-quarter of total disposable income.

Debt levels in 2003 were at historic highs. **Figure 4Ka** graphs all debt and mortgage debt as a share of disposable personal income from 1947 to 2003. All debt rose from about 20% of disposable personal income at the end of World War II to over 60% by the early 1960s. Overall debt levels then remained roughly constant through the mid-1980s, when they began to increase rapidly again. By 2003, overall debt was 114.5% of annual disposable income. In 1947 mortgage debt was about 16% of all debt, but by 2003 that share had increased to 74%. Home equity loans have increased along with consumer credit, as shown in Figure **4Kb**, indicating that households were increasingly spending their accumulated equity rather than saving it.

FIGURE 4Ka Debt as a percentage of disposable personal income, 1947-2003

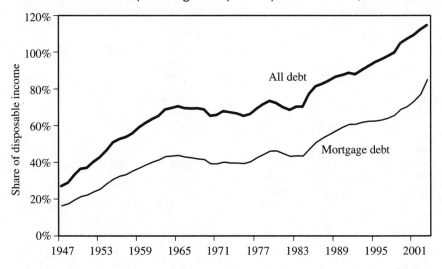

Source: Authors' analysis of Federal Reserve Board (2004c).

FIGURE 4Kb Debt as a percentage of disposable personal income, 1947-2003

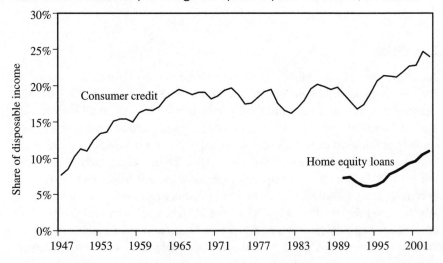

Source: Authors' analysis of Federal Reserve Board (2004c).

Note: Data for home equity loans are unavailable prior to 1990.

FIGURE 4L Distribution of growth in debt, 1998-2001

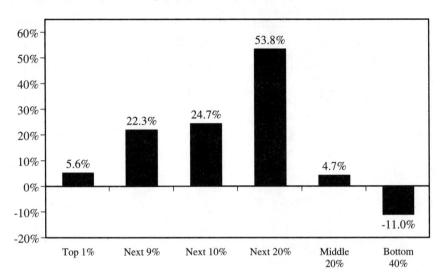

Source: Wolff (2004).

Although aggregate debt is now a more important feature of the household economy than at any time in modern history, aggregate data do not describe the distribution of the debt, which can be seen by revisiting Table 4.9. The debt distribution (described in the third section of Table 4.9) has several striking features. First, debt is more equally distributed than either assets or net worth. In 2001, for example, the average household in the top 1% had a net worth 168 times greater than that of a household in the middle 20%. In the same year, however, the average debt held by the top 1% was only five and a half times greater than the average for the middle 20%. Second, for typical households, debt levels are high compared to the value of assets. In 2001, the average outstanding debt of households in the middle 20% was $50,500 (typically mortgage debt plus credit-card debt). This debt level is about four times greater than the corresponding $12,000 average for stock holdings and about 45% of the total value of other assets such as the family home.

The data in Table 4.9 also illustrate how the increase in household debt was distributed among households of different wealth levels. **Figure 4L** divides the total increase in debt between 1998 and 2001 among households at different points in the wealth distribution. (The approach here is identical to that used in

TABLE 4.14 Household debt service burden,* 1980-2002
(as a percentage of disposable personal income)

	Total	Consumer	Mortgage
1980	12.9%	8.4%	4.5%
1989	13.6	7.6	6.0
1995	12.7	6.8	5.9
2000	13.9	7.8	6.1
2001	14.1	7.9	6.3
2002	14.0	7.8	6.2
Percentage-point change			
1980-89	13.4	7.5	5.9
1989-2000	0.3	0.2	0.1
2000-02	0.1	0.0	0.1

* Debt service consists of the estimated required payments on outstanding mortgage and consumer debt.

Source: Federal Reserve Board (2003).

Figure 4F, which looked at the distribution of growth in stock holdings.) As overall household debt increased, the share of debt held by the top 1% of households increased only slightly by 5.6%. Debt for the next 9% and next 10% grew by roughly 23% for each group. The brunt of the increase in debt was borne by the next 20% (or the second fifth of the distribution), as debt increased by 53.8% for this income group. Debt increased modestly for the middle class, by 4.7%, and debt decreased 11% for the bottom 40%.

Debt service

There is both good debt and bad debt; in and of itself, debt is not a problem for households. In fact, credit generally represents a tremendous economic opportunity for households, since they can use it to buy houses, cars, and other big-ticket consumer goods and necessities that provide services over many years. Debt can also be used to cope with short-term economic setbacks such as unemployment or illness or to make important investments in education or small businesses. Debt becomes a burden only when required debt payments begin to crowd out other economic obligations or opportunities.

Table 4.14 reproduces estimates from the Federal Reserve Board on the average household debt service burden (the minimum required payments on outstanding debt, as a share of household disposable income) from 1980 through

2002 (the latest data available). It is important to note that many households rent their homes, and this rent is not included as debt, although rent payments can easily be a very high share of disposable income. In addition, the Federal Reserve Board does not include as debt a plethora of costs incurred by low-income people who can not secure loans through traditional lending institutions. For example, leasing a car often becomes the only option for those who are unable to secure a car loan, but this is not considered debt. Or, to secure a loan, those with financial insecurity often have to turn to predatory lenders. Nontraditional lending services such as pawn shops and rapid-cash providers such as non-bank check-cashing services—which charge extraordinary fees compared to traditional lending institutions—constitute significant sources of "debt" for many low-income families.

As shown in Table 4.14, in 2002, minimum debt payments totaled about 14.0% of all household disposable income, and about half of these payments were for consumer debt (7.8% of disposable personal income). Mortgage payments made up another 6.2% of disposable income. Over the full period from 1980 to 2002, the debt service burden increased by only a small margin, which was perhaps surprising given that household debt levels rose so much over the same period. The main reason for the relatively constant debt service burden was the low nominal interest rates at the end of the 1990s and into the 2000s compared to the interest rates of the early 1980s. But with debt levels higher than they were 20 years ago, the household sector is more vulnerable now than in the past to rising interest rates.

However, the aggregate debt service figures in Table 4.14 do not show how debt service varies across households. **Table 4.15** shows household debt payments as a share of income for households at different income levels. (These numbers, also from the Federal Reserve Board, use a different underlying source of data than that used in Table 4.14. The definitions of payments and incomes also differ slightly. As a result, the aggregate numbers in Tables 4.14 and 4.15 do not match exactly.) In 2001 (the latest year for which data are available), households with annual incomes of $90,000-$100,000 spent 8.0% of their income meeting the minimum required debt payments, compared to 15.3% of income for those in households with less than $20,000 in annual income and 15.1% for middle-income groups (those in the $20,000-$39,999 range). Those paying the highest household debt service percentages were the three cohorts in the $40,000-$89,999 range, all of which had debt burdens just over 16%. Between 1998 and 2001, debt service burdens for all households fell, except for an increase of 0.1 percentage points for those in the $80,000-$89,999 range.

TABLE 4.15 Household debt service as a share of income by income level, 1992-2001 (percent of households)

Household income*	1992	1995	1998	2001	Percentage-point change 1992-2001	1998-2001
$90,000-100,000	11.2%	9.3%	10.2%	8.0%	-3.2	-2.2
$80,000-89,999	15.2	16.2	16.4	16.5	1.3	0.1
$60,000-79,999	16.3	17.4	18.5	16.3	0.0	-2.2
$40,000-59,999	15.5	14.9	17.8	16.5	1.0	-1.3
$20,000- 39,999	15.2	16.1	15.7	15.1	-0.1	-0.6
Less than $20,000	15.8	18.0	17.9	15.3	-0.5	-2.6
Average	14.0%	13.6%	14.4%	12.5%	-1.5	-1.9

* Constant 2001 dollars.

Source: Aizcorbe, Kennickell, and Moore (2003).

Hardship

Table 4.16 takes a slightly different look at the distribution of debt service payments by showing the share of each household income group that had debt service payments equal to more than 40% of household income, a level that is generally considered to represent economic hardship. In 2001, 16% of households in the $20,000-$39,999 range were making debt service payments in excess of 40% of their income, as were 27% of those in the less than $20,000 range. Between 1998 and 2001, the share of households facing high debt burdens decreased for all income ranges, with the exception of a 0.1 percentage-point increase for those in the $80,000-$89,999 range.

Table 4.17 shows another measure of the impact of debt on economic hardship: the share of households, by income level, that are late paying bills. In 2001, 7% (about one in 14) of all households were 60 days or more late in paying at least one bill. Not surprisingly, the share of households behind on their bills was strongly related to income. Very few (1.3%) of the highest income group were late in paying bills, while one in seven (13.4%) in the lowest income range were behind on at least one bill. Table 4.17 also illustrates a rise in the percentage of late-paying households between 1998 and 2001 for the lowest income groups (up 0.5 percentage points), while all other income cohorts had lower late-paying household percentages.

TABLE 4.16 Households with high debt burdens by income level, 1992-2001 (percent of households)

Household income*	1992	1995	1998	2001	Percentage-point change	
					1992-2001	1998-2001
$90,000 - 100,000	2.5%	2.0%	2.6%	2.0%	-0.5	-0.6
$80,000 - 89,999	2.9	4.6	3.4	3.5	0.6	0.1
$60,000 - 79,999	7.6	7.1	8.6	5.6	-2.0	-3.0
$40,000 - 59,999	10.1	8.1	15.3	11.7	1.6	-3.6
$20,000 - 39,999	15.1	16.0	17.2	16.0	0.9	-1.2
Less than $20,000	26.4	26.2	28.2	27.0	0.6	-1.2
Average	10.8%	10.6%	12.8%	11.0%	0.2	-1.8

* Constant 2001 dollars.

Source: Aizcorbe, Kennickell, and Moore (2003).

TABLE 4.17 Households late paying bills by income level, 1992-2001 (percent of households)

Household income*	1992	1995	1998	2001	Percentage-point change	
					1992-2001	1998-2001
$90,000 - 100,000	1.0%	1.0%	1.6%	1.3%	0.3	-0.3
$80,000 - 89,999	1.8	2.8	3.9	2.6	0.8	-1.3
$60,000 - 79,999	4.4	6.6	5.9	4.0	-0.4	-1.9
$40,000 - 59,999	6.9	8.7	10.0	7.9	1.0	-2.1
$20,000 - 39,999	9.3	10.1	12.3	11.7	2.4	-0.6
Less than $20,000	11.0	10.2	12.9	13.4	2.4	0.5
Average	6.0%	7.1%	8.1%	7.0%	1.0	-1.1

* Constant 2001 dollars.

Source: Aizcorbe, Kennickell, and Moore (2003).

FIGURE 4M Consumer bankruptcies per 1,000 adults, 1980-2003

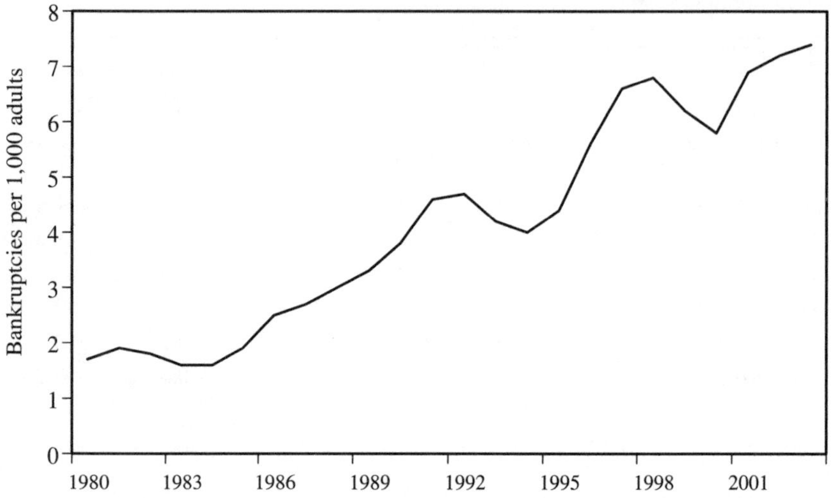

Note: Population figure for 2003 was estimated from the revised seasonally adjusted civilian CPS employment and civilian labor force data from the Bureau of Labor Statistics.

Source: Authors' analysis of American Bankruptcy Institute (2004).

The ultimate indicator of debt-related difficulties is personal bankruptcy. **Figure 4M** graphs the rate of personal bankruptcies from 1980 through 2003. In 2003, more than seven out of every 1,000 adults declared personal bankruptcy. Bankruptcy rates continued to increase throughout the weak recovery period that followed the 2001 recession.

Conclusion

In sum, this analysis reveals three distinct aspects of wealth in the United States. First, data presented here establish that the distribution of wealth is highly unequal, much more so than the distribution of wages and income. For instance, while stock ownership greatly affected net worth for some higher-wealth households, a majority of households held either no stock or very small amounts of stock, and were therefore largely unaffected by stock market fluctuations.

Second, there have been gains in wealth and asset holdings for all income classes, although the gains are concentrated at the top of the wealth distribution. However, more middle-income households are better prepared for retirement than they use to be. Also, between 1998 and 2001 there was a decrease in the percentage of households with extremely low net wealth. These latest data show that middle-class households gained more in average wealth than they gained in average debt between 1998 and 2001. However, almost 18% of households had zero or negative net worth in 2001, and it is middle- and lower-income households that are more apt to have high debt burdens.

The inequality of debt burdens is indicative of the third important characteristic regarding wealth: there is plenty of room to improve wealth, asset, and debt distributions by class, race, and other socioeconomic characteristics. Although there were some significant improvements in wealth and asset holdings by race—such as home ownership rates that went from 42.9% in 1989 to 48.1% in 2003 for black households—it is still the fact that less than half of all black households actually own their own homes. Hence, race and other socioeconomic characteristics continue to be critical factors that exacerbate the skewed distribution of wealth in the United States.

Poverty: rising in this business cycle

While the United States is the richest of the industrialized nations, it has always, to a greater or lesser degree over time, suffered the problem of poverty amidst prosperity. In recent decades, the growth of inequality has meant that much of the nation's economic growth was channeled to higher-income families, while incomes at the bottom stagnated. For example, the official poverty rate—the share of Americans living in households with incomes below the federal poverty threshold—was about the same in 1973 (11.1%) as in 2000 (11.3%), despite the fact that real per capita income grew 66% over that period.

To some, the fact that more than one-tenth of the population—12.5% or 35.9 million persons in 2003—faces material deprivation may be disheartening, but not particularly alarming. But many poverty analysts believe that the official poverty statistics underestimate the extent of material hardship in America. The thresholds used to determine poverty status were developed almost half a century ago, and have been updated only for inflation. They are widely criticized for failing to represent either the changing needs of the population or rising relative incomes. As a benchmark for what is needed to avoid material deprivation in America, the thresholds are unrealistically low. In 2003, for example, a single parent with two children was officially considered poor if the family income (before taxes but counting cash transfers like welfare benefits) was below $14,824; for two parents with two children, the income threshold was $18,660. The income concept used by the Census Bureau (which leaves out the effect of taxes, near-cash benefits, and necessary expenses, such as child care, incurred by working families) represents an incomplete measure of the resources available to families to meet their consumption needs.

This chapter thus uses various alternative measures to expand the scope of the analysis. One useful measure simply doubles the poverty thresholds. This seems arbitrary—if the official thresholds are so inferior, what do we gain by doubling them? However, the authors' own work on family budgets reveals that twice the poverty thresholds corresponds closely to more rigorously defined measures of a family's ability to meet its basic needs. These budget thresholds are developed by adding up the costs of basic consumption components, including food, shelter, clothing, health care, taxes, and child care (for working families). The fact that these measures generate family budget poverty rates that are close to the rates of families at or below twice the official poverty line gives some validity to this measure.

For example, consider the so-called "fair-market rent" (FMR) in various cities relative to the poverty threshold. These data are developed by the U.S. Department of Housing and Urban Development for its Section 8 housing assistance program, and typically capture the rental value of two-bedroom apartments at the 40th percentile of the rent distribution. In much family budget work, these values serve as reliable proxies for what low-income families need to spend for housing of acceptable quality. In Boston in 2001, the FMR was 65% of the poverty threshold for a family of four, and 82% for a family of three. In Los Angeles, the comparable percentages were 52% and 66%; in Detroit, 44% and 56%. These percentages imply that, according to the official poverty thresholds, poor families have to pay impossibly high shares of their income on housing, leaving far too little to meet their other consumption needs. However, once we double the poverty thresholds, and thus halve the shares devoted to rent, families under these thresholds have a much better chance of paying for their other necessities, including food, health care, and child care.

For a number of good reasons, though, we cannot ignore the official measure. First, it has a long history, and many informative time-series analyses use that metric. Second, while the official statistics omit many families whose incomes are arguably insufficient to meet their basic needs, those statistics are certainly informative about the most economically disadvantaged families. Thus, we examine numerous measures of material deprivation, a strategy that enables us to view poverty through a broader lens than would be the case if we were restricted to only the official measure.

Regardless of the metric, a few trends emerge clearly from the data that follow. First, impressive progress against poverty in the 1960s stalled in the early 1970s to the mid-1990s. The 1995-2000 period was one of dramatic progress, as poverty fell by 2.5 percentage points, and twice-poverty fell by 4.3 points (corresponding to 4.8 million fewer poor and 8.6 million fewer "near-poor" persons). The 2001 recession and the jobless recovery that followed partially reversed these gains.

As is always the case in a recession, the ranks of the poor and near-poor expanded in the recent downturn, as poverty rates rose from 11.3% in 2000 to 12.5% in 2003, while twice-poverty rates rose from 29.3% to 31.1%. These rate increases translate into over 4 million more officially poor and over 8 million more near-poor over this three-year period. At the same time, the social safety net was somewhat less effective at catching those economically vulnerable families hurt by the recession. Among low-income single-mother families, for example, welfare benefits, which fell steeply throughout the latter 1990s, continued to slide in the recession, thus failing to play their historical counter-cyclical role. What's more, the slowing economy led to significant reductions in the hours of work by these women, and that drop led to lower earnings and less income from the earned income tax credit (EITC), a generous wage subsidy that is key to lifting the incomes of low-income, working families. In this regard, for some groups of poor and near-poor persons the safety net is less counter-cyclical than it used to be. A related finding is that the EITC fails to reach many families between the one- and two-times poverty range.

One factor that has been implicated to explain the lack of progress against poverty over the past 30 years is the increase in mother-only families, who at any given point in time have considerably lower income and higher poverty rates than families with two earners (see Chapter 1). While this argument has some merit, the upward pressure on poverty rates by the formation of single-parent families has diminished considerably over time, while the economic determinants—growth, inequality, and unemployment—have, if anything, grown more important. Over the 1970s, for example, had all else remained constant, the shift to mother-only families would have contributed two percentage points to the poverty rate (in fact, poverty fell slightly over the decade). But the effect of mother-only families fell steeply after that, and so by the 1990s this factor contributed only 0.3 points to higher poverty.

Far more important in explaining the lack of progress against poverty is the role of inequality and weak low-wage labor markets. Over the 1980s, when poverty rates were particularly unresponsive to growth, the effect of inequality was to drive poverty up by 2.9 percentage points (poverty rose 1.1 points over the decade because other factors, such as the improved education of low-income family heads, offset the inequality effect). That effect was significantly dampened in the 1990s, but it appears poised to return in the current business cycle, creating potentially strong headwinds against poverty reduction.

As regards low-wage labor markets, the fast productivity growth of the latter 1990s combined with low unemployment gave a significant boost to the earnings of low-wage workers. But by itself, fast economic growth is unlikely to move the wages of the lowest-paid workers. In the last five years of the 1980s cycle, productivity grew 1.5% per year, but average unemployment was high—6.4%. As a result of a labor market too slack to ensure growth in the wages of low-wage workers, the real wages of this group barely budged. By contrast, over the last five years of the 1990s business cycle, productivity grew a point faster per year (2.5%), and, equally important, average unemployment was 4.8%. Under these conditions, 20th percentile real wages grew as employers needed to bid up even low wages to get and keep the workers they needed to meet strong demand in these years. In fact, low wages grew at almost the rate of productivity, an unprecedented trend over the last 30 years.

The most recent trends in low wages corroborate the view that fast productivity growth alone will not suffice to fuel the growth of low wages. Between 2001 and 2003, productivity grew far more quickly than in the earlier periods mentioned above. Yet unemployment was high, on average, compared to the latter half of the 1990s. Under these conditions, the extra income generated by the fast growth of productivity did not flow to low-wage workers, as earnings growth at the 20th percentile slowed to 0.5% per year.

Thus, we conclude that it takes a combination of fast growth and very low unemployment to ensure that the benefits of growth are distributed broadly enough to connect the fortunes of the poor with those of the rest of working America. At the same time, we need to be mindful of the historically important role of an effective safety net in a dynamic economy in which business cycle downturns can do great damage to the living standards of the most economically vulnerable.

The trends and the composition of poverty and near-poverty

In 2003, the poverty rate stood at 12.5% and the twice-poverty rate was 31.1%, meaning that 35.9 million persons were officially poor and 89.7 million lived in households with income less than two times their poverty threshold (**Table 5.1** and **Figure 5A**). As is often the case, the ranks of the poor and near-poor expanded in the recent downturn, as poverty rates rose from 11.3% in 2000 to 12.5% in 2003, while twice-poverty rates rose from 29.3% to 31.1%. These rate increases translate into over 4 million more officially poor and over 8 million more near-poor over this two-year period. Chapter 1 explored the factors that lead to income losses in a recession, particularly the decline of labor market income. Since poverty status is a function of income, the same factors hold here as well.

Figure 5B quantifies the effect of labor market income by simulating the impact of different unemployment trends than those that actually occurred over the boom and recent bust. Specifically, we construct a simple statistical model

TABLE 5.1 Percent and number of persons in poverty and twice poverty, 1959-2002

Year	Poverty rate	Number in poverty (in thousands)	Twice-poverty rate	Number in twice-poverty (in thousands)
1959	22.4%	39,490		
1967	14.2	27,769		
1973	11.1	22,973		
1979	11.7	26,072	31.3%	70,501
1989	12.8	31,528	31.4	78,150
1995	13.8	36,425	33.6	89,642
2000	11.3	31,581	29.3	81,026
2003	12.5	35,861	31.1	89,655
Averages over business cycles				
1959-67	19.1%	35,505		
1967-73	12.5	25,102		
1973-79	11.6	24,641		
1979-89	13.6	31,954	33.7%	79,724
1989-2000	13.5	35,295	32.6	86,236
1989-95	14.1	36,083	33.5	86,760
1995-2000	12.8	34,563	31.6	86,193
2000-2003	11.9	33,730	30.3	85,770

Source: U.S. Bureau of the Census.
For detailed information on table source, see Table Notes.

that adequately predicts poverty rates given trends in unemployment, productivity, and inequality (the roles of these variables on poverty trends are examined in greater detail later in the chapter). The first two bars show the actual 2.5 percentage-point fall in poverty between 1995 and 2000; the third bar shows a simulated rate based on the assumption that unemployment, instead of falling from 5.6% in 1995 to 4.0% in 2000, stayed at 5.6% over these years. Poverty still declines under this scenario, but by less than half as much (1.1 points instead of 2.5). Had unemployment not risen in 2001 and 2002, poverty would have ticked up only slightly over these years, by 0.1 percentage points instead of 0.8. Though we do not yet have poverty data for 2003, unemployment went up slightly in that year as well, from 5.8% in 2002 to 6.0%, suggesting that poverty may have nudged up further in 2003 as well.

The trend in poverty shown in Figure 5A reveals two fairly distinct periods. The first runs from 1959 to 1973, when the poverty rate fell by half, from about 22% to about 11%. From 1973 on, however, the poverty rate moves in a gener-

FIGURE 5A Poverty and twice-poverty rates, 1959-2003

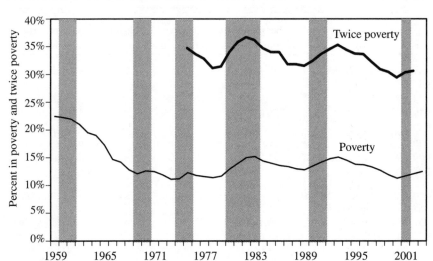

Note: Periods of recession are shaded.

Source: U.S. Bureau of the Census. For detailed information on figure sources, see Figure Notes.

ally cyclical manner, ending up in 2000 just about where it started, at 11.3%. Yet, despite the downward drift in the business cycles of the 1970s and 1980s, the poverty rate trend appears only moderately responsive to growth, certainly less so than the twice-poverty measure. Table 5.1 shows that poverty rates grew successively higher in the business cycle peaks of 1973, 1979, and 1989, implying a structural (as opposed to cyclical) increase in poverty over time. The bottom part of the table shows that poverty rates averaged two percentage points higher in the 1980s than in the 1973-79 period, and a half percentage point higher in the early 1990s than in the 1980s. Rising poverty rates in 1989-95 gave way to a steep decline in 1995-2000.

Have we reached a limit as to how much we can hope to reduce poverty rates, or is there something unique about these last few decades that has weakened the link between economic growth and poverty? We explore this question throughout the chapter, and it seems that the absence of full employment and the presence of growing inequality over these years is part of the answer.

We have fewer years of data for the twice-poverty rate, but the available data show that it is somewhat more responsive to growth, falling further during booms and rising more in busts. When the labor market moved toward full employment

FIGURE 5B Actual and simulated poverty rates under different unemployment trends, 1995-2002

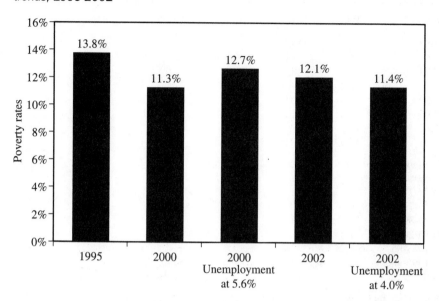

Source: Authors' analysis of U.S. Bureau of the Census and BLS data.

in the latter half of the 1990s, the twice-poverty rate fell by 4.3 percentage points, while poverty fell by 2.5 points; conversely, poverty is up 1.2 points since 2000 while twice-poverty is up 1.8 points. Part of this trend is attributable to the fact that this group is more connected to the labor market, and thus more susceptible to its ups and downs. But we also see evidence here of the fact that the safety net—the system of cash and near-cash transfer intended to dampen the effect of recessions—fails to reach many families in the twice-poverty category.

Table 5.2—poverty rates for persons by race—shows that poverty rates for minorities are higher at any given point in time than those for whites, but that they have also been much more responsive to growth and recession (**Figure 5C** plots these series over time). Rates for African Americans are historically the highest, though Hispanic rates (unavailable for 1959 and 1967) rose more quickly than the other groups during the 1980s, in part due to increased immigration of low-income Hispanic families over this period. Yet the gains made by minorities over the 1990s, particularly the latter 1990s, were extraordinary. Between 1995 and 2000, poverty fell by 6.8 points among African Americans and by 8.8 points among Hispanics.

TABLE 5.2 Persons in poverty by race/ethnicity, 1959-2003

Year	Total	White	Black	Hispanic
1959	22.4%	18.1%	n.a.	n.a.
1967	14.2	11.0	39.3%	n.a.
1973	11.1	8.4	31.4	21.9%
1979	11.7	9.0	31.0	21.8
1989	12.8	10.0	30.7	26.2
1995	13.8	11.2	29.3	30.3
2000	11.3	9.5	22.5	21.5
2003	12.5	10.5	24.4	22.5
Percentage-point changes				
1959-67	-8.2	-7.1	n.a.	n.a.
1967-73	-3.1	-2.6	-7.9	n.a.
1973-79	0.6	0.6	-0.4	-0.1
1979-89	1.1	1.0	-0.3	4.4
1989-2000	-1.5	-0.5	-8.2	-4.7
1989-95	1.0	1.2	-1.4	4.1
1995-2000	-2.5	-1.7	-6.8	-8.8
2000-02	1.2	1.0	1.9	1.0

Source: U.S. Bureau of the Census.

FIGURE 5C Poverty rates by race/ethnicity, 1973-2003

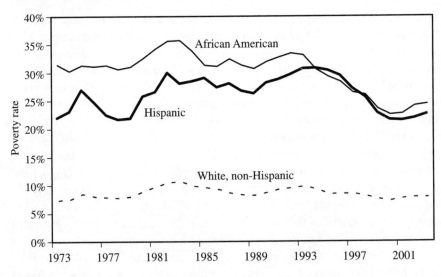

Source: U.S. Bureau of the Census; see also Chapman and Bernstein (2002).

The 1995-2000 Hispanic trend is particularly notable as it regards the impact of immigration. The influx of poor, low-skilled immigrants is one factor leading to higher poverty rates, but it is often mistakenly elevated as a key determinant explaining the lack of progress against poverty over the last few decades. However, the fact that Hispanic rates fell 3.5 times faster than the overall rate from 1995 to 2000 reveals that, when the tide rises quickly enough, most boats can be lifted, even those dominated by immigrants. More formal analysis of this question shows that the poverty-reducing growth of immigrant incomes over this period far surpassed poverty-increasing effects of the increase in the immigrant population.

The larger-than-average decline in minority poverty led to a closing of the gap between poverty rates for whites and minorities (Figure 5C). In 1989, the incidence of black poverty was 3.7 times that for non-Hispanic whites; for Hispanics, the ratio was 3.2-to-1. By 2000, the gap had closed to 2.9-to-1 for blacks (the lowest on record) and 2.8-to-1 for Hispanics.

Figure 5D provides data since 1995 on the twice-poverty rate by race/ethnicity. Most white and Asian families (about three-quarters in 2002) have incomes above twice-poverty. But even with the positive trend of the latter 1990s, about half of African American and Hispanic families have incomes below this threshold, suggesting that half of minority populations are likely to have some difficulties meeting their basic consumptions needs. As noted, the decline for minorities in twice-poverty in the 1995-2000 period was significant, and even larger than that shown in the previous table. Thus, while incomes grew relatively quickly for poor minority families over this period, they grew even more quickly for minority families between one- and two-times poverty.

The recent recession had a far more negative effect on African American poverty rates than on rates for whites (a predictable outcome) or, surprisingly, Hispanics. In fact, Hispanic rates rose much less than average in the 2000-02 period (0.3 points versus 0.8 for poverty, and 0.4 points versus 1.2 for twice-poverty). More research is needed to explain this result for Hispanics, but it is likely related to the relatively better labor market outcomes for Hispanics over this period (see Chapter 3). More typically, because of more precarious labor market status and lower average incomes among minorities, minority poverty tends to rise more in downturns than it does for whites, as shown in the figure. In the deeper recession of the early 1980s (actually two recessions with only a year between them), rates for blacks and Hispanics rose 3.2 and 2.3 percentage points, respectively, while rates for whites went up 1.7 points (1980-83). We look more closely at the factors behind the increase in poverty over the downturn in a later section focusing on single-mother families.

This discussion of trends and point changes can obscure the important and persistent gap in the level of minority poverty rates compared to those of whites.

FIGURE 5D Twice-poverty by race/ethnicity, 1995-2002

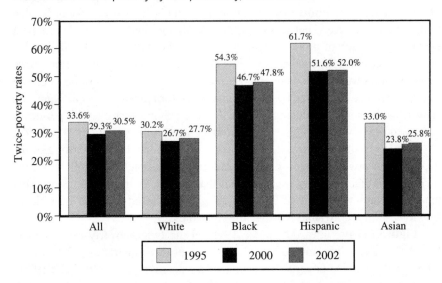

Source: Authors' analysis of March CPS data.

As can be seen in Figure 5C, though highly favorable economic conditions narrowed the gap between minorities and whites, even in 2000 considerable space remained between the trend lines. And in that peak year, more than one-fifth of each of these populations were poor. Given the inadequacy of the poverty line as a measure of deprivation, the fact that so many minority families were poor at the end of the longest and strongest recovery since the 1960s provides a stark reminder of the urgency of the poverty problem.

This sense of urgency is heightened when we examine child poverty. Given the importance of adequate income during a child's formative years, the high poverty rates for children in the U.S. has long been considered a far greater socioeconomic problem here than in other advanced nations, where child poverty is lower (**Table 5.3**; see Chapter 7 for international poverty comparisons).

In 2003, 17.6% (almost 13 million) of the nation's children (persons less than age 18) were poor. Since the damage done by child poverty is particularly severe for younger children, we examine the rates for children under 6 as well, and these are consistently higher than the overall child rates. In 2003, 20.1% of children (4.4 million) under 6 were poor, and the rates for minorities were far higher: 35.7% for young black children and 29.1% for Hispanics (these values are for 2002).

TABLE 5.3 Percent of children in poverty by race, 1979-2003

Year	Total	White	Black	Hispanic
Children under 18				
1979	16.4%	11.8%	41.2%	28.0%
1989	19.6	14.8	43.7	36.2
1995	20.8	16.2	41.9	40.0
2000	16.2	13.1	31.2	28.4
2003	17.6	14.3	34.1	29.7
Percentage-point changes				
1979-1989	3.2	3.0	2.5	8.2
1989-2000	-3.4	-1.7	-12.5	-7.8
1989-95	1.2	1.4	-1.8	3.8
1995-2000	-4.6	-3.1	-10.7	-11.6
2000-03	1.4	1.2	2.9	1.3
Children under 6				
1979	18.1%	13.3%	43.6%	29.2%
1989	22.5	16.9	49.8	38.8
1995	24.1	18.6	49.2	42.8
2000	17.2	14.1	32.9	28.9
2002	18.8	15.4	36.8	29.1
2003	20.1	n.a.	n.a.	n.a.
Percentage-point changes				
1979-1989	4.4	3.6	6.2	9.6
1989-2000	-5.3	-2.8	-16.9	-9.9
1989-95	1.6	1.7	-0.6	4.0
1995-2000	-6.9	-4.5	-16.3	-13.9
2000-03	2.9	1.4	3.9	0.2

Source: U.S. Bureau of the Census.

Most recently, child poverty trended up after falling steeply, particularly for minorities, in the latter 1990s. Poverty among African American and Hispanic children fell by 10.7 and 11.6 percentage points from 1995 to 2000, with even faster declines among younger children. The rate for black children in 2000—31.2%—is the lowest recorded rate for this group since these data were first collected in the mid-1970s. For Hispanic children, the large decline after 1995 brought them back to just above their 1979 rate. Yet here again the data reveal positive trends but disappointingly high levels. The most recent data show that more than one-third of black children and about three out of every 10 Hispanic children were poor in 2002.

TABLE 5.4 Family poverty by race/ethnicity of family head and for different family types, 1959-2003

	Race/ethnicity of family head:				Families with children:	
	All	White	Black	Hispanic	Married couples	Female head
1959	18.5%	15.2%	n.a.	n.a.	n.a.	59.9%
1967	11.4	9.1	33.9%	n.a.	n.a.	44.5
1973	8.8	6.6	28.1	19.8%	n.a.	43.2
1979	9.2	6.9	27.8	20.3	6.1%	39.6
1989	10.3	7.8	27.8	23.4	7.3	42.8
1995	10.8	8.5	26.4	27.0	7.5	41.5
2000	8.7	7.1	19.3	19.2	6.0	33.0
2003	10.0	8.1	22.3	20.8	7.0	35.5
Percentage-point changes						
1959-73	-9.7	-8.6	n.a.	n.a.	n.a.	-16.7
1973-79	0.4	0.3	-0.3	0.5	n.a.	-3.6
1979-89	1.1	0.9	0.0	3.1	1.2	3.2
1989-2000	-1.6	-0.7	-8.5	-4.2	-1.3	-9.8
1989-95	0.5	0.7	-1.4	3.6	0.2	-1.3
1995-2000	-2.1	-1.4	-7.1	-7.8	-1.5	-8.5
2000-03	1.3	1.0	3.0	1.6	1.0	2.5

Source: U.S. Bureau of the Census.

Child poverty rates are fully a function of a family's income. **Table 5.4** shifts the unit of observation from persons to families, which in Census terminology refers to two or more persons related through blood, marriage, or adoption (i.e., one-person units are excluded). In general, family poverty rates are lower than poverty rates for persons, reflecting both the relatively high number of poor children and unrelated individuals included in the person counts.

The patterns over time are similar to those shown in the previous tables, with consistently increasing rates of family poverty at business cycle peaks from 1973 to 1989. The poverty rates for African American families were essentially unchanged over these years at about 28%. Over the 1990s, however, they fell by 8.5 percentage points; the 2000 rate of 19.3% is the lowest on record and the first time poverty for black families fell below 20%. Poverty among Hispanic families grew sharply, by 3.6 points, through 1995, but thereafter reversed course and fell even more quickly than the rate for blacks; by 2000, Hispanics too posted the lowest rate on record.

Between 2000 and 2003, family poverty rose by 1.3 percentage points overall. For African Americans, family poverty rates went up by more than twice that amount—3 points—while Hispanic rates rose 1.6 points. This table also presents data on two family types with children: married couples and families headed by a single mother. The latter, on whom we focus later in the chapter, experienced the largest decline in family poverty rates between 1995 and 2000 and a slightly lower-than-average increase in the downturn. Below, we explore this finding in the context of how labor market opportunities evolved over the boom and bust for these single mothers. Married-couple families consistently have the lowest rates in the table—only 6% of such families were poor at the peak year of 2000.

We now turn to two measures of the depth of poverty: the poverty gap and the share of the poor with incomes less than half the poverty threshold, i.e., the deeply impoverished.

Since a poverty threshold is a fixed-income level, families are considered poor whether they are one dollar or a thousand dollars below the poverty line. Thus, another useful way to gauge the depth of poverty is the "poverty gap": the average income deficit (the dollar gap between a poor family's income and its poverty threshold) experienced by poor families or individuals.

Figure 5E plots both family poverty rates and the average family poverty gap. Over the 1960s through the mid-1970s, both the poverty rate and the poverty gap declined, meaning that fewer families were poor and, of those who were, were on average less poor over time. The strong labor market, along with the expansion of cash transfers over this period, including both Social Security (which significantly reduced the poverty of the elderly) and welfare benefits, contributed to these trends. As shown in **Table 5.5**, the average family poverty gap fell 0.8% annually over this period, and twice that much for individuals.

Both family poverty and the poverty gap rose steeply over the recessionary period in the early 1980s, and, as shown in the figure, the two series diverged in the mid-1980s. In fact, the growth rates in the bottom section of the table reveal that the poverty gap has risen consistently over business cycle peaks. Thus, while the 1973 and 2000 poverty rates were about the same (8.8% in 1973 and 8.6% in 2000), the average poor family was over $1,281 (2003 dollars) worse off at the end of the period.

The poverty gap series shows an interesting divergence from much of the trends observed thus far in that it shows no improvement over the latter 1990s. In fact, the average poor family was slightly worse off in 2000 than in 1995 (this was more so the case for the average poor individual). This finding suggests that the families who exited poverty over this period were those whose incomes placed

FIGURE 5E Family poverty gap and family poverty rates, 1959-2003

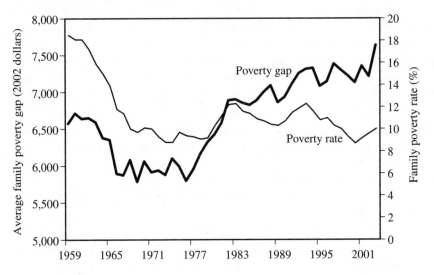

Source: Authors' analysis of U.S. Bureau of the Census data.

TABLE 5.5 Average poverty gap, 1967-2003 (2003 dollars)

Years	Families	Persons not in families
1959	$6,715	$4,462
1973	6,005	3,555
1979	6,453	3,575
1989	7,010	4,066
1995	7,237	4,509
2000	7,286	4,687
2003	7,627	5,024
Annual growth rates		
1959-73	-0.8%	-1.6%
1973-79	1.2	0.1
1979-89	0.8	1.3
1989-2000	0.4	1.3
1989-95	0.5	1.7
1995-2000	0.1	0.8
2000-03	1.5	2.3

Source: U.S. Bureau of the Census data.

FIGURE 5F   Percent of the poor below half the poverty line

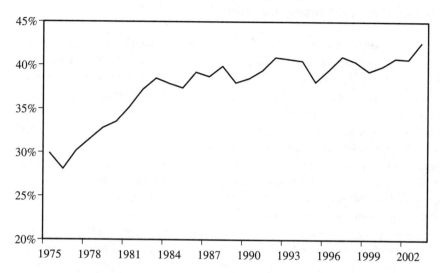

Source: U.S. Bureau of the Census.

them closer to the poverty threshold, leaving behind the least well-off among the poor, and raising the average poverty gap. **Figure 5F**, the share of the poor below half the poverty line, corroborates this interpretation. For a family of four with two children, this threshold amounted to $9,330 in 2003. After increasing from around 30% to around 40% through the 1980s, the share of the deeply poor has changed little, reinforcing the notion that the poor of today have lower average income levels than the poor in earlier periods. Note also the sharp uptick in the most recent year, 2003, as the share of deeply poor rose by about 2 percentage points, the largest one-year jump since 1982. Below, we examine the extent to which safety net programs have reduced the poverty gap over time.

To some extent, the trend toward poorer families within the poverty population is to be expected, given the strong shift of public policy toward work instead of cash assistance. The families most able to take advantage of both the strong labor market of the latter 1990s and the income supports tied to work, like the EITC, were likely to both climb out of poverty and do so from relatively close to the income threshold. Those left behind are probably the least likely to be able to take advantage of either a strong market economy or work-based supports.

We now turn to a more comprehensive examination of this shift in policy and its impact on poverty.

Recent trends in poverty and near-poverty:
the 1990s and the recent downturn

In the latter 1990s, the movement toward full employment boosted incomes and reduced the income gap between middle- and low-income families. As discussed in the previous section, tight labor markets and broad-based wage growth reduced poverty, particularly among minorities. **Table 5.6** examines these years more closely by tracking poverty and twice-poverty among working-age families (families headed by someone age 25-54), with children, under different income definitions. We focus on such families because, unlike, for example, elderly families who are less connected to the labor market, their incomes should be most responsive to the boom of the latter 1990s and the recession/jobless recovery that followed. In later analysis, we offer a more detailed examination of the poverty-reducing effects of taxes and transfers over time. Here, we are largely interested in earnings and earnings-related transfers, such as the EITC.

Table 5.6 shows that, while poverty rates based solely on earnings for prime-age families with children are higher than official rates, both poverty and twice-poverty fell further under this income definition between 1995 and 2000 than under the official income measure. Official poverty fell 3.4 percentage points (5.1 for twice-poverty), while poverty based solely on earnings fell 4.6 points (5.9 for twice-poverty). Adding the EITC reduces the level of poverty at each point in time. For example, in 1995, the refundable credit reduced the share of persons in these families who were poor based on earnings alone from 19.3% to 16.9%. Note, however, that the reduction in poverty from 1995 to 2000 based on earnings (and earnings plus the EITC) is greater in columns 2 and 3 compared to column 4, which includes cash and near-cash transfers (-4.6 and -4.7 compared to -3.0). This difference is a result of declining transfers over this period, a subject discussed below. Taking all these income sources together leads to a reduction in earnings-based poverty, as shown in the final column. In 2002, for example, taxes and transfers lowered poverty rates by 5.9 percentage points, less than in 1995 (6.6 points) but more than in 2000 (4.9).

In terms of twice-poverty, the difference between columns 2 and 3 suggests that the EITC has almost no effect on twice-poverty rates. This is a function of the rules of the policy, which cause its benefits to fade as incomes move toward twice the poverty threshold. Thus, the tax credit as structured provides little aid to these near-poor families, despite the fact that the gap between their incomes and their needs means they are often constrained in their spending on necessities like rent, food, transportation, or child care.

In fact, as shown in the last column, for the twice-poverty group, taking account of the full spate of income sources and taxes actually leads to higher

TABLE 5.6 Prime-age families (household head age 25-54) with children, poverty and twice-poverty by various income definitions

	(1) Official	(2) Earnings only	(3) Earnings +EITC	(4) After tax +other inc. sources	(4)-(2)
Poverty					
1995	15.0%	19.3%	16.9%	12.7%	-6.6
2000	11.6	14.6	12.2	9.7	-4.9
2002	12.2	15.9	13.1	10.0	-5.9
1995-2000	-3.4	-4.6	-4.7	-3.0	1.6
2000-02	0.6	1.2	0.8	0.3	-0.9
Twice-poverty					
1995	35.1%	39.2%	39.0%	42.9%	3.8
2000	30.0	33.2	32.9	35.9	2.7
2002	31.4	34.7	34.3	36.7	2.1
1995-2000	-5.1	-5.9	-6.0	-7.0	-1.1
2000-02	1.4	1.4	1.3	0.8	-0.6

Source: Authors' analysis of March CPS data.

poverty rates, though less so over time. In 1995, 35.1% of prime-age families with children had incomes below two times their poverty threshold; after taxes and other income sources, that rate rose to 42.9%, presumably because these families had positive tax liabilities and their incomes were too high for most means-tested transfers. Thanks to the progressive tax system, this effect diminished as incomes fell in the recession, and the increase in twice-poverty after taxes was held to 2.1 points in 2002.

One particular family type—the mother-only family—has been the focus of much attention regarding poverty policy. Over the 1990s low-income single mothers, defined here as those with incomes below two times the poverty threshold, sharply increased their hours in the paid labor market, along with their earnings. Pulled by the tightening of the job market, the higher value of the minimum wage, and an expanded EITC, and pushed by welfare reform, increasing numbers of single mothers went to work. Their earnings, including the EITC, grew quickly over this period, while their welfare income declined sharply.

Figure 5G plots the annual changes in some key variables regarding income growth over the recent boom and ensuing downturn. Note first the annual

FIGURE 5G Labor market and real income trends for low-income single mothers, 1994-2002

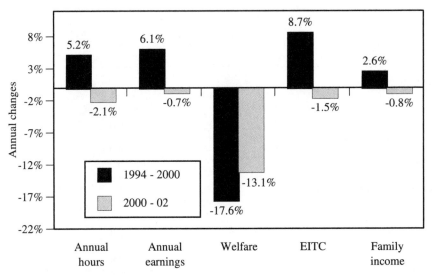

Source: Authors' analysis of March CPS data.

5.2% increase in hours worked per year by low-income single mothers between 1994 and 2000, a sharp gain in hours worked. As shown in **Figure 5H**, the annual hours worked by these women rose from about 900 per year in 1994 to over 1,200 six years later, in 2000, an increase of 320 hours per year. This amounts to two more months of full-time work, a historically large shift over a relatively short time period. In contrast, among married mothers we see no upward trend at all, supporting the notion that policies such as the expanded EITC, a higher minimum wage, and welfare reform made a real difference in the labor supply of single mothers. In fact, by the end of the period, single mothers were working more hours per year than married mothers.

Turning back to Figure 5G, real annual earnings grew even more quickly than hours between 1994 and 2000, implying a rising hourly wage (this pace of earnings growth was three times that of low-income married mothers). Yet, while hours and earnings were rising, real income from welfare was falling at double-digit rates. On the other hand, EITC benefits grew even faster than earnings. Putting it all together, real income rose 2.6% per year between 1994 and 2000 for low-income single mothers, a trend that helps to explain the decline in their poverty rates (shown in Table 5.4).

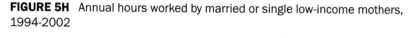

FIGURE 5H Annual hours worked by married or single low-income mothers, 1994-2002

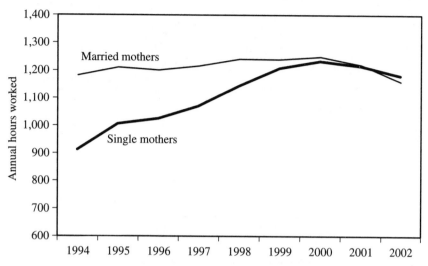

Source: Authors' analysis of March CPS data.

Figure 5I, which shows the levels behind these trends, reveals that the average real income of this group grew from about $14,000 to $16,300 (2002 dollars) from 1994 to 2000, driven by increases in earnings and EITC benefits that outpaced welfare losses (the relatively large "other" category includes income from other family members and from other cash transfers, like Social Security; it shows little change). The stacked bars in the figure show the diminished role of welfare benefits and the increased role of earnings and the EITC.

As Figure 5G showed, low-income single-mother families lost ground between 2000 and 2002, as their real income fell 0.8%, losing $245 in income. Their welfare benefits continued to decline sharply, at 13.1% per year, implying that this aspect of the safety net did not serve to catch those hurt by the downturn. Equally important is the fact that real EITC income also declined over these years. This important wage subsidy is tied to work, and the decline in labor market activity experienced by these mothers meant the loss of EITC dollars as well as welfare income. As shown in Figure 5I, another component of safety net income, unemployment insurance compensation, expanded in the downturn, replacing some of the income lost. But despite the fact that the average real income from UI more than doubled, from $110 in 2000 to $279 in

FIGURE 5I   Income components for low-income single mothers, 1994-2002

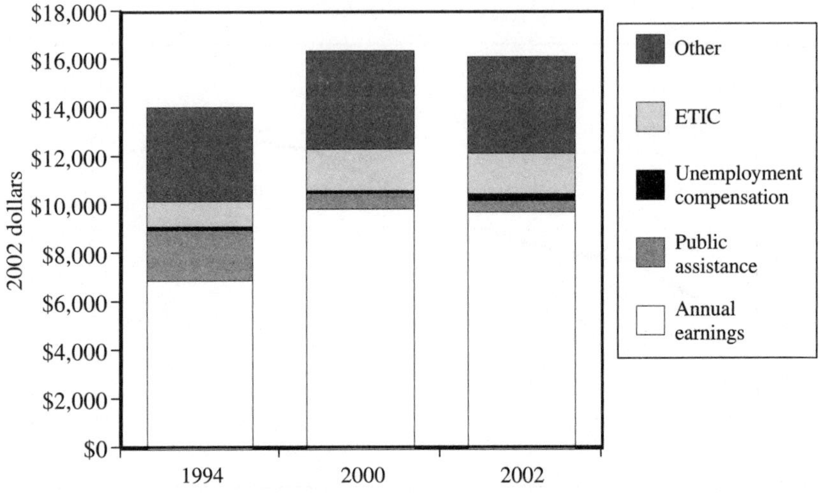

Source: Authors' analysis of March CPS data.

2002, that $169 increase was almost wholly offset by the $160 decline in welfare benefits.

These three figures combine to show that, despite prodigious work effort, low-income single mothers lost ground over the downturn. As revealed in Chapter 1, they were not alone: other families lost ground as well, including the median family, at a rate similar to these families. And the safety net, a set of policies designed to protect economically vulnerable families when the economy stumbles, failed to prevent their incomes from falling. It helped a bit—welfare benefits fell more slowly over these two years and UI provided some extra cash to job losers—but not enough to reverse the loss in earnings. We look more closely at this issue below.

Poverty, growth, and the inequality wedge

As shown in Figure 5A, despite some periods of intermittent progress, the United States has made few long-term gains against poverty since the mid-1970s. Analysts point to shifts in family structure and immigration to explain the trend, but, while these factors play a role, they are secondary to the main factor that has created a wedge between economic growth and poverty reduction since 1973:

TABLE 5.7 Changes in poverty rates and various correlates, 1959-2003

Year	Poverty rates	Annual growth rates		Unem-ployment	Gini co-efficient**	Mother-only families as share of all families
		Produc-tivity*	Per capita income			
1959-73	-11.3	2.8%	3.3%	-0.6	-0.9%	2.7
1973-89	1.7	1.3	2.0	0.4	10.7	2.9
1989-2000	-1.5	1.7	2.0	-1.8	3.9	1.8
1989-95	1.0	1.6	0.8	0.3	2.4	1.3
1995-2000	-2.5	2.5	2.8	-1.6	1.5	-0.6
2000-03	1.2	3.8	1.4	2.0	0.9	0.1

* Non-farm business sector.
** We use the trend values shown in Figure 1I. See that Figure Note for more details.

Source: Poverty rates, family share, and Gini coefficients from U.S. Bureau of the Census; productivity, BLS; real per capita income, BEA.

the rise of income inequality. While average incomes grew more slowly after 1973, the fact that the growth that occurred was shared unequally meant that incomes at the bottom of the income scale fell (or grew less quickly) than those at the top. This factor, more than any other, has slowed the progress that could have been made over a 30-year period of economic growth.

Table 5.7 looks at key macroeconomic variables to paint a broad picture of the trends in poverty and the economy over various periods: 1959-73, when poverty fell sharply, the mid-1970s through the 1980s, when it increased slightly; 1989-2000, when, in the latter half of that period, it fell steeply; and 2000-03, when the economic downturn led to higher poverty rates.

The contrast between these periods yields useful insights. In the 1960s and early 1970s, macroeconomic growth, falling unemployment (particularly, a low average unemployment rate of 5% over those years), and slightly falling inequality helped to reduce poverty by 11.3 percentage points (part of this reduction was also due to expanded cash transfers, especially to the elderly). Note that the share of mother-only families grew relatively quickly over this period, yet poverty rates fell steeply, a phenomenon we explore in the next table. Essentially, in this period the benefits of historically fast productivity growth were broadly shared, both in the form of rising real wages for workers throughout the wage scale as well as in transfers, such as Social Security and welfare benefits. The low employment rates that prevailed over the period also helped to dampen the growth of inequality and ensure that growth was broadly distributed.

From the perspective of these economic indicators and poverty reduction, in the 1973-89 period slower growth and higher inequality led to a 1.1 point increase in poverty. Both productivity (1.3% per year) and real per capita income (2.0%) grew more slowly, unemployment rose and was high on average (7%), and inequality expanded most quickly relative to the other time periods in the table. The share of mother-only families grew at about the same pace as in the earlier period.

The 1989-2000 business cycle can be broken down into two periods, one dominated by a recession and jobless recovery (during which poverty rose 1 point), and the other featuring the strongest economy in decades (during which poverty fell 2.5 points). The latter 1990s was characterized by two factors that together proved to be a potent force to distribute growth to lower-income families and thus dampen inequality's rise: faster productivity growth and low unemployment. As in the 1960s, these factors combined to channel more income to lower-income families through more labor market opportunities, higher wages, and more transfers (in this case through the EITC, not through welfare, as shown in Figure 5G). The impact of these forces on poverty among minority families was even more dramatic (see Figure 5C).

The years 2000-03 witnessed the predictable increase in poverty that typically accompanies a recession (and like the early 1990s, a jobless recovery). Even though this is too short a period to identify any potentially persistent trends, the data provide some interesting implications. An unusual feature of this period was the further acceleration of productivity growth, from the already accelerated rate of 2.5% per year in 1995-2000 to 3.8%. Yet the decline in labor market opportunities led to higher unemployment and more poverty. Some economists have noted that the unemployment level remained low in these years, and compared to earlier decades this is true (recall, however, that depressed labor force growth reduced measured unemployment; see Chapter 3). However, the three-year increase in unemployment was historically large, and this significant rise in joblessness was one factor driving up poverty over these years.

Clearly, the strength of economic growth and the level of unemployment are key determinants of poverty rates. But perhaps most importantly, the extent of inequality at a given point in time determines how this growth is distributed. When inequality is growing, it acts as a wedge between growth and poverty reduction. In other periods, when inequality is contracting, growth is effectively channeled to low-income and disadvantaged families, leading to poverty reduction. We now turn to another poverty determinant, demographic change.

The impact of demographic change

Poverty in the United States is a complicated phenomenon, with many determinants that interact with one another. For example, minorities have higher poverty rates than whites, and they also face considerable economic barriers, such as labor market discrimination and less access to quality education. Thus, in terms of poverty's determinants, economic factors interact with race. Thus far, we have focused largely on economic causes, but another explanation offered for the failure of poverty to fall despite growth—one that has historically received a great deal of attention from poverty analysts and policy makers—is the increase in family types more vulnerable to poverty. This argument points to the increase in the share of families headed by single mothers, since these families have considerably lower income and higher poverty rates than families with two earners (see Chapter 1). While this argument has some merit, the upward pressure on poverty rates by formation of single-parent families has diminished considerably over time, while the economic determinants—growth, inequality, and unemployment—have, if anything, grown more important.

Table 5.8 shows the percent of persons in three different family types in the 1959-2003 period, along with the poverty rates of persons in those families. Clearly, there has been a shift over time into family types more vulnerable to poverty. For instance, the percentage of persons in married-couple and male-headed families, which have the lowest poverty rates, has consistently fallen, from 85.9% in 1959 to 69.1% in 2003. Conversely, the share of female-headed families and households consisting of single individuals has expanded.

By itself, we would expect this pattern of family structure changes to increase poverty rates. Single-parent families typically have only one major earner to depend on, and, in the case of single mothers, are further disadvantaged by the fact that women tend to earn less than men (individuals also have much higher poverty rates on average). However, changes in poverty rates within these groups also play a determining role. While growth in vulnerable family types as a share of all families will put upward pressure on poverty rates, rising incomes within this growth would be a countervailing factor. Though the composition effect—the fact that the formation of these families in and of itself raises poverty—has gotten most of the attention is this debate, the income and poverty trends within this family type have gotten less attention.

In fact, the poverty rates for persons by family type show that all family types saw their poverty rates fall over the 1960s and 1970s, with single persons showing the largest drop (12 percentage points in both decades). The poverty rates of persons in female-headed families fell 11.2 points over the 1960s, another 3.3 points over the 1970s, and 7.4 more points over the 1990s, for a cumu-

TABLE 5.8 Changing family structure and poverty, 1959-2003

Year	Percent of persons in:				Poverty rate of persons in:			
	Female-headed families	Married-couple and male-headed families*	Not living in families	Total	Female-headed families	Married-couple and male-headed families*	Not living in families	All persons
1959	8.0%	85.9%	6.1%	100.0%	49.4%	18.2%	46.1%	22.4%
1969	9.0	83.7	7.3	100.0	38.2	7.4	34.0	12.1
1979	12.1	76.2	11.7	100.0	34.9	6.4	21.9	11.7
1989	13.2	72.5	14.3	100.0	35.9	7.3	19.2	12.8
2000	13.8	69.9	16.4	100.0	28.5	6.2	19.0	11.3
2003	14.4	69.1	16.5	100.0	30.0	6.9	20.4	12.5
Percentage-point changes								
1959-69	1.0	-2.3	1.3		-11.2	-10.8	-12.1	-10.3
1969-79	3.1	-7.5	4.4		-3.3	-0.9	-12.1	-0.4
1979-89	1.1	-3.7	2.6		1.0	0.9	-2.7	1.1
1989-2000	0.5	-2.6	2.1		-7.4	-1.2	-0.2	-1.5
2000-03	0.6	-0.8	0.2		0.3	0.6	1.4	0.8
1959-2003	6.4	-16.8	10.5		-19.4	-11.3	-25.7	-9.9

* From 1979 forward, this group includes a small residual number of persons in unrelated subfamilies.

Source: U.S. Bureau of the Census, P60-198.

lative decline of 19.4 points. In fact, with the exception of the 1980s, the poverty rates of mother-only families have fallen faster than those of married-couple and male-headed families in each time period.

In terms of poverty dynamics, these patterns push the overall poverty rate in different directions, with family structure shifts leading to more poverty and within-group income growth leading to less poverty. The timing of the changes is also important. When the demographic shifts were occurring most rapidly, in the 1969-79 period, the overall poverty rate dropped from 12.1% to 11.7%, with declines occurring for each family type but declining most for those with the highest poverty rates: individuals and those in female-headed families. Conversely, when demographic forces were less poverty-inducing over the 1980s, the trend reversed, and poverty grew by one point for those in mother-only families. Thus, while demographic shifts to single-parent families are associated with higher poverty at any point in time, these trends suggest that such shifts might not go far in explaining why poverty rates are much the same now as they were in the early 1970s.

Another variable that needs to be brought into the mix is education level. Often overlooked, the educational upgrading of heads of families over time has been an important countervailing trend to the shift to lower-income family types. As Americans from all walks of life become more highly educated, they and their families are less likely to be poor (holding all else equal). This relationship can be seen in **Table 5.9**, which shows family poverty rates and twice-poverty rates for families with children in 1969 by the education level of the family head, along with the shares of families in each category. Families headed by persons with higher levels of education are less likely to be poor. Note, for example, that families with children headed by a college graduate have poverty rates under 3% in both years. On the other end of the scale, the rates for families headed by someone with less than a high school education (one-third in 2000) reveal the increased importance of education as an antipoverty tool.

In fact, the importance of this determinant has increased over time, as fewer pathways out of poverty exist for those with the least education. Families headed by such persons were always most likely to be poor, but in 1969 their rates were less than twice the overall average and about 10 times that of families headed by a college graduate. By 2000, the poverty rates for families headed by high school dropouts were about 2.6 times the overall rate and 13 times the college rate. The point changes in twice-poverty status are even larger than those for poverty; in fact, for twice-poverty, rates fell over the period for those with a college degree or more, and the overall rate fell as well. Clearly, the inverse relationship between education and poverty status has strengthened considerably over time, a fact highlighted in the analysis that follows.

TABLE 5.9 Poverty rates for families with children by education level of family head, 1969-2000

Education level of family head	Poverty		
	1969	2000	Percentage-point changes
Less than high school	19.6%	33.3%	13.7
High school	6.9	15.1	8.2
Some college	5.1	8.6	3.5
College or more	2.1	2.7	0.6
All	10.6	12.7	2.1
	Twice-poverty		
	1969	2000	Percentage-point changes
Less than high school	52.8%	66.8%	14.0
High school	30.9	39.6	8.7
Some college	22.9	26.5	3.6
College or more	11.2	8.2	-3.0
All	34.9	31.8	-3.2
Shares			
Less than high school	36.9%	15.0%	-21.9
High school	33.9	30.3	-3.6
Some college	14.6	28.6	13.9
College or more	14.5	26.1	11.5
All	100.0	100.0	

Source: Authors' analysis of March CPS data.

The bottom section of the table shows the persistent shift toward higher levels of educational attainment by families with children. For instance, the full 1969-2000 period saw a 25.5 percentage-point shift out of the bottom two education categories into the "some college" and college graduate categories. What was the impact of these shifts on poverty rates? If we calculate a hypothetical poverty rate using poverty rates from 2000 and education shares from 1969, we derive a poverty rate approximating the prevailing rate had no education upgrading occurred (of course, this is a simplistic, one-variable analysis intended to show only the impact of educational shifts). This rate comes to 19.1%, and the difference between this rate and the actual 2000 rate of 12.7%, i.e., 6.4 percentage points, represents the poverty-reducing impact of educational upgrading. A similar exercise for twice-poverty yields a much larger education effect of 11.4 points.

Thus, while family structure shifts may have put upward pressure on poverty rates over time, educational shifts have helped to reduce poverty. Simulta-

TABLE 5.10 The impact of economic, demographic, and educational factors on poverty rates, 1969-2002

	1969-79	1979-89	1989-2000	2000-02
Actual change	-0.5	1.1	-1.5	0.8
Total demographic effect	0.6	-0.3	-0.7	0.2
Race	0.3	0.4	0.4	0.1
Education	-1.6	-1.2	-1.2	0.1
Family structure	2.0	0.7	0.3	0.1
Interaction	-0.2	-0.1	-0.2	0.0
Economic change	-1.0	1.4	-0.8	0.6
Growth	-1.3	-1.5	-1.6	0.4
Inequality	0.2	2.9	0.8	0.2

Source: EPI analysis of March CPS data.

neously, as we have emphasized throughout, the rate of economic growth and inequality also matter. What is needed is a method to parcel out the relative contributions.

Table 5.10 provides a breakdown, or decomposition, of poverty's growth that separately accounts for these factors (and adds race of the household head). This table separates the growth in poverty rates into three demographic factors—the education level and race of the family head and family structure—and two economic components—the poverty-reducing effect of overall economic growth and the poverty-increasing effect of growing inequality. Thus, it highlights the relative importance of these factors in the growth of poverty in each time period. If the conventional wisdom is correct—that family structure changes are the key factor breaking the link between economic growth and poverty— then this decomposition should reveal a consistent increase in this factor's role over time. Similarly, the role of economic factors—such as the overall growth of the economy and especially the increase in inequality—should have diminished. In fact, as the table shows, the opposite is the case: the poverty-inducing role of family structure shifts fell steeply over time.

Family structure changes played the largest role in poverty's growth in the 1970s, adding two points to poverty's growth in those years. Over the next few decades, however, its contribution diminished considerably (from adding 2 points in the 1970s to adding 0.7 and 0.3 points in the 1980s and 1990s). Though the poverty-reducing impact of educational upgrading fell by 0.4 points from the

1970s to the latter two decades, it remained a relatively large determinant of poverty outcomes. By the 1990s, the impact of education was four times that of family structure (1.2 points compared to 0.3).

Additionally, while family structure was having its most negative impact on poverty's growth in the 1970s, poverty rates actually fell by 0.5 percentage points, thanks to economic growth that was only partially offset by slightly increasing income inequality (income inequality grew little in this period relative to later periods). Poverty rose in the 1980s, and the largest contributor was faster-growing inequality that was only partially offset by overall growth. The increase in inequality over this decade added 2.9 points to the growth of poverty, by far the largest poverty-inducing factor of any variable in any year in the table. Had inequality risen half that much (and thus had half that effect on poverty rates), it still would have been the most unequal decade, yet poverty would have fallen slightly (by 0.3 points), all else equal.

Over the 1990s, inequality slowed and its large poverty-inducing effect fell significantly, to 0.8 percentage points. Educational upgrading took 1.2 points off poverty over the decade and overall economic growth removed another 1.6 points. But both these effects were of similar magnitudes to earlier periods. The difference in the 1990s was that inequality's impact fell, as did that of family structure.

The last time period in the table, 2000-02, is too short to reveal much change in variables such as family structure and educational upgrading, factors that need more years to evolve. We include it, however, to show the recession-induced impact of negative income growth. Note that this is the only period where "growth" (in this case, declining average real incomes) is poverty-inducing.

Figure 5J plots the summary rows from the previous table for each period, excluding the last one because it is not a comparable cycle. The demographic effect includes race, education, and family structure (and a small residual category accounting for interactions between these factors), and the economic effect includes the offsetting effects of growth and inequality. The best business cycle in terms of poverty reduction was the 1990s, where the net effects of both components was poverty-reducing. The patterns in these bars are suggestive of an important insight regarding poverty reduction. With the poverty-inducing role of family structure somewhat diminished, net demographics, due to educational upgrading, are a negative (i.e., poverty-reducing) factor. Thus, the greatest force in reducing poverty is continued, or even accelerated, educational upgrading, along with stronger, more equal growth. Most importantly, this decomposition underscores the fact that the inequality wedge can have large poverty-inducing effects. One of the most important poverty determinants moving forward will be the extent to which economic growth is or is not broadly shared.

FIGURE 5J The contribution of demographics (including education), growth, and inequality to changes in poverty, 1969-2000

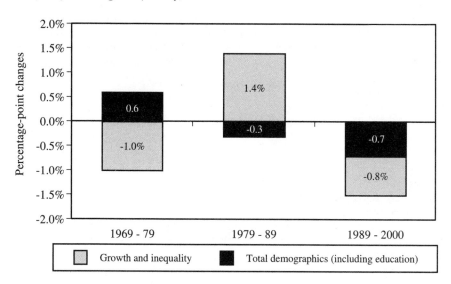

Source: Table 5.10.

The changing effects of taxes and transfers

Another important determinant of the poverty rate is the tax and transfer system that serves to collect and redistribute resources throughout the economy. Cash and near-cash benefits, such as welfare payments and food stamps, increase the resources available to the poor and thus lower poverty. (While the value of food stamps is not counted in the official poverty rate, we correct for that omission below). Payroll taxes paid by low-income workers can raise poverty rates that measure such costs (recall that the official measure is pretax), while EITC benefits can lower after-tax poverty rates. Also, all of these programs vary over time and by family type, so we need to track the trend in their impact on poverty rates for different types of persons.

The impact of the tax and transfer system on poverty is broadly a function of two forces: changes in market-driven poverty rates and changes in the magnitude and incidence of benefits. If the market (pre-tax, pre-transfer distribution) generates less poverty (say, due to stronger and more equal growth), then the transfer system has less work to do to reduce poverty rates. Conversely, when

337

TABLE 5.11 Poverty-reducing effects of transfers over downturns, 1979-2002

All persons	(1) Before taxes and transfers	(2) After taxes	(3) Plus non- means tested (including Medicare)*	(4) Plus means tested (including Medicaid)*	(5) Change in poverty due to taxes and transfers	(5)/(1) Reduction effective- ness rate
1979	19.5%	19.3%	12.4%	8.9%	10.6	54.4%
1981	22.0	22.4	14.8	11.5	10.5	47.7
1989	20.0%	20.3%	13.5%	10.4%	9.6	48.0%
1991	21.8	21.8	14.7	11.4	10.4	47.7
2000	18.6%	17.6%	10.8%	8.65%	10.0	53.8%
2002	20.0	19.1	11.6	9.4	10.6	53.0
Persons in female-headed families with children under 18						
1979	53.4%	52.3%	47.3%	28.1%	25.3	47.4%
1981	55.3	55.2	50.6	35.7	19.6	35.4
1989	51.45%	51.1%	47.0%	34.9%	16.5	32.1%
1991	56.5	55.1	50.9	38.0	18.5	32.7
2000	40.9%	35.3%	31.9%	23.4%	17.5	42.8%
2002	41.7	36.6	32.0	24.6	17.1	41.0

* Includes fungible value of Medicare and Medicaid benefits; see Table Note.

Source: EPI analysis of U.S. Bureau of the Census, P-60, No. 182-RD and Ferret table:
http://ferret.bls.census.gov/macro/032001/rdcall/2_001.htm.

inequality rises and incomes fall, the transfer system must expand if poverty levels are to be maintained, let alone be further reduced.

Given that the most recent data cover the 2001 recession and the following year of jobless recovery, we switch from our usual peak-to-peak focus to a peak-to-trough focus. This switch enables us to examine the impact of the safety net on market outcomes over those precise times when we most expect the safety net to ameliorate market-induced income losses among disadvantaged families. **Table 5.11** thus examines the changes in market poverty and the impact of taxes and transfers for all persons and for persons in mother-only families over the three downturns for which we have data.

The first entry in the table, 19.5%, represents the poverty rate before any government intervention, i.e., the poverty rate delivered by the market. Moving

FIGURE 5K Poverty-reducing effect of taxes and means-tested transfers on members of mother-only families, 1981 and 2002

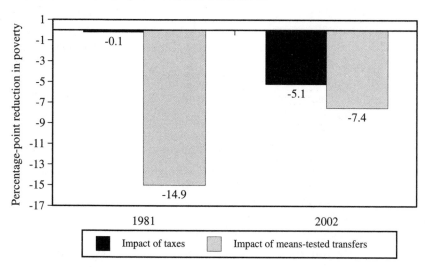

Source: Authors' analysis of U.S. Bureau of the Census data.

left to right, the table introduces different transfers and taxes and shows how poverty is affected by each. In the most recent peak year, 2000, moving from column 1 to 2 shows the effect of taxes reducing poverty by one point for all persons (18.6% to 17.6%) but by 5.6 points (40.9% to 35.3%) for persons in female-headed families. Due to the expansion of the EITC, these effects are much larger than those that occurred in earlier years. On the other hand, means-tested transfers have fallen steeply over these years. In fact, they reduced the poverty of those in single-mother families by only half as much in 2002 as in 1981.

Figure 5K shows how these effects of taxes and means-tested transfers have changed significantly over time for persons in mother-only families. The first bar shows that taxes had almost no impact on poverty in the recessionary year of 1981, though transfers based on income reduced poverty by almost 15 points. In 2002, however, the expanded EITC helped reduce poverty by 5.1 points, while the effect of means-tested transfers was cut by half. Taken together, the joint poverty-reducing effect of these programs was greater in the earlier period (15.0 points in 1981 versus 12.5 points in 2002). In other words, by this metric, the loss from means-tested benefits was greater than the gains from more progressive taxation among the poor. These findings suggest that, for persons in mother-only families, the counter-cyclical component of the safety net—its ability to compensate for the recession-induced loss of market income—has been diminished by changes that favor labor market income over transfers. This theme was suggested in Figure 5G, which showed that EITC benefits fell for low-income single mothers between 2000 and 2002, partly as a function of their loss of labor market opportunities over these years.

But what about the total effect of all transfers? Column 5, which shows the cumulative effects of government tax and transfer policies, indicates that in 2002 they reduced market-generated poverty by 10.6 points. The final column in Table 5.11 represents the share of market poverty reduced by government tax and transfer policy. For all persons, the total change in poverty has been constant, hovering around 10 percentage points. Thus, any difference in the poverty-effectiveness rate is largely a function of changes in the market rates shown in column 1. Thus, the point reduction in market poverty for all persons was essentially the same in 1981, 1991, and 2002 (10.5, 10.4, and 10.6 points, respectively). But the increased poverty effectiveness rate, from 47.7% in both of the earlier years to 53.0% in 2002, was due to the fact that the market rate was about two points lower in the latter year.

The story is a bit more complex for persons in mother-only families. Whether we look at peaks or troughs, the poverty-reducing impact of taxes and transfers has fallen over time, from 25.3 points in 1979 to 17.5 points in 2000 (or from 19.6 points in 1981 to 17.1 points in 2002). However, the drop in market poverty was very steep for these families, and at 41.7% was 13.6 points lower in 2002 than in 1981. Thus, the reduction effectiveness rate was higher in 2002 than in 1981.

The low-wage labor market

Given the elevated role of work in the lives of poor and near-poor families (recall the hours trend in Figure 5H), conditions in low-wage labor markets play an increasingly important role in evaluating the nation's progress against poverty. This section examines the characteristics of low-wage workers and their historical wage trends.

Table 5.12 looks at the characteristics of low-wage workers, defined the same way as in Table 2.9 (as earning the hourly wage that, with full-time, full-year work, would lift a family of four above the poverty threshold). Just under one-quarter of the workforce earned this wage level in 2003, and their average hourly wage was just above seven dollars. Comparing the percentages in the two columns reveals categories in which low-wage workers are over-represented. Such workers are disproportionately female, minority, non-college educated,

TABLE 5.12 Characteristics of low-wage workers, 2003

	Low wage	Total workforce
Share of workforce	24.3%	100.0%
Number	28,280,343	116,288,910
Average wage	7.09	17.15
Gender		
Female	58.2%	48.2%
Male	41.8	51.8
Race/ethnicity		
White	58.4%	69.6%
African American	14.0	11.2
Hispanic	21.9	13.4
Asian	3.7	4.2
Other	2.0	1.7
Education		
Less than high school	23.5%	10.6%
High School	36.8	30.6
Associate degree	6.4	9.3
Some college	24.5	20.4
College or more	8.9	29.1
Industry		
Financial and information services	5.9%	9.9%
Manufacturing	9.0	13.6
Durable	4.6	8.5
Non-durable	4.4	5.1
Construction	4.2	6.4
Transportation and utilities	3.0	5.4
Services	52.7	43.5
Trade	20.7	14.6
Wholesale	2.1	3.2
Retail	18.6	11.4
Government	2.2	5.2
Other industries	2.2	1.3
Occupations		
Managers/professionals	11.8%	34.1%
Admin/office support	14.6	15.5
Blue collar	21.6	23.3
Services	34.5	15.8
Sales	15.6	10.6
Other occupations	1.9	0.7
Union status		
Non-union	93.6%	85.4%
Union	6.4	14.6

Source: Authors' analysis of CPS ORG data.

FIGURE 5L Real hourly wages of low-wage workers, 1973-2003

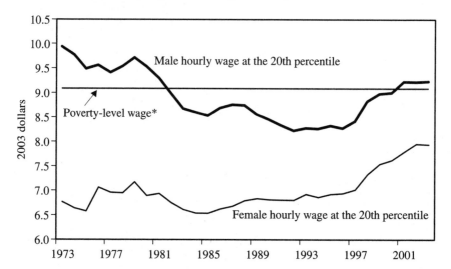

* This value is the poverty-level wage used in Table 2.9, updated to 2003 dollars.

Source: Authors' analysis of CPS data.

and young. They also are more likely to work in low-wage industries such as retail trade and service industries, and less likely to work in durable manufacturing (non-durable manufacturing—the manufacture of things like food and apparel— pays much less than durable), transportation and utilities, finance, information services, and government. By occupation, low-wage workers are over-represented in sales (e.g., cashiers) and services, where they staff the low-paying jobs such as security guards, food preparation, or home health aides in health services. They are least likely to be managers and professionals. Finally, they are significantly less likely to either be union members or covered by union contracts.

The tight labor market of the latter 1990s—particularly the low-wage sector—turned out to be a key determinant of the progress against poverty over these years. **Figure 5L** show the real value of wages, by gender, at the 20th percentile, a good proxy for the typical wage in the low-wage labor market. The straight line in the figure is the poverty-level wage used in Table 2.9, included here as a benchmark of the wage needed to lift a family of four above the poverty line with full-time, full-year work.

The real hourly earnings for low-wage males drifted down through most of the period, reversing course only in the latter half of the 1990s. The trend for low-wage women has been more positive, but from a much lower level; they too enjoyed a positive boost from the tight labor market of the latter 1990s. In fact, the wage momentum from that period lasted through 2002 (at least for women), when the recession and particularly the jobless recovery caught up with low earners by 2003 and real wage growth flattened. It is clear that the significant progress made against poverty and near-poverty in these years was closely tied to these low-wage trends, as well as with sharply increased employment opportunities and the expanded EITC.

Among low-income single-mother families (whose labor market experience is illustrated in Figures 5G-5I) annual hours of work peaked at about 1,230 in 2000. That year, the 20th percentile female wage (in 2003 dollars) was $7.62. The product of these two values leads to annual earnings of about $9,400. Assuming that full EITC benefits could add about another $3,800 to this income, a single mother's income still falls below the poverty threshold for a family with two children and, of course, far below the twice-poverty threshold. A more complete accounting would add the value of food stamps, subtract payroll taxes, factor in child care costs, etc., but the point is a simple one: even in good times, many working families remain vulnerable to some degree of material deprivation.

Economists often stress the role of productivity growth as a primary driver of wage trends. While this is usually true on average, in the recent history of growing wage inequality it has been all too common to experience growing productivity and declining real wages among certain classes of workers. Note, for example, the negative trend for males shown in Figure 5L, which occurred as the economy was expanding and productivity growth was positive.

Figure 5M illustrates that, while productivity growth is necessary for real wages to grow in the low-wage sector, it is not sufficient. Low unemployment is the other necessary ingredient, as only tight labor markets can ensure that the benefits of faster growth will be broadly shared. The figure plots the annual growth rates of three variables in three time periods: productivity, real 20th percentile wages (for all workers), and the average unemployment rate over the period. The first two sets of bars show the growth rates of these variables in the last five years of the 1980s and 1990s expansions; the final set of bars, for 2001-03, shows the most recent trend over the recession and jobless recovery.

Over the last five years of the 1980s expansion, productivity grew at an annual rate of 1.5%, but average unemployment was 6.4%, and as a result of a labor market too slack to ensure low-wage growth, wages at the 20th percentile barely budged. Over the last five years of the last business cycle, productivity grew a point faster per year (2.5%), and average unemployment was 4.8%. Under these conditions, 20th percentile real wages grew as employers needed to

FIGURE 5M Productivity, unemployment, and real low-wage growth

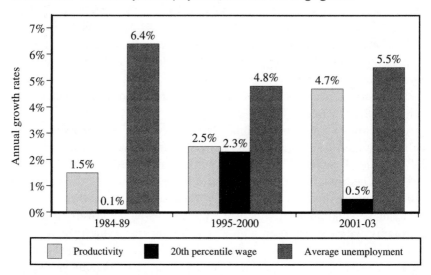

Source: Authors' analysis of BLS, Census, and ORG data.

bid up even low wages to get and keep the workers they needed to meet strong demand in these years. In fact, low wages grew at almost the rate of productivity, an unprecedented trend over the full time series shown in Figure 5M.

The last set of bars provides an interesting corroboration of the contention that fast productivity growth alone will not suffice to fuel the growth of low wages. Between 2001 and 2003, productivity grew far more quickly than in the other periods. Yet unemployment was high, on average, compared to the latter half of the 1990s. Under these conditions, the extra income generated by the fast growth of productivity did not flow to low-wage workers, as earnings at the 20th percentile slowed to 0.5% per year. In fact, as shown in Chapter 1, little of the faster productivity growth over this recession/jobless recovery went to compensation in general, as labor's share of national income fell to a historic low point.

Conclusion

Tremendous changes have transpired in the U.S. economy and society over the course of the past quarter century. Some have been positive, such as the increase in productivity growth and the full employment labor market that prevailed over the latter 1990s. (But faster productivity growth remains an apparent fixture of the economy; full employment does not.) Others have been negative, such as the sharp increase in income inequality. Yet, despite these momentous developments, the poverty rate in 1973 was almost identical to that of 2000, the peak year of the previous business cycle.

Why have we failed to make progress against poverty? The most important consideration is that low unemployment, just as it does for income and wages, matters for poverty, especially given the policy changes that emphasize work as the primary pathway out of poverty. And since families between poverty and twice-poverty are more attached to the labor force, labor market conditions matter even more for twice-poverty.

The recession of 2001 and the ensuing jobless recovery—the longest on record—predictably ended the conditions that lowered poverty in the 1990s. Poverty rose 0.8 points between 2000 and 2002, and twice-poverty was up 1.2 points. Hours declined for low-wage workers, and their hourly wage growth flattened. What's more, the safety net was somewhat less effective in this downturn in that it shaved fewer points off market-based poverty than in the past.

Putting it all together, the message of the last few decades comes across clearly: to make lasting progress against poverty, it is necessary to ensure that the benefits of the growing economy are broadly shared, and the best way to meet this goal is to maintain tight labor markets. Yet, the dynamic U.S. economy will continue to stumble and recessions are endemic. What's more, the two most recent recession were both followed by jobless recoveries, with the last one particularly protracted. This is a critically important development in that poverty policy now stresses work as a pathway out of poverty more so than in the past. However, the lack of jobs and the absence of full employment presents a challenge to such a policy, and reminds us that a strong safety nets remains a critical component of an advanced economy's strategy for dealing with poverty amidst plenty.

CHAPTER 6

Regional analysis:
labor market slump widespread in most states

by Jeff Chapman

Previous chapters have focused exclusively on information of national scope. This chapter examines the state of the economy in each of the nation's regions, Census divisions (groups of states within regions), and states. A regional focus is important because, in many ways, state or regional data more accurately represent the economy faced by workers in a particular area than do broad national data.

This chapter focuses on what happened to state labor markets between 2001 and 2003, a period of weak labor markets in nearly every state. As of mid-2004, the national labor market has finally started to show signs of recovery. While this is welcome news, it comes three years after the recession started and over two years since the economy purportedly entered the recovery. For many states, it will take numerous consecutive months of robust job growth to return to the employment levels of three years ago.

The contrast between the late 1990s and the last three years is sharp in most states. Expanding payrolls, full employment, and strong, broad-based wage growth have been replaced by fewer jobs, higher unemployment, and stagnating wages.

A state-by-state analysis of labor markets reveals that the recent slump has been uniquely geographically pervasive, but that the plight of the manufacturing sector has been a central factor in states with the most severe job losses: while most states' economies have suffered in the last three years, states with heavy reliance on manufacturing have generally done worse.

Job losses have been accompanied by rising unemployment in nearly every state. In addition, most states have seen a sharp increase in long-term unemployment and an increase in involuntary part-time employment. The wage gains of the last half of the 1990s relied on the benefits of full employment. With unemployment on the rise, wage growth has slowed in most states.

Finally, this chapter also addresses three additional economic issues that have been important in recent years at the state level: the growing number of states that have set minimum wages above the federal rate, the state fiscal crisis, and state and local tax distribution.

Job loss

As discussed in Chapter 3, job growth nationwide accelerated in the latter half of the 1990s. **Table 6.1** shows that nine states, including six Western states, achieved annual employment growth rates of at least 3% across this period. More than half of the states had annual growth rates of at least 2%.

From 2000 to 2001, when national employment grew by only 41,000 jobs, employment contracted in 23 states, led by states in the Midwest and South. Of the remaining states, all but two and the District of Columbia saw job growth slow compared to the earlier period.

In 39 states, the two years following the recession's official end in November 2001 proved to be worse in terms of job growth than 2001. By 2003, 36 states had fewer jobs than they did three years earlier. These states were spread out in every region and division of the country (see **Figure 6A**.)

The geographic pervasiveness of the recent jobless recovery stands in sharp contrast to the jobless recovery of the early 1990s. In 1992, only 13 states and the District of Columbia still had fewer jobs than three years earlier. Of those states, only California was not located in the Eastern corridor spanning Virginia to Maine (see the top panel of **Figure 6A**).

As noted in Chapter 3, one of the key factors in the recession and jobless recovery was the travails of the manufacturing sector: making up 13.1% of jobs in 2000, this industry lost 15.9% of its jobs in the next three years, compared to slight job *growth* of 0.8% in the other industries combined. (Even without the manufacturing crisis, this 0.8% growth in the recovery would still have been very weak in historical terms.) As shown in **Table 6.2**, 20 of the 35 states that had fewer jobs in 2003 than in 2000 experienced job growth outside of manufacturing. For example, while Arkansas lost 14.2% of manufacturing jobs, all other industries grew by 2.1%.

While most states experienced job loss between 2000 and 2003 (and severe job losses in manufacturing), there was considerable variation among the states. As shown in **Figure 6B**, the level of job growth (or loss) by state correlates powerfully with each state's reliance on manufacturing. Given the severity of losses in this sector, it is not surprising to find such a strong relationship.

TABLE 6.1 Non-farm payroll employment by state, division, and region, 1979-2003 (in thousands)

	1979	1989	1995	2000	2001	2003	Annual average percent change				
							1979-89	1989-2000	1995-2000	2000-01	2000-03
UNITED STATES	89,932	108,014	117,298	131,785	131,826	129,931	1.8%	1.8%	2.4%	0.0%	-0.5%
NORTHEAST	20,406	23,644	23,072	25,338	25,297	24,821	1.5%	0.6%	1.9%	-0.2%	-0.7%
New England	5,394	6,569	6,326	7,017	7,026	6,835	2.0	0.6	2.1	0.1	-0.9
Maine	416	542	538	603	608	606	2.7	1.0	2.3	0.8	0.1
New Hampshire	379	529	540	622	627	617	3.4	1.5	2.9	0.8	-0.3
Vermont	198	262	270	299	302	299	2.8	1.2	2.0	1.1	0.0
Massachusetts	2,604	3,109	2,977	3,323	3,329	3,186	1.8	0.6	2.2	0.2	-1.4
Rhode Island	400	462	440	477	478	484	1.5	0.3	1.6	0.4	0.5
Connecticut	1,398	1,666	1,562	1,693	1,681	1,643	1.8	0.1	1.6	-0.7	-1.0
Middle Atlantic	15,013	17,075	16,746	18,321	18,271	17,986	1.3%	0.6%	1.8%	-0.3%	-0.6%
New York	7,179	8,247	7,892	8,635	8,592	8,404	1.4	0.4	1.8	-0.5	-0.9
New Jersey	3,027	3,690	3,601	3,995	3,997	3,980	2.0	0.7	2.1	0.1	-0.1
Pennsylvania	4,806	5,139	5,253	5,691	5,683	5,602	0.7	0.9	1.6	-0.2	-0.5
MIDWEST	24,172	26,580	29,350	32,039	31,682	30,990	1.0%	1.7%	1.8%	-1.1%	-1.1%
East North Central	17,198	18,670	20,433	22,177	21,841	21,296	0.8	1.6	1.7	-1.5	-1.3
Ohio	4,485	4,818	5,221	5,625	5,543	5,391	0.7	1.4	1.5	-1.5	-1.4
Indiana	2,236	2,479	2,787	3,000	2,933	2,897	1.0	1.7	1.5	-2.2	-1.2
Illinois	4,880	5,214	5,593	6,045	5,995	5,818	0.7	1.4	1.6	-0.8	-1.3
Michigan	3,637	3,922	4,274	4,674	4,556	4,412	0.8	1.6	1.8	-2.5	-1.9
Wisconsin	1,960	2,236	2,559	2,834	2,814	2,779	1.3	2.2	2.1	-0.7	-0.6
West North Central	6,973	7,911	8,917	9,862	9,841	9,694	1.3%	2.0%	2.0%	-0.2%	-0.6%
Minnesota	1,767	2,087	2,379	2,676	2,680	2,651	1.7	2.3	2.4	0.2	-0.3
Iowa	1,132	1,200	1,358	1,478	1,466	1,440	0.6	1.9	1.7	-0.9	-0.9
Missouri	2,011	2,315	2,521	2,749	2,726	2,676	1.4	1.6	1.7	-0.8	-0.9
North Dakota	244	260	302	328	330	333	0.6	2.1	1.7	0.6	0.5

(cont.)

TABLE 6.1 (cont.) Non-farm payroll employment by state, division, and region, 1979-2003 (in thousands)

	1979	1989	1995	2000	2001	2003	Annual average percentage change				
							1979-89	1989-2000	1995-2000	2000-01	2000-03
West North Central (cont.)											
South Dakota	241	276	344	378	379	378	1.4%	2.9%	1.9%	0.2%	0.0%
Nebraska	631	708	816	908	913	904	1.2	2.3	2.2	0.5	-0.2
Kansas	947	1,064	1,198	1,345	1,348	1,312	1.2	2.2	2.3	0.2	-0.8
SOUTH	28,571	35,989	40,652	46,235	46,255	45,862	2.3%	2.3%	2.6%	0.0%	-0.3%
South Atlantic	14,392	19,433	21,453	24,595	24,628	24,548	3.0	2.2	2.8	0.1	-0.1
Delaware	257	345	366	420	419	414	3.0	1.8	2.8	-0.1	-0.5
Maryland	1,691	2,155	2,183	2,450	2,467	2,483	2.5	1.2	2.3	0.7	0.4
District of Columbia	613	681	643	650	654	665	1.1	-0.4	0.2	0.5	0.7
Virginia	2,115	2,862	3,070	3,517	3,517	3,500	3.1	1.9	2.8	0.0	-0.2
West Virginia	659	615	688	736	735	726	-0.7	1.6	1.4	-0.1	-0.4
North Carolina	2,373	3,074	3,460	3,934	3,899	3,803	2.6	2.3	2.6	-0.9	-1.1
South Carolina	1,176	1,500	1,646	1,859	1,823	1,813	2.5	2.0	2.5	-1.9	-0.8
Georgia	2,128	2,941	3,402	3,949	3,943	3,860	3.3	2.7	3.0	-0.2	-0.8
Florida	3,381	5,261	5,996	7,081	7,171	7,286	4.5	2.7	3.4	1.3	1.0
East South Central	5,223	6,121	7,020	7,638	7,531	7,442	1.6%	2.0%	1.7%	-1.4%	-0.9%
Kentucky	1,245	1,433	1,643	1,825	1,804	1,783	1.4	2.2	2.1	-1.1	-0.8
Tennessee	1,777	2,167	2,499	2,729	2,688	2,668	2.0	2.1	1.8	-1.5	-0.8
Alabama	1,362	1,601	1,804	1,931	1,909	1,875	1.6	1.7	1.4	-1.2	-1.0
Mississippi	838	919	1,075	1,154	1,130	1,117	0.9	2.1	1.4	-2.0	-1.1
West South Central	8,957	10,436	12,180	14,001	14,096	13,872	1.5%	2.7%	2.8%	0.7%	-0.3%
Arkansas	750	893	1,069	1,159	1,154	1,144	1.8	2.4	1.6	-0.4	-0.4
Louisiana	1,517	1,539	1,772	1,920	1,918	1,905	0.1	2.0	1.6	-0.1	-0.3
Oklahoma	1,088	1,164	1,316	1,489	1,507	1,451	0.7	2.3	2.5	1.2	-0.9
Texas	5,602	6,840	8,023	9,433	9,518	9,373	2.0	3.0	3.3	0.9	-0.2

(cont.)

TABLE 6.1 (cont.) Non-farm payroll employment by state, division, and region, 1979-2003 (in thousands)

	1979	1989	1995	2000	2001	2003	Annual average percent change				
							1979-89	1989-2000	1995-2000	2000-01	2000-03
WEST	17,276	21,844	24,035	28,130	28,322	28,097	2.4%	2.3%	3.2%	0.7%	0.0%
Mountain	4,414	5,621	7,053	8,489	8,585	8,598	2.4	3.8	3.8	1.1	0.4
Montana	284	291	351	388	392	400	0.2	2.6	2.0	1.1	1.1
Idaho	338	366	477	560	568	572	0.8	3.9	3.2	1.5	0.7
Wyoming	201	193	219	239	245	250	-0.4	2.0	1.8	2.5	1.5
Colorado	1,218	1,482	1,834	2,213	2,225	2,150	2.0	3.7	3.8	0.6	-0.9
New Mexico	461	562	682	745	757	776	2.0	2.6	1.8	1.7	1.4
Arizona	980	1,455	1,795	2,243	2,265	2,289	4.0	4.0	4.6	1.0	0.7
Utah	548	691	908	1,075	1,081	1,074	2.3	4.1	3.5	0.5	0.0
Nevada	384	581	786	1,027	1,051	1,087	4.2	5.3	5.5	2.4	1.9
Pacific	12,863	16,224	16,982	19,641	19,737	19,499	2.3%	1.8%	3.0%	0.5%	-0.2%
Washington	1,581	2,047	2,347	2,711	2,697	2,659	2.6	2.6	2.9	-0.5	-0.6
Oregon	1,056	1,206	1,418	1,607	1,594	1,562	1.3	2.6	2.5	-0.8	-0.9
California	9,665	12,239	12,422	14,488	14,602	14,410	2.4	1.5	3.1	0.8	-0.2
Alaska	167	227	262	284	289	300	3.1	2.1	1.6	1.9	1.8
Hawaii	394	506	533	551	555	567	2.5	0.8	0.7	0.7	1.0

Note: Payroll employment is estimated for states and the nation separately, so the state estimates do not sum to the U.S. totals. Region and division estimates are not provided by the BLS. Estimates here are simply the sum of the component states and are presented only for comparison.

Source: Authors' analysis of BLS data.

FIGURE 6A Job growth by state, 1989-92 and 2000-03

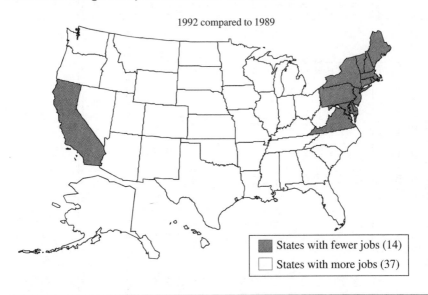

1992 compared to 1989

States with fewer jobs (14)
States with more jobs (37)

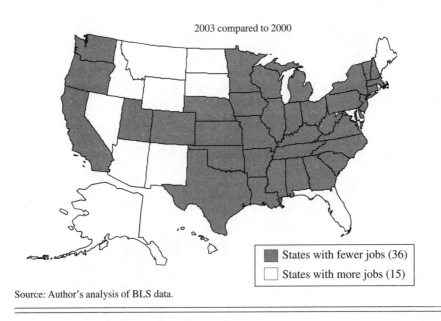

2003 compared to 2000

States with fewer jobs (36)
States with more jobs (15)

Source: Author's analysis of BLS data.

TABLE 6.2 Comparison of job growth in manufacturing and all other industries by state, division, and region, 2000-03

	Manufacturing share of total payroll employment, 2000	Manufacturing share of total payroll employment, 2003	Change in payroll employment, 2000-03		
			Actual manu-facturing	All other industries	Total
UNITED STATES	13.1%	11.2%	-15.9%	0.8%	-1.4%
NORTHEAST	11.8%	9.9%	-17.8%	0.1%	-2.0%
New England	13.4	11.2	-18.8	-0.1	-2.6
Maine	13.2	10.5	-19.7	3.5	0.4
New Hampshire	16.5	13.0	-21.9	3.3	-0.9
Vermont	15.5	12.6	-18.8	3.4	0.0
Massachusetts	12.3	10.2	-20.0	-1.9	-4.1
Rhode Island	14.9	12.2	-17.2	4.7	1.5
Connecticut	13.9	12.1	-15.3	-0.9	-2.9
Middle Atlantic	11.1%	9.4%	-17.3%	0.1%	-1.8%
New York	8.7	7.3	-18.1	-1.2	-2.7
New Jersey	10.6	8.8	-16.6	1.6	-0.4
Pennsylvania	15.2	12.8	-17.0	1.2	-1.6
MIDWEST	17.0%	14.8%	-15.8%	-0.7%	-3.3%
East North Central	18.2	15.8	-16.8	-1.1	-4.0
Ohio	18.2	15.7	-17.3	-1.2	-4.2
Indiana	22.1	19.8	-13.7	-0.5	-3.4
Illinois	14.4	12.3	-17.6	-1.4	-3.8
Michigan	19.2	16.5	-18.9	-2.5	-5.6
Wisconsin	21.0	18.2	-14.8	1.5	-1.9
West North Central	14.1%	12.5%	-12.9%	0.1%	-1.7%
Minnesota	14.8	13.0	-13.2	1.2	-0.9
Iowa	17.0	15.3	-12.5	-0.5	-2.6
Missouri	13.2	11.7	-13.5	-1.0	-2.6
North Dakota	7.3	7.0	-2.1	1.8	1.5
South Dakota	11.6	10.0	-13.9	2.0	0.1
Nebraska	12.6	11.3	-10.7	1.0	-0.5
Kansas	14.9	13.1	-14.1	-0.4	-2.5
SOUTH	12.5%	10.5%	-16.2%	1.4%	-0.8%
South Atlantic	11.1	9.3	-16.8	1.9	-0.2
Delaware	9.9	8.6	-14.0	-0.2	-1.5
Maryland	7.1	5.9	-15.1	2.6	1.3
District of Columbia	0.6	0.4	-29.7	2.4	2.2
Virginia	10.3	8.7	-16.1	1.3	-0.5
West Virginia	10.3	8.9	-14.8	0.3	-1.3
North Carolina	19.3	15.9	-20.3	0.7	-3.3
South Carolina	18.1	15.3	-17.6	0.8	-2.5
Georgia	13.4	11.7	-14.9	-0.3	-2.3
Florida	6.4	5.3	-14.5	4.1	2.9

(cont.)

TABLE 6.2 *(cont.)* Comparison of job growth in manufacturing and all other industries by state, division, and region, 2000-03

	Manufacturing share of total payroll employ-ment, 2000	Manufacturing share of total payroll employ-ment, 2003	Change in payroll employment, 2000-03		
			Actual manu-facturing	All other industries	Total
SOUTH *(cont.)*					
East South Central	18.0%	15.5%	-16.0%	0.4%	-2.6%
Kentucky	17.0	14.9	-14.2	0.2	-2.3
Tennessee	17.9	15.5	-15.1	0.6	-2.2
Alabama	18.2	15.7	-16.4	0.1	-2.9
Mississippi	19.3	16.0	-19.9	0.8	-3.2
West South Central	11.9%	10.1%	-15.5%	1.0%	-0.9%
Arkansas	20.7	18.0	-14.2	2.1	-1.3
Louisiana	9.2	8.2	-12.2	0.4	-0.8
Oklahoma	11.9	9.9	-19.4	-0.3	-2.6
Texas	11.3	9.6	-15.6	1.3	-0.6
WEST	11.2%	9.4%	-16.1%	1.9%	-0.1%
Mountain	8.4	7.1	-14.2	2.7	1.3
Montana	5.8	4.7	-16.0	4.4	3.3
Idaho	12.5	10.8	-11.3	4.1	2.2
Wyoming	4.3	3.7	-10.6	5.2	4.5
Colorado	8.6	7.3	-18.3	-1.3	-2.8
New Mexico	5.6	4.7	-12.9	5.1	4.1
Arizona	9.4	7.6	-17.1	4.1	2.1
Utah	11.7	10.4	-10.7	1.2	-0.1
Nevada	4.2	4.0	2.3	6.0	5.9
Pacific	12.4%	10.4%	-16.7%	1.5%	-0.7%
Washington	12.2	10.0	-19.7	0.6	-1.9
Oregon	13.9	12.5	-12.3	-1.2	-2.8
California	12.8	10.7	-16.8	1.9	-0.5
Alaska	4.2	3.9	-0.8	5.9	5.6
Hawaii	3.0	2.6	-9.1	3.3	2.9

Note: Payroll employment is estimated for states and the nation separately, so the state estimates do not sum to the U.S. totals. Region and division estimates are not provided by the BLS. Estimates here are simply the sum of the component states and are presented only for comparison.

Source: Authors' analysis of BLS data.

The 21 states in the upper left quadrant of Figure 6B (e.g., Hawaii) are those with lower-than-average reliance on manufacturing and higher-than-average job growth. The 18 states in the lower right quadrant (e.g., Indiana) are those with higher-than-average reliance on manufacturing and lower-than-average job growth. The remaining 12 states cluster fairly close to the linear rela-

FIGURE 6B Job loss by state (2000-03) compared to reliance on manufacturing employment in 2000

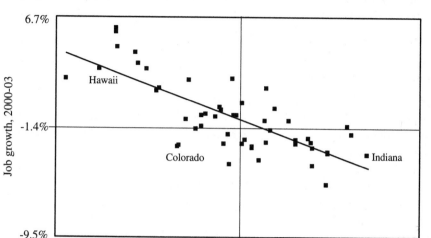

Source: Authors' analysis of BLS data.

tionship suggested by the downward-sloping line. Colorado is one important example of a state that appears to be in opposition to this relationship between job loss and the manufacturing industry because it has a lower-than-average reliance on manufacturing and worse-than-average job loss (placing it in the lower left quadrant). However, while Colorado's manufacturing sector was only 8.6% of total employment, it suffered more than most sectors, with a decline of 18.3%, compared to losses of 1.3% in the remaining sectors.

Also noted in Chapter 3 is the fact that the loss of manufacturing jobs, if not reversed, will have a significant impact on the living standards of working families. This is especially the case in those states that have relied heavily on the manufacturing industry. In Michigan, for example, the average weekly wage in manufacturing was $1,001 in 2002—52% above the average in the state's fastest growing industry (education and health services), which indicates a combination of lower hourly wages and scarcer full-time work in education and health services. In addition, manufacturing firms covered about 75% of their workers with health insurance, compared to 55% in education and health services.

Table 6.1 also provides historical data showing that, while the pace of national employment growth was the same in the 1980s and the 1990s (1.8% per year), there was considerable regional variation. Job growth was generally faster in the Northeast and Pacific regions over the 1980s and slower in the 1990s. Job growth in the Midwest and the East and West South Central divisions was faster in the 1990s than in the 1980s.

Labor market slack

The national unemployment rate hit a 31-year low of 4% in 2000. This national trend was reflected throughout the states, all of which reached historically low unemployment in 2000. Twenty-eight states had unemployment below 4% and only one state (Alaska) had unemployment above 6%. By comparison, in 1989 (the economic peak prior to 2000), 13 states had unemployment above 6% and only nine states had rates below 4% (the national rate was 5.4%).

Not surprisingly, the recession and jobless recovery led to increased unemployment. From 2000 to 2001 the unemployment rate of 16 states rose by one percentage point or more, mostly in those states affected strongly by manufacturing losses, including North Carolina, Michigan, Oregon, and Washington. By 2003, all but nine states had unemployment rates of one percentage point or more above their 2000 rates (**Table 6.3**).

Table 6.3 also shows the increase in unemployment from 1989 to 1992 compared to the 2000 to 2003 period. In the Northeast and most South Atlantic states, the change in unemployment was greater between 1989 and 1992, but in most of the rest of the country the increase in unemployment has been worse in the recent period.

There was also a sharp increase in long-term unemployment between 2000 and 2003 (**Table 6.4**). The share of the unemployed that had been out of work for more than 26 weeks went from 11.4% in 2000 to 22.1% in 2003. Since state unemployment benefits usually run out at 26 weeks (there were temporary extensions in recent years), the share of the unemployed without work for more than 26 weeks is a useful measure of the extent of the hardship caused by persistent joblessness. It is also a sign of weak demand and feeble job creation, since it shows that many workers are unable to leave unemployment for work. Long-term unemployment rose considerably in every state except Hawaii and Delaware between 2000 and 2003. For example, in North Carolina, the share of unemployed workers that had been unemployed for more than half a year rose from 10.6% in 2000 to 23.8% in 2003.

Another limitation of the unemployment rate is that it does not account for changes in the quality of employment. One aspect of job quality that has been declining in recent years is the availability of full-time employment. After declining in every state during the last half of the 1990s, the 2000 to 2003 period

TABLE 6.3 Unemployment rate during two jobless recoveries by state, division, and region

	Unemployment rate		Percentage-point difference	Unemployment rate		Percentage-point difference
	1989	1992		2000	2003	
UNITED STATES	5.3%	7.5%	2.2	4.0%	6.0%	2.0
NORTHEAST	4.5%	8.2%	3.7	3.8%	5.8%	2.0
New England	3.9	8.1	4.2	2.8	5.4	2.7
Maine	4.2	7.4	3.2	3.5	5.1	1.6
New Hampshire	3.4	7.5	4.1	2.8	4.3	1.5
Vermont	3.6	6.6	3.0	2.9	4.6	1.7
Massachusetts	4.0	8.6	4.6	2.6	5.8	3.2
Rhode Island	4.1	9.1	5.0	4.1	5.3	1.2
Connecticut	3.8	7.7	3.9	2.2	5.5	3.3
Middle Atlantic	4.7%	8.2%	3.5	4.2%	6.0%	1.8
New York	5.1	8.5	3.4	4.6	6.3	1.8
New Jersey	4.0	8.4	4.4	3.7	5.9	2.1
Pennsylvania	4.5	7.6	3.1	4.1	5.6	1.4
MIDWEST	5.4%	6.7%	1.3	3.6%	5.9%	2.3
East North Central	5.7	7.4	1.7	3.8	6.3	2.5
Ohio	5.6	7.4	1.8	4.0	6.1	2.1
Indiana	4.8	6.8	2.0	3.2	5.1	1.9
Illinois	6.0	7.5	1.5	4.3	6.7	2.4
Michigan	7.0	8.9	1.9	3.5	7.3	3.8
Wisconsin	4.3	5.2	0.9	3.6	5.6	2.1
West North Central	4.5%	4.9%	0.4	3.2%	5.0%	1.8
Minnesota	4.3	5.3	1.0	3.3	5.0	1.7
Iowa	4.2	4.7	0.5	2.6	4.5	1.9
Missouri	5.5	5.8	0.3	3.4	5.6	2.2
North Dakota	4.3	5.2	0.9	3.0	4.0	1.0
South Dakota	4.2	3.3	-0.9	2.3	3.6	1.3
Nebraska	3.1	3.0	-0.1	3.0	4.0	1.1
Kansas	4.1	4.4	0.3	3.7	5.4	1.7
SOUTH	5.7%	7.3%	1.6	3.9%	5.8%	1.9
South Atlantic	4.8	7.2	2.4	3.5	5.2	1.7
Delaware	3.5	5.4	1.9	3.9	4.4	0.4
Maryland	3.7	6.7	3.0	3.8	4.5	0.7
District of Columbia	5.1	8.5	3.4	5.7	7.0	1.3
Virginia	3.8	6.4	2.6	2.2	4.1	1.9
West Virginia	8.7	11.3	2.6	5.5	6.1	0.6
North Carolina	3.5	6.0	2.5	3.6	6.5	2.8
South Carolina	4.8	6.5	1.7	3.8	6.8	3.0
Georgia	5.6	7.1	1.5	3.7	4.7	1.0
Florida	5.7	8.3	2.6	3.6	5.2	1.6

(cont.)

TABLE 6.3 *(cont.)*   Unemployment rate during two jobless recoveries by state, division, and region

	Unemployment rate		Percentage-point difference	Unemployment rate		Percentage-point difference
	1989	1992		2000	2003	
SOUTH *(cont.)*						
East South Central	6.3%	7.1%	0.8	4.4%	6.0%	1.6
Kentucky	6.1	6.9	0.8	4.1	6.2	2.1
Tennessee	5.1	6.4	1.3	3.9	5.8	1.9
Alabama	6.9	7.5	0.6	4.5	5.8	1.3
Mississippi	7.8	8.3	0.5	5.6	6.3	0.8
West South Central	6.9%	7.6%	0.7	4.3%	6.6%	2.3
Arkansas	7.3	7.3	0.0	4.4	6.2	1.8
Louisiana	8.0	8.3	0.3	5.4	6.6	1.1
Oklahoma	5.5	5.8	0.3	3.1	5.7	2.6
Texas	6.8	7.8	1.0	4.2	6.8	2.5
WEST	5.3%	8.2%	2.9	4.6%	6.5%	1.9
Mountain	5.5	6.5	1.0	3.8	5.7	1.9
Montana	5.8	6.7	0.9	5.0	4.7	-0.2
Idaho	5.3	6.5	1.2	4.9	5.4	0.5
Wyoming	6.3	5.7	-0.6	3.9	4.4	0.5
Colorado	5.8	6.0	0.2	2.8	6.0	3.3
New Mexico	6.7	7.0	0.3	5.0	6.4	1.4
Arizona	5.3	7.5	2.2	4.0	5.6	1.7
Utah	4.7	5.1	0.4	3.3	5.6	2.4
Nevada	5.1	6.7	1.6	4.0	5.2	1.2
Pacific	5.2%	8.8%	3.6	5.0%	6.9%	1.9
Washington	6.1	7.5	1.4	5.2	7.5	2.3
Oregon	5.6	7.5	1.9	4.9	8.2	3.3
California	5.1	9.4	4.3	4.9	6.7	1.8
Alaska	6.7	9.1	2.4	6.7	8.0	1.3
Hawaii	2.4	4.6	2.2	4.3	4.3	0.0

Source: Authors' analysis of BLS data.

has seen a rise in part-time employment in most states, as shown in **Table 6.5**. Moreover, involuntary part-time work (meaning the part-time jobs held by workers who would take full-time work if it was available) increased in all but three states. For example, Nevada, which saw some of the strongest job growth in the nation, also saw an increase in part-time employment of 2.7 percentage points between 2000 and 2003. Involuntary part-time employment in Nevada grew by 8.2 percentage points across this period.

TABLE 6.4 Long-term unemployment by state, division, and region, 2000-03

	2000	2003	Percentage-point change, 2000-03
UNITED STATES	11.4%	22.1%	10.7
NORTHEAST	14.4%	25.4%	11.0
New England	8.9	24.4	15.5
Maine	*	17.4	*
New Hampshire	*	24.4	*
Vermont	*	13.0	*
Massachusetts	*	26.6	*
Rhode Island	*	21.1	*
Connecticut	*	25.0	*
Middle Atlantic	15.8%	25.7%	9.9
New York	17.8	28.7	10.9
New Jersey	16.7	23.2	6.5
Pennsylvania	11.8	22.4	10.6
MIDWEST	9.8%	21.9%	12.1
East North Central	10.5	23.8	13.3
Ohio	11.5	20.9	9.4
Indiana	*	28.0	*
Illinois	13.0	25.8	12.8
Michigan	6.5	24.5	18.0
Wisconsin	*	19.4	*
West North Central	8.0%	16.7%	8.7
Minnesota	*	14.9	*
Iowa	*	16.9	*
Missouri	*	19.8	*
North Dakota	*	10.7	*
South Dakota	*	14.9	*
Nebraska	*	17.3	*
Kansas	*	14.5	*
SOUTH	10.8%	20.9%	10.1
South Atlantic	11.5	22.2	10.7
Delaware	18.0	17.3	-0.7
Maryland	14.7	21.8	7.1
District of Columbia	24.4	32.8	8.4
Virginia	*	18.7	*
West Virginia	15.9	24.8	8.9

(cont.)

TABLE 6.4 *(cont.)* Long-term unemployment by state, division, and region, 2000-03

	2000	2003	Percentage-point change, 2000-03
South Atlantic (cont.)			
North Carolina	10.6%	23.8%	13.2
South Carolina	*	21.9	*
Georgia	7.6	27.7	*
Florida	12.1	19.2	7.1
East South Central	10.0%	22.4%	12.4
Kentucky	*	19.5	*
Tennessee	*	22.7	*
Alabama	14.1	22.0	7.9
Mississippi	11.9	26.3	14.4
West South Central	10.2%	18.4%	8.2
Arkansas	*	18.0	*
Louisiana	13.1	18.3	5.2
Oklahoma	*	21.4	*
Texas	9.5	18.0	8.5
WEST	11.5%	21.4%	9.9
Mountain	8.7	18.2	9.5
Montana	10.0	13.2	3.2
Idaho	*	12.0	*
Wyoming	*	14.1	*
Colorado	*	22.7	*
New Mexico	*	18.1	*
Arizona	*	19.0	*
Utah	*	14.2	*
Nevada	*	16.1	*
Pacific	12.3%	22.4%	10.1
Washington	10.8	22.7	11.9
Oregon	*	20.0	*
California	13.0	23.0	10.0
Alaska	*	14.1	*
Hawaii	21.0	17.2	-3.8

* Due to small sample sizes, statistic cannot be calculated.

Note: Long-term unemployment is defined here as those who have been unemployed for longer than 26 weeks.

Source: Authors' analysis of BLS data.

TABLE 6.5 Growth in part-time work by state, 1995-2003

	Part-time work as share of total employment					Working part time for economic reasons as share of total part-time employment				
				Percentage-point change					Percentage-point change	
	1995	2000	2003	1995-2000	2000-03	1995	2000	2003	1995-2000	2000-03
UNITED STATES	24.6%	21.8%	23.1%	-2.8	1.3	14.6%	10.8%	14.7%	-3.8	3.9
NORTHEAST	25.1%	22.5%	23.8%	-2.6	1.4	14.1%	9.6%	11.8%	-4.5	2.2
New England	27.2	24.0	26.6	-3.2	2.6	13.4	7.7	10.8	-5.7	3.1
Maine	28.6	25.7	29.1	-2.9	3.4	18.9	11.8	12.5	-7.1	0.7
New Hampshire	25.6	25.2	25.1	-0.4	-0.1	14.4	6.5	9.3	-7.9	2.8
Vermont	27.7	26.1	27.8	-1.6	1.7	15.7	9.2	10.1	-6.5	0.9
Massachusetts	27.7	23.6	26.2	-4.1	2.6	12.1	7.4	9.4	-4.7	2.0
Rhode Island	28.8	26.8	29.4	-2.0	2.6	14.6	8.0	9.8	-6.6	1.9
Connecticut	25.8	22.5	25.9	-3.3	3.4	12.3	6.4	13.8	-5.9	7.4
Middle Atlantic	24.3%	21.9%	22.8%	-2.4	0.9	14.4%	10.4%	12.3%	-4.0	1.9
New York	23.4	21.1	22.7	-2.3	1.6	15.3	11.2	13.0	-4.1	1.8
New Jersey	23.0	20.5	21.0	-2.5	0.5	12.8	9.0	11.0	-3.8	2.1
Pennsylvania	26.4	24.0	24.1	-2.4	0.1	14.1	10.2	11.9	-3.9	1.8
MIDWEST	25.7%	23.4%	25.0%	-2.3	1.6	11.7%	8.7%	13.4%	-3.0	4.7
East North Central	25.2	23.1	24.6	-2.1	1.5	12.1	9.1	14.1	-3.0	5.0
Ohio	24.9	24.1	26.4	-0.8	2.3	11.9	8.7	13.9	-3.2	5.2
Indiana	24.2	22.6	22.3	-1.6	-0.3	10.9	7.9	13.7	-3.0	5.8
Illinois	24.0	21.1	22.1	-2.9	1.0	12.2	9.9	14.6	-2.3	4.7
Michigan	26.0	23.7	26.4	-2.3	2.7	13.1	9.4	15.2	-3.7	5.7
Wisconsin	27.8	25.0	26.1	-2.8	1.1	11.6	9.1	12.4	-2.5	3.3
West North Central	26.9%	24.2%	25.7%	-2.7	1.6	10.9%	7.9%	11.8%	-3.0	4.0
Minnesota	27.6	27.0	27.4	-0.6	0.4	12.3	7.2	11.7	-5.1	4.5
Iowa	28.1	24.5	26.2	-3.6	1.7	10.7	7.8	10.0	-2.9	2.1

(cont.)

361

TABLE 6.5 (cont.) Growth in part-time work by state, 1995-2003

	Part-time work as share of total employment					Working part time for economic reasons as share of total part-time employment				
				Percentage-point change					Percentage-point change	
	1995	2000	2003	1995-2000	2000-03	1995	2000	2003	1995-2000	2000-03
West North Central (cont.)										
Missouri	25.3%	20.6%	22.9%	-4.7	2.3	10.2%	8.1%	12.9%	-2.1	4.9
North Dakota	29.1	27.0	27.2	-2.1	0.2	11.4	9.8	11.5	-1.6	1.7
South Dakota	27.3	25.7	25.6	-1.6	-0.1	10.2	8.6	10.9	-1.6	2.3
Nebraska	26.3	24.5	26.1	-1.8	1.7	9.6	8.2	11.8	-1.4	3.5
Kansas	27.5	24.3	27.1	-3.2	2.8	10.6	8.0	12.6	-2.6	4.6
SOUTH	23.0%	19.7%	21.0%	-3.3	1.3	14.8%	11.5%	15.9%	-3.3	4.3
South Atlantic	22.6	19.2	20.5	-3.4	1.3	14.5	10.5	15.0	-4.0	4.5
Delaware	23.1	21.3	21.6	-1.8	0.3	12.2	8.3	9.3	-3.9	1.0
Maryland	22.6	21.3	22.2	-1.3	0.9	10.5	6.1	10.2	-4.4	4.1
District of Columbia	21.2	17.2	16.8	-4.0	-0.4	18.6	13.2	15.4	-5.4	2.2
Virginia	24.2	19.7	21.3	-4.5	1.6	13.2	7.2	10.3	-6.0	3.0
West Virginia	26.0	23.2	21.8	-2.8	-1.5	21.3	16.7	17.0	-4.6	0.3
North Carolina	22.7	18.9	22.5	-3.8	3.6	13.5	11.0	17.2	-2.5	6.2
South Carolina	22.2	19.2	21.5	-3.0	2.3	13.3	12.5	16.5	-0.8	4.0
Georgia	21.0	18.6	17.9	-2.4	-0.7	15.5	10.0	15.0	-5.5	5.0
Florida	22.4	18.1	19.6	-4.3	1.5	16.2	12.7	17.8	-3.5	5.2
East South Central	23.6%	21.5%	21.8%	-2.1	0.4	13.6%	12.4%	14.1%	-1.2	1.8
Kentucky	23.7	22.2	23.9	-1.5	1.7	12.7	9.2	13.0	-3.5	3.8
Tennessee	24.5	21.3	21.6	-3.2	0.3	11.7	12.3	14.4	0.6	2.1
Alabama	23.0	21.2	21.0	-1.8	-0.3	15.4	14.4	12.9	-1.0	-1.5
Mississippi	22.5	20.9	20.5	-1.6	-0.4	16.5	14.2	17.3	-2.3	3.1

(cont.)

TABLE 6.5 *(cont.)*   Growth in part-time work by state, 1995-2003

	Part-time work as share of total employment			Percentage-point change		Working part time for economic reasons as share of total part-time employment			Percentage-point change	
	1995	2000	2003	1995-2000	2000-03	1995	2000	2003	1995-2000	2000-03
West South Central	23.1%	19.6%	21.4%	-3.5	1.7	16.0%	12.8%	18.2%	-3.2	5.4
Arkansas	22.0	19.5	22.1	-2.5	2.6	14.8	13.7	16.1	-1.1	2.4
Louisiana	25.3	20.2	20.4	-5.1	0.2	17.1	13.7	15.3	-3.4	1.5
Oklahoma	24.3	22.2	23.1	-2.1	1.0	14.0	10.8	13.0	-3.2	2.1
Texas	22.7	19.1	21.2	-3.6	2.0	16.3	12.9	19.9	-3.4	7.0
WEST	25.5%	22.8%	24.0%	-2.7	1.2	18.1%	13.2%	17.2%	-4.9	4.0
Mountain	25.5	22.5	24.6	-3.0	2.1	14.5	10.8	15.8	-3.7	5.0
Montana	28.6	27.9	28.0	-0.7	0.1	18.4	15.1	16.3	-3.3	1.1
Idaho	28.4	26.1	27.9	-2.3	1.8	15.2	11.8	16.3	-3.4	4.5
Wyoming	26.1	23.7	24.4	-2.4	0.8	15.6	11.8	12.7	-3.8	0.9
Colorado	25.0	21.9	24.2	-3.1	2.3	12.4	8.3	15.8	-4.1	7.5
New Mexico	28.4	22.3	25.7	-6.1	3.4	16.9	14.6	14.8	-2.3	0.2
Arizona	24.8	21.2	22.9	-3.6	1.7	15.6	10.9	15.0	-4.7	4.0
Utah	29.0	28.0	30.6	-1.0	2.7	8.9	8.2	14.4	-0.7	6.2
Nevada	18.0	15.8	18.5	-2.2	2.7	20.8	14.4	22.6	-6.4	8.2
Pacific	25.5%	22.9%	23.7%	-2.6	0.8	19.6%	14.2%	17.8%	-5.4	3.6
Washington	26.6	26.2	27.1	-0.4	0.9	17.7	14.1	17.4	-3.6	3.3
Oregon	26.9	26.0	25.9	-0.9	-0.1	13.8	12.1	19.6	-1.7	7.6
California	25.1	22.0	22.9	-3.1	0.9	20.8	14.2	17.7	-6.6	3.4
Alaska	24.9	22.1	25.8	-2.8	3.7	18.1	19.5	18.6	1.4	-0.9
Hawaii	26.6	24.3	23.4	-2.3	-0.9	16.0	17.2	16.3	1.2	-0.9

Source: Authors' analysis of BLS data.

Stagnant wage growth

A weak labor market affects the living standards of working families directly when workers lose jobs or are unable to find work that pays well and provides adequate hours and benefits. Another impact of high unemployment is that workers have less bargaining power and wage growth can either decline or disappear.

Alternatively, full employment can lead to substantial wage gains as employers need to pay more to attract and retain workers. This was the case during the last half of the 1990s—from 1995 to 2000, low-wage workers in all but nine states saw annual real wage growth of 1% or higher (**Table 6.6**).

Because wages are "sticky" (meaning they rarely fall in nominal terms), we wouldn't expect the weakened labor market of 2001 through 2003 to immediately result in dramatic wage declines. For the most part, the momentum of the latter 1990s fueled continued low-wage growth. However, the effect of rising unemployment has been noticeable. After rising at an annual rate of 2.3% from 1995 to 2000, the growth in low wages slowed to less than 1% annually from 2000 to 2003.

Wage growth for low-wage workers slowed even further in some areas. In the West North Central division, for example, wage growth slowed from 3.1% annually from 1995 to 2000 to less than 1% annually from 2000 to 2003 (top panel of **Figure 6C**). There were some states, primarily in the Northeast, where wage growth was faster in the 2000 to 2003 period than between 1995 and 2000, but the overall picture was one of wage stagnation.

Table 6.7 shows the potential impact of wage stagnation during this period on the paycheck of full-time, year-round workers. For example, in Ohio, if 20th percentile wage growth had continued to grow at its 1995-2000 rate, full-time, year-round workers at the 20th percentile would have earned over $1,700 more than they did.

Wage stagnation in recent years is especially troubling if it proves to be the precursor to a return to 1980s wage trends. Because the U.S. labor market was far from reaching full employment, the wages of most low-wage workers fell across most the country in the 1980s. In many states, the decline was severe. For example, the 20th percentile wage fell by 15% in Michigan and 12% in Washington state. This trend of falling or stagnant wages continued into the early 1990s.

Because of a decade and a half of stagnant or negative wage growth, the strong growth of the 1995-2000 period served, in many cases, only to make up for previous losses. Between the economic peak years of 1979 and 2000, low-wage workers in every single state experienced wage growth of less than

TABLE 6.6 Low wages (20th percentile) by state, 1979-2003 (2003 dollars)

	1979	1989	1995	2000	2003	Annualized percent changes				
						1979-89	1989-2000	1995-2000	1979-2003	2000-03
UNITED STATES	$7.91	$7.42	$7.41	$8.30	$8.46	-0.6%	1.0%	2.3%	0.2%	0.7%
NORTHEAST	$8.19	$8.56	$8.27	$8.62	$9.07	0.4%	0.1%	0.8%	0.2%	1.7%
New England	8.04	9.22	8.57	9.12	9.69	1.4	-0.1	1.2	0.6	2.0
Maine	7.35	8.06	7.34	8.38	8.56	0.9	0.4	2.7	0.6	0.7
New Hampshire	7.91	9.03	8.41	9.11	9.90	1.3	0.1	1.6	0.7	2.8
Vermont	7.29	8.29	8.13	8.48	9.01	1.3	0.2	0.8	0.7	2.0
Massachusetts	8.14	9.67	8.84	9.27	9.89	1.7	-0.4	0.9	0.6	2.2
Rhode Island	7.92	8.42	8.18	8.94	8.75	0.6	0.6	1.8	0.6	-0.7
Connecticut	8.52	10.01	9.34	9.70	9.88	1.6	-0.3	0.8	0.6	0.6
Middle Atlantic	$8.25	$8.35	$8.17	$8.47	$8.90	0.1%	0.1%	0.7%	0.1%	1.6%
New York	8.24	8.40	8.15	8.33	8.63	0.2	-0.1	0.4	0.0	1.2
New Jersey	8.28	9.26	8.89	9.22	9.81	1.1	0.0	0.7	0.5	2.1
Pennsylvania	8.25	7.67	7.65	8.29	8.76	-0.7	0.7	1.6	0.0	1.9
MIDWEST	$8.18	$7.30	$7.55	$8.62	$8.76	-1.1%	1.5%	2.7%	0.2%	0.5%
East North Central	8.41	7.39	7.65	8.62	8.73	-1.3	1.4	2.4	0.1	0.4
Ohio	8.21	7.42	7.36	8.49	8.42	-1.0	1.2	2.9	0.2	-0.3
Indiana	7.90	7.00	7.55	8.70	8.77	-1.2	2.0	2.9	0.5	0.3
Illinois	8.79	7.77	7.86	8.42	8.77	-1.2	0.7	1.4	-0.2	1.3
Michigan	8.78	7.46	8.05	8.77	8.90	-1.6	1.5	1.7	0.0	0.5
Wisconsin	8.12	7.18	7.52	9.00	8.95	-1.2	2.1	3.7	0.5	-0.2
West North Central	$7.74	$7.08	$7.39	$8.63	$8.81	-0.9%	1.8%	3.1%	0.5%	0.7%
Minnesota	8.16	7.90	8.45	9.59	9.95	-0.3	1.8	2.6	0.8	1.2
Iowa	7.71	6.82	7.35	8.60	8.72	-1.2	2.1	3.2	0.5	0.4
Missouri	7.65	6.97	7.31	8.76	8.66	-0.9	2.1	3.7	0.6	-0.4

(cont.)

365

TABLE 6.6 (cont.) Low wages (20th percentile) by state, 1979-2003 (2003 dollars)

	1979	1989	1995	2000	2003	Annualized percent changes				
						1979-89	1989-2000	1995-2000	1979-2003	2000-03
West North Central (cont.)										
North Dakota	$7.33	$6.58	$6.56	$7.54	$7.86	-1.1%	1.3%	2.8%	0.1%	1.4%
South Dakota	7.12	6.20	6.92	8.23	8.07	-1.4	2.6	3.5	0.7	-0.7
Nebraska	7.52	6.74	7.14	7.99	8.39	-1.1	1.6	2.3	0.3	1.6
Kansas	7.89	7.07	6.85	7.93	8.19	-1.1	1.1	3.0	0.0	1.1
SOUTH	$7.43	$7.00	$7.10	$7.85	$8.08	-0.6%	1.0%	2.0%	0.3%	1.0%
South Atlantic	7.48	7.35	7.40	8.24	8.49	-0.2	1.0	2.2	0.5	1.0
Delaware	8.36	8.20	7.95	8.64	9.14	-0.2	0.5	1.7	0.2	1.9
Maryland	8.47	8.70	8.52	9.21	9.92	0.3	0.5	1.6	0.4	2.5
District of Columbia	9.25	8.71	8.46	9.54	10.03	-0.6	0.8	2.4	0.1	1.7
Virginia	7.58	7.83	7.79	8.63	8.76	0.3	0.9	2.1	0.6	0.5
West Virginia	7.73	5.96	6.62	7.15	7.47	-2.6	1.7	1.5	-0.4	1.5
North Carolina	7.35	7.17	7.46	8.35	8.23	-0.2	1.4	2.3	0.6	-0.5
South Carolina	7.21	6.89	7.25	8.33	8.09	-0.4	1.7	2.8	0.7	-1.0
Georgia	7.46	7.25	7.29	8.24	8.70	-0.3	1.2	2.5	0.5	1.8
Florida	7.28	7.23	7.12	7.69	8.20	-0.1	0.6	1.6	0.3	2.2
East South Central	$7.30	$6.43	$6.83	$7.65	$8.09	-1.3%	1.6%	2.3%	0.2%	1.9%
Kentucky	7.58	6.39	6.96	7.84	8.08	-1.7	1.9	2.4	0.2	1.0
Tennessee	7.36	6.71	7.17	8.00	8.33	-0.9	1.6	2.2	0.4	1.4
Alabama	7.26	6.62	6.51	7.47	8.08	-0.9	1.1	2.8	0.1	2.7
Mississippi	7.00	5.74	6.17	7.18	7.76	-2.0	2.0	3.1	0.1	2.6
West South Central	$7.45	$6.58	$6.69	$7.49	$7.53	-1.2%	1.2%	2.3%	0.0%	0.2%
Arkansas	7.17	6.18	6.45	7.32	7.43	-1.5	1.6	2.5	0.1	0.5
Louisiana	7.41	6.21	6.37	7.29	7.24	-1.7	1.5	2.7	-0.1	-0.2
Oklahoma	7.72	6.85	6.59	7.65	7.78	-1.2	1.0	3.0	0.0	0.5
Texas	7.48	6.68	6.81	7.53	7.56	-1.1	1.1	2.0	0.0	0.1

(cont.)

TABLE 6.6 (cont.)   Low wages (20th percentile) by state, 1979-2003 (2003 dollars)

| | 1979 | 1989 | 1995 | 2000 | 2003 | Annualized percent changes | | | | |
						1979-89	1989-2000	1995-2000	1979-2003	2000-03
WEST	$8.46	$7.74	$7.44	$8.20	$8.47	-0.9%	0.5%	2.0%	-0.2%	1.1%
Mountain	7.87	7.13	7.37	8.21	8.29	-1.0	1.3	2.2	0.2	0.3
Montana	7.54	6.59	6.91	7.04	7.43	-1.3	0.6	0.4	-0.3	1.8
Idaho	7.58	6.44	7.03	7.70	7.82	-1.6	1.6	1.8	0.1	0.5
Wyoming	8.40	6.77	6.74	7.45	7.97	-2.1	0.9	2.0	-0.6	2.3
Colorado	8.14	7.28	7.96	9.08	9.65	-1.1	2.0	2.7	0.5	2.0
New Mexico	7.42	6.32	6.98	7.37	7.49	-1.6	1.4	1.1	0.0	0.5
Arizona	7.84	7.31	7.16	8.17	8.60	-0.7	1.0	2.7	0.2	1.7
Utah	7.93	7.29	7.35	8.26	7.95	-0.8	1.1	2.4	0.2	-1.3
Nevada	8.24	7.98	8.11	8.31	8.36	-0.3	0.4	0.5	0.0	0.2
Pacific	$8.70	$8.12	$7.48	$8.19	$8.55	-0.7%	0.1%	1.8%	-0.3%	1.5%
Washington	9.13	8.05	8.11	9.04	8.97	-1.3	1.1	2.2	0.0	-0.2
Oregon	8.79	7.80	7.83	8.38	8.18	-1.2	0.7	1.4	-0.2	-0.8
California	8.65	8.12	7.32	7.96	8.47	-0.6	-0.2	1.7	-0.4	2.1
Alaska	12.26	10.48	9.54	9.57	10.10	-1.6	-0.8	0.1	-1.2	1.8
Hawaii	7.58	8.34	8.34	7.82	8.71	1.0	-0.6	-1.3	0.1	3.7

Source: Authors' analysis of BLS data.

367

FIGURE 6C Growth in wages by division, 1995-2000 and 2000-03

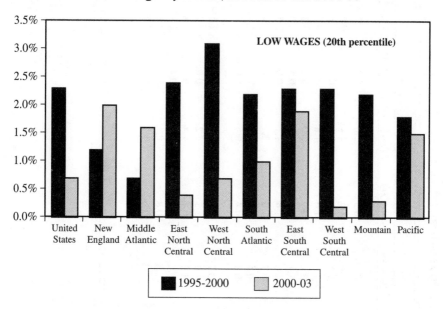

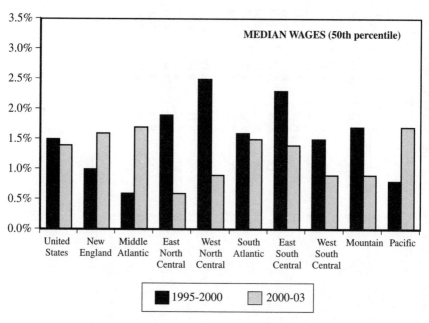

Source: Authors' analysis of BLS data.

TABLE 6.7 Potential impact of hourly wage growth stagnation

	20th percentile wage in 2003		Impact of change in hourly wage growth on paycheck of a full-time, year-round worker
	Actual	If wage growth had remained at 1995-2000 level	
UNITED STATES	$8.46	$8.87	-$860
NORTHEAST	$9.07	$8.83	$506
New England	9.69	9.47	466
Maine	8.56	9.07	-1,059
New Hampshire	9.90	9.56	716
Vermont	9.01	8.70	653
Massachusetts	9.89	9.53	748
Rhode Island	8.75	9.44	-1,417
Connecticut	9.88	9.93	-84
Middle Atlantic	$8.90	$8.66	$489
New York	8.63	8.43	408
New Jersey	9.81	9.42	815
Pennsylvania	8.76	8.69	150
MIDWEST	$8.76	$9.34	-$1,212
East North Central	8.73	9.26	-1,106
Ohio	8.42	9.25	-1,739
Indiana	8.77	9.47	-1,464
Illinois	8.77	8.78	-38
Michigan	8.90	9.24	-708
Wisconsin	8.95	10.03	-2,242
West North Central	$8.81	$9.47	-$1,364
Minnesota	9.95	10.35	-847
Iowa	8.72	9.45	-1,520
Missouri	8.66	9.77	-2,313
North Dakota	7.86	8.20	-705
South Dakota	8.07	9.14	-2,217
Nebraska	8.39	8.55	-322
Kansas	8.19	8.66	-968
SOUTH	$8.08	$8.33	-$534
South Atlantic	8.49	8.79	-617
Delaware	9.14	9.08	127
Maryland	9.92	9.66	546
District of Columbia	10.03	10.25	-447
Virginia	8.76	9.18	-884
West Virginia	7.47	7.48	-15
North Carolina	8.23	8.93	-1,447
South Carolina	8.09	9.05	-1,994
Georgia	8.70	8.87	-336
Florida	8.20	8.05	298

(cont.)

TABLE 6.7 *(cont.)* Potential impact of hourly wage growth stagnation

	20th percentile wage in 2003		Impact of change in hourly wage growth on paycheck of a full-time, year-round worker
	Actual	If wage growth had remained at 1995-2000 level	
East South Central	$8.09	$8.18	-$202
Kentucky	8.08	8.41	-692
Tennessee	8.33	8.54	-423
Alabama	8.08	8.11	-70
Mississippi	7.76	7.86	-195
West South Central	$7.53	$8.02	-$1,013
Arkansas	7.43	7.89	-956
Louisiana	7.24	7.91	-1,388
Oklahoma	7.78	8.37	-1,239
Texas	7.56	7.99	-904
WEST	$8.47	$8.68	-$441
Mountain	8.29	8.76	-996
Montana	7.43	7.11	651
Idaho	7.82	8.13	-635
Wyoming	7.97	7.91	125
Colorado	9.65	9.83	-370
New Mexico	7.49	7.61	-248
Arizona	8.60	8.85	-522
Utah	7.95	8.86	-1,886
Nevada	8.36	8.43	-135
Pacific	$8.55	$8.65	-$198
Washington	8.97	9.64	-1,397
Oregon	8.18	8.73	-1,143
California	8.47	8.37	197
Alaska	10.10	9.59	1,073
Hawaii	8.71	7.53	2,467

Source: Authors' analysis of BLS data.

1% annually, with all of that growth occurring in the last five years in most states.

Median wages have followed similar trends. Wage growth at the median did slightly better than low wages in the 1980s, but did not grow as quickly during the late 1990s boom (**Table 6.8**). Median wage growth was slower from 2000 to 2003 than from 1995 to 2000 in most of the country, with the Northeast again being the exception (**Figure 6C**).

TABLE 6.8 Median wage (50th percentile) by state, 1979-2003 (2003 dollars)

						Annualized percent changes				
	1979	1989	1995	2000	2003	1979-89	1989-2000	1995-2000	1979-2003	2000-03
UNITED STATES	$12.36	$12.36	$12.14	$13.07	$13.62	0.0%	0.5%	1.5%	0.3%	1.4%
NORTHEAST	$12.66	$14.03	$13.66	$14.12	$14.89	1.0%	0.1%	0.7%	0.5%	1.8%
New England	12.02	14.18	13.99	14.72	15.46	1.7	0.3	1.0	1.0	1.6
Maine	10.07	11.47	10.98	11.81	12.41	1.3	0.3	1.5	0.8	1.7
New Hampshire	11.48	13.66	12.99	14.03	15.03	1.8	0.2	1.6	1.0	2.3
Vermont	10.76	11.94	12.07	12.49	13.62	1.1	0.4	0.7	0.7	2.9
Massachusetts	12.12	14.51	14.31	15.05	16.20	1.8	0.3	1.0	1.0	2.5
Rhode Island	11.62	12.64	13.12	14.04	14.09	0.8	1.0	1.4	0.9	0.1
Connecticut	12.89	15.11	15.69	16.00	17.04	1.6	0.5	0.4	1.0	2.1
Middle Atlantic	12.96	13.98	13.54	13.97	14.69	0.8%	0.0%	0.6%	0.4%	1.7%
New York	12.93	14.21	13.82	13.91	14.54	1.0	-0.2	0.1	0.3	1.5
New Jersey	13.25	15.09	15.25	15.45	16.89	1.3	0.2	0.3	0.7	3.0
Pennsylvania	12.84	12.35	12.35	13.15	13.59	-0.4	0.6	1.3	0.1	1.1
MIDWEST	$13.12	$12.21	$12.13	$13.44	$13.74	-0.7%	0.9%	2.1%	0.1%	0.8%
East North Central	13.59	12.56	12.39	13.59	13.83	-0.8	0.7	1.9	0.0	0.6
Ohio	13.44	12.43	12.08	13.51	13.14	-0.8	0.8	2.3	0.0	-0.9
Indiana	12.26	11.30	11.49	12.78	13.22	-0.8	1.1	2.1	0.2	1.2
Illinois	13.89	13.21	13.26	13.93	14.39	-0.5	0.5	1.0	0.0	1.1
Michigan	14.43	13.13	13.16	14.00	14.22	-0.9	0.6	1.2	-0.1	0.5
Wisconsin	12.88	11.80	12.18	13.07	13.77	-0.9	0.9	1.4	0.1	1.8
West North Central	12.00	11.46	11.63	13.14	13.48	-0.5%	1.3%	2.5%	0.4%	0.9%
Minnesota	12.89	12.69	12.89	15.33	15.52	-0.2	1.7	3.5	0.8	0.4
Iowa	12.03	11.03	10.99	12.71	13.01	-0.9	1.3	2.9	0.3	0.8
Missouri	11.99	11.43	11.62	13.30	13.47	-0.5	1.4	2.7	0.5	0.4

(cont.)

TABLE 6.8 (cont.) Median wage (50th percentile) by state, 1979-2003 (2003 dollars)

	1979	1989	1995	2000	2003	Annualized percent changes				
						1979-89	1989-2000	1995-2000	1979-2003	2000-03
West North Central (cont.)										
North Dakota	$11.25	$10.19	$9.84	$10.78	$11.16	-1.0%	0.5%	1.8%	-0.2%	1.2%
South Dakota	9.94	9.50	10.16	11.57	11.48	-0.4	1.8	2.6	0.7	-0.3
Nebraska	11.30	10.41	10.72	11.36	12.12	-0.8	0.8	1.2	0.0	2.2
Kansas	11.80	11.61	10.88	12.42	12.80	-0.2	0.6	2.7	0.2	1.0
SOUTH	$11.34	$11.23	$11.26	$12.24	$12.71	-0.1%	0.8%	1.7%	0.4%	1.2%
South Atlantic	11.28	11.64	11.79	12.77	13.34	0.3	0.8	1.6	0.6	1.5
Delaware	12.63	13.08	12.65	13.90	14.47	0.3	0.6	1.9	0.5	1.4
Maryland	13.63	14.10	14.40	14.87	16.07	0.3	0.5	0.6	0.4	2.6
District of Columbia	14.10	14.25	14.21	15.90	16.77	0.1	1.0	2.3	0.6	1.8
Virginia	11.95	12.99	12.39	14.13	14.55	0.8	0.8	2.7	0.8	1.0
West Virginia	13.12	10.47	10.92	11.56	12.01	-2.2	0.9	1.2	-0.6	1.3
North Carolina	10.31	10.80	11.17	12.31	12.48	0.5	1.2	2.0	0.8	0.5
South Carolina	9.97	10.75	10.86	12.77	12.53	0.8	1.6	3.3	1.2	-0.6
Georgia	11.11	11.59	11.51	12.29	13.45	0.4	0.5	1.3	0.5	3.0
Florida	10.50	11.16	11.10	11.81	12.52	0.6	0.5	1.3	0.6	2.0
East South Central	$11.12	$10.37	$10.61	$11.87	$12.36	-0.7%	1.2%	2.3%	0.3%	1.4%
Kentucky	11.96	11.08	11.17	11.98	12.26	-0.8	0.7	1.4	0.0	0.8
Tennessee	10.81	10.30	10.85	12.25	12.48	-0.5	1.6	2.5	0.6	0.6
Alabama	11.32	10.65	10.23	11.59	12.84	-0.6	0.8	2.5	0.1	3.5
Mississippi	9.58	9.23	9.87	11.08	11.63	-0.4	1.7	2.3	0.7	1.6
West South Central	$11.56	$10.90	$10.79	$11.63	$11.94	-0.6%	0.6%	1.5%	0.0%	0.9%
Arkansas	9.68	9.43	10.09	10.72	11.24	-0.3	1.2	1.2	0.5	1.6
Louisiana	11.67	10.34	10.53	11.53	11.85	-1.2	1.0	1.8	-0.1	0.9
Oklahoma	12.08	11.06	10.75	11.29	12.02	-0.9	0.2	1.0	-0.3	2.1
Texas	11.73	11.21	10.96	11.81	12.01	-0.4	0.5	1.5	0.0	0.6

(cont.)

TABLE 6.8 (cont.) Median wage (50th percentile) by state, 1979-2003 (2003 dollars)

	1979	1989	1995	2000	2003	Annualized percent changes				
						1979-89	1989-2000	1995-2000	1979-2003	2000-03
WEST	$13.62	$13.41	$12.66	$13.44	$14.08	-0.2%	0.0%	1.2%	-0.1%	1.6%
Mountain	12.45	11.68	11.74	12.77	13.12	-0.6	0.8	1.7	0.1	0.9
Montana	12.29	10.69	10.66	10.70	11.35	-1.4	0.0	0.1	-0.7	2.0
Idaho	11.83	10.42	11.04	11.75	11.65	-1.3	1.1	1.3	0.0	-0.3
Wyoming	13.93	11.70	11.17	11.62	12.45	-1.7	-0.1	0.8	-0.9	2.3
Colorado	13.26	12.37	13.06	14.69	14.99	-0.7	1.6	2.4	0.5	0.7
New Mexico	11.84	10.31	10.81	11.47	11.40	-1.4	1.0	1.2	-0.1	-0.2
Arizona	12.04	11.96	11.40	12.64	13.40	-0.1	0.5	2.1	0.2	2.0
Utah	12.57	11.66	11.26	12.64	12.20	-0.8	0.7	2.3	0.0	-1.2
Nevada	12.42	12.58	11.94	12.27	12.43	0.1	-0.2	0.6	-0.1	0.4
Pacific	$13.91	$14.07	$13.24	$13.82	$14.52	0.1%	-0.2%	0.8%	0.0%	1.7%
Washington	14.49	13.64	13.05	14.42	14.86	-0.6	0.5	2.0	0.0	1.0
Oregon	13.74	13.00	12.63	12.98	13.52	-0.6	0.0	0.5	-0.3	1.4
California	13.80	14.16	13.36	13.82	14.61	0.3	-0.2	0.7	0.0	1.9
Alaska	19.55	16.92	15.69	15.54	15.90	-1.4	-0.8	-0.2	-1.1	0.8
Hawaii	12.44	13.46	12.67	12.62	13.70	0.8	-0.6	-0.1	0.1	2.8

Source: Authors' analysis of BLS data.

TABLE 6.9 Median family income by Census division, 1995-2003 (2003 dollars)

	1995	2000	2003	Annualized percent changes	
				1995-2000	2000-03
UNITED STATES	$48,689	$54,263	$52,758	2.2%	-0.9%
New England	$54,608	$64,065	$64,585	3.2%	0.3%
Middle Atlantic	51,842	58,076	57,882	2.3	-0.1
East North Central	53,003	58,252	54,697	1.9	-2.1
West North Central	50,250	57,631	57,644	2.8	0.0
South Atlantic	46,098	52,692	50,730	2.7	-1.3
East South Central	40,219	45,218	44,238	2.4	-0.7
West South Central	42,419	44,556	43,771	1.0	-0.6
Mountain	47,562	53,600	51,603	2.4	-1.3
Pacific	51,729	55,436	56,951	1.4	0.9

Source: Authors' analysis of U.S. Bureau of the Census data.

Family income

The growing economy of the last half of the 1990s provided a boost to the incomes of working families across the country. **Table 6.9** shows real median family income by Census divisions (groups of states by geographic location). This key economic indicator—the income of the family at the center of the income scale—grew in all nine divisions from 1995 to 2000. Incomes grew fastest in New England, where the median family's income grew by an average rate of 3.2% per year, after adjusting for inflation. Income growth was slowest in the West South Central division (Arkansas, Louisiana, Oklahoma, and Texas), but was still above the rate of inflation.

The share of Americans living in households with incomes below the official poverty threshold (the poverty rate) improved over this period as well (**Table 6.10**), with poverty rates falling in all nine divisions. The Southeast and West saw the largest declines in poverty.

The top panel of **Figure 6D** breaks down how the strong economy of this period affected the average family income of the bottom 60% of families. For example, hourly wage growth added an annual average of $531 between 1995 and 2000 in the South Atlantic division. Also, the unemployment rate fell and workers were able to work more hours during the year, which added to family incomes as well. Additional hours of work added an average of $410 annually in the South Atlantic division.

TABLE 6.10 Poverty rates by Census division, 1995-2003 (2003 dollars)

	1995	2000	2003	Percentage-point changes	
				1995-2000	2000-03
UNITED STATES	13.8%	11.3%	12.5%	-2.5	1.1
New England	10.1%	8.9%	9.5%	-1.2	0.6
Middle Atlantic	13.4	10.8	11.9	-2.5	1.1
East North Central	11.3	9.9	11.2	-1.4	1.4
West North Central	10.3	8.0	9.5	-2.3	1.5
South Atlantic	13.9	10.8	12.4	-3.1	1.6
East South Central	17.9	13.5	14.7	-4.4	1.2
West South Central	17.5	15.7	16.6	-1.8	0.9
Mountain	13.7	11.1	12.0	-2.6	0.8
Pacific	15.4	12.1	12.9	-3.3	0.7

Source: Authors' analysis of U.S. Bureau of the Census data.

The labor market troubles of 2001-03 turned the corner on family incomes. Median family incomes fell or stagnated across the country and poverty rates rose or remained constant. The bottom panel of Figure 6D shows the effects of the labor market slump on family incomes. As previously noted, hourly wage growth slowed over this period. In the East North Central division wage growth had added $438 per year to family income from 1995-2000, but was essentially flat in the following three years.

The key component of falling family incomes between 2001 and 2003 was the declining availability of work. As previously noted, many workers lost jobs or were forced to cut back their hours. All nine divisions felt the brunt of declining work hours, but the South and Midwest suffered the worst. In the East North Central division, which was hit hard by the manufacturing crisis, reduced hours took an average of $811 from the average family incomes of the bottom 60% of families.

State minimum wages

The minimum wage is a key policy affecting the living standards of working families. The decline of the federal minimum wage in recent decades has had a very direct impact on workers, particularly for women in the workforce.

Previous analysis has focused exclusively on the federal minimum wage,

FIGURE 6D Impact of wage growth and changes in hours worked on average income of working families

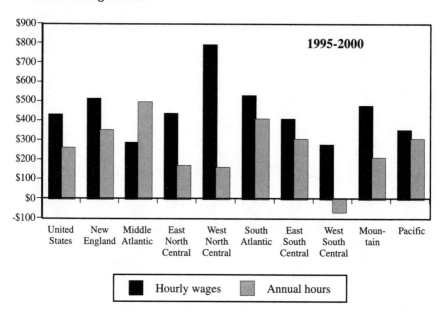

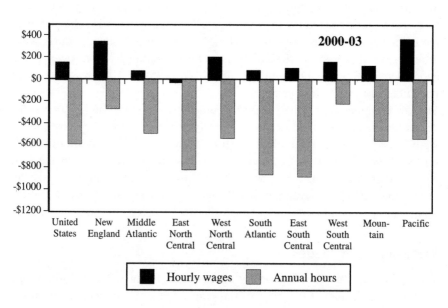

Source: Authors' analysis of U.S. Bureau of the Census data.

FIGURE 6E Real value of federal minimum wage and number of states with minimum wages above the federal rate, 1979-2004

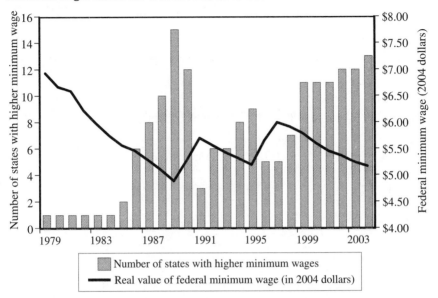

Note: In some years, Connecticut had a minimum wage set at two to three cents above the federal rate. This is not included here as a higher rate.

Source: Authors' analysis.

but states have played an important role as well. By setting their own wage floors, states can alleviate the impact of federal neglect as well as account for regional differences in wage levels and the cost of living. For example, the Alaska minimum wage has been set above the federal rate for decades in recognition of the higher cost of living in that state.

From 1979 to 1989, the value of the federal minimum wage fell by 29.5%, from $6.81 to $4.80 (in 2003 dollars). In 1979, only one state (Alaska) had a higher minimum wage than the federal level. In response to inaction at the federal level, however, by 1989 there were 15 states with higher minimum wages (**Figure 6E**).

As of this writing, the federal minimum wage—fixed at $5.15—has not been raised since 1997. Once again, some states have stepped in and raised their minimum wage rates in the absence of a federal increase. The number of states with minimum wages higher than the federal level has more than doubled, from five in 1997 to 13 in 2004.

TABLE 6.11   States with minimum wages above the federal level, 2004

Washington	$7.16	(Annually adjusted for inflation)
Alaska	7.15	
Connecticut	7.10	
Oregon	7.05	(Annually adjusted for inflation)
California	6.75	
Massachusetts	6.75	
Rhode Island	6.75	
Vermont	6.75	(Scheduled to rise to $7.00 in 2005)
Hawaii	6.25	
Maine	6.25	
District of Columbia	6.15	(Set at $1.00 above federal rate)
Delaware	6.15	
Illinois	5.50	(Scheduled to rise to $6.50 in 2005)

Source: U.S. Department of Labor.

The wage levels set by the states range from $5.50 in Illinois to $7.16 in Washington state (**Table 6.11**). Voters in Oregon and Washington have passed ballot initiatives setting moderate annual adjustments to the state minimum wage to account for the rising cost of living. This policy ensures that the value of a minimum wage paycheck in those two states is not eroded by inflation.

The state fiscal crisis

A discussion of recent economic trends at the state level would be incomplete without a mention of the state fiscal crisis. Following particularly strong fiscal conditions in the late 1990s, most states and many localities faced large budget shortfalls beginning in fiscal year 2002 that, in many cases, continue to this day.

The key cause of this crisis was the drop in state tax revenue illustrated in **Figure 6F**. The bars in Figure 6E represent the percentage change in tax revenue by quarter over the same quarter in the previous year from 1997 to 2003. Changes are adjusted for inflation and for state policy changes. Figure 6E shows the results of the recession, which brought with it a drop in family incomes (as discussed in Chapter 1) and a decline in stock market value that affected tax receipts. Figure 6E also demonstrates the ongoing effects of the erosion of state tax bases as economic activity moves from goods (which are generally taxed) to services (which are generally not taxed). These problems were exacerbated in

FIGURE 6F Year-over-year change in quarterly state tax revenue, 1997-2003

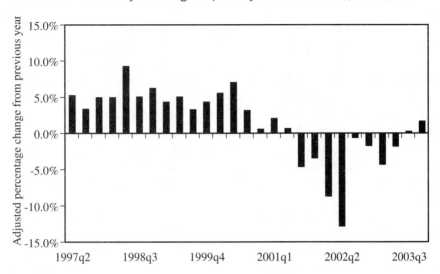

Note: Revenue changes have been adjusted for inflation as well as legislated tax changes.

Source: Rockefeller Institute of Government.

some cases by significant tax rate cuts in the late 1990s, but these effects are netted out in Figure 6E. Even after netting out the effect of policy changes, year-over-year state tax revenue fell below zero for eight straight quarters, from the third quarter of 2001 to the third quarter of 2003.

Federal policies exacerbated state budget troubles in a number of ways (Lav 2003). For example, federal tax cuts enacted in the last three years have reduced state revenues because of linkages between federal and state tax codes, and federal policies bar states from imposing certain kinds of taxes (such as Internet sales taxes). Additionally, for more than a decade, states have been picking up more of the cost of health care for the elderly and disabled. Probably the most important federal contribution to state budget woes has been an increase in federal laws that place demands on states without providing funding. These unfunded mandates, including laws related to homeland security, election reform, and education, have cost states in the tens of billions of dollars per year.

Unlike the federal government, all but one state government have laws that prevent them from responding to falling revenue by running deficits. Instead, states must employ tactics such as cutting spending, increasing taxes, raising fees, selling bonds, depleting budget reserves, and decoupling from federal tax laws.

State (and local) governments play a key role in the provision of important public services. The largest spending areas for state governments are public education and Medicaid, the latter of which provides health care for a substantial number of children, adults, and the elderly. Other important spending areas include higher education and transportation. For many Americans, state budget troubles can have a very direct impact on their living standards as educational quality declines and health care benefits are cut.

With many states desperate to raise revenue—and doing so with tax and fee increases that have disproportionately affected working families—it is useful to consider the evidence concerning the fairness of state and local tax systems.

Table 6.12 illustrates the imbalance of state and local tax burdens. Nationwide, the poorest 20% of families pay 11.4% of their incomes in state and local taxes—more than double the effective tax rate on the richest 1%.

Since broad-based income taxes tend to be progressive, states without them tend to have more regressive tax distributions. For example, in Washington state the poorest 20% of families pay more than five times as much in taxes as the richest 1% in terms of share of their income (17.6% compared to 3.1%, respectively). States that rely more on progressive income taxes and less on sales and excise taxes have flatter structures. For example, in Vermont the poorest 20% pay 10.0% of their income in state and local taxes compared to 7.1% for the richest 1%. Because of heavy reliance of a flat income tax and low reliance on sales taxes, Delaware is the only state where the richest 1% pay as much as the poorest 20%

TABLE 6.12 State and local taxes as a share of total family income by income group by state, 2002

	Lowest 20%	Middle 20%	Top 1%	Top 1% versus lowest 20%	Top 1% versus middle 20%
				Percentage-point difference	
UNITED STATES	11.4%	9.6%	5.2%	-6.2	-4.4
NORTHEAST					
New England					
Maine	10.0%	9.9%	6.8%	-3.2	-3.1
New Hampshire*	8.1	5.4	1.9	-6.2	-3.5
Vermont	10.0	9.5	7.1	-2.9	-2.4
Massachusetts	9.3	8.6	4.6	-4.7	-4.0
Rhode Island	13.0	10.3	6.0	-7.0	-4.3
Connecticut	10.2	9.5	4.4	-5.8	-5.1
Middle Atlantic					
New York	12.6%	11.6%	6.5%	-6.1	-5.1
New Jersey	12.4	9.3	5.9	-6.5	-3.4
Pennsylvania	11.4	8.8	3.5	-7.9	-5.3
MIDWEST					
East North Central					
Ohio	10.9%	10.3%	6.7%	-4.2	-3.6
Indiana	11.7	9.7	4.7	-7.0	-5.0
Illinois	13.1	10.0	4.6	-8.5	-5.4
Michigan	13.3	10.8	5.0	-8.3	-5.8
Wisconsin	10.2	11.3	5.9	-4.3	-5.4
West North Central					
Minnesota	10.5%	9.9%	6.4%	-4.1	-3.5
Iowa	10.6	9.9	5.8	-4.8	-4.1
Missouri	9.9	9.3	5.3	-4.6	-4.0
North Dakota	10.2	9.0	5.1	-5.1	-3.9
South Dakota*	10.0	9.0	2.1	-7.9	-6.9
Nebraska	10.2	9.8	6.4	-3.8	-3.4
Kansas	11.5	10.3	5.7	-5.8	-4.6
SOUTH					
South Atlantic					
Delaware	4.7%	5.2%	4.8%	0.1	-0.4
Maryland	9.4	8.8	5.1	-4.3	-3.7
District of Columbia	8.4	10.8	5.8	-2.6	-5.0
Virginia	9.0	8.1	4.8	-4.2	-3.3
West Virginia	9.3	9.7	6.5	-2.8	-3.2
North Carolina	10.6	10.0	6.1	-4.5	-3.9
South Carolina	7.9	8.8	5.5	-2.4	-3.3
Georgia	11.9	10.3	5.4	-6.5	-4.9
Florida*	14.4	9.8	2.7	-11.7	-7.1

(*cont.*)

TABLE 6.12 *(cont.)* State and local taxes as a share of total family income by income group by state, 2002

	Lowest 20%	Middle 20%	Top 1%	Percentage-point difference	
				Top 1% versus lowest 20%	Top 1% versus middle 20%
East South Central					
Kentucky	9.8%	10.1%	5.6%	-4.2	-4.5
Tennessee*	11.7	8.7	3.0	-8.7	-5.7
Alabama	10.6	9.6	3.8	-6.8	-5.8
Mississippi	10.0	9.7	5.3	-4.7	-4.4
West South Central					
Arkansas	10.7%	10.5%	5.8%	-4.9	-4.7
Louisiana	11.5	9.5	4.9	-6.6	-4.6
Oklahoma	12.0	11.1	5.7	-6.3	-5.4
Texas*	11.4	8.2	3.2	-8.2	-5.0
WEST					
Mountain					
Montana	6.1%	6.8%	5.2%	-0.9	-1.6
Idaho	9.7	9.0	6.1	-3.6	-2.9
Wyoming*	7.6	5.4	1.6	-6.0	-3.8
Colorado	9.9	8.7	4.4	-5.5	-4.3
New Mexico	12.1	10.4	6.3	-5.8	-4.1
Arizona	12.5	9.5	4.9	-7.6	-4.6
Utah	11.4	10.7	5.5	-5.9	-5.2
Nevada*	8.3	6.1	1.8	-6.5	-4.3
Pacific					
Washington*	17.6%	11.1%	3.1%	-14.5	-8.0
Oregon	9.4	8.1	6.1	-3.3	-2.0
California	11.3	9.2	7.2	-4.1	-2.0
Alaska*	3.8	2.9	2.5	-1.3	-0.4
Hawaii	12.6	11.1	5.8	-6.8	-5.3

* States without broad-based income tax.

Note: Tax rates shown are after federal deduction offset.

Source: McIntyre et al. (2003).

International comparisons:
beyond the U.S. model

In the preceding chapters, the U.S. economy was judged using domestic historical data as a benchmark. In this chapter, the economic performance of the United States is compared to that of 19 other rich, industrialized countries that, like the United States, belong to the Paris-based Organization for Economic Cooperation and Development (OECD). This analysis—which allows a comparison of the U.S. economy with similar economies facing the same global conditions with respect to trade, investment, technology, the environment, and other factors that shape economic opportunities—provides another useful yardstick for gauging the strengths and weaknesses of the U.S. economy.

Because of high productivity growth and low unemployment in the United States during the 1990s relative to Europe, many have argued that Europe should emulate key features of the U.S. economy, including weaker unions, lower minimum wages, less-generous social benefit systems, and lower taxes. The international comparisons in this analysis can shed light on the ongoing debate about the advisability of exporting this "U.S. model" to other countries.

The United States experienced tremendous income and productivity growth in the economic "golden age" that lasted from the end of World War II through the first oil shock in 1973. But by the 1980s, several OECD countries had caught up to U.S. productivity levels, and by 2002 many OECD countries had surpassed relative U.S. levels of productivity and income. In the 2000s, real annual compensation growth in the United States was less than the OECD average.

Regardless of productivity and income levels, the U.S. economy has consistently produced the highest levels of economic inequality. Moreover, inequality in the United States (along with the United Kingdom) has shown a strong tendency to rise, even as inequality was relatively stable or declining in most of the rest of the OECD. The United States also has a higher level of overall poverty, and poverty is deeper and more difficult to escape in the United States than in the rest of the OECD countries. The lack of redistributive social policies only exacerbates the high levels of poverty and income inequality in the United States.

Income and productivity: U.S. lead narrows

For the entire post-World War II period, the average standard of living in the United States has been among the highest in the world. **Tables 7.1** and **7.2** summarize data on the most common measure of average living standards: per capita income, or the total value of goods and services produced in the domestic economy per member of the population. Table 7.1 converts the value of foreign goods and services, measured in foreign currency, to U.S. dollars using the market-determined exchange rate in each year. By this measure, in 1960, the United States had one of the highest standards of living among the 20 countries examined here, trailing only Switzerland, Sweden, and Denmark, and it was well ahead of most of the European economies that were still rebuilding after World War II. Per capita income grew rapidly in the United States in the 1960s and 1970s, but it rose even more rapidly in almost all the other economies. As a result, almost all of the OECD economies narrowed the income gap with the United States. In the 1980s and again in the 1990s, growth in per capita income decelerated sharply in comparison to the previous two decades throughout most of the OECD. The deceleration was less severe for the United States during this time. In the 1990s, growth in U.S. per capita income was slightly above average compared to the other rich countries. By 2002, the latest data available, annual growth rates in per capita income had slowed considerably for the United States and most other OECD countries. Per capita income in the United States was $36,102 per year, higher than the non-U.S. population-weighted average of $34,957, but below that of Switzerland ($52,624), Japan ($50,611), Norway ($45,177), Denmark ($44,740), Austria ($38,477), Sweden ($37,870), Germany ($37,150), and Finland ($36,659).

Using market exchange rates to convert the cost of goods and services in other countries to a U.S. value can, in some cases, give a misleading picture of relative standards of living. The relatively high level of income in Japan, for example, reflects fluctuations in market exchange rates in response to short-term international capital flows and other macroeconomic factors. However, this does not necessarily reflect long-term differences in national prices and the relative standard of living in Japan and the United States. In reality, prices vary considerably across countries. For example, land and housing prices are generally much lower in the wide-open United States, Canada, and Australia than they

TABLE 7.1 Per capita income using market exchange rates,* 1960-2002 (2002 dollars)

Country	Per capita income					Annual growth rates (%)			
	1960	1979	1989	2000	2002	1960-79	1979-89	1989-2000	2000-02
United States	$13,947	$23,980	$29,234	$35,819	$36,102	2.9%	2.0%	1.9%	0.4%
Japan	5,807	31,298	42,951	50,532	50,611	9.3	3.2	1.5	0.1
Germany	10,165	26,166	31,543	36,904	37,150	5.1	1.9	1.4	0.3
France	10,099	23,325	28,015	33,013	33,755	4.5	1.8	1.5	1.1
Italy	7,952	15,946	20,114	23,599	24,004	3.7	2.3	1.5	0.9
United Kingdom	10,075	16,382	20,306	25,009	26,225	2.6	2.2	1.9	2.4
Canada	11,024	18,788	22,136	26,157	26,979	2.8	1.7	1.5	1.6
Australia	$10,003	$17,762	$21,335	$26,369	$27,471	3.1%	1.8%	1.9%	2.1%
Austria	8,992	24,733	30,033	37,871	38,477	5.5	2.0	2.1	0.8
Belgium	8,976	23,043	28,436	34,870	35,049	5.1	2.1	1.9	0.3
Denmark	13,979	31,033	35,612	43,526	44,740	4.3	1.4	1.8	1.4
Finland	11,268	22,189	30,391	35,618	36,659	3.6	3.2	1.5	1.5
Ireland	5,303	12,044	15,676	31,545	34,814	4.4	2.7	6.6	5.1
Netherlands	10,280	23,746	27,275	35,318	35,332	4.5	1.4	2.4	0.0
New Zealand	9,879	15,454	17,702	20,138	21,183	2.4	1.4	1.2	2.6
Norway	11,975	25,481	32,025	44,375	45,177	4.1	2.3	3.0	0.9
Portugal	2,248	7,991	10,766	14,333	14,429	6.9	3.0	2.6	0.3
Spain	4,673	12,206	15,326	19,940	20,607	5.2	2.3	2.4	1.7
Sweden	14,873	25,172	30,656	37,036	37,870	2.8	2.0	1.7	1.1
Switzerland	21,856	42,766	50,473	52,836	52,624	3.6	1.7	0.4	-0.2
Average excluding U.S.	$8,700	$22,781	$28,880	$34,473	$34,957	5.3%	2.3%	1.7%	0.9%

* At the price levels and exchange rates of 1995 except for 1960, which is calculated at 1990 exchange rates.

Source: Authors' analysis of OECD (2001a, 2003a) data. For detailed information on table sources, see Table Notes.

TABLE 7.2 Per capita income using purchasing-power-parity exchange rates, 1970-2002 (2002 dollars)

Country	Per capita income				
	1970	1979	1989	2000	2002
United States	$19,060	$23,980	$29,234	$35,819	$36,102
Japan	12,859	17,323	22,841	26,898	26,940
Germany	14,439	18,604	21,512	26,342	26,517
France	13,961	18,023	22,212	26,187	26,775
Italy	12,722	16,754	21,811	25,589	26,028
United Kingdom	12,967	15,875	20,728	25,406	26,641
Canada	16,523	21,804	24,767	29,365	30,287
Australia	$15,998	$18,616	$21,694	$26,998	$28,126
Austria	13,159	18,156	23,057	29,208	29,675
Belgium	14,153	18,489	22,309	27,641	27,784
Denmark	17,624	20,657	23,227	28,388	29,180
Finland	12,593	16,530	23,199	26,702	27,483
Ireland	8,770	11,835	15,189	30,567	33,736
Netherlands	15,370	18,807	22,045	28,490	28,502
New Zealand	15,144	16,051	18,145	20,888	21,971
Norway	12,253	17,654	22,530	31,189	31,753
Portugal	7,395	10,140	13,250	17,640	17,759
Spain	9,776	12,467	16,069	21,087	21,792
Sweden	15,944	18,457	23,823	28,041	28,672
Switzerland	23,551	25,148	29,680	31,070	30,945
Average excluding U.S.	$13,477	$17,309	$21,634	$26,197	$26,680

* At the price levels and purchasing-power-parity exchange rates of 1995.

Source: Authors' analysis of OECD (2003a) data.

are in more crowded European countries and in Japan. To account for price variations among countries, Table 7.2 uses an alternative set of criteria for converting the value of each country's goods and services into U.S. dollars. These alternative exchange rates, known as purchasing-power parities (PPPs), are not based on international currency market exchange rates, but rather on the price of buying an equivalent "basket" of goods and services in all countries. While calculation of PPPs presents many practical and conceptual problems, PPPs are a reasonable indicator of the relative price of consumption and arguably a better measure of relative living standards than market exchange rates.

When per capita income is measured on a PPP basis rather than by market exchange rates, the United States appears to provide an average standard of

FIGURE 7A Annual growth rates of per capita income using market exchange rates,* 1960-2002 (2002 dollars)

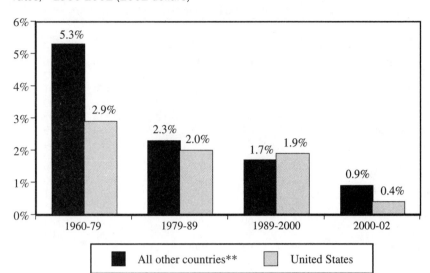

* For detailed information on figure and figure sources, see Figure Notes.
** Average of all countries listed in Table 7.1, not including the United States.

Source: Authors' analysis of OECD (1999a, 2001a, 2003a).

living that is well above that of the rest of the OECD economies. By this measure, in 1970 the United States ($19,060) was surpassed only by Switzerland ($23,551). In 2002, the United States had the highest per capita income, using PPPs, of all the OECD countries. This ranking suggests that consumption goods (housing, food, transportation, clothing, and others) are generally cheaper in the United States than in the other economies, and these lower prices help to raise the standard of living in the United States relative to other "more expensive" economies. It is worth noting, however, that PPPs do not account for the cost of non-market social goods, such as education, health care, or child care, which are much lower in many European countries relative to the United States.

The pattern of growth in per capita income was similar regardless of whether PPPs or market exchange rates were used, (for this reason, per capita income growth is only reported in Table 7.1). **Figure 7A** graphically illustrates annual per capita income growth rates for four time periods: 1960-79, 1979-89, 1989-2000, and 2000-2002. Growth rates for the United States are compared to the average growth of all the other OECD countries. Annual growth rates were

TABLE 7.3 Income and productivity levels in the OECD, 1950-2002

	GDP per hour worked (United States = 100)					
Country	1950	1973	1980	1990	1995	2002
United States	100	100	100	100	100	100
Japan	15	47	55	68	72	72
Germany	39	76	88	94	104	101
France	46	77	88	103	106	103
Italy	43	83	97	104	115	105
United Kingdom	61	64	70	74	80	79
Canada	85	86	88	85	86	84
Australia	72	69	72	71	73	76
Austria	—	—	—	—	—	96
Belgium	59	85	102	110	113	111
Denmark	60	81	89	94	97	95
Finland	35	60	64	74	80	84
Ireland	—	46	58	74	83	103
Netherlands	59	92	106	112	113	106
New Zealand	—	81	71	65	63	61
Norway	57	79	101	115	128	131
Portugal	19	40	—	44	50	51
Spain	25	56	69	82	87	74
Sweden	58	79	83	81	84	85
Switzerland	86	96	101	95	86	81
Average excluding U.S.	41	68	78	85	91	88

Source: Authors' analysis of OECD (2003c) data.

much higher, on average, for other OECD countries (5.3%) compared to the United States (2.9%) from 1960-79. In the 1989-2000 period, annual growth rates for the United States (1.9%) were above the average rates of all other OECD countries (1.7%). The growth rate fell to just 0.4% annually from 2000 to 2002 in the United States, while it fell to 0.9% for the other OECD countries.

The main determinant of an economy's current and future standard of living is the level and rate of growth of productivity—the value of goods and services that the economy can produce on average in an hour of work. Productivity is the starting point in any explanation of differences in the level and growth of income across countries. **Table 7.3** presents other nations' productivity levels as a percentage of the U.S. level. In 1950, the U.S. economy was far more productive than other economies. The United States produced more than six times as many goods and services in an hour than Japan and over twice as

TABLE 7.4 Labor productivity* growth per year in the OECD, 1960-2003

Country	1960-73	1973-79	1979-1989	1989-2000	2000-03
United States	2.6%	0.3%	1.2%	1.7%	2.6%
Japan	8.4	2.8	2.8	1.3	1.7
Germany	4.5	3.1	1.4	1.7	0.9
France	5.3	2.9	2.5	1.5	0.2
Italy	6.4	2.8	1.9	1.7	-0.4
United Kingdom	4.0	1.6	1.8	1.8	1.2
Canada	2.5	1.1	1.0	1.5	0.7
Australia	3.0%	2.5%	1.1%	2.0%	1.1%
Austria	5.9	3.1	2.4	2.5	0.9
Belgium	5.2	2.7	2.4	1.6	0.4
Denmark	3.9	2.3	1.3	2.4	1.7
Finland	5.0	3.2	3.4	2.9	1.2
Ireland	4.8	4.3	4.1	3.7	3.5
Netherlands	4.8	2.6	1.6	1.4	0.0
New Zealand	2.1	-1.1	1.9	0.7	1.1
Norway	3.8	2.7	1.0	2.7	1.5
Portugal	7.5	0.5	2.2	2.1	0.0
Spain	5.9	2.8	2.7	1.4	0.9
Sweden	3.7	1.4	1.8	2.8	1.1
Switzerland	3.3	0.8	0.4	0.3	-0.1

* See Table Notes for source of productivity data.

Source: OECD (1998, 2001d, and 2003a).

much in an hour as France. The nearest competitors were other economies that had escaped massive dislocation during World War II—Switzerland (86% of the U.S. level), Canada (85%), Australia (72%), and Denmark (60%). All economies narrowed the productivity gap with the United States between 1950 and 2002 except Canada and Switzerland. Seven nations—Norway (131%), Belgium (111%), the Netherlands (106%), Italy (105%), France (103%), Ireland (103%), and Germany (101%)—exceeded U.S. productivity levels in 2002.

The pattern of productivity growth summarized in **Table 7.4** and **Figure 7B** closely resembles that of per capita income. The first key feature of productivity growth was the dramatic slowdown after the mid-1970s. Growth was much more rapid in the 1960s than it was in the 1980s and 1990s. A second key feature was the comparably poor performance of the United States before productivity growth rebounded between 2000 and 2003. All OECD countries had decreases in labor productivity growth from the 1989-2000 to 2000-03 periods

FIGURE 7B Productivity growth rates, 1960-2003

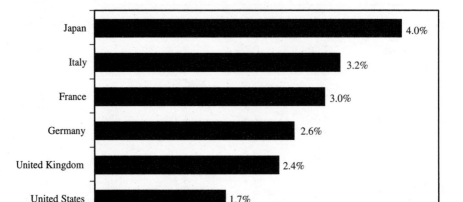

Source: Authors' analysis of OECD (1998, 2001d, and 2003a) data.

except for the United States (1.7% to 2.6%), Japan (1.3% to 1.7%), and New Zealand (0.7% to 1.1%). (The estimate for the United States for the period between 1979 and 2002, taken from the OECD, is slightly lower than the official U.S. government rate because the estimates in Table 7.4 do not take into account recent changes in the method that the Bureau of Labor Statistics uses to calculate labor productivity. The figures here, however, are comparable across countries).

Figure 7B illustrates that, over the past four decades, Japan has had the highest average annual productivity growth rates. Productivity growth rates for the United States (1.7%) and Canada (1.6%) were significantly less than Japan (4.0%), Italy (3.2%), France (3.0%), Germany (2.6%), and the United Kingdom (2.4%).

Economists explain the poor U.S. performance prior to 1995 by arguing that it is much harder to lead than to follow, to innovate than to imitate. In this view, productivity growth was faster outside the United States because other economies were engaged in a constant game of catch-up in which they rapidly assimilated technological improvements pioneered in the United States. While this view may have made sense as late as the 1960s or 1970s, the data on productivity levels in Table 7.3 suggest otherwise. By the end of the 1990s, several European economies had matched or exceeded U.S. productivity levels, and many others had narrowed the gap considerably—even with the relatively rapid productivity gains of the late 1990s in the United States. The ability of Norway, Belgium, the Netherlands, Italy, France, Ireland, and Germany to reach U.S. productivity levels in 2002 suggests that these countries' comprehensive welfare and collective-bargaining systems have not stymied income growth or improvements in economic efficiency relative to the more free-market-oriented United States.

Some economists have also dismissed the evidence of high European productivity levels as simply a by-product of high European unemployment rates. These economists argue that low-productivity workers find jobs in the low-unemployment United States, thus pulling down the average productivity level of the U.S. economy. Indeed, in Europe, which generally has higher unemployment rates than the United States, low-productivity workers are less likely to work and therefore don't pull down average productivity levels. This argument, however, has several flaws. First, three of the European economies in Table 7.3 with 2002 productivity levels above the U.S. level—Ireland, the Netherlands, and Norway—actually have *lower* unemployment rates than the United States. (See Table 7.21, which shows that in 2002 the unemployment rate was 4.3% in Ireland, 2.7% in the Netherlands, and 3.9% in Norway). The very low unemployment rates in these countries did not prevent them from achieving high productivity levels. Second, in the United States in the late 1990s, even as the unemployment rates of low-skill workers fell to historic depths, productivity rose. Third, in high-unemployment European economies, an important share of unemployed workers had mid- to high levels of formal education. (See, for example, Table 7.22 and the related discussion). This suggests that unemployed workers finding employment would not have had a significant negative impact on average productivity.

Table 7.5 combines 2002 data from Table 7.3 and 7.21 to illustrate how productivity levels would potentially change if currently unemployed workers in each country were included in the workforce and each had zero productivity. The adjusted income and productivity levels are calculated by subtracting income and productivity levels in column one from the difference in unemployment between each country and the United States. In France, for example—a country that in 2002 had high unemployment (8.8%) and productivity 103% of the U.S. level—adjusted productivity is calculated by subtracting the U.S. unemployment rate of 5.8% from France's 8.8% unemployment rate, which leaves 3.0%. Second, subtract the 3.0% from the initial productivity level of France: 103% - 3.0% = 100% adjusted productivity. This 100% indicates that the high unemployment rate in France did not greatly affect its productivity level. If high European productivity levels were simply a by-product of high European unemployment rates, the adjusted productivity level of France would be expected to fall substantially behind the U.S. level of 100. It is also worth noting

TABLE 7.5 Productivity and unemployment rates in the OECD, 2002*

Country	Income and productivity (U.S. = 100)	Unemployment rate	Adjusted income and productivity**
United States	100	5.8%	—
Japan	72	5.4	73
Germany	101	8.6	98
France	103	8.8	100
Italy	105	9.0	102
United Kingdom	79	5.1	80
Canada	84	7.7	82
Australia	76	6.3%	76
Austria	96	4.3	98
Belgium	111	7.3	109
Denmark	95	4.6	96
Finland	84	9.1	81
Ireland	103	4.3	104
Netherlands	106	2.7	109
New Zealand	61	5.2	61
Norway	131	3.9	133
Portugal	51	5.1	52
Spain	74	11.3	68
Sweden	85	4.9	86
Switzerland	81	3.2	83

* See Table Notes.
** Assumes unemployment above U.S. rate corresponds to employed workers with no output.

Source: Authors' analysis of OECD (2003b, 2003c) data.

that France achieved its relatively high productivity even as it lowered the standard workweek to 35 hours. Thus, adjusting for differences in unemployment did not alter the basic conclusion that a number of advanced countries now have higher productivity levels than the United States.

Of the seven countries that had productivity levels higher than the United States in 2002, six of them had adjusted productivity levels as high or higher than U.S. levels. Germany was the only county with higher productivity than the United States that had an adjusted productivity level that was only slightly lower than the U.S. level, with 98% adjusted productivity. The adjusted productivity of Spain—which had an unemployment rate of 11.3%—fell the most, from 74% to 68% of the U.S. level.

TABLE 7.6 Real compensation growth per year in the OECD,* 1979-2003

Country	1979-89	1989-2000	2000-03
United States	-0.3%	0.9%	0.3%
Japan	1.3	0.3	-0.5
Germany*	1.1	1.7	0.0
France	1.1	0.1	0.9
Italy	1.3	0.8	0.1
United Kingdom	1.8	1.5	1.9
Canada	0.6	0.2	0.0
Australia	0.4%	0.4%	0.4%
Austria	1.8	1.5	0.3
Belgium	0.8	2.2	2.0
Denmark	1.0	1.5	2.4
Finland	3.0	1.3	1.3
Ireland	1.9	1.3	0.7
Netherlands	0.0	0.5	0.6
New Zealand	-0.4	-1.5	-0.8
Norway	0.5	1.2	4.3
Portugal	0.1	3.6	0.4
Spain	1.0	2.3	1.2
Sweden	1.3	0.8	2.1
Switzerland	1.4	0.5	1.6
Average excluding U.S.	1.1%	0.9%	0.5%

* See Table Notes.

Source: Authors' analysis of OECD (2001d and 2003a) data.

Workers' wages and compensation: unequal growth

Wages and other work-related benefits are by far the most important source of income for the vast majority of people in the United States and the other countries analyzed here. The level, growth, and distribution of wages and benefits are important starting points for international economic comparisons. **Table 7.6** shows the inflation-adjusted annual growth rates of compensation per worker (wages plus fringe benefits) in the private sector for 20 countries from 1979-89, 1989-2000, and 2000-03. In the 1980s, 1990s, and into the new century, growth rates varied considerably across countries. In the 1980s, the United States put in the second-worst performance, with average compensation falling about 0.3% per year—only New Zealand saw a worse decline, with a drop of

TABLE 7.7 Relative hourly compensation of manufacturing production workers, 1979-2002, using market exchange rates (U.S. = 100)

Country	Hourly compensation			
	1979	1989	2000	2002
United States	100	100	100	100
Japan	60	88	111	88
Germany*	124	123	121	123
France	85	88	83	82
Italy	78	101	74	70
United Kingdom	63	74	80	82
Canada	87	103	81	75
Australia	83	87	71	73
Austria	88	99	98	99
Belgium	131	108	106	107
Denmark	117	102	103	114
Finland	83	118	98	101
Ireland	55	68	63	71
Netherlands	126	105	96	102
New Zealand	51	53	41	42
Norway	114	128	111	128
Portugal	19	21	24	—
Spain	59	63	55	56
Sweden	125	122	101	95
Switzerland	117	117	107	113
Average excluding U.S.	82	93	92	88

* Western Germany.

Source: Authors' analysis of BLS (2001a and 2003) data.

0.4% annually. Compensation grew most in Finland (3.0% per year), the United Kingdom (1.8% per year), and Ireland (1.9% per year). From 1989 to 2000, the United States had a 0.9% annual growth rate of real compensation, which was right at the average for all other countries. The U.S. average from 2000 to 2003 was 0.3%, below the OECD average of 0.5% in real compensation growth. Thirteen countries fared better than the United States, most notably Norway with 4.3% growth.

The most extensive international data on compensation covers the narrower group of workers in manufacturing, which included between 13% and 23% of employed workers in OECD countries. **Tables 7.7** and **7.8** compare hourly compensation in manufacturing in 19 OECD countries to the corresponding levels

TABLE 7.8 Relative hourly compensation of manufacturing production workers, 1979-2002, using purchasing-power parities (U.S. = 100)

Country				
	1979	1989	2000	2002
United States	100	100	100	100
Japan	53	62	80	79
Germany*	99	120	126	127
France	68	88	98	95
Italy	97	107	96	86
United Kingdom	67	78	83	86
Canada	88	96	101	97
Australia	73	80	92	98
Austria	83	102	114	111
Belgium	99	114	126	123
Denmark	84	84	98	103
Finland	67	89	107	107
Ireland	56	71	68	74
Netherlands	97	109	112	112
New Zealand	60	59	61	62
Norway	73	92	106	108
Portugal	34	37	39	—
Spain	64	74	78	76
Sweden	85	93	98	95
Switzerland	87	97	93	94
Average excluding U.S.	75	87	95	92

Hourly compensation

* Prior to 1999, Western Germany.

Source: Authors' analysis of BLS (2001b and 2004) and OECD (2003a) data.

in the United States in 1979, 1989, 2000, and 2002. In Table 7.7 national compensation rates are converted into U.S. dollars using market exchange rates. Market exchange rates reflect the relative value of American goods, services (including labor), and assets in international markets; therefore, the compensation figures here capture the relative costs to an employer of hiring U.S. labor. Seven of the 19 countries had total compensation levels higher than those in the United States in 2002. From 1979 to 2002, manufacturing wages converged closer to the U.S. average. In 1979, eight countries had manufacturing wages within 20% of the U.S. average. By 2002, 10 countries fell within this range.

In terms of purchasing-power parities (which better reflect the ability of the compensation levels in each country to guarantee a specific standard of living), U.S. workers fared better in the international comparison. In 1979, manufacturing compensation on a PPP basis was higher in the United States than in every other country examined in Table 7.8. Several countries—Belgium and Germany with 99 and Italy and the Netherlands with 97—were the only countries within 10% of the U.S. level. But all of the OECD economies except Italy closed the compensation gap between 1979 and 2002. By 2002, manufacturing compensation in the United States (100) had fallen behind that of Germany (127), Belgium (123), the Netherlands (112), Austria (111), Norway (108), Finland (107), and Denmark (103). Italy surpassed the United States in 1989, but has been slipping ever since—down to 86 in 2002.

Table 7.9 looks more carefully at the growth of hourly compensation in manufacturing. Growth in compensation was determined on a purchasing-power basis over the periods 1979-89, 1989-2000, and 2000-02. The table examines growth in compensation over the three periods separately for all manufacturing employees and for production workers only. During the 1980s, the United States, at just 0.2% per year, had one of the lowest rates of growth in hourly compensation in manufacturing among OECD countries where data were available. Among U.S production workers in the 1980s, real hourly compensation actually fell 0.8% per year, compared to average growth in the other advanced economies of 1.1% per year. Production worker compensation also fell in New Zealand (-0.7% per year), and Denmark (-0.1% per year), but rose in every other country examined here. Between 1989 and 2000, the United States again turned in one of the worst performances in compensation growth for all manufacturing employees, with a 0.8% per year growth rate (only Italy was lower at 0.2%). At the same time, there was no change in compensation for production workers in the United States. Outside the United States, hourly compensation for production workers grew 0.9% on average per year. The beginning of the new millennium saw several countries with large increases in annual compensation growth rates for all manufacturing employees, including Japan (4.8%), Belgium (4.3%), and Norway (3.6%). Compensation increases were much less, in most cases, for production workers. Italy (-2.9%) and Canada (-0.1%) posted negative growth in compensation for production workers from 2000 to 2002. The United States (1.4%) was just below the average of 1.5% growth for all employees, but was above the OECD average (0.6%) for production workers, with a growth rate of 1.5%.

The positive growth rates in hourly compensation for all manufacturing employees (which includes both production, or nonsupervisory, workers and nonproduction, or supervisory, workers) and the negative-to-stagnant growth rates for production workers in the United States through the 1980s and 1990s were another manifestation of growing wage inequality in the United States.

TABLE 7.9 Annual growth in real hourly compensation in manufacturing in the OECD, 1979-2002

| Country | 1979-89 | | 1989-2000 | | 2000-02 | |
	All employees	Production workers	All employees	Production workers	All employees	Production workers
United States	0.2%	-0.8%	0.8%	0.0%	1.4%	1.5%
Japan	1.8	1.4	1.8	1.9	4.8	0.5
Germany*	2.5	2.0	2.2	1.4	1.4	1.8
France	1.9	2.4	1.4	1.3	1.9	0.2
Italy	0.9	1.8	0.2	0.1	0.4	-2.9
United Kingdom	3.4	1.8	2.2	0.9	2.3	3.6
Canada	0.4	0.2	1.2	0.7	0.6	-0.1
Australia	—	0.5%	—	1.4%	—	4.8%
Austria	—	2.0	—	1.7	—	0.7
Belgium	1.3%	1.0	1.0%	1.7	4.3%	0.6
Denmark**	1.2	-0.1	—	1.9	—	5.0
Finland	—	3.1	—	2.9	—	2.1
Ireland	—	1.9	—	1.6	—	3.8
Netherlands	1.4	0.5	1.4	0.9	1.5	1.8
New Zealand	—	-0.7	—	0.6	—	1.0
Norway	1.0	1.0	1.9	1.5	3.6	3.9
Portugal	—	1.5	—	1.8	—	—
Spain	—	1.4	—	1.6	—	0.8
Sweden	1.1	0.9	1.8	1.3	1.9	0.5
Switzerland	—	1.3	—	0.2	—	1.4
Average excluding U.S.	1.2%	1.1%	1.0%	0.9%	1.5%	0.6%

* Western Germany.
* Number for all employees in second period is 1989-93.

Source: Authors' analysis of BLS (2003, 2004) and OECD (2003a) data.

The majority of manufacturing workers are production workers. The wide disparity between growth in production workers' wages and wages overall means that manufacturing supervisors and other, non-production workers' wages have far outpaced production workers' wages. In short, the hourly compensation data suggest that manufacturing compensation grew more slowly and more unequally in the United States than it did in other OECD countries over the 1979 to 2000 period. Whether the more positive trends of 2000 through 2002 are maintained despite the long labor slump and persistent manufacturing job losses will be interesting to observe.

Table 7.10 uses data on full-time employees in all sectors of the economy to take a broader look at international earnings inequality. The table measures

TABLE 7.10 Earnings inequality in OECD countries, 1979-2000

Country	Years*	90th percentile relative to the 10th percentile**		90th percentile relative to the 10th percentile		Real wages lowest decile
		Men	Women	Men	Women	
				Average annual percentage changes		
United States	1979-2000	4.8	4.1	1.4%	1.6%	-0.8%
Japan	1979-99	2.7	2.3	0.3	0.1	0.9
Germany	1984-98	2.9	2.8	0.9	-0.2	1.5
France	1979-98	3.3	2.7	-0.2	-0.1	1.3
Italy	1986-96	2.4	2.1	1.6	-0.6	1.2
United Kingdom	1979-2000	3.4	3.1	1.3	1.2	2.0
Canada	1981-94	3.8	4.0	0.6	0.5	-0.1
Australia	1979-2000	3.2	2.7	0.7%	0.5%	-0.2%
Austria	1996	2.9	2.3	—	—	—
Belgium	1985-95	2.2	2.2	—	—	0.6
Denmark	1980-90	—	—	—	—	0.5
Finland	1980-99	2.5	2.0	0.1	-0.1	2.2
Ireland	1987-97	4.1	3.3	2.3	-1.1	2.1
Netherlands	1979-99	2.8	2.6	0.9	0.2	0.0
New Zealand	1984-97	3.5	2.8	2.1	1.1	-1.3
Norway	1980-91	—	—	—	—	1.6
Sweden	1980-98	2.3	1.9	0.6	0.7	0.5
Switzerland	1991-98	2.4	2.4	0.8	-0.8	—

* Latest range available.
** Data for last year in the range.

Source: Glyn (2001) and authors' analysis of unpublished OECD data.

inequality by the ratio of the earnings of high-wage workers (those making 90% or more of the total workforce) to the earnings of low-wage workers (those making only 10% or less of the workforce). By this measure, the United States had the highest earnings inequality of all OECD countries (4.8 for men and 4.1 for women). Inequality grew in most economies among both men and women. Among men, the ratio of earnings of the 90th-percentile worker to those of the 10th-percentile worker (the "90-10 ratio") increased by an annual rate of 1.4% in the United States. This was surpassed only by Ireland (2.3% per year), New Zealand (2.1% per year), and Italy (1.6% per year), and was well above most of the rest of the OECD economies examined. Among women, inequality in the 90-10 ratio increased most in the United States (1.6% per year), with the United Kingdom following at 1.2% per year.

One of the most troubling aspects of U.S. inequality is that it has been driven, in part, by absolute, not just relative, declines in the standard of living for those at the bottom. The last column of Table 7.10 shows that, despite relatively high levels of average productivity in the U.S. economy, workers at the 10th percentile of the earnings distribution experienced a decline in inflation-adjusted wages of 0.8% per year. This decline was more than any other country experienced except New Zealand (-1.3% per year). Wages for workers in the lowest decile increased in most other countries, with highs of 2.2% per year in Finland and 2.1% per year in Ireland, countries with relatively low unemployment rates.

The available data show that inequality in wages by gender slowed from the mid-1980s to the mid-1990s except in Sweden, where there was acceleration. **Figure 7C** shows the gap in pay among men and women across countries. Japan had the widest gender pay gap for all three periods, although there has been some improvement over time. In 1985 the gap in Japan was 46.5—meaning that among full-time workers, women earned an average of 46.5 cents less than men for every dollar earned. This wage gap had decreased to 39.2 by 1999. In the United States the gender pay gap was 25.2 in 2000, which was down from 31.8 in 1985, but up from 24.5 in 1995. A similar story can be told about France, Australia, and Sweden, where there has not been consistent erosion in the gender wage gap.

Household income: unequal growth

The per capita income figures in Tables 7.1 and 7.2 were economy-wide, annual averages. Since individuals make many important decisions about consumption as part of a family or broader household, and since, as we have seen, averages can be deceiving because they mask inequality, it is important to review international data on the distribution of household income. Labor compensation accounts for the largest share of household income, therefore, the basic pattern of inequality that occurred with earnings repeats itself here: income inequality is high (and rising) in the United States compared to the rest of the OECD. At the bottom of the income scale, U.S. inequality yields poverty rates that are higher and living standards that are lower than those at the bottom in comparable economies. Moreover, income mobility appears to be *lower* in the United States than in other OECD countries.

Household income in this analysis is measured after taxes and transfers, including refundable tax credits. **Table 7.11** uses two measures of household income inequality for OECD countries. The first measure is the "90-10 ratio," which measures how many times more income a household in the 90th percentile has compared to a household in the 10th percentile. The second inequality measure is the Gini coefficient, a special inequality scale that ranges from zero (perfect equality of income across households) to one (all income is concentrated at the very top of the income distribution). The United States has the

FIGURE 7C Gender wage gaps in the OECD,* 1985, 1995, and 1999

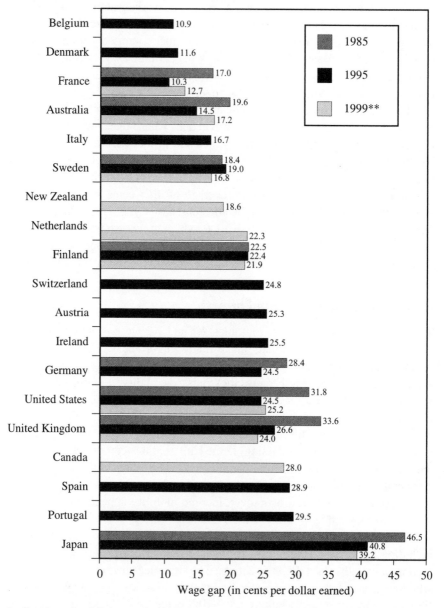

* Female median full-time earnings as a percentage of male median full-time earnings.
** Australia, United Kingdom, and the United States are 2000 data.

Source: OECD (2001g).

TABLE 7.11 Household income inequality in the OECD*

| Country | Year | Gini coefficient | Percent of median income | | Ratio of 90th to 10th percentile |
			Low income (10th percentile)	High income (90th percentile)	
United States	2000	0.368	39%	210%	5.5
Japan	1992	0.315	46	192	4.2
Germany	2000	0.252	54	173	3.2
France	1994	0.288	54	191	3.5
Italy	2000	0.333	44	199	4.5
United Kingdom	1999	0.345	47	215	4.6
Canada	1998	0.305	46	188	4.1
Australia	1994	0.311	45%	195%	4.3
Austria	1997	0.266	53	178	3.4
Belgium	1997	0.250	53	170	3.2
Denmark	1992	0.236	54	155	2.9
Finland	2000	0.247	57	164	2.9
Ireland	1996	0.325	46	201	4.3
Netherlands	1999	0.248	56	167	3.0
Norway	2000	0.251	57	159	2.8
Spain	1990	0.303	50	197	4.0
Sweden	2000	0.252	57	168	3.0
Switzerland	1992	0.307	52	188	3.6
Average excluding U.S.		0.284	49%	171%	3.6

* See Table Notes.

Sources: Smeeding (2004).

most unequal household income by both measures (see also **Figure 7D**). In the United States, a household in the 10th percentile of the income distribution receives just 39% of the income of the median household (the household exactly in the middle of the income distribution). In the other 17 economies, the 10th percentile household receives between 44% (Italy) and 57% (Finland, Norway, and Sweden) of the median national income. At the other extreme, the 90th percentile household in the United States makes 210% of the median national income, a level surpassed only by the United Kingdom (215%). Denmark (155%) and Norway (159%) are well below the OECD average of 171%. Subsequently, the ratio of the 90th to the 10th percentile is largest for the United States (5.5) and smallest for Norway (2.8) and Denmark (2.9).

The income inequality shown in Table 7.11 compares the position of low- and high-income households relative to the median income in each country. **Table 7.12** and **Figure 7E** compare low- and high-income households to the

FIGURE 7D Relative income comparisons in the OECD*

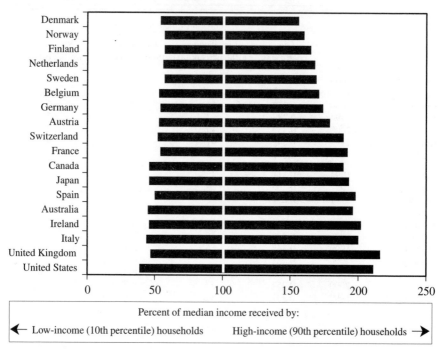

Percent of median income received by:

← Low-income (10th percentile) households   High-income (90th percentile) households →

* The gap between the income of the top 10% and the bottom 10% of households in each nation.

Source: Smeeding (2004).

median in the United States, an analysis that illustrates differences in the absolute standard of living across countries. Low-income (10th percentile) households in the United States made only 39% of the U.S. median income in 2000.
Four countries—Australia, the United Kingdom, Finland, and Sweden—had
household income at the 10th percentile, less than 39% of the U.S. median. To
the extent that these countries provide more social and economic support to
their citizens, these numbers are somewhat misleading as direct comparisons
regarding living standards of low-income people.

Not surprisingly, high-income households were much better off in the United
States (210% of the median income) than in the rest of the countries. The next
closest is Switzerland, where high-income households were 185% of the U.S.
median. The 90-10 ratio of 5.5 for the United States is still the highest compared to the U.S. median. Compared to U.S. median incomes, Denmark and
Norway (2.9) had the lowest 90-10 ratio.

TABLE 7.12 Household income inequality relative to U.S. median income*

| Country | Year | Percent of U.S. median income | | Ratio of 90th to 10th percentile |
		Low income (10th percentile)	High income (90th percentile)	
United States	2000	39%	210%	5.5
Germany	2000	41	131	3.2
France	1994	43	148	3.4
United Kingdom	1999	35	157	4.5
Canada	1998	45	180	4.0
Australia	1994	34%	148%	4.4
Belgium	1997	43	136	3.2
Denmark	1995	43	123	2.9
Finland	2000	38	111	2.9
Netherlands	1999	41	133	3.3
Norway	1995	50	143	2.9
Sweden	2000	38	113	3.0
Switzerland	1992	55	185	3.4
Average excluding U.S.		39%	130%	3.4

* See Table Notes.

Source: Smeeding and Rainwater (2001); Smeeding (2004).

Figure 7E further illustrates the differences between countries in the percentage of U.S. median income received by low-income households. This figure also shows the vast differences in the percentage of U.S. median income received by high-income households across OECD countries. Finland's high-income households received 111% of the U.S. median, while high-income U.S. households received 210% of the U.S. median.

Table 7.13 shows that since the end of the 1970s income inequality has been growing in many rich, industrialized countries—inequality increased in 10 countries but declined in six. In absolute terms (see the far-right column of Table 7.13), the annual increase in income inequality has been strongest in the United States and the United Kingdom. Income inequality has grown more slowly in Belgium, Norway, and Italy, and has fallen over the same period in Germany, Spain, Canada, the Netherlands, France, and Switzerland. Given the lower initial levels of inequality in most countries other than the United States, the absolute increases in other economies represent much larger relative increases in inequality than they would in the United States. In terms of percentage-point changes, the United States saw the second-largest increase in inequal-

FIGURE 7E Composition of low and high incomes compared to U.S. median*

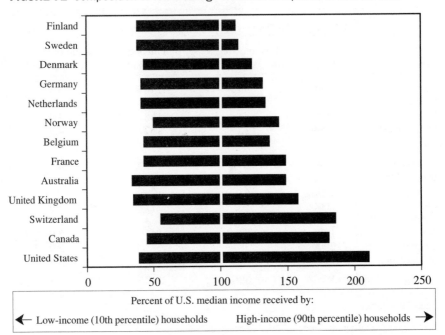

Percent of U.S. median income received by:

← Low-income (10th percentile) households   High-income (90th percentile) households →

* These relative income measures compare the gap between the top 10% and the bottom 10% of household income in each country to the 2000 U.S. median income in purchasing-power-parity terms.

Source: Smeeding and Rainwater (2001) and Smeeding (2004).

ity, second only to the United Kingdom. In terms of percent change, the United States had the fifth-largest increase (15.7%), while the United Kingdom had a very large 29.2% increase in income inequality.

Intergenerational earning mobility is another important aspect of inequality and the persistence of inequality. The degree of association between fathers' and sons' earnings is shown in **Figure 7F** for several OECD countries. In this figure, a measure of 0.6 is indicative of a high association between fathers' and sons' incomes, signifying low economic mobility. A lower value (e.g., 0.2) implies that the two earnings are not highly correlated, which is suggestive of greater mobility. The United Kingdom (0.57) had the least amount of mobility as shown in Figure 7F, while Finland (0.22) had the most.

Figures 7G and **7H** show the historical distribution of the top decile and the top 0.1% income share. The top-decile income share was larger in France than in the United States, for the most part, after World War II until the late

TABLE 7.13 Change in income inequality in the OECD after 1968

Country	Time period	Change in Gini coefficient*	
		Percent change	Percentage-point change
United States	1974-2000	15.7%	0.050
Germany	1973-2000	-7.0	-0.019
France	1979-94	-1.7	-0.005
Italy	1986-2000	8.8	0.027
United Kingdom	1969-99	29.2	0.078
Canada	1971-2000	-4.4	-0.014
Australia	1981-94	10.7%	0.030
Austria	1987-97	17.2	0.039
Belgium	1985-97	10.1	0.023
Denmark	1987-97	1.2	0.003
Finland	1987-2000	18.2	0.038
Netherlands	1983-99	-4.6	-0.012
Norway	1979-2000	12.6	0.028
Spain	1980-90	-4.7	-0.015
Sweden	1975-2000	17.2	0.037
Switzerland	1982-92	-0.6	-0.002

* See Table Notes.

Source: Authors' analysis of Luxembourg Income Study (2004a) data.

1970s, when the top decile of income share in the United States grew considerably. The U.S. top decile share of income was close to an all-time high in 1998, at 44% (Figure 7G). France's top-decile income share held steady throughout the 1990s, and was 32.5% in 1998. A look at the top 0.1% (Figure 7H) income share shows a similar pattern, although the post-WW II fall is not as drastic as in Figure 7G. There was a steady decline in the top 0.1% income share for all three countries (France, United States, and United Kingdom) from 1913 through WW II until the mid-1980s. In 1998, the top 0.1% income share was 2.0% in France; this percentage has been somewhat stable and slightly decreasing since the 1940s. The top 0.1% income share was 3.3% in 1998 for the United Kingdom, and it has been trending upward since the late 1970s. For the United States, the top 0.1% income share was 7.4% in 1998—this share increased enormously from the late 1970s to 1998. Both of these figures illustrate the income inequality that exists in developed countries and how it has worsened much more in the United States relative to France or the United Kingdom.

FIGURE 7F Intergenerational earnings mobility in OECD countries

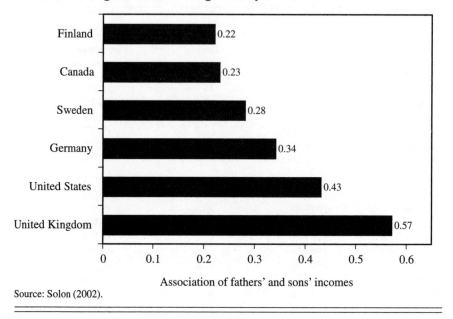

Source: Solon (2002).

FIGURE 7G Top decile family income share in France and in the United States, 1913-98

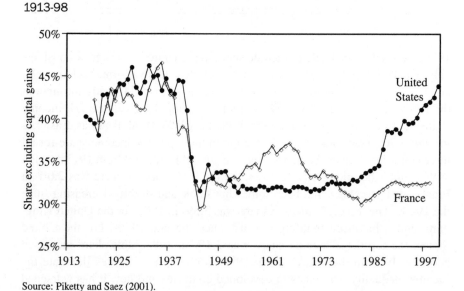

Source: Piketty and Saez (2001).

FIGURE 7H Top 0.1% family income share in France, the United States, and the United Kingdom, 1913-98

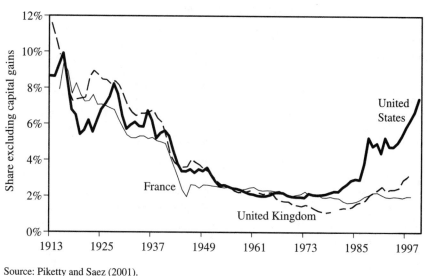

Source: Piketty and Saez (2001).

Poverty: deeper and more enduring in the United States

Higher inequality in the United States is associated with higher levels of poverty relative to the rest of the OECD, even though per capita income in the United States is high. **Table 7.14** summarizes international data on poverty rates. Following the standard methodology for international comparisons, the table defines the poverty rate as the share of households that received 50% or less of the median income in each country. In the United States, this threshold amounted to an income that was much higher than the official poverty rate (see Chapter 5). (Table 7.12, which compares the income of the 10th percentile household in each country to the U.S. median income, provides an indication of the absolute standard of living of low-income families across the OECD countries). Like the official U.S. definition of poverty, the poverty rates in Table 7.14 take into account cash transfers and are adjusted for family size, but unlike the U.S. definition, they also account for taxes and tax credits. The United States, with 17.0% of its total population living in poverty, had the highest level of overall poverty among the 17 countries examined here. Australia (14.3%), Italy (12.7%), the United Kingdom (12.5%), and Ireland (12.3%) followed the United States. The United States was also unique in that it had the

TABLE 7.14 Poverty rates in OECD countries

Country	Poverty line (50% of median)*		
	Total poverty	Children	Elderly
United States	17.0%	21.9%	24.7%
Japan	—	—	—
Germany	8.3	6.8	11.6
France	8.0	7.9	9.8
Italy	12.7	16.6	13.7
United Kingdom	12.5	15.4	20.9
Canada	11.4	14.9	5.9
Australia	14.3%	15.8%	29.4%
Austria	8.0	10.2	10.5
Belgium	8.0	7.7	11.7
Denmark	9.2	8.7	6.6
Finland	5.4	2.8	8.5
Ireland	12.3	14.4	24.3
Netherlands	7.3	9.8	2.4
New Zealand	—	—	—
Norway	6.4	3.4	11.9
Portugal	—	—	—
Spain	10.1	12.2	11.3
Sweden	6.5	4.2	7.7
Switzerland	9.3	10.0	8.4

* See Table Notes.

Source: Luxembourg Income Study (2004b) data.

highest rate of child poverty (21.9%) and the second-highest rate of elderly poverty (24.7%). Finland (5.4%), Norway (6.4%), and Sweden (6.5%) had the lowest overall poverty rates.

Table 7.15 provides three other definitions of poverty: poor at least once over the three years examined, poor in all three years, and "permanent-income poverty," which shows the proportion of people whose average income over the entire three-year period was less than the average of the poverty level over the three years. Individuals who moved in and out of poverty but whose incomes did not rise much above the poverty level were captured by the permanent income poverty measure. The United States was not much higher than other countries in terms of the proportion of people who were poor at least once over the three-year period. However, the United States had a much higher rate of

TABLE 7.15 Poverty in the OECD countries, 1993 to 1995

Country	Poor at least once	Poor in all three years	Permanent-income poverty*
United States	23.5%	9.5%	14.5%
Japan	—	—	—
Germany	19.2	4.3	8.1
France	16.6	3.0	6.6
Italy	21.5	5.6	10.4
United Kingdom	19.5	2.4	6.5
Canada	18.1	5.1	8.9
Australia	—	—	—
Austria	—	—	—
Belgium	16.0%	2.8%	5.2%
Denmark	9.1	0.8	1.8
Finland	25.1	6.5	12.2
Ireland	15.3	1.3	5.3
Netherlands	12.9	1.6	4.5
New Zealand	—	—	—
Norway	—	—	—
Portugal	24.2	7.8	13.4
Spain	21.3	3.7	8.7
Sweden	—	—	—
Switzerland	—	—	—

* See Table Notes.

Source: OCED (2001e).

people who were poor over all three years—at 9.5%, it was over twice as high as most other countries, which range from 0.8% (Denmark) to 7.8% (Portugal). The United States also had the highest rate of permanent-income poverty (14.5%). The relatively large number of people in poverty for long durations in the United States indicates that mobility out of poverty is more limited here than in other OECD countries.

"Family-friendly" and educational policies in many OECD countries may explain lower incidences of poverty in those countries, especially childhood poverty. Though the United States had a high proportion of children five years of age in formal school or center-based education programs (**Table 7.16**), a relatively low proportion of children under age five were in such programs. The percentage of children that received publicly supported child care was very low in the United States for children under age three and relatively low for

TABLE 7.16 Maternity and child care policies in the OECD*

Country	Maternity/child care leave indicators			Proportion of young children using school/center-based education programs		Percentage of children in publicly supported care	
	Duration maternity leave (weeks)	Maternity (% of average wages)	Total maternity/child care leave	Age 3 and 4	Age 5	Age under 3	Age 3 to mandatory school age
United States	0	0%	12	47%	79%	6%	53%
Japan	14	60	48	77	—	—	—
Germany	14	100	156	70	—	5	77
France	16	100	144	100	—	20	99
Italy	20	80	60	99	98	—	—
United Kingdom	52	90 for 6 wks	48	81	100	2	77
Canada	17	55	48	21	—	5	53
Australia	0	0%	48	38%	81%	—	—
Austria	16	100	160	62	—	—	—
Belgium	15	75 to 80	28	100	99	42%	99%
Denmark	18	90	76	85	94	74	90
Finland	18	65	144	39	48	22	66
Ireland	18	80	24	26	—	—	—
Netherlands	16	100	40	49	100	17	71
New Zealand	0	0	12	85	—	—	—
Norway	—	—	96	76	81	37	78
Portugal	26	100	120	68	74	—	—
Spain	16	100	144	100	—	—	—
Sweden	—	—	96	73	75	48	82
Switzerland	16	—	16	22	—	—	—

* See Table Notes.

Source: Waldfogel (2004).

children between age three and the mandatory school age. Thus, paying for child care presents a financial burden for American families unlike that experienced in many other countries. It is also more difficult for parents to afford time off to care for their children in the United States, since it is one of just three countries (the others are New Zealand and Australia) that do not mandate paid maternity or paternity leave. The majority of workers in the United States are not even eligible for unpaid family leave. In six countries, 100% of wages are covered during maternity leave, and the leave lasts a minimum of three months.

Figure 7I shows the real incomes at the 50th percentile of households with children. Cash and non-cash measures are indexed to the United States. Households with children in Norway had 57% more cash than U.S. households and

FIGURE 7I Real incomes of low-income households with children*:
cash and non-cash

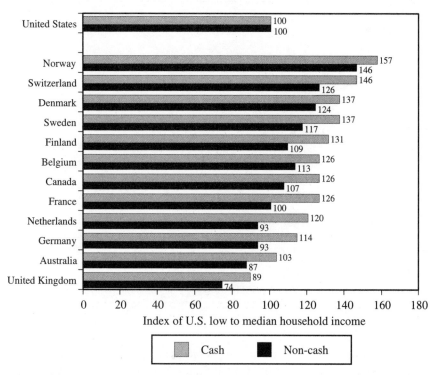

* Indexed to U.S. low to median household income for households with children; all other currencies converted to 1997 U.S. dollars using purchasing-power parities.

Source: Smeeding (2002).

46% more non-cash benefits. Another eight of the OECD countries had better cash and non-cash incomes than the United States, while only the United Kingdom was worse than the United States in both categories. These and other relatively low expenditures on social welfare are implicated in the high poverty rates in the United States.

The diagonal line in **Figure 7J** illustrates how countries with higher social expenditures as a percentage of GDP had lower poverty rates among children. The negative relationship between social expenditures and child poverty is clearly evident. The United States stands out as the country with the lowest expenditures and the highest child poverty rate. The paucity of social expenditures addressing high poverty and growing income inequality in the United

FIGURE 7J Social expenditures versus child poverty in the OECD

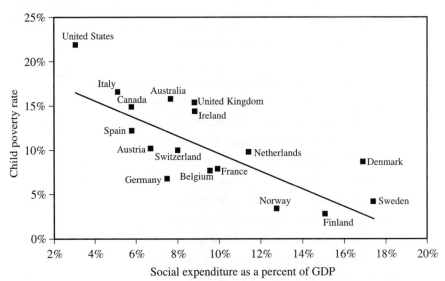

Note: R² = 0.58.

Source: Authors' analysis of OECD (2002) and Luxembourg Income Study (2004b) data.

States is not due to a lack of resources—high per capita income and high productivity make it possible for the United States to afford social welfare spending. Moreover, other OECD countries that spend more on both poverty reduction and family-friendly policies have done so while maintaining competitive rates of productivity and income growth. Growth, then, has benefited a broader spectrum of workers in those countries. Although strong growth in the United States over the late 1990s benefited low-wage workers and their families, inequality continued to rise, following its long-term trend. In the United States, growth has generally not been shared equally either in terms of wages paid by firms or through redistributive social policies.

Employment and hours worked: problems with the U.S. model

The per capita income figures in Tables 7.1 and 7.2 appear, at face value, to be at odds with the international estimates of productivity levels in Table 7.3. Per capita income in the United States—the value of goods and services produced annually per person—is generally much higher relative to the other OECD economies than is the U.S. productivity level (i.e., the value of goods and services produced in one hour of work in the United States). These differences between per capita income and productivity levels stem from two important differences across countries: the share of the total population employed and the average number of hours worked each year by those with jobs.

The U.S. economy employed a greater share of its working-age population, and its workers worked, on average, more hours per year than workers in any other rich, industrialized economy. This additional work raises per capita income in the United States relative to other economies with roughly similar productivity levels but lower levels of employment and lower average annual hours worked. Supporters of the U.S. model have long argued that the ability of the United States to generate a greater volume of work, whether measured in terms of number of jobs or hours of work, is an essential feature of the U.S. model. To address this contention, this section takes a closer look at international employment rates, average hours worked, and unemployment rates.

The United States, indeed, employed a greater share of its working-age population (men and women combined) than did seven of the other nine countries listed in **Table 7.17**. In 2002, the United States employed 69.7% of its male working-age population—third only to Japan (70.4%) and the Netherlands (73.5%). That same year, 56.3% of women were employed in the United States—third to Sweden (57.1%) and Canada (56.9%). Employment rates may vary because of differences across economies in school enrollment rates for adults, early retirement rates, and women's non-market responsibilities, especially child care.

Table 7.17 shows a different pattern over time for employment rates of men and women. Among working-age men, employment rates fell in every country during the 1980s and in every country in the 1990s except the Netherlands. There were some fairly large changes in the short period from 2000 to 2002. For this period, six countries had negative percentage-point changes in male employment rates and four countries had positive changes. The largest percentage-point change was the 2.2 percentage-point decline in male employment rates for the United States and Germany. Among working-age women, employment rates rose between 1979 and 1989 in every country, and increased by more than eight percentage points for Canada, the Netherlands, and Australia. From 1989 to 2000, all countries, most exceptionally the Netherlands (14.8), had increases in female employment rates, with the exception of Sweden (-5.6) and Japan (-1.0). Employment rates for women from 2000 to 2002 were negative for two countries—the U.S. with -1.4 and Japan with -1.0—and positive for the other eight countries.

Table 7.18 is a listing of average annual hours worked in OECD countries. In 2002, workers in the United States worked, on average, more hours per year

TABLE 7.17 Employment rates* in OECD countries

	1979	1989	2000	2002	Percentage-point change		
					1979-89	1989-2000	2000-02
Male							
United States	73.8%	72.5%	71.9%	69.7%	-1.3	-0.6	-2.2
Japan	78.2	75.1	72.5	70.4	-3.1	-2.6	-2.1
Germany	69.8	65.9	61.7	59.5	-3.9	-4.2	-2.2
France	69.6	61.2	59.0	59.6	-8.4	-2.2	0.6
Italy	66.3	59.9	56.5	57.2	-6.4	-3.4	0.7
United Kingdom	74.5	70.4	67.5	66.7	-4.1	-2.9	-0.8
Canada	74.3	71.7	68.3	68.2	-2.6	-3.4	-0.1
Australia	75.3%	72.1%	68.7%	68.2%	-3.2	-3.4	-0.5
Netherlands	74.3	65.1	71.9	73.5	-9.2	6.8	1.6
Sweden	73.7	70.9	64.3	64.4	-2.8	-6.6	0.1
Female							
United States	47.5%	54.3%	57.7%	56.3%	6.8	3.4	-1.4
Japan	45.7	47.4	46.4	45.4	1.7	-1.0	-1.0
Germany	38.4	39.7	44.6	45.4	1.3	4.9	0.8
France	40.5	41.2	43.9	45.2	0.7	2.7	1.3
Italy	27.3	28.6	30.5	32.2	1.3	1.9	1.7
United Kingdom	45.3	49.7	52.5	53.0	4.4	2.8	0.5
Canada	45.6	53.9	56.1	56.9	8.3	2.2	0.8
Australia	40.7%	48.8%	52.6%	53.1%	8.1	3.8	0.5
Netherlands	29.2	37.4	52.2	54.7	8.2	14.8	2.5
Sweden	57.2	61.7	56.1	57.1	4.5	-5.6	1.0

* See Table Notes.

Source: Authors' analysis of BLS (2004).

(1,815 hours) than workers in any of the other countries, except Australia (1,824 hours) and New Zealand (1,816 hours). The historic leader in annual hours worked—Japan—worked fewer hours than the United States (1,821 hours compared to 1,834 hours) in 2000, the most recent year in which a comparison can be made. Between 1979 and 1989, on average, OECD countries (excluding the United States) reduced annual hours of work by 103 hours, while hours worked in the United States decreased by one hour. During this same time period, Sweden increased its average hours worked by 32, but only to a level that kept it close to the bottom in average hours worked per year. Three countries—Sweden (76 hours), Canada (19 hours), and Denmark (13 hours)—increased hours of work between 1989 and 2000. On average, OECD countries decreased hours

TABLE 7.18 Average annual hours worked in the OECD,* 1979-2002

| | 1979 | 1989 | 2000 | 2002 | Change in hours | | |
					1979-89	1989-2000	2000-02
United States	1,838	1,837	1,834	1,815	-1	-3	-19
Japan	2,126	2,031	1,821	—	-95	-210	—
Germany	1,708	1,541	1,463	1,444	-167	-78	-19
France	1,764	1,618	1,500	1,459	-146	-118	-41
Italy	1,717	1,675	1,631	1,619	-42	-44	-12
United Kingdom	1,815	1,767	1,708	1,707	-48	-59	-1
Canada	1,832	1,788	1,807	1,778	-44	19	-29
Australia	1,904	1,866	1,855	1,824	-38	-11	-31
Austria	—	—	—	—	—	—	—
Belgium	—	1,677	1,530	1,559	—	-147	29
Denmark	—	1,491	1,504	1,499	—	13	-5
Finland	1,837	1,728	1,727	1,711	-109	-1	-16
Ireland	—	1,920	1,690	1,668	—	-230	-22
Netherlands	—	1,437	1,371	1,340	—	-66	-31
New Zealand	—	1,820	1,817	1,816	—	-3	-1
Norway	1,514	1,432	1,380	1,342	-82	-52	-38
Portugal	—	1,881	1,718	1,719	—	-163	1
Spain	2,022	1,824	1,814	1,807	-198	-10	-7
Sweden	1,517	1,549	1,625	1,581	32	76	-44
Switzerland	—	—	1,568	—	—	—	—
Average excluding U.S.	1,870	1,760	1,665	1,602	-103	-45	-18

* See Table Notes.

Source: OECD (2001e) and (2003b).

of work (-18 hours) from 2000 to 2002, whereas the decrease in U.S. hours worked (-19 hours) was close to the overall average.

The data on employment rates and average hours worked suggest that more U.S. workers (as a share of the U.S. working population) contribute more hours to GDP than was the case in most other OECD countries. European nations, on the other hand, chose to take their productivity gains in the form of reduced hours—through shorter workweeks, longer vacations, and earlier retirements. This is an explicit policy choice—France, for example, reduced its workweek from 39 to 35 hours in January 2000.

The calculations in **Table 7.19** help to reconcile the differences between the United States and the other economies' productivity levels on the one hand, and their per capita income levels on the other. The last three columns in Table

TABLE 7.19 Per capita income compared to OECD average

	Per capita income (OECD average = 100)	Difference from OECD average attributed to:		
		Productivity	Hours worked per person	Labor utilization
United States	131.1%	13.8%	13.9%	3.4%
Japan	97.8	-17.6	9.2	6.2
Germany	96.3	13.0	-12.1	-4.6
France	97.2	20.7	-12.0	-11.5
Italy	94.5	15.3	-1.5	-19.3
United Kingdom	96.7	-11.0	4.4	3.3
Canada	110.0	-5.3	9.1	6.2
Australia	102.1%	-11.4%	11.3%	2.2%
Denmark	105.9	5.4	11.4	-10.9
Finland	99.8	-4.5	6.2	-2.0
Ireland	122.5	23.2	0.5	-1.3
Netherlands	103.5	16.8	-21.2	8.0
New Zealand	79.8	-30.8	8.5	2.1
Norway	115.3	28.5	-23.6	10.4
Portugal	64.5	-42.6	3.2	3.9
Spain	79.1	-17.7	7.9	-11.1
Sweden	104.1	4.3	-0.5	0.3

Source: Bivens (2004).

7.19 break down the variation in per capita income that diverges from the OECD average of 100. For example, the per capita income in the United States was 131.1% of the OECD average of 100. Therefore, per capita income in the United States was 31.1% higher than the OECD average. The 31.1% is further broken down by productivity, hours worked per person, and labor utilization (number of workers in the economy). For the United States, 13.8% of the 31.1% of per capita income above the OECD average is attributable to higher productivity, 13.9% to more hours worked per person, and 3.4% to slightly higher employment rates. Portugal had the lowest per capita income—64.5% of the OECD average. Conversely, Portugal's per capita income is 35.5% less than the OECD average. The -35.5% divergence from the OECD average of 100 can mostly be attributed to a -42.6% productivity gap. Norway's per capita income is 115.3% of the OECD average; their productivity difference was the highest (28.5%), but they also had the lowest hours worked per person (-23.6% of the OECD average). The basic lesson of these employment and hours data is that an important portion of the apparently higher standard of living in the United States comes not from working more efficiently than other comparable economies, but simply from working longer.

The capacity of the U.S. economy to sustain high employment rates is an important economic accomplishment. **Table 7.20** puts U.S. job creation into historical and international context. The table shows the annual employment growth rate in 20 OECD economies over three periods: 1979-89, 1989-2000, and 2000-01. Australia (2.4%) had the highest annual growth rate in employment from 1979 to 1989. The United States, at 1.7%, was above the OECD average of 0.7%, but was lower than four other countries. During this period only Ireland (-0.5%) had a negative annual growth rate in employment. During the 1990s, the United States again had better than average growth (1.3% versus the average of 1.1%), but seven countries had as strong or better annual growth rates in employment—most notably Ireland at 4.0%. From 2000 to 2001, the United States managed to sustain higher than average growth rates in employment—1.3% versus the average of 0.9%. Twelve countries had higher annual growth rates in employment compared to the United States from 2000 to 2001, with Switzerland leading the list with high annual increases of 6.2% over this period.

The employment growth data, therefore, suggest that the U.S. job creation rate in the 1990s was not particularly high either by its own historical terms or when compared with several other economies with different labor market institutions. These job creation data are consistent with the earlier data on employment rates, which showed that the United States was not able to prevent the male employment rate from falling in the 1980s and 1990s (though it did a better job than other economies), and that several economies raised their female employment rates by larger margins than did the United States over the same period. The high starting point for female employment rates in the United States played a role in the lagging U.S. performance, as did the lack of adequate policies—such as paid maternity/paternity leave and child care—to address the needs of working women to balance work and family.

Table 7.21 reports the unemployment rate in 20 OECD countries for 1979, 1989, 2000, and 2002. Over the late 1990s, many OECD countries experienced falling unemployment rates. The jobless rate remained low in the United States in 2000 (4.0%), and eight other countries had rates below 5%—Switzerland (2.7%), the Netherlands (2.9%), Norway (3.4%), Austria (3.7%), Portugal (4.1%), Ireland (4.3%), Denmark (4.4%), and Japan (4.7%). In 2002, unemployment rates in 10 countries were worse than they were in 2000. For that same year, 11 countries had unemployment rates lower than the 5.8% U.S. rate.

TABLE 7.20 Employment in OECD countries, 1979-2001

	Employment (thousands)					Employment change (thousands)			Annual growth rate (%)		
	1979	1989	1995	2000	2001	1979-89	1989-2000	2000-01	1979-89	1989-2000	2000-01
United States	98,824	117,342	124,900	135,219	136,941	18,518	17,877	1,722	1.7%	1.3%	1.3%
Japan	54,790	61,280	64,570	64,458	64,121	6,490	3,178	-337	1.1	0.5	-0.5
Germany	26,120	27,469	35,780	38,706	38,917	1,349	11,237	211	0.5	3.2	0.5
France	21,395	21,842	21,908	24,139	24,517	447	2,297	378	0.2	0.9	1.6
Italy	20,057	20,833	19,851	20,874	21,300	776	41	426	0.4	0.0	2.0
United Kingdom	25,080	26,549	25,891	27,938	27,505	1,469	1,389	-433	0.6	0.5	-1.5
Canada	10,658	12,986	13,357	14,911	15,076	2,328	1,925	165	2.0	1.3	1.1
Australia	6,079	7,715	8,219	9,097	9,188	1,636	1,382	91	2.4%	1.5%	1.0%
Austria	3,051	3,342	3,729	4,019	4,077	291	677	58	0.9	1.7	1.4
Belgium	3,660	3,670	3,715	3,970	4,198	10	300	228	0.0	0.7	5.7
Denmark	2,439	2,610	2,566	2,726	2,721	171	116	-5	0.7	0.4	-0.2
Finland	2,246	2,494	2,090	2,326	2,359	248	-168	33	1.1	-0.6	1.4
Ireland	1,151	1,099	1,272	1,692	1,741	-52	593	49	-0.5	4.0	2.9
Netherlands	4,821	6,065	6,838	6,959	7,064	1,244	894	105	2.3	1.3	1.5
New Zealand	1,262	1,468	1,668	1,779	1,823	206	311	44	1.5	1.8	2.5
Norway	1,862	2,014	2,047	2,269	2,278	152	255	9	0.8	1.1	0.4
Portugal	3,854	4,377	4,382	4,877	5,063	523	500	186	1.3	1.0	3.8
Spain	11,902	12,260	12,049	15,370	15,946	358	3,110	576	0.3	2.1	3.7
Sweden	4,180	4,466	3,986	4,157	4,239	286	-309	82	0.7	-0.6	2.0
Switzerland	3,095	3,704	3,800	3,910	4,154	609	206	244	1.8	0.5	6.2
Average excluding U.S.	25,606	27,891	29,640	30,873	30,903	2,230	3,212	64	0.7%	1.1%	0.9%

Source: Authors' analysis of OECD (2001d, 2002, and 2003b).

TABLE 7.21 Unemployment rates in the OECD, 1979-2002 (percent of civilian labor force)

Country	Standardized unemployment*			
	1979	1989	2000	2002
United States	5.8%	5.3%	4.0%	5.8%
Japan	2.1	2.3	4.7	5.4
Germany	2.7	5.6	7.8	8.6
France	5.3	9.1	9.5	8.8
Italy	5.8	9.7	10.4	9.0
United Kingdom	4.7	7.1	5.4	5.1
Canada	7.5	7.5	6.8	7.7
Australia	6.1%	6.0%	6.3%	6.3%
Austria	—	—	3.7	4.3
Belgium	9.1	7.4	6.9	7.3
Denmark	—	6.8	4.4	4.6
Finland	6.5	3.1	9.8	9.1
Ireland	—	14.7	4.3	4.3
Netherlands	5.8	6.6	2.9	2.7
New Zealand	—	7.1	6.0	5.2
Norway	2.0	5.4	3.4	3.9
Portugal	—	5.2	4.1	5.1
Spain	7.7	13.9	11.3	11.3
Sweden	2.1	1.5	5.6	4.9
Switzerland	—	—	2.7	3.2
Average excluding U.S.	4.2%	6.6%	6.9%	7.0%

* See Table Notes.

Source: OECD (2001e and 2003b).

Table 7.22 assesses an important claim about the causes of higher unemployment rates in some European countries; specifically, that Europe's labor market institutions, such as strong unions, high minimum wages, and generous benefits, have priced less-skilled workers out of jobs. If this were the case, we would expect the unemployment rates of less-educated workers and better-educated workers to be relatively close to one another in the United States, where relatively weak unions, low minimum wages, and poor benefits would have less of an effect on the employment prospects of less-educated workers (in other words, where compensation can fall so as to promote more jobs for the less skilled). Conversely, we would expect the unemployment rates of less-

TABLE 7.22 Unemployment rates in the OECD by education level, 2001

	Unemployment rate*			Ratio of	
Country	Less than high school	High school	College	Less than high school/ college	High school/ college
United States	8.1%	3.8%	2.1%	3.9	1.8
Japan	5.9	4.8	3.1	1.9	1.5
Germany	13.5	8.2	4.2	3.2	2.0
France	11.9	6.9	4.8	2.5	1.4
Italy	9.1	6.8	5.3	1.7	1.3
United Kingdom	7.6	3.9	2.0	3.8	2.0
Canada	10.2	6.2	4.5	2.3	1.4
Australia	7.6%	4.7%	3.1%	2.5	1.5
Austria	6.4	3.0	1.5	4.3	2.0
Belgium	8.5	5.5	2.7	3.1	2.0
Denmark	5.0	3.3	3.2	1.6	1.0
Finland	11.4	8.5	4.4	2.6	1.9
Ireland	5.4	2.5	1.7	3.2	1.5
Netherlands	3.1	1.8	1.3	2.4	1.4
New Zealand	6.7	3.2	3.2	2.1	1.0
Norway	3.4	2.7	1.7	2.0	1.6
Portugal	3.6	3.2	2.8	1.3	1.1
Spain	10.2	8.4	6.9	1.5	1.2
Sweden	5.9	4.6	2.6	2.3	1.8
Switzerland	3.6	2.0	1.3	2.8	1.5
Average excluding U.S.	8.4%	5.6%	3.7%	2.4	1.6

* See Table Notes.

Source: Authors' analysis of OECD (2003b).

educated and better-educated workers to be relatively farther apart in Europe, where labor market institutions would, by conventional thinking, dispropor-tionately hurt job creation for less-educated workers. Yet the data in Table 7.22 run completely counter to this expectation. The unemployment rate for work-ers with less than a high school education in the United States in 2001 was almost four times higher than the rate for college-educated workers—only Austria's ratio was higher at 4.3. The ratio of high school to college unem-ployment rates was 1.8 in the United States, which was higher than 13 other OECD countries and only slightly lower than the ratios in five countries. Thus, Europe's strong labor market institutions do not appear to have priced less-skilled workers out of the market. If anything, the European institutions appear to be associated with substantially *lower* relative unemployment rates for less-educated workers.

Evaluating the U.S. model

The United States suffers from greater earnings and income inequality, higher poverty rates, and less movement out of poverty than almost every other OECD economy. Due to the highly unequal distribution of income in the United States, low-wage workers and low-income households are almost universally worse off in absolute terms than their low-wage, low-income counterparts in other, less-affluent OECD countries. Further, American workers work longer hours and have less in the way of social supports for families than workers in other OECD countries.

Supporters of the U.S. economic model generally acknowledge the relative inequality in the United States but argue that the model provides greater mobility, greater employment opportunities, and greater dynamism than do more interventionist economies. The evidence, however, provides little support for this view. First, there is less mobility out of poverty in the United States than in other nations. Poverty is deeper and harder to escape in the United States, and much less is available in the way of adequate social policy relative to other OECD countries. Although the gender wage gap is lower, there is much less support for working parents in the United States. The vaunted "flexibility" of the U.S. model serves to benefit mostly employers, not to help employees balance work and family.

Second, U.S. success in employment creation is often exaggerated. U.S. job growth rates in the 2000s were lackluster by their own historical standards and far worse than several other OECD countries with different kinds of labor market institutions. In 2000, unemployment was low in the United States, but it was falling across the OECD, and many countries had jobless rates lower than the U.S. rate. Perhaps most importantly, the pattern of unemployment rates in OECD countries was completely inconsistent with the idea that labor market institutions had priced less-educated workers out of jobs—the "flexible" U.S. labor market had the highest relative unemployment rate for less-educated workers among all the OECD countries.

Third, the data on growth rates in per capita income and productivity suggest that, although the U.S. economy saw increased productivity in the last few years, it underperformed relative to other OECD economies for most of the past 20 years. In the 1980s and the early 1990s, nearly all of the OECD economies— including the United States—suffered a dramatic deceleration in the growth rates of both per capita income and productivity. The especially slow growth rates in the United States, however, allowed all the OECD countries to narrow the U.S. lead, and several have eliminated the productivity gap altogether.

The best interpretation of the available international evidence is that, while the late 1990s were a period of low unemployment and overall economic growth, many OECD economies still faced labor market challenges. Economic growth and productivity growth rates across the entire OECD were lower in the 1990s than they were in the 1960s. Inequality rose sharply, especially in the United States, the United Kingdom, and a few other countries. Social policy and policy makers have not stepped up to address pressing social needs and the rise in poverty in the United States. Other OECD countries should be wary of pursuing similar policies for social spending. The evidence in this chapter underscores the diversity of international experience in providing wage, income, and employment security. Many OECD countries have economic and social policies, which differ from those in the United States, and they have not been detrimental to productivity. In fact, in many cases, these alternative policies have been pursued in economies with productivity levels that surpass U.S. levels. This suggests that those formulating policy may benefit from looking beyond the U.S. model.

The family income data series

This appendix explains the various adjustments made to the March Current Population Survey data and the methodology used to prepare the data in the tables discussed on the following pages.

The data source used for our analyses of family incomes and poverty is the U.S. Bureau of the Census's March Current Population Survey (CPS) microdata set. Each March, approximately 60,000 households are asked questions about their incomes from a wide variety of sources in the prior year (the income data in the 2004 March CPS refer to 2003). For the national analysis in Chapter 1, we use the data relevant to the year in question.

In order to preserve the confidentiality of respondents, the income variables on the public-use files of the CPS are top-coded, i.e., values above a certain level are suppressed. Since income inequality measures are sensitive to changes in the upper reaches of the income scale, this suppression poses a challenge to analysts interested in both the extent of inequality in a given time period and the change in inequality over time. We use an imputation technique, described below, that is commonly used in such cases to estimate the value of top-coded data. Over the course of the 1990s, Census top-coding procedures underwent significant changes, which also must be dealt with to preserve consistency. These methods are discussed below.

For most of the years of data in our study, a relatively small share of the distribution of any one variable is top-coded. For example, in 1989, 0.67% (i.e., two-thirds of the top 1%) of weighted cases are top-coded on the variable "earnings from longest job," meaning actual reported values are given for over 99% of those with positive earnings. Nevertheless, the disproportionate influence of the small group of top-coded cases means their earnings levels cannot be ignored.

Our approach has been to impute the average value above the top-code for the key components of income using the assumption that the tails of these distributions follow a Pareto distribution. (The Pareto distribution is defined as $c/(x^{(a+1)})$, where c and a are positive constants that we estimate using the top 20% of the empirical distribution (more precisely, c is a scale parameter assumed known; a is the key parameter for estimation). We apply this technique to three key variables: income from wage and salary (1968-1987), earnings from longest job (1988-2000), and income from interest (1968-1992). Since the upper tail of empirical income distributions closely follows the general shape of the Pareto, this imputation method is commonly used for dealing with top-coded data (West, undated). The estimate uses the shape of the upper part of the distribution (in our case, the top 20%) to extrapolate to the part that is unobservable due to the top-codes. Intuitively, if the shape of the observable part of the distribution suggests that the tail above the top-code is particularly long, implying a few cases with very high income values, the imputation will return a high mean relative to the case where it appears that the tail above the top-code is rather short.

Polivka (1998), using an uncensored dataset (i.e., without top-codes), shows that the Pareto procedure effectively replicates the mean above the top-code. For example, her analysis of the use of the technique to estimate usual weekly earnings from the earnings files of the CPS yields estimates that are generally within less than 1% of the true mean.

As noted, the Census Bureau has lifted the top-codes over time in order to accommodate the fact that nominal and real wage growth eventually renders the old top-codes too low. For example, the top-coded value for "earnings from longest job" was increased from $50,000 in 1979 to $99,999 in 1989. Given the growth of earnings over this period, we did not judge this change (or any others in the income-component variables) to create inconsistencies in the trend comparisons between these two time periods.

However, changes made in the mid- and latter 1990s data did require consistency adjustments. For these years, the Census Bureau both adjusted the top-codes (some were raised, some were lowered; the new top-codes were determined by using whichever value was higher: the top 3% of all reported amounts for the variable, or the top 0.5% of all persons), and used "plug-in" averages above the top-codes for certain variables. "Plug-ins" are group-specific average values taken above the top-code, with the groups defined on the basis of gender, race, and worker status. We found that the Pareto procedure was not feasible with unearned income, given the empirical distributions of these variables, so for March data (survey year) 1996 forward we use the plug-in values. Our tabulations show that, in tandem with the procedure described next regarding earnings, this approach avoids trend inconsistencies.

The most important variable that we adjust (i.e., the adjustment with the largest impact on family income) is "earnings from longest job." The top-code on this variable was raised sharply in survey year 1994, and this change leads to an upward bias in comparing estimates at or around that year to earlier years. (Note that this bias is attenuated over time as nominal income growth "catches up" to the new top-code, and relatively smaller shares of respondents again fall into that category.) Our procedure for dealing with this was to impose a lower top-code on the earnings data that we grew over time by the rate of inflation, and to calculate Pareto estimates based on these artificial top-codes. We found that this procedure led to a relatively smooth series across the changes in Census Bureau methodology.

For example, we find that, while our imputed series generates lower incomes among, say, the top 5% of families (because we are imposing a lower top-code) in the mid-1990s, by the end of the 1990s our estimates were only slightly lower than those from the unadjusted Census data. For 2001 forward we do not have any top-code adjustments.

Table 1.2. We decompose the growth of average family income in the following manner. We begin with log changes in family income over the relevant time periods—this is the value to be decomposed between annual hours, hourly wages, and other (non-labor) income. For example, in Table 1.2, this equals 12.8% for the 1994–2000 period. Family earnings grew 15.2% over this period, and we multiply this value by earnings/income averaged over the two years. For this period, that ratio is 0.813. This result represents the earnings contribution (12.4%). In order to decompose this value further into the wage and hours shares, we use weights derived from their growth over the period as shown in the table. The wage share, 1994–2000, is thus computed as (9.9%/ 15.2%)*12.4%, or 8.1%. The share of income growth attributed to the change in "other" is derived by multiplying its growth over the period by the ratio of other/income, again averaged over the two years (note that this is simply one minus the 0.813 value noted above). It is the nature of this type of log decomposition that if the "other" category is a relatively large share of the total, the decomposition will not perfectly sum to the total, but this is not the case here.

Tables 1.26–1.28: The source for these tables is the March CPS datasets described above. The analysis focuses on married-couple families with children, spouse present, where both spouses were between 25 and 54 years of age. The distributional analysis places 20% of families, not persons, in each fifth.

The annual hours variable in the March data is the product of two variables: weeks worked per year, and usual hours per week. Since allowable values on the latter variable go up to 99, this product can be over 5,000. Such values are clearly outliers, and we decided to exclude cases with annual hours greater than 3,500, which led to the exclusion of between 2% and 5% of cases over the years of our analysis.

Wives' wages in this analysis (Table 1.28) are constructed differently than in most of the analysis in this book, i.e., they are "hour-weighted" in this section and "person-weighted" elsewhere. Whereas we usually calculate averages by summing the wages and dividing by the weighted number of earners, in this case we calculate annual hours by dividing annual earnings by annual hours. Since earnings levels and number of hours worked are positively correlated, hour-weighted wage levels tend to be slightly higher than person-weighted wages.

Table 5.10: The methodology for this decomposition is taken from Danziger and Gottschalk (1995, chapter 5). The change to be explained is the difference in poverty rates between t_0 and t_1. We first isolate the effect of average income growth by assigning the average growth between the two time periods to all families in t_0 and recalculate the poverty rate (we adjust each family's poverty line for the increase in the CPI over this period). This procedure holds the demographic composition and the shape of the income distribution constant in t_0 while allowing incomes to grow equally for all families. Thus, the difference between this simulated poverty rate and the actual t_0 poverty rate is attributable to the growth in average income.

We repeat this exercise for each demographic group in t_0 (we use the three family types in Table 5.8, two races—white and non-white—and three education categories of the family head—less than high school, high school and some college, and college or more). By weighting each of these simulated t_0 rates by their t_1 population shares, we can simulate a t_0 poverty rate that reflects the average income growth and demographic composition of t_1. The difference between this simulated rate and the one discussed in the above paragraph gives the contribution of demographic change over the time period. Finally, since this second simulated rate incorporates the mean growth and demographic change between the two periods, but not the change in the shape of the distribution, the difference between this second simulated rate and the actual rate for t_1 equals the change in poverty rates attributable to changes in inequality over the two periods.

Wage analysis computations

by Danielle Gao

This appendix provides background information on the analysis of wage data from the Current Population Survey (CPS), which is prepared by the Bureau of the Census for the Bureau of Labor Statistics (BLS). Specifically, for 1979 and beyond, we analyze microdata files provided by the BLS that contain a full year's data on the outgoing rotation groups (ORG) in the CPS. (For years prior to 1979, we use the CPS May files; our use of these files is discussed below.) We believe that the CPS ORG files allow for a timely, up-to-date, and accurate analysis of wage trends keeping within the familiar labor force definitions and concepts employed by BLS.

The sampling framework of the monthly CPS is a "rolling panel," in which households are in the survey for four consecutive months, out for eight, and then back in for four months. The ORG files provide data on those CPS respondents in either the fourth or eighth month of the CPS (i.e., in groups four or eight, out of a total of eight groups). Therefore, in any given month the ORG file represents a quarter of the CPS sample. For a given year, the ORG file is equivalent to three months of CPSs (one-fourth of 12). For our analysis, we use a sample drawn from the full-year ORG sample, the size of which ranges from 160,000 to 180,000 observations during the 1979 to 1995 period. Due to a decrease in the overall sample size of the CPS, the ORG was shrunk to 145,000 cases from 1996 to 1998, and our current sample comes in at about 170,000 cases.

Changes in annual or weekly earnings can result from changes in hourly earnings or from more working time (either more hours per week or weeks per year). Our analysis is centered around the hourly wage, which represents the pure price of labor (exclusive of benefits), because we are interested in changing pay levels for the workforce and its sub-groups. We do this to be able to clearly distinguish changes in earnings resulting from more (or less) work rather than more (or less) pay. Most of our wage analysis, therefore, does not take into account that weekly or annual earnings may have changed because of longer or shorter working hours or lesser or greater opportunities for employment. An exception to this is Table 2.1, where we present annual hours, earnings, and hourly weighted wages from the March CPS.

In our view, the ORG files provide a better source of data for wage analysis than the traditionally used March CPS files. In order to calculate hourly wages from the March CPS, analysts must make calculations using three retrospective variables: the annual earnings, weeks worked, and usual weekly hours worked in the year prior to the survey. In contrast, respondents in the ORG are asked a set of questions about hours worked, weekly wages, and (for workers paid by the hour) hourly wages in the week prior to the survey. In this regard, the data from the ORG are likely to be more reliable than data from the March CPS. See Bernstein and Mishel (1997) for a detailed discussion of these differences.

Our subsample includes all wage-and-salary workers with valid wage and hour data, whether paid weekly or by the hour. Specifically, in order to be included in our sub-sample, respondents had to meet the following criteria:

- age 18-64;

- employed in the public or private sector (unincorporated self-employed were excluded);

- hours worked within the valid range in the survey (1-99 per week, or hours vary—see discussion below); and,

- either hourly or weekly wages within the valid survey range (top-coding discussed below).

For those who met these criteria, an hourly wage was calculated in the following manner. If a valid hourly wage was reported, that wage was used throughout our analysis. For salaried workers (those who report only a weekly wage), the hourly wage was their weekly wage divided by their hours worked. Outliers, i.e., persons with hourly wages below 50 cents or above $100 in 1989 CPI-U-X1-adjusted dollars, were removed from the analysis. Starting from year 2002, we use CPI-RS adjusted dollars instead. These yearly upper and lower bounds are presented in **Table B-1**. CPS demographic weights were applied to make the sample nationally representative.

TABLE B-1 Wage earner sample, hourly wage upper and lower limits, 1973-2003

Year	Lower	Upper
1973	$0.19	$38.06
1974	0.21	41.85
1975	0.23	45.32
1976	0.24	47.90
1977	0.25	50.97
1978	0.27	54.44
1979	0.30	59.68
1980	0.33	66.37
1981	0.36	72.66
1982	0.39	77.10
1983	0.40	80.32
1984	0.42	83.79
1985	0.43	86.77
1986	0.44	88.39
1987	0.46	91.61
1988	0.48	95.40
1989	0.50	100.00
1990	0.53	105.40
1991	0.55	109.84
1992	0.57	113.15
1993	0.58	116.53
1994	0.60	119.52
1995	0.61	122.90
1996	0.63	126.53
1997	0.65	129.54
1998	0.66	131.45
1999	0.67	134.35
2000	0.69	138.87
2001	0.71	142.82
2002	0.70	140.05*
2003	0.72	143.26*

* adjusted by CPI_RS

Source: Authors' analysis.

The hourly wage reported by hourly workers in the CPS is net of any overtime, tips, or commissions (OTTC), thus introducing a potential undercount in the hourly wage for workers who regularly receive tips or premium pay. OTTC is included in the usual weekly earnings of hourly workers, which raises

THE STATE OF WORKING AMERICA

the possibility of assigning an imputed hourly wage to hourly workers based on the reported weekly wage and hours worked per week. Conceptually, using this imputed wage is preferable to using the reported hourly wage because it is more inclusive. We have chosen, however, not to use this broader wage measure, because the extra information on OTTC seems unreliable. We compared the imputed hourly wage (reported weekly earnings divided by weekly hours) to the reported hourly wage; the difference presumably reflects OTTC. This comparison showed that significant percentages of the hourly workforce appeared to receive negative OTTC. These error rates range from a low of 0% of the hourly workforce in the period 1989-93 to a high of 16-17% in 1973-88, and persist across the survey change from 1993 to 1994. Since negative OTTC is clearly implausible, we rejected this imputed hourly wage series and rely strictly on the hourly rate of pay as reported directly by hourly workers, subject to the sample criteria discussed above.

For tables that show wage percentiles, we "smooth" hourly wages to compensate for "wage clumps" in the wage distributions. The technique involves creating a categorical hourly wage distribution, where the categories are 50-cent intervals, starting at 25 cents. We then find the categories on either side of each decile and perform a weighted, linear interpolation to locate the wage precisely on the particular decile. The weights for the interpolation are derived from differences in the cumulative percentages on either side of the decile. For example, suppose that 48% of the wage distribution of workers by wage level are in the $9.26-9.75 wage "bin," and 51% are in the next higher bin $9.76-10.25. The weight for the interpolation (in this case the median or 50th percen-

tile) is $\dfrac{(50-48)}{(51-48)}$ or 2/3. The interpolated median equals this weight, times

the width of the bin ($.50), plus the upper bound of the previous bin ($9.75), or $10.08 in this example.

For the survey years 1973-88, the weekly wage is top-coded at $999.00; an extended top-code value of $1,923 is available in 1986-97; the top-code value changes to $2,884.61 in 1998-2003. Particularly for the later years, this truncation of the wage distribution creates a downward bias in the mean wage. We dealt with the top-coding issue by imputing a new weekly wage for top-coded individuals. The imputed value is the Pareto-imputed mean for the upper tail of the weekly earnings distribution, based on the distribution of weekly earnings up to the 80th percentile. This procedure was done for men and women separately. The imputed values for men and women appear in **Table B-2**. A new hourly wage, equal to the new estimated value for weekly earnings, divided by that person's usual hours per week, was calculated.

TABLE B-2 Pareto-imputed mean values for top-coded weekly earnings, and share top coded, 1973-2003

Year	Share			Value	
	All	Men	Women	Men	Women
1973	0.11%	0.17%	0.02%	$1,365	$1,340
1974	0.16	0.26	0.01	1,385	1,297
1975	0.21	0.35	0.02	1,410	1,323
1976	0.30	0.51	0.01	1,392	1,314
1977	0.36	0.59	0.04	1,384	1,309
1978	0.38	0.65	0.02	1,377	1,297
1979	0.57	0.98	0.05	1,388	1,301
1980	0.72	1.23	0.07	1,380	1,287
1981	1.05	1.82	0.10	1,408	1,281
1982	1.45	2.50	0.18	1,430	1,306
1983	1.89	3.27	0.25	1,458	1,307
1984	2.32	3.92	0.42	1,471	1,336
1985	2.78	4.63	0.60	1,490	1,343
1986	0.80	1.37	0.15	2,435	2,466
1987	1.06	1.80	0.20	2,413	2,472
1988	1.30	2.19	0.29	2,410	2,461
1989	0.48	0.84	0.08	2,710	2,506
1990	0.60	1.04	0.11	2,724	2,522
1991	0.71	1.21	0.17	2,744	2,553
1992	0.77	1.28	0.22	2,727	2,581
1993	0.86	1.43	0.24	2,754	2,580
1994	1.25	1.98	0.43	2,882	2,689
1995	1.34	2.16	0.43	2,851	2,660
1996	1.41	2.27	0.46	2,863	2,678
1997	1.71	2.67	0.65	2,908	2,751
1998	0.63	0.97	0.24	4,437	4,155
1999	0.71	1.18	0.21	4,464	4,099
2000	0.83	1.37	0.24	4,502	4,179
2001	0.91	1.44	0.33	4,477	4,227
2002	1.05	1.66	0.38	4,555	4,252
2003	1.07	1.69	0.40	4,546	4,219

Source: Authors' analysis.

In January 1994, a new survey instrument was introduced into the CPS; many labor force items were added and improved. This presents a significant challenge to the researcher who wishes to make comparisons over time. The most careful research on the impact of the survey change has been conducted by BLS researcher Anne Polivka (1996, 1997). Interestingly, Polivka does not find that the survey changes had a major impact on broad measures of unemployment or wage levels, though significant differences did surface for some sub-groups (e.g., weekly earnings for those with less than a high school diploma and those with advanced degrees, the unemployment rate of older workers). However, a change in the reporting of weekly hours did call for the alteration of our methodology. In 1994 the CPS began allowing people to report that their usual hours worked per week vary. In order to include non-hourly workers who report varying hours in our wage analysis, we estimated their usual hours using a regression-based imputation procedure, where we predicted the usual hours of work for "hours vary" cases based on the usual hours worked of persons with similar characteristics. An hourly wage was calculated by dividing weekly earnings by the estimate of hours for these workers. The share of our sample that received such a wage in the 1994-97 period is presented in **Table B-3**. The reported hourly wage of hourly workers was preserved.

BLS analysts Ilg and Hauzen (2000), following Polivka (1999), do adjust the 10th percentile wage because "changes to the survey in 1994 led to lower reported earnings for relatively low-paid workers, compared with pre-1994 estimates." We make no such adjustments for both practical and empirical reasons. Practically, the BLS has provided no adjustment factors for hourly wage trends that we can use—Polivka's work is for weekly wages. More importantly, the trends in 10th percentile hourly wages differ from those reported by Ilg and Hauzen for 10th percentile weekly earnings. This is perhaps not surprising, since the composition of earners at the "bottom" will differ when measured by weekly rather than hourly wages, with low-weekly earners being almost exclusively part-timers. Empirically, Ilg and Hauzen show the unadjusted 50/10 wage gap jumping up between 1993 and 1994, when the new survey begins. In contrast, our 50/10 wage gap for hourly wages falls between 1993 and 1994. Thus, the pattern of wage change in their data differs greatly from that in our data. In fact, our review of the 1993-94 trends across all of the deciles shows no discontinuities whatsoever. Consequently, we make no adjustments to account for any effect of the 1994 survey change. Had we made the sort of adjustments suggested by Polivka, our measured 1990s' fall in the 50/10 wage gap would be even larger and the overall pattern—falling 50/10, rising 90/50, and especially the 95/50 wage gaps—would remain the same.

When a response is not obtained for weekly earnings, or an inconsistency is detected, an "imputed" response is performed by CPS using a "hot deck" method, whereby a response from another sample person with similar demographic and economic characteristics is used for the nonresponse. This procedure for imputing missing wage data appears to bias between union and non-

TABLE B-3 Share of wage earners assigned an hourly wage from imputed weekly hours, 1994-2003

Year	Percent hours vary
1994	2.0%
1995	2.1
1996	2.4
1997	2.4
1998	2.5
1999	2.4
2000	2.4
2001	2.5
2002	2.5
2003	2.5

Source: Authors' analysis.

union members. We restrict our sample to the observations with non-imputed wages only for union wage premium analysis (table 2.35).

Demographic variables are also used in the analysis. Our race variable comprises four mutually exclusive categories:

- white, non-Hispanic;

- black, non-Hispanic;

- Hispanic, any race;

- all others.

Beginning in 1992, the CPS employed a new coding scheme for education, providing data on the respondent's highest degree attained. The CPS in earlier years provided data on years of schooling completed. The challenge to make a consistent wage series by education level is to either make the new data consistent with the past or to make the old "years of schooling" data consistent with the new, educational attainment measures. In prior versions of *The State of Working America*, we achieved a consistent series by imputing years of schooling for 1992 and later years, i.e., making the "new" consistent with the "old." In this version, however, we have converted the "old" data to the new coding following Jaeger (1997). However, Jaeger does not separately identify four-year college and "more than college" categories. Since the wages of these sub-groups of the "college or more" group have divergent trends, we construct pre-1992 wages and employment separately for "four-year college" and "advanced." To do so, we compute wages, wage premiums, and employment separately for those with 16, 17, and 18-plus years of schooling completed. The challenge is to distribute the "17s" to the 16 years (presumably a four-year degree) and 18-plus years (presumably advanced) groups. We do this by using the share of the "17s" that have a terminal four-year college degree, as computed in the February 1990 CPS supplement that provides both education codings: 61.4%. We then assume that 61.4% of all of the "17s" are "college-only" and compute a weighted average of the "16s" and 61.4% of the "17s" to construct "college-only" wages and wage premiums. Correspondingly, we compute a weighted average of 38.6% (or 1 less 61.4%) of the "17s" and the "18s" to construct advanced "wages and wage premiums." Distributing the "17s" affects each year differently depending on the actual change in the wages and premiums for "17s" and the changing relative size of the "17s" (which varies only slightly from 2.5% of men and women from 1979 to 1991).

We employ these education categories in various tables in Chapter 2, where we present wage trends by education over time. For the data for 1992 and later, we compute the "some college" trends by aggregating those "with some college but no degree beyond high school" and those with an associate or other degree that is not a four-year college degree.

Table notes

FREQUENTLY CITED SOURCES

The following abbreviations are used throughout the table and figure notes.
BLS—Bureau of Labor Statistics.
CES—Current Establishment Survey, a survey of U.S. businesses conducted by the BLS.
CPI—Consumer price index.
CPI-U-RS—Consumer price index for all urban consumers, research series.
CPS—Current Population Survey, a survey of U.S. households conducted by the BLS.
Employment and Earnings—U.S. Department of Labor, Employment and Earnings, monthly and historical supplements.
ERP—President of the United States. Economic Report of the President.
NIPA—U.S. Department of Commerce, National Income and Product Accounts.
ORG—Outgoing Rotation Group, a segment of the March CPS.
P-60—Poverty in the United States. U.S. Department of Commerce, Bureau of the Census.
SCB—U.S. Department of Commerce, Survey of Current Business, monthly.

The following agencies and their respective web sites are referenced throughout the text.
Bureau of Labor Statistics (BLS)—www.bls.gov
    Current Employment Survey (CES)—http://www.bls.gov/data/home.htm
    Current Population Survey (CPS)—http://www.bls.gov/data/home.htm
Bureau of Economic Analysis (BEA)—www.bea.gov
    NIPA Tables—www.bea.gov/bea/dn/nipaweb/index.asp
U.S. Bureau of the Census—www.census.gov
    Historical Poverty Tables—www.census.gov/hhes/income/histinc/histpovtb.html
    Historical Income Tables—www.census.gov/hhes/income/histinc/histinctb.html

INTRODUCTION

1   *Labor market indicators since the recession and recovery began.* Payroll employment—BLS, CES (http://www.bls.gov/CES Historical tables B3); Unemployment, underemployment, employment rate, labor force participation rate, share long-term unemployment—BLS, CPS (http://www.bls.gov/CPS Tables A1, Table A9, Table A12). This table draws on the material in Chapter 3.

2   *Deceleration of wage growth in 2003.* The real hourly wage measures are those presented in Tables 2.6 and 2.7. Productivity growth is for the nonfarm business sector. Inflation is computed from the CPI-RS.

3   *Compensation, wages and benefits in expanding and contracting industries.* Compensation, wages and benefits are from BEA, NIPA tables and computed per full-time equivalent employee, with data for 64 industries; corresponding employment counts by industry—BLS, CES http://www.bls.gov/CES—are used to compute shares of total employment in March and November 2001 and in June 2004. Expanding industries are those whose share of total employment expands. The average pay of expanding industries is a weighted average of expanding industries, with the change in employment shares as the weights. Corresponding computations are made for contracting industries, defined as industries whose employment shares have declined.

4   *Growth of income in corporate sector.* Analysis is based on the data presented in Table 1.25. To compute shares of real corporate income growth, the compensation data were deflated by the consumption expenditures index and capital income by the GDP deflator: their sum in real terms is used as total real corporate income

CHAPTER 1

1.1   *Median family income.* Census homepage, Historical Income Tables, Families, Table F-5.

1.2   *Average family income and its components for the middle quintile.* Authors' analysis of March CPS data. See appendix A for description of decomposition in bottom panel.

1.3   *Length of time to recovery of median family income after recession.* See note to Table 1.1. Peaks based on National Bureau of Economic Research business cycle dating (http://www.nber.org/cycles.html).

1.4   *Growth of real median family income and productivity.* Census homepage, Historical Income Tables, Families, Table F-5; BLS "Productivity and Costs" Table 1.

1.5   *Annual family income growth for the middle fifth, unadjusted and adjusted for family size.* The unadjusted (for family size) values come from Census Income Table F-3; however, instead of using the deflator CPI-U-RS (the standard deflator in this edition) we use CPI-U in order to maintain greater consistency with the growth rates labeled "adjusted for family size." These values are derived by dividing family income by the poverty threshold for that family size, which is deflated using the CPI-U (Census Table F-21).

1.6   *Median family income by race/ethnic group.* Census homepage, Historical Income Tables, Families, Table F-5.

1.7   *Median family income by age of household head.* Census homepage, Historical Income Tables, Families, Table F-11.

1.8   *Median family income growth by 10-year cohorts, starting in 1949.* Census homepage, Historical Income Tables, Families, Table F-11.

1.9   *Median family income by family type.* Census homepage, Historical Income Tables, Families, Table F-7.

1.10   *Average real income levels and shares by income group and share of growth accruing to each group.* CBO (2004) data, *Effective Federal Taxes Rates 1979 to 2001*, Table B1-C.

1.11   *Income ratios, comprehensive income data.* See notes for Table 1.10.

1.12   *Shares of family income going to income fifths and to the top 5%.* Census homepage, Historical Income Tables, Families, Table F-2.

1.13   *Real family income by income group, upper limit of each group.* Census homepage, Historical Income Tables, Families, Table F-1.

1.14   *Family income mobility over three decades.* Bradbury and Katz, 2002.

1.15   *Income mobility for white and black families.* Hertz, 2003.

1.16   *Effective federal tax rates for all households by comprehensive household income quintile.* CBO (2004), *Effective Federal Taxes Rates 1979 to 2002*, Table B-1A.

1.17   *Effective tax rates for selected federal taxes.* CBO (2004), Effective Federal Taxes Rates 1979 to 2002Table B-1A

1.18   *Composition of federal and state/local tax revenue, by progressive and regressive components.* NIPA Tables 3.2 and 3.3.

1.19   *Federal and state local revenue as a share of GDP.* NIPA tables 1.1.5, 3.2, and 3.3.

1.20   *Impact of recent tax changes on effective rates and after-tax income shares.* Data provided by Robert McIntyre, Institute on Taxation and Economic Policy.

1.21   *Family income by real and relative income brackets.* Authors' analysis of Census homepage, Historical Income Tables, Families, Table F-23; bottom panel from unpublished Census Bureau data provided by Jack McNeil and Charles Nelson.

1.22   *Sources of household income by income type.* Unpublished data provided by the Institute on Economic and Tax Policy.

1.23   *Shares of market-based personal income by income type.* From NIPA Table 2.1 Capital gains data are from the Internal Revenue Services Statistics on Income series and include gains as well as losses. The capital gains data for 2003 are an estimate based on the growth in CBO forecasts for capital gains.

1.24   *Shares of income by type and sector.* Based on NIPA Table 1.15 (unrevised -2003). The "corporate and business" sector includes "corporate," "other private business," and "rest of world." The "government/nonprofit" sector includes the household, government enterprise, and government sectors, all of which generate no capital income. Capital income consists of profits, interest, and rental income.

1.25   *Corporate sector profit rates and shares.* Uses capital income and tax data from NIPA Table 1.14. "Pre-tax profit rates" are the sum of corporate profits with inventory valuation and capital consumption adjustments and net interest (lines 11 and 9) as a share of corporate capital (created by Christian Weller based on methodology presented in Baker (1996)). "After-tax profit rates" account for a tax rate based on the quotient of taxes on corporate income and corporate profits with inventory valuation and capital consumption adjustments (lines 12 and 11). The denominator for "profit share" is capital income as defined above (sum of lines 11 and 9); the denominator for "labor share" is compensation to employees (line 4); the denominator for both is their sum. The "capital-output ratio" is corporate capital divided by capital income (both as defined above).

1.26　*Annual hours worked by husbands and wives, 25-54, with children.* Authors' analysis of March CPS data; see Appendix A.

1.27　*Average income by quintile, married-couple families with children and wives' contribution to income growth, 2002 dollars.* Authors' analysis of March CPS data; see Appendix A.

1.28　*Annual hours, wages, and earnings for prime-age wives with children.* Authors' analysis of March CPS data; see Appendix A.

CHAPTER 2

2.1　*Trends in average wages and average hours.* Productivity data are from the BLS and measure output per hour in the non-farm business sector. The wage-level data are based on the authors' tabulations of March CPS files using a series on annual, weekly, and hourly wages for wage and salary workers (the sample definition in the CPS ORG wage analysis is used; see Appendix B). The weekly and hourly wage data are "hour weighted," obtained by dividing annual wages by weeks worked and annual hours worked. The 1967 and 1973 values are derived from unpublished tabulations provided by Kevin Murphy from an update of Murphy and Welch (1989). Their values include self-employment as well as wage and salary workers. The values displayed in this table were bridged from CPS 1979 values using the growth rates in the Murphy and Welch series. Hours of work were derived from differences between annual, weekly, and hourly wage trends.

2.2　*Growth of average hourly wages, benefits, and compensation.* These data are computed from the NIPA tables, which are available online. "Wages and salaries" are calculated by dividing wage and salary accruals (Table 6.3) by hours worked by full-time and part-time employees (Table 6.9). "Total compensation" is the sum of wages and salaries, and social insurance. Social insurance is total compensation minus the sum of volunteer benefits (sum of health and non-health benefits; see Table 6.11) and wages and salaries. "Benefits" is the difference between total compensation and wages and salaries. These data were deflated using the NIPA personal consumption expenditure (PCE, chain-weighted) index, with health insurance adjusted by the PCE medical care (chained) index.

2.3　*Growth in private-sector average hourly wages, benefits, and compensation.* Based on employment cost levels from the BLS Employer Costs for Employee Compensation (ECEC) data for March for private-industry workers. We categorize wages and salaries differently than BLS, putting all wage-related items (including paid leave and supplemental pay) into the hourly wage. Benefits, in our definition, include only payroll taxes, pensions, insurance, and "other" benefits. The sum of wages and salaries and benefits makes up total compensation. It is important to use the current-weighted series rather than the fixed-weighted series because composition shifts (in the distribution of employment across occupations and industries) have a large effect. Employer costs for insurance are deflated by the medical care component of the CPI-U-RS (unpublished series from Stephen Reed at BLS). All other pay is deflated by the CPI-U-RS for "all items." Inflation is measured for the first quarter of each year.

2.4 *Hourly and weekly earnings of private production and nonsupervisory workers.* BLS Current Establishment Survey data. Available online. Deflated using CPI-U-RS.

2.5 *Changes in hourly wages by occupation.* Based on analysis of CPS wage data described in Appendix B.

2.6 *Wages for all workers by wage percentile.* Based on analysis of CPS wage data described in Appendix B.

2.7 *Wages for male workers by wage percentile.* Based on analysis of CPS wage data described in Appendix B.

2.8 *Wages for female workers by wage percentile.* Based on analysis of CPS wage data described in Appendix B.

2.9 *Distribution of total employment by wage level.* Based on analysis of CPS wage data described in Appendix B. The poverty-level wage is calculated using the preliminary estimate of the four-person weighted average poverty threshold in 2003 ($[xx]) divided by 2,080 hours and deflated by CPI-U-RS to obtain levels for other years. The threshold is available at the Census Web site. We calculated more intervals than we show but aggregated for simplicity of presentation (no trends were lost).

2.10 *Distribution of white employment by wage level.* See note to Table 2.9. These are non-Hispanic whites.

2.11 *Distribution of black employment by wage level.* See note to Table 2.9. These are non-Hispanic blacks.

2.12 *Distribution of Hispanic employment by wage level.* See note to Table 2.9. Hispanics may be of any race.

2.13 *Growth of specific fringe benefits.* Based on NIPA data described in note to Table 2.2 and ECEC data described in note to Table 2.3.

2.14 *Change in private-sector employer-provided health insurance coverage.* Based on tabulations of March CPS data samples of private wage-and-salary earners ages 18-64 who worked at least 20 hours per week and 26 weeks per year. Coverage is defined as being included in an employer-provided plan where the employer paid for at least some of the coverage.

2.15 *Change in private-sector employer-provided pension coverage.* See note to Table 2.14.

2.16 *Dimensions of wage inequality.* All of the data are based on analyses of the ORG CPS data described in Appendix B. The measures of "total wage inequality" are natural logs of wage ratios (multiplied by 100) computed from Tables 2.7 and 2.8. The exception is that the 1979 data for women are 1978-80 averages. This was done to smooth the volatility of the series, especially at the 10th percentile. The "between group inequalities" are computed from regressions of the log of hourly wages on education categorical variables (high school omitted), experience as a quartic, marital status, race, and region (4). The college/high school and high school/less-than-high-school premiums are simply the coefficient on "college" and "less than high school." The experience differentials are the differences in the value of age (calculated from the coefficients of the quartic specification) evaluated at 25, 35, and 50 years. "Within-group wage inequality" is measured as the root mean square error from the same log wage regressions used to compute age and education differentials.

2.17 *Real hourly wage for all by education.* Based on tabulations of CPS wage data described in Appendix B. See Appendix B for details on how a consistent measure of education was developed to bridge the change in coding in 1992.

2.18 *Real hourly wage for men by education.* See note to Table 2.17.

2.19 *Real hourly wage for women by education.* See note to Table 2.17.

2.20 *Educational attainment of the labor force.* Based on analysis of CPS wage earners. The data are described in Appendix B. The categories are as follows: "less than high school" is grade 1-12 or no diploma; "high school/GED" is high school graduate diploma or equivalent; "some college" is some college but no degree; "associate college" is occupational or academic associate's degree; "college B.A." is a bachelor's degree; and "advanced degree" is a master's, professional, or doctorate degree.

2.21 *Hourly wages of entry-level and experienced workers by education.* Based on analysis of CPS wage data described in Appendix B.

2.22 *Hourly wages by decile within education groups.* Based on analysis of CPS wage data described in Appendix B.

2.23 *Decomposition of total and within-group wage inequality.* All of the data are from the ORG CPS data sample described in Appendix B. "Overall wage inequality" is measured as the standard deviation of log wages. "Within-group wage inequality" is the mean square error from log wage regressions (the same ones used for Table 2.16). "Between-group wage inequality" is the difference between the overall and within-group wage inequalities and reflects changes in all of the included variables: education, age, marital status, race, ethnicity, and region.

2.24 *Hourly wage growth among men by race/ethnicity.* Based on analysis of CPS wage data described in Appendix B.

2.25 *Hourly wage growth among women by race/ethnicity.* Based on analysis of CPS wage data described in Appendix B.

2.26 *Gender wage ratio.* Uses 50th percentile for Tables 2.7 and 2.8.

2.27 *Impact of rising and falling unemployment on wage levels and wage ratios.* The unemployment rate is from BLS. Wage data are based on analysis of quarterly CPS wage data (see Appendix B). The "simulated effect of change on unemployment" was calculated by regressing the log of nominal wages on lagged wages, unemployment, productivity growth, and seasonal dummies for each included percentile, by gender. Using these models, wages were predicted given a simulated unemployment rate series where in one case the unemployment rate maintained its 1979 level through the third quarter of 1987 (preventing its actual increase), and in the other case maintained its 1995 level through the fourth quarter of 2000 (preventing its actual decrease). "Unemployment contribution to change" shows the wage simulated by the model in the final quarter of the simulation period compared to the actual wage.

2.28   *Employment growth and compensation by sector.* Employment levels by industry are from the BLS Current Establishment Survey (CES). Compensation by industry is per full-time equivalent worker based on NIPA data (Tables 6.2D and 6.5D). College intensity by industry is computed form the CPS-ORG data described in Appendix B.

2.29   *Employment growth by sector.* Based on data in Table 2.28.

2.30   *The effect of industry shifts on the growth of the college/high school wage differential.* The industry shift effect is calculated from estimated college/high school wage differentials using the model described in the note to Table 2.16, "industry composition actual," and a model that adds a set of industry controls (12), which gives "industry composition constant." The difference in the growth of these estimates is the industry shift effect.

2.31   *Net trade in U.S. manufactures by factor intensity and trading partner.* This is an update of Cline (1997), Table 4.3, p. 188, presented in Bivens (2004).

2.32   *Trade-deficit-induced job loss by wage and education level.* This is an update of Scott et al. (1997), Tables 1 and 2, presented in Bivens (2004).

2.33   *Changes in immigration by education.* Based on Borjas (2003) Appendix 2, pp. 1372-3.

2.34   *Union wage and benefit premium.* Employment cost index pay-level data in *Employer Costs for Employee Compensation,* March 2003, Table 13, for private industry.

2.35   *Union wage premium by demographic group.* "Percent union" is tabulated from CPS ORG data (see Appendix B) and includes all those covered by unions. "Union premium" values are the coefficients on union in a model of log hourly wages with controls for education, experience as a quartic, marital status, region, industry (12) and occupation (9), and race/ethnicity and gender where appropriate. For this analysis we only use observations that do not have imputed wages. This is because the imputation process does not take union status into account and therefore biases the union premium toward zero. See Mishel (2003).

2.36   *Union premiums for health, retirement, and paid leave.* Based on Table 4 in Mishel (2004), which draws on Buchmueller, Di Nardo, and Valletta (2001).

2.37   *Union impact on paid leave, pension, and health benefits.* Based on Table 3 in Mishel (2003) which draws on Pierce (1999b), Tables 4, 5, and 6.

2.38   *Effect of deunionization on male wage differentials.* This analysis replicates, updates, and expands on Freeman (1991), Table 2. The analysis uses the CPS ORG sample used in other analyses (see Appendix B). The year 1978, rather than 1979, is the earliest year analyzed because we have no union membership data in our 1979 sample. The "union wage premium" for a group is based on the coefficient on collective bargaining coverage in a regression of hourly wages on a simple human capital model (the same one used for estimating education differentials, as described in note to Table 2.16), with major industry (12) and occupation (9) controls in a sample for that group. The change in union premium across years, therefore, holds industry and occupation composition constant. "Percent union" is the share covered by collective bargaining. Freeman's analysis assumed the union premium was unchanged over time. We allow the union premium to differ across years so changes in the union effect are driven by changes in the unionization rate and the union wage premium. The analysis compares the change in the union effect on relative wages to the actual change in relative wages (regression-adjusted with simple human capital controls plus controls for other education or occupation groups).

2.39 *Union wage premium for subgroups.* Based on Table 2 in Mishel (2003), which draws on Gundersen (2003), Table 5.1 and Appendix C, and Card (1991), Table 8.

2.40 *Illustration of impact of unions on average wages of high school graduates.* Based on Table 5 in Mishel (2003).

2.41 *Value of the minimum wage.* Historical values of minimum wage from Shapiro (1987), p. 19. Deflated using CPI-U-RS.

2.42 *Characteristics of minimum wage and other workers.* Bernstein and Schmitt (1998), Table 1.

2.43 *Impact of lower minimum wage on key wage differentials among women.* The impact of the change in the minimum wage since 1979 is based on comparing the actual changes from 1979 to simulated wage distributions in 1989 and 1997 where the real value of the minimum wage in 1979 is imposed on the data. This analysis is based on the CPS ORG data described in Appendix B. The simulated microdata are obtained by setting the hourly wages of those in the "sweep" (earning between the current minimum wage and the 1979 value) at the 1979 value (inflation-adjusted by CPI-U-RS) of the minimum wage. Those earning less than the legislated minimum wage were assigned a wage at the same proportionate distance to the 1979 level as they were to the existing minimum. In 1997, the existing minimum was based on a weighted average by month of the prevailing minimum of $4.75 for nine months and $5.15 for three months. The counterfactual returns to education were estimated on the simulated microdata with a simple human capital model and compared to the actual change (based on the same model) presented in Table 2.17. The other wage differentials are based on logged differentials computed from the actual and simulated microdata. The shares earning less than the 1979 minimum are computed directly from the data.

2.44 *Distribution of minimum wage gains and income shares by fifth for various household types.* Bernstein and Schmitt (1998), Table 2.

2.45 *Use of computers at work.* Card and DiNardo (2002).

2.46 *Executive annual pay.* The 1992-2003 data are from a *Wall Street Journal*/William M. Mercer survey (of 350 large companies) of CEO compensation. "Realized direct compensation" includes salary, bonus, gains from options exercised, value of restricted stock at grant, and other long-term incentive award payments. "Cash compensation" data, also from Mercer, go back to 1989. The average compensation for 1989 is backed out of the 1995 data by extrapolating the 1989-95 trend in the Pearl Meyer/ *Wall Street Journal* data.

2.47   *CEO pay in advanced countries.* Total CEO compensation in dollars and the ratio of CEO to production-worker pay are from Towers Perrin (1988 and 2003).

2.48   *Changes in pay and education requirements.* This is a shift-share analysis based on the changes in the employment shares of 775 occupations as projected in the most recent BLS projections (Hecker 2004). The education intensities and median annual wage for each occupation were in a spreadsheet supplied by BLS.

CHAPTER 3

3.1   *Unemployment rates.* BLS (2004c), Table A-1.

3.2   *Effect of a 1% higher unemployment rate on mean annual earnings, mean annual income, and share of total family income, by family income quintile.* Bartik (2002). Observations are on region-year-cells, with the United States divided into 21 groupings of states. Quintiles are defined by family income, with an "unrelated individual" included as "family." All regressions and calculations are weighted by 2000 population for region. All regressions include year and regional dummies.

3.3   *Unemployment rates by gender, race, and educational status (persons 25 years or older).* Data are taken from BLS (2004c), Table A-4.

3.4   *Change in unemployment rates 13 quarters after business cycle peak.* Monthly seasonally adjusted unemployment data are from BLS (2004c), Tables A-1 and A-2. Data analysis is from the peak of the recession to the current quarter.

3.5   *Change in unemployment rates 10 quarters after business cycle trough.* Monthly seasonally adjusted unemployment data are from BLS (2004c), Tables A-1 and A-2. Data analysis is from the trough of the recession to the current quarter.

3.6   *Unemployment and long-term unemployment by education.* Data are taken from Allegretto and Stettner (2004).

3.7   *Long-term unemployment growth.* Data are taken from Allegretto and Stettner (2004).

3.8   *Underemployment, 2001 recession to current period.* Data taken from BLS (2004c), Table A-12. "Discouraged workers" are individuals not in the labor force who wanted a job, had searched for work in the previous year, or were available to work but were not actively searching for work because of discouragement over job prospects. "Other marginally attached" individuals are in identical circumstances, but are not actively searching for work for reasons other than discouragement, including family responsibilities, school or training commitments, or ill health or disabilities. "Involuntary part-time" workers cite "economic reasons" for working fewer than 35 hours per week.

3.9   *Employment rates.* Non-seasonally adjusted annual data are from BLS (2004c).

3.10   *Change in employment rates over recession and recovery.* Monthly seasonally adjusted employment-to-population ratio data are from BLS (2004c). Seasonally adjusted data for Hispanic men and women are not available. Data analysis is from the peak of the recession to the current quarter.

3.11   *Change in employment rates for economic recoveries.* Monthly seasonally adjusted employment-to-population ratio data are from BLS (2004c). Seasonally adjusted data for Hispanic men and women are not available. Data analysis is from the trough of the recession to the current quarter.

3.12   *Employed workers by work arrangement.* Data for 1997 through 2001 are taken from Wenger (2002). Data for 1995 are from Kalleberg et al. (1997), Table 1, p. 9.

3.13   *Characteristics of nonstandard workers.* Wenger (2002).

3.14   *Hourly wages of nonstandard workers, compared to regular full-time workers by gender and work arrangement.* Wenger (2002).

3.15   *Health and pension coverage by nonstandard work arrangement.* Wenger (2002).

3.16   *Workers preferring standard employment by type of nonstandard work arrangement.* Data for 1995 are from Kalleberg et al. (1997), Table 36, p. 61. Data for 2001 are from Wenger (2002), Table 12.

3.17   *Nonagricultural employment by full-time and part-time status.* Data are taken from BLS (2004c), Table A-5. Note that the definition of "part time" used here differs from the earlier analysis of nonstandard work. Here, part-time workers include any of the work types in the earlier table, including temporary workers and the self-employed who work part-time schedules. In the earlier tables a temp or self-employed worker who generally worked part time would have been classified as a temp or as self-employed regardless of hours. Industries reflect the introduction of the 2002 Census industry classification system derived from the 2002 North American Industry Classification System (NAICS) into the Current Population Survey (CPS). Beginning in January 2003, data reflect revised population controls used in the CPS.

3.18   *Workers feeling overworked.* Galinsky, Kim, and Bond (2001), Table 2, p. 19.

3.19   *Multiple job holders.* Data from 1994 to 2003 are from BLS (2004a), Table A-13. Data from 1971 to 1989 are from BLS (1997), Table 1. All figures are for May of the given year.

3.20   *Self-employment.* Data for nonagricultural self-employed workers and total nonagricultural employment are from the BLS (2004c), Table A-5.

3.21   *Employment in personnel services industry.* Data on personnel services industry employment (SIC 736) and total employment are from BLS (2004d).

3.22   *Perceptions of job security.* General Social Survey (GSS) data provided by The Roper Center for Public Opinion Research at the University of Connecticut (2004).

CHAPTER 4

4.1   *Distribution of income and wealth.* Unpublished analysis of Survey of Consumer Finances (SCF) data prepared in April 2004 by Edward Wolff for the Economic Policy Institute.

4.2   *Growth of household wealth.* Net worth and asset data are from the Federal Reserve Bank (2004a), Table B.100, p 94. Nonprofit organizations, a small component judging from the breakout on tangible assets, were included because the Federal Reserve does not give breakouts for financial assets. Data were converted to real dollars using the CPI-RS. The number of households is based on Census Bureau (2004), Table HH-1. We used the number of families in 1950 for the number of families in 1949. The number of households in 2003 was forecasted by using 1.0% growth over 2002 as cited in Economy.com (2004a) forecast detail of demographics and labor markets.

4.3   *Changes in the distribution wealth.* See note to Table 4.1.

4.4   *Change in average wealth by wealth class.* See note to Table 4.1.

4.5   *Households with low net wealth.* See note to Table 4.1.

4.6   *Wealth by race.* See note to Table 4.1.

4.7   *Distribution of asset ownership across households.* See notes to Table 4.1.

4.8   *Share of households owning stock.* See note to Table 4.1.

4.9   *Average household assets and liabilities by wealth class.* See note to Table 4.1.

4.10   *Concentration of stock ownership by income level.* See note to Table 4.1.

4.11   *Home ownership rates by race and income.* Authors' analysis of Bureau of Census data from the American Housing Survey. Data for home ownership by race and for all Americans for 1999 and 2003 are taken from Housing Vacancy Survey, 2003, Tables 13 and 20, Bureau of Census (1999 and 2003). Other yearly data are taken from the American Housing Survey. Average home ownership rates by income quintile estimated using ownership rates and population shares by discrete income categories. These data are taken from American Housing Survey, Bureau of Census (1999, 2003), Tables 3-12 and 4-12. Data for home ownership rates for all and by race for 2000 and 2002 are taken from Economy.com (2004b).

4.12   *Retirement income adequacy.* See note to Table 4.1.

4.13   *Household debt by type.* Data are from the Federal Reserve Board (2004b) and Economagic (2004).

4.14   *Household debt service burden.* Federal Reserve Board (2003). Annual averages of seasonally adjusted quarterly data.

4.15   *Household debt service as a share of income by income level.* Aizcorbe, Kennickell, Moore (2003), Table 14, p. 28.

4.16   *Households with high debt burdens by income level.* Aizcorbe, Kennickell, Moore (2003), Table 14, p. 29.

4.17   *Households late paying bills by income level.* Aizcorbe, Kennickell, Moore (2003). See note to Table 4.16.

CHAPTER 5

5.1   *Percent and number of persons in poverty and twice poverty.* Census homepage, Historical Poverty Tables, Persons, Table 2, Table 5, and Table P-1.

5.2   *Persons in poverty by race/ethnicity.* See note to Table 5.1.

5.3   *Percent of children in poverty by race.* Census homepage, Historical Poverty Tables, Persons, Table 3. Data on children under six are from FERRET Poverty Table 1 for 2001-02 and from P-60 poverty publications for earlier years.

5.4   *Family poverty by race/ethnicity of family head and for different family types.* Census homepage, Historical Poverty Tables, Persons, Table 4.

5.5   *Average poverty gap.* Recent years from: http://ferret.bls.census.gov/macro/032004/pov/toc.htm. Prior to 1987, data are from annual Census P-60 poverty reports.

5.6   *Prime-age families (household head age 25-54) with children, poverty and twice poverty by various income definitions.* Authors' analysis of March CPS data.

5.7   *Changes in poverty rates and various correlates.* For "poverty rates" see note to Table 5.1; for "productivity" see BLS, measures of output per hour in the non-farm business sector; for "per capita income" see NIPA Table 2.1; for "unemployment" see BLS, monthly CPS; for "Gini coefficient" see U.S. Bureau of the Census, Historical Income Tables, Families, Table F-4, and note to Figure 1I; for "mother-only families as a share of all families" see note to Table 5.8.

5.8   *Changing family structure and poverty.* U.S. Bureau of the Census, P60-214, Appendix Table A-1.

5.9   *Poverty rates for families with children by education level of family head.* Authors' analysis of March CPS data.

5.10   *The impact of economic, demographic, and educational factors on poverty rates.* See Appendix A.

5.11   *Poverty-reducing effects of transfers over downturns.* U.S. Bureau of the Census, P-60, No. 182-RD, and the FERRET, Experimental Measures of Income and Poverty, Table 2.

5.12   *Characteristics of low-wage workers.* Authors' analysis of CPS ORG data; see Appendix B.

CHAPTER 6

6.1   *Non-farm payroll employment by state, division, and region (in thousands).* BLS, available online (see Current Employment Statistics survey).

6.2   *Comparison of job growth in manufacturing and all other industries by state, division, and region.* BLS, available online (see Current Employment Statistics survey).

6.3   *Unemployment rate during two jobless recoveries by state, division, and region.* Authors' analysis of basic CPS data.

6.4   *Long-term unemployment by state, division, and region.* Authors' analysis of basic CPS data.

6.5   *Growth in part-time work by state.* Authors' analysis of basic CPS data.

6.6   *Low wages (20th percentile) by state (2003 dollars).* Based on analysis of CPS wage data as described in Appendix B.

6.7   *Potential impact of hourly wage growth stagnation.* Based on analysis of CPS wage data as described in Appendix B.

6.8   *Median wage (50th percentile) by state (2003 dollars).* Based on analysis of CPS wage data as described in Appendix B.

6.9   Median family income by Census division. Based on analysis of CPS March supplement data as described in Appendix A.

6.10   Poverty rates by Census division. Based on analysis of CPS March supplement data as described in Appendix A.

6.11   *States with minimum wages above the federal level.* U.S. Department of Labor. http://www.dol.gov/esa/minwage/america.htm.

6.12   *State and local taxes as a share of total family income by income group by state.* McIntyre et.al. (2003).

CHAPTER 7

7.1   *Per capita income using market exchange rates.* At the price level and exchange rates of 1995, except 1960, which is calculated at 1990 exchange rates. GDP per capita for 1960 is from OECD (1999a), Table 20, p. 146, converted to 2002 dollars (from 1990 dollars in original) using a GDP deflator constructed using data from the *Bureau of Economic Analysis* (2004b), Table 1.1.4., available online at www.bea.gov. GDP per capita for the other years is taken from OECD (2001a and 2003a), Table A9, p. 322 and available online at www.oecd.org., converted to 2002 dollars (from 1995 dollars in original) by a GDP deflator constructed using data from the *Bureau of Economic Analysis* (2004), Table 1.1.4. (available online at www.bea.gov). Population for 1960 for all other OECD countries with the exception of Germany, and 1970 for Germany, is from the Penn World Table, available online at www.pwt.econ.upenn.edu/php_site/pwt_index.php (2004). Population-weighted averages excluding the United States computed using annual national population data from OECD (2003a), *Annual National Accounts, Volume 1* (available online at www.oecd.org).

7.2   *Per capita income, using purchasing-power-parity exchange rates.* At the price level and PPP exchange rates of 1995. GDP per capita for all years is taken from OECD (2001a and 2003a), *National Accounts: Main Aggregates, Volume 1,* Table B7, p. 338, converted to 2002 dollars (from 1995 dollars in original) using a constructed GDP deflator that applied data from the *Bureau of Economic Analysis* (2004), Table 1.1.4. (available online at www.bea.gov). Population-weighted averages excluding the United States computed using annual national population data from OECD (2003a).

7.3   *Income and productivity levels in the OECD.* GDP data taken from the OECD (2003c), Table D.2. GDP per capita table indexed relative to U.S. data for the same year. Data adjusted for PPP by source. The methodology has two levels. The first level involves converting annual snapshots of GDP per hour worked into PPP adjusted GPD per hour worked. The second level involves creating a time series using the converted PPP GPD per hour worked. Population-weighted averages excluding the United States computed using annual population data from the OECD (2003a), for 1980 to 2002. For 1950, 1960 population data was used to calculate the population-weighted average excluding the United States for 1950. The population data for 1960 is from the Penn World Table, which is available online at www.pwt.econ.upenn.edu/php_site/ pwt_index.php (2004). Of this Penn World population data, for Germany, the data are for 1970, while for all the other OECD countries represented in Table 7.3 the data are for 1960.

7.4   *Labor productivity growth per year in the OECD.* Business sector. For the 1960-73 column, data are for earliest available year: 1961 for Australia and Ireland; 1962 for Japan and the U.K.; 1964 for Spain; 1965 for France and Sweden; 1966 for Canada and Norway; 1967 for New Zealand; 1969 for the Netherlands; and 1970 for Belgium. The data in first two columns are taken from OECD (1998), Annex Table 59, p. 284, and begin in 1960 or earliest available year: 1961 for Australia and Ireland; 1962 for Japan and the U.K.; 1964 for Spain; 1965 for France and Sweden; 1966 for Canada and Norway; 1967 for New Zealand; 1969 for the Netherlands; and 1970 for Belgium. Data from 1985 to 2000 were taken from OECD (2001d), Annex Table 13, p. 217. Data for 1979 to 1985 were calculated from the SourceOECD (2002) Economic Outlook Database, table entitled *Labour Productivity in the Business Sector.* Data for 2001 to 2003 were taken from OECD (2003a), Annex Table 13. For Germany, the first two columns refer to Western Germany. Population-weighted averages excluding the United States computed using annual population data from OECD (2003a).

7.5   *Productivity and unemployment rates in the OECD.* This table is constructed from data in Tables 7.3 and 7.21. For further details on sources, see notes for Tables 7.3 and 7.21.

7.6   *Real compensation growth per year in the OECD.* Compensation per employee in the business sector. Nominal compensation per employee in the business sector for years 2001 to 2003 is from OECD (2003a), Annex Table 12 (available online at www.oecd.org). Data for 1985 to 2000 is from OECD (2001d), Annex Table 12, p. 216. Data for 1979 to 1985 are from OECD (1999), Annex Table 12, p. 206. The data were deflated by changes in consumer prices from OECD (2001d and 2003a), Annex Table 16, p. 220 and online for 2001 to 2003 Consumer Price Changes figures. For Germany, growth rate reported uses data for western Germany for 1979 and data for Germany for 1980 to 2003. Population-weighted averages excluding the United States computed using annual population data from the OCED (2003a).

7.7   *Relative hourly compensation of manufacturing production workers, using market exchange rates.* Index of hourly compensation costs for production workers in manufacturing from BLS (2001a and 2003), Table 1. Population-weighted averages excluding the United States computed using annual population data from the OECD

(2003a).In the OECD, between 1979 and 2002, 13 to 23 percent of workers were in manufacturing. Data are rom the BLS (2004), Tables 2 and 5.

7.8   *Relative hourly compensation of manufacturing production workers, using purchasing-power parities.* Hourly compensation costs in national currency for production workers in manufacturing from BLS (2001b and 2004), Table 3, converted to U.S. dollars using purchasing-power parities for GDP from OECD (2003a). Population-weighted averages excluding the United States computed using annual population data from the OECD (2003a).

7.9   *Annual growth in real hourly compensation in manufacturing in the OECD.* Compensation for all workers in manufacturing is hourly compensation in manufacturing, on a national currency basis, from BLS (2004), Table 7.1. The hourly compensation in manufacturing data refer to employees (wage and salary earners) in Belgium, Denmark, Italy, and the Netherlands, and to all employed persons (employees and self-employed workers) in the other countries. Compensation for production workers is hourly compensation costs in national currency for production workers in manufacturing from BLS (2003), Table 4. Data for 1979 and 1989 are from BLS (2000c), and data for 1995 and 2000 are taken from BLS (2003). Both are deflated using consumer price indexes derived from OECD (2003a), Table 16. Population-weighted averages excluding the United States computed using annual population data from the OECD (2003a).

7.10   *Earnings inequality in OECD countries.* Data for the last three columns are taken from Glyn (2001), Table 1, p. 4. Medians are constructed for 10 countries with data for at least six years in both the 1980s and 1990s. Real wages are calculated from real average earnings in manufacturing (OECD Historical Statistics) increased (or reduced) by the rise (or fall) in wages at bottom deciles compared to median. Real wage deciles are calculated for the latest year available which is the last number in the "years" column. These data are calculated from the unpublished OECD Wage Dispersion Database.

7.11   *Household income inequality in the OECD.* For each country, the latest year available is used. Data for the Gini coefficients and the percentile ratios are taken from Smeeding (2004), Figure 1. Gini coefficients are based on incomes which are bottom coded at 1% of disposable income and top coded at 10 times the median disposable income. Gini coefficient for Japan is calculated from 1993 Japanese Survey of Income Redistribution. Averages excluding the United States calculated as simple averages.

7.12   *Household income inequality relative to the U.S. median income.* Data taken from Smeeding and Rainwater (2001) and Smeeding (2004), Figure 2. Household income at the 10th and 90th percentiles in each country is compared to median income. For France, Australia, Denmark, Norway, and Switzerland, data are represented as percent of overall U.S. 1997 medium equivalent income in purchasing-power-parity terms. For the United States., Germany, the United Kingdom, Canada, Belgium, Finland, the Netherlands, and Sweden, data are represented as percent of U.S. 2000 median equivalent income in purchasing-power-parity terms. Income inequality measured as disposable household income per equivalent adult. Averages excluding the United States calculated as simple averages.

7.13 *Change in income inequality in the OECD after 1968.* Data are taken from Luxembourg Income Study Web site (2004a). Calculations were made by computing the percentage change between the earliest and latest years, as well as the percentage-point change between the same years. The change in the Gini coefficient column is measured as the relative change in the Gini coefficient, where growth reflects more inequality. Belgium data has been updated by source.

7.14 *Poverty rates in OECD countries.* Data represent annual snapshots of poverty in the OECD countries. Poverty data for the total population, children, and the elderly are taken from Luxembourg Income Study Web site (2004b). For Spain, the data are from 1994; for Switzerland, the data are from 1992; for Ireland, the data are from 1996; for Australia and France, the data are from 1994; for Austria, Belgium, and Denmark, the data are from 1997; for the U.K. and the Netherlands, the data are for 1999; and for Finland, Italy, Norway, Sweden, Canada, the United States, and Germany, the data are from 2000. All data are based on household-level analysis.

7.15 *Poverty in the OECD countries.* Data are taken from the OECD (2001e) poverty study, Table 2.1, p. 45. Data are taken over a three-year period. Permanent-income poverty is the proportion of individuals with total income over the three-year period less than the sum of the poverty level over that period.

7.16 *Maternity and child care policies in the OECD.* Data for proportion of young children using formal child care arrangements and maternity/child care leave indicators, as well as data for percentage of children in publicly supported care and share of child care costs covered by government are taken from Waldfogel (2004), Tables 1, 2, and 3 of unpublished data. Data presented are from the latest available year: Data for maternity/child care leave are for the period 1998 to 2002. Data on share of three- to four-year-old children using formal center or school-based early childhood education programs are from 2001. Data on share of five-year-old children using formal school-based education programs are from 1999. Data on share of children in publicly supported care are from 2000.

7.17 *Employment rates in OECD countries.* BLS (2004), Table 4 (available online at www.bls.gov). Employment rates calculated from total employment as a percentage of working-age population. For Germany, 1979 and 1989 data are for Western Germany; 2000 and 2002 data are for Germany.

7.18 *Average annual hours worked in the OECD.* OECD (2001e and 2003b), Table F. Hours are calculated as the total number of hours worked over the year divided by the average number of people employed. The data are intended for comparisons of trends over time. Data are from the electronic version of the *OECD Employment Outlook* (2003), Table F. This electronic version of Table F has been corrected as compared with the original printed publication. All data refer to total employment. For Germany, Western Germany data are used for 1979. For France, new data used from the national accounts of the Institut national de la statistique et des études économiques (INSEE) for the period 1990 to 2001. 2002 is an estimate. Population-weighted averages excluding the United States computed using annual population data from the OECD (2003a).

7.19 *Per capita income compared to OECD average.* Bivens (2004), Unpublished data.

7.20 *Employment in OECD countries.* All data are taken from OECD (2001h, 2002, and 2003b), Civilian Employment tables. Population-weighted averages excluding the United States computed using annual population data from the OECD (2003a).

7.21 *Unemployment rates in the OECD.* Unemployment based on comparable definitions. Data for 1979 are from OECD (2001e) Table A, p. 208. Data for 1989, 2001, and 2002 are from OECD (2003b), Basic Structural Statistics table, p. 268. According to the OECD, in so far as possible, these data have been adjusted to ensure comparability over time and to conform to the guidelines of the International Labour Office (ILO). All series are benchmarked to labor-force-survey-based estimates. In countries with annual surveys, monthly estimates are obtained by interpolation/extrapolation and by incorporating trends in administrative data, where available. The annual figures are then calculated by averaging the monthly estimates (for both unemployed and the labor force). For countries with monthly or quarterly surveys, the annual estimates are obtained by averaging the monthly or quarterly estimates, respectively. For several countries, the adjustment procedure used is similar to that of the Bureau of Labor Statistics, U.S. Department of Labor. For European Union (EU) countries, the procedures are similar to those used in deriving the Comparable Unemployment Rates (CURs) of the Statistical Office of the European Communities. Minor differences may appear mainly because of various methods of calculating and applying adjustment factors, and because EU estimates are based on the civilian labor force. For Germany, West Germany data are used for 1979 and 1989. Population-weighted averages excluding the United States using annual population data from the OECD (2003a).

7.22 *Unemployment rates in the OECD by education level.* Unemployment rates measures using OECD's standardized unemployment rate. OECD describes educational categories as: "Less than upper secondary," "Upper secondary," and "Tertiary." OECD (2003b), Table D, pp. 316-18. For Germany, data is for Eastern and Western Germany. Population-weighted averages excluding the United States computed using annual population data from the OECD (2003a).

Figure notes

INTRODUCTION

A   *Percent change in employment 39 months after business cycle peak.* See notes for Table 3D.

B   *Gross job gains and gross job losses.* See notes for Table 3F.

C   *Real hourly wages since recession ended.* BLS homepage, Table B. Inflation is computed using CPI-U.

D   *Real weekly wages since recession ended.* BLS homepage, Table B. Inflation is computed using CPI-U

E   *Change in real income by income percentile.* Authors' analysis of Census data.

F   *Real growth of compensation and capital income in the corporate sector, 12 quarters after peak, current cycle versus average of prior cycles.* Based on data developed for Table 4.

CHAPTER 1

1A   *Real median family income.* See note to Table 1.1.

1B   *Annual growth in nominal median family income and inflation.* Census homepage, Historical Income Tables, Families, Table F-5, Inflation: RS deflator from BLS.

1C   *Ratio of black and Hispanic to white median family income.* Census homepage, Historical Income Tables, Families, Table F-5.

1D   *Effect of a one-percentage-point increase in unemployment on median family income by age.* The figure shows the coefficients on the unemployment rate from a regression of the change in the log of real median family income for families headed by persons within the age brackets shown in the figure (plus a constant).

1E   *Income share of the top 1%.* Piketty and Saez (2003), updated to 2002 from Saez Web site: http://emlab.berkeley.edu/users/saez/.

1F   *Composition of income share for the top 0.01%.* Piketty and Saez (2003).

1G   *Real income growth by income group (comprehensive income data).* CBO (2004) data, Effective Federal Taxes Rates 1979 to 2002, Table B1-C.

1H   *Low-, middle-, and high-income growth.* Census homepage, Historical Income Tables, Families, Table F-1.

1I   *Family income inequality, Gini coefficient.* Census homepage, Historical Income Tables, Families, Table 4. The steep jump in the figure in 1993 is in part due to the lifting of the Census top-codes. In order to discount this change, we ran a time-series regression with a dummy variable for the 1993-2000 period. The regression uses the state-space model approach, described in Koopman et al. 2000. STAMP software was used to run the structural model, with a fixed-level, stochastic slope and AR(1) terms to model the unobserved trend and cycle components.

1J   *Ratio of family income of top 5% to lowest 20%.* Census homepage, Historical Income Tables, Families, Table F-3, deflated using CPI-U-RS.

1K   *Real family income growth by quintile.* See notes for Figure 1J. 1947 data provided by Census Bureau.

1L   *Income and consumption inequality, Gini coefficients indexed to 1981.* Johnson and Smeeding (1998), with updates provided by Johnson.

1M   *Share of families remaining in the top fifth income bracket at start and end of decade.* Bradbury and Katz (2002).

1N   *Pretax and post-tax growth of real household income, by income group.* CBO (2004) data, Effective Federal Taxes Rates 1979 to 2002.

1O   *Components of effective federal tax rate, bottom fifth income quintile.* CBO (2004) data, Effective Federal Taxes Rates 1979 to 2002.

1P   *Change in family income shares over the past two recessions.* Census homepage, *Income, Poverty, and Health Coverage in the United States: 2003*, Appendix A.

1Q   *Income shares in the corporate sector.* Analysis is based on the data from NIPA Table 1.14.

1R   *Before- and after-tax return to capital.* See note for figure 1N, FRB data.

1S   *Growth of family work hours compared to average weekly hours.* Family hours are from authors' analysis of March CPS data (see Appendix A). Average weekly hours are for all workers, provided by BLS.

1T   *Annual work hours, middle-income wives, age 25-54, with children.* Authors' analysis of March CPS data. See Appendix A

CHAPTER 2

2A   *Hourly wage and compensation growth for production/nonsupervisory workers.* See note to Table 2.4. Hourly compensation was estimated based on multiplying hourly wages by the ratio of compensation to wages for all workers in each year. The compensation/wage ratio is drawn from the NIPA data used in Table 2.2. The compensation/wage ratio for 2003 was set equal to the 2002 level.

2B   *Change in real hourly wages for men by wage percentile.* See note to Table 2.7.

2C   *Change in real hourly wages for women by wage percentile.* See note to Table 2.8.

2D   *Share of workers earning poverty-level wages by gender.* See note to Table 2.9

2E   *Share of workers earning poverty-level wages by race/ethnicity.* See note to Table 2.9

2F   *Private-sector employer-provided health insurance coverage by race/ethnicity.* See note to Table 2.14.

2G   *Share of pension participants in defined-contribution and defined-benefit plans.* U.S. Department of Labor (2001-02), Table E4b.

2H   *Men's wage inequality.* Based on ratios of wages by decile in annual data presented in Table 2.7.

2I   *Women's wage inequality.* Based on ratios of wages by decile in annual data presented in Table 2.8.

2J   *95/50 percentile wage inequality.* Based on ratios of wages by percentile presented in Tables 2.7, and 2.8.

2K   *College/high school wage premium.* Differentials estimated with controls for experience (as a quartic), region (4), marital status, race/ethnicity, and education, which is specified as dummy variables for less than high school, some college, college, and advanced degree. Estimates were made on the CPS ORG data as described in Appendix B and presented in Table 2.16.

2L   *Productivity and hourly compensation growth.* Average hourly productivity and compensation are for the non-farm business sector and available from the BLS Web site (see major sector productivity and cost index). The compensation series is deflated by the CPI-U-RS. The median compensation of female, male, and all workers is derived by multiplying the compensation/wage ratio (based on the NIPA data discussed in the note to Table 2.2) by the real median wage series for each in Tables 2.6, 2.7, and 2.8.

2M   *Entry-level wages of male and female high school graduates.* See note to Table 2.21.

2N   *Entry-level wages of male and female college graduates.* See note to Table 2.21.

2O   *Health and pension coverage for recent high school graduates.*

Computed from the same data as used in tables 2.14 and 2.15.

2P   *Health and pension coverage for recent college graduates.* Computed from the same data as used in tables 2.14 and 2.15.

2Q   *Gender wage ratio by percentile.* The gender wage ratio is calculated by dividing the female wage by the male wage at the respective wage level. See note to Tables 2.6, 2.7, and 2.8 for wage derivations.

2R   *Unemployment.* The unemployment rate is available at the BLS Web site (see Current Population Survey).

2S   *Share of intermediate inputs supplied by imports.* Update of Feenstra and Hanson (2001) presented in Bivens (2004).

2T   *Employment in IT software industries and software investment.* From Bivens and Price (2004).

2U   *Change in software-related jobs since 2000.* From Bivens and Price (2004).

2V   *Union membership in the United States.* Hirsch and Macpherson (1997) and BLS (Employment and Earnings).

2W   *Real value of the minimum wage.* Series compiled by authors and deflated using CPI-U-RS.

2X   *Minimum wage as percentage of average hourly earnings.* Calculated from values of minimum wage (Table 2.41) and average hourly earnings (Table 2.4).

2Y   *Ratio of CEO to average worker pay.* Calculated by dividing the CEO average annual pay (see note to Table 2.46) by production nonsupervisory workers' average annual pay (hourly average multiplied by 2,080 multiplied by the compensation/ wage ratio discussed in note to Table 2.2). The production nonsupervisory worker's average hourly pay is available online from the BLS (see Current Establishment Survey).

CHAPTER 3

3A   *Unemployment rate and its trend.* Authors' calculation for trend of annual unemployment data (using Hodrick-Prescott filter) from BLS (2004c).

3B   *Family income gained due to lower unemployment between 1995 and 2000, by quintile.* Bartik (2002).

3C   *Employment: 2001 recession and recovery.* Total non-farm seasonally adjusted monthly data are taken from BLS (2004d).

3D   *Percent change in employment 39 months after business cycle peak.* Total non-farm seasonally adjusted data are taken from BLS (2004d). 1980 recession is not included.

3E   *Change in private-sector employment 31 months after recovery began.* Seasonally adjusted monthly total private employment data are taken from BLS (2004d), Table B-1.

3F   *Gross job gains and losses.* Seasonally adjusted data are taken from BLS (2004f) and Faberman (2004). Data from 1990q2 to 2003q1 are from Faberman (2004) and data from 2003q2 to 2003q3 are from BLS (2004f). Gross job gains and gross job losses are expressed as rates by dividing their levels by the average employment in the current and previous quarters. This provides a symmetric growth rate. The rates are calculated for the components of gross job gains and gross job losses and then summed to form their respective totals. These rates can be added and subtracted just as their levels can. These data are Business Employment Dynamics data and are from the administrative records of the regularly collected establishment employment data (Quarterly Census of Employment and Wages program). This program is a quarterly census of all establishments under state unemployment insurance programs, representing about 98% of employment on non-farm payrolls.

3G   *Percent change in employment by industry 10 quarters after business cycle trough.* Monthly seasonally adjusted data are from BLS (2004d), Table B-1.

3H   *Percentage-point change in unemployment 13 quarters after peak for the two most recent recessions, by educational status.* EPI seasonally adjusted data from 1990q1 to 1991q4. Data are taken from BLS (2004c).

3I   *Unemployment by selected occupational classifications.* Data are taken from BLS (2004c), Table A-10. 2004 occupational data use non-seasonally adjusted quarterly data from BLS (2004c) on aggregated unemployment rates by occupations. We do not suspect that there is any seasonal component attached to these occupations. 2004 data calculated by averaging first- and second-quarter data. The 2004 unemployment rate uses seasonally adjusted quarterly data from BLS (2004c). White-collar unemployment calculated by taking the average of the broader Management and Sales occupation categories in BLS (2004c) Table A-10; blue-collar employment calculated from taking the average of the broader Natural Resources and Production occupation categories from Table A-10. Services data are taken directly from BLS 92004c), Table A-10.

3J   *Unemployment by information technology occupations.* Data for computer programmers and software engineers are taken from unpublished data from BLS. Data for the unemployment rates are taken from BLS (2004c). 2004 occupational data use non-seasonally adjusted quarterly data from unpublished BLS data on disaggregated unemployment rates by occupations. We do not suspect that there is any seasonal component attached to these occupations. 2004 calculated by averaging first- and second-quarter data. The unemployment rate for 2004 uses seasonally adjusted quarterly data from BLS (2004c).

3K   *Mean duration of unemployment in weeks.* Data are monthly seasonally adjusted from BLS (2004c), Tables A-1 and A-9.

3L   *Long-term unemployment as a share of total unemployment compared to the unemployment rate.* Data are taken from BLS (2004c).

3M   *Long-term unemployment 31 months from the start of the recovery.* Data are taken from BLS (2004c).

3N   *Percentage-point change in share of unemployment and long-term unemployment by education.* Allegretto and Stettner (2004).

3O   *Monthly underemployment and unemployment rates.* See note to Table 3.8.

3P   *Annual labor force participation rate.* Data are taken from BLS (2004c), Table A-2.

3Q   *Labor force participation rates for men by race/ethnicity.* See note to Figure 3P.

3R   *Labor force participation rates for women by race/ethnicity.* See note to Figure 3P.

3S   *Effects of lower labor force participation rates on the size of the civilian labor force.* Seasonally adjusted monthly data are taken from BLS (2004c). The estimated labor force is constructed by holding the labor force participation rate constant at the March 2001 rate of 67.0%.

3T   *Missing labor force and its effect on the unemployment rate.* Data are taken from BLS (2004c). This analysis assumes that the individuals who make up the missing labor force want jobs and, if they were actively searching for employment, would be counted as unemployed.

3U   *Change in employment rates during economic recoveries by gender and race.* Data are taken from BLS (2004c).

3V   *Annual employment rates by age group.* Data are taken from BLS (2004c).

3W   *Employment rates of college graduates by age group.* See note to Figure 3V.

3X   *Responsibility for determining own hours of work by family type.* McCrate (2002), Figure F, p. 8.

3Y   *Employment in temporary help industry as share of total employment.* Data are taken from BLS (2004d).

3Z   *Part-time employment as a percent of all employment.* Seasonally adjusted monthly data are taken from BLS (2004c).

3AA   *Employment and average weekly overtime hours in manufacturing.* Data are taken from BLS (2004d), Tables B-1 and B-2.

3BB   *Manufacturing output.* Seasonally adjusted manufacturing production (GMF [NAICS] series) data are taken from the Federal Reserve Board (2004), Tables 1, 2, and 10.

CHAPTER 4

4A   *Distribution of wealth by wealth class.* Data taken from Wolff (2004). Data for 1986 calculated by taking half of the difference between 1983 and 1989 and adding it to 1983 to get a linear approximation.

4B   *Annual net worth of "Forbes 400" wealthiest individuals.* Data for 1982 to 2001 adapted from Broom and Shay (2000), Table 2, p. 15; updated to 2000 and 2001 by Broom and Shay (via personal correspondence). Data for 2002 and 2003 are from Forbes.com (2004), Forbes 400 list.

4C   *Growth of U.S. stock market.* Standard & Poor's Composite Index from Economic Report of the President (2004), Table B-95, p. 430, deflated by the CPI-U-RS (Table B-62).

4D   *Distribution of stock market holdings by wealth class.* See note to Table 4.9.

4E   *Distribution of stock market wealth by wealth class.* See note to Table 4.9.

4F   *Distribution of growth in stock market holdings by wealth class.* See note to Table 4.9.

4G   *Average home ownership rates.* Yearly average of data published by the Bureau of Census, Housing Vacancy Survey, (2003), Historical tables, Table 13. Home ownership rates for the U.S. and Regions.

4H   *Home ownership rates by race.* See note to Table 4.11.

4I   *Average rate of home ownership by income.* See note to Table 4.11.

4J   *Change in mean retirement wealth by income class.* See note to Table 4.1.

4K   *Debt as percentage of disposable personal income.* See note to Table 4.13.

4L   *Distribution of growth in debt.* Calculated from Table 4.8.

4M   *Consumer bankruptcies per 1,000 adults.* Data on consumer bankruptcies from the American Bankruptcy Institute Web page (2004), U.S. Bankruptcy Filings table. Data on adult population from the Economic Report of the President, (2002), Table B-35 (available online at http://www.gpoaccess.gov/eop/); Bureau of Labor Statistics (2004a); and data from the A tables on Household Data from the current population survey by the Bureau of Labor Statistics (2004b).

CHAPTER 5

5A   *Poverty and twice-poverty rates.* See note to Table 5.1.

5B   *Actual and simulated poverty rates under different unemployment trends.* Based on a simple time-series model where the change in poverty rates from 1959 to 2003 are regressed on a constant, the log changes in three variables: productivity, the trend in the Gini coefficient, and the change in the unemployment rate. The simulations hold unemployment constant in the values shown in the figure.

5C   *Poverty rates by race/ethnicity.* See note to Table 5.2.

5D   *Twice-poverty by race/ethnicity.* Authors' analysis of March CPS data. Racial/ethnic categories are exclusive, i.e., Hispanics are not in other categories.

5E   *Family poverty gap and family poverty rates.* See notes to Table 5.4 and 5.5.

5F   *Percent of the poor below half the poverty line.* Census homepage, Historical Poverty Tables, Table 5, Table 22.

5G   *Labor market and real income trends for low-income single mothers.* Authors' analysis of March CPS data. Sample is single-mother families (primary families only) headed by women age 18 to 65 with incomes below twice the poverty line.

5H   *Annual hours worked by married or single low-income mothers.* See previous note.

5I   *Income components for low-income single mothers.* See note 5G.

5J   *The contribution of demographics (including education), growth, and inequality to changes in poverty.* Data are from Table 5.10. See Appendix A for methods.

5K   *Poverty-reducing effect of taxes and means-tested transfers on persons in mother-only families.* See note to Table 5.11.

5L   *Real hourly wages of low-wage workers.* Wages are based on analysis of CPS wage data as described in Appendix B. The poverty-level wage is the hourly wage that, at full-time, full-year work, would lift a family of four above the poverty line. This equals $ 9.04 in 2003 dollars.

5M   *Productivity, unemployment, and real low-wage growth.* Productivity and unemployment from BLS, low-wage growth from CPS-ORG series described in Appendix B.

CHAPTER 6

6A   *Job growth by state.* BLS, available online (see Current Employment Statistics survey).

6B   *Job loss by state (2000-03) compared to reliance on manufacturing employment in 2000.* BLS, available online (see Current Employment Statistics survey).

6C   *Growth in wages by division.* Based on analysis of CPS wage data as described in Appendix B.

6D   Impact of wage growth and changes in hours worked on average income of working families. Based on analysis of CPS March supplement as described in Appendix A. The total change in average family income for the bottom 60% of working families is broken into two components—wage and salary income and other income. The total number of annual hours is summed across families. The average hourly wage for each family is simply total annual earnings divided by total annual hours. The effect of hourly wage growth on average family income is equal to the change in family income if annual hours were held constant and vice versa.

6E   *Real value of federal minimum wage and number of states with minimum wages above the federal rate.* Department of Labor.

6F   *Year-over-year change in quarterly state tax revenue.* Changes are adjusted for inflation and state policy changes. See Nicholas (2004) for the Rockefeller Institute of Government.

CHAPTER 7

7A   *Annual growth rates of per capita income using market exchange rates.* At the price level and exchange rates of 1995 (except for 1960 which is at 1990 exchange rates). See note to Table 7.1.

7B   *Productivity growth rates.* See note to Table 7.4.

7C   *Gender wage gaps in the OECD.* Data are taken from OECD (2001g), *Society at a Glance 2001,* Annex Table B4. Note that the data for the chart only appear in the Web version, not in the book itself. For Australia, the U.K., and the United States, we used 2000 data because these countries had up to 2000 data available and the difference between the data for 1999 and 2000 was minimal.

7D   *Relative income comparisons in the OECD.* Data are from Smeeding (2004), Figure 1.

7E   *Composition of low and high incomes compared to U.S. median.* See notes to Table 7.12.

7F   *Intergenerational earnings mobility in OECD countries.* Data are taken from Solon (2002), Table 1. For the United States, the data represent average value of many U.S. studies on intergenerational earnings elasticity (Solon 2002). For the other countries, the data represent the most conservative estimate of the intergenerational earnings elasticity.

7G   *Top decile income share in France and in the United States.* Data are taken from Piketty and Saez (2001), Figure 19. Authors' computations based on income tax returns (France: see Piketty 2001, Table A1, col. P90-100; U.S.: see Piketty and Saez 2001, Table A1, col. P90-100).

7H   *Top 0.1% income share in France, the United States, and the United Kingdom.* Data are taken from Piketty and Saez (2001), Figure 21. Authors' computations based on income tax returns (France: see Piketty 2001, Table A1, col. P99-100; U.S.: see Piketty and Saez 2001, Table A1, col. P99-100; U.K.: see Atkinson 2001).

7I   *Real incomes of low-income households with children: cash and non-cash.* Data taken from Smeeding (2002).

7J   *Social expenditures versus child poverty in the OECD.* Data on child poverty taken from Luxembourg Income Study Web site at www.lisproject.org (2004b) and are taken for the latest year possible and for the 50th percentile (same years that were used in table 7.13). Data for social expenditures are calculated from OECD (2002) Annex Table B6. $R^2 = 0.5784$. Note that, like figure 7C, the data for the chart only appear in the Web version, not in the book itself. The social expenditure data are for 1997 and here social expenditure is calculated by subtracting out pensions and health benefits from public social expenditure.

Bibliography

Aizcorbe, Ana M., Arthur B. Kennickell, and Kevin B. Moore. 2003. Recent changes in U.S. family finances: Evidence from the 1998 and 2001 Survey of Consumer Finances. *Federal Reserve Bulletin.* January. <http://www.federalreserve.gov/pubs/bulletin/2003/0103lead.pdf>

Allegretto, Sylvia and Andy Stettner. 2004. *Educated, Experienced, and Out of Work.* EPI) Issue Brief, no.198. Washington, D.C.: Economic Policy Institute.

American Bankruptcy Institute. 2004. *Annual, Total Business and Non-Business Bankruptcy Filings.* Alexandria, Va.: American Bankruptcy Institute.

Atkinson, Anthony B. 2001. *Top Incomes in the United Kingdom Over the Twentieth Century.* Oxford, England: Nuffied College.

Bartik, Timothy J. 2002. *Jobs for the Poor: Can Labor Demand Policies Help?* New York, N.Y.: Russell Sage Foundation and the Upjohn Institute.

Bivens, Josh. Forthcoming (2004). *Globalization, Jobs, Wages, and Inequality.* Washington, D.C.: Economic Policy Institute.

Bivens, L. Josh, and Lee Price. 2004. *Offshoring Issue Guide.* Washington, D.C.: Economic Policy Institute. <http://www.epinet.org/content.cfm/issueguide_offshoring>

Bernstein, Jared, and John Schmitt. 1998. *Making Work Pay: The Impact of the 1996-97 Minimum Wage Increase.* Washington, D.C.: Economic Policy Institute.

Borjas, George J. 2003. The labor demand curve is downward sloping. *Quarterly Journal of Economics.* November.

Bradbury, Katherine, and Jane Katz. 2002. Are lifetime incomes growing more unequal? Looking at new evidence on family income mobility. *Regional Review.* Federal Reserve Bank of Boston, Vol. 12, No. 4.

Broom, Leonard, and Shay, William. 2000. "Discontinuities in the distribution of great wealth: Sectoral forces old and new." Paper prepared for the Conference on Saving, Intergenerational Transfer, and the Distribution of Wealth held by the Jerome Levy Economics Institute at Bard College, June 7-9, 2000.

463

Buchmueller, Thomas C., John DiNardo, Robert G. Valletta. 2001. "Union effects on health insurance provision and coverage in the United States." National Bureau of Economic Research, Working Paper No. 8238. Cambridge, Mass.: NBER.

Card, David. 1991. "The effect of unions on the distribution of wages: Redistribution or re-labeling?" Working Paper No. 287. Princeton, N.J.: Department of Economics, Princeton University.

Card, David and John E. DiNardo. "Skill-biased technological change and rising wage inequality: Some problems and puzzles." National Bureau of Economic Research Working Paper No. W8769. Cambridge, Mass.: NBER.

Cline, William R. 1997. *Trade and Income Distribution*. Washington, D.C.: Institute for International Economics.

Congressional Budget Office. 2004. *Effective Federal Tax Rates, 1979-2001*. Washington, D.C.: CBO. April. <http://www.cbo.gov/showdoc.cfm? index= 5324&sequence=0>

Economagic. 2004. *Economic Time Series Page*. Washington, D.C.: Economagic.com. < http://www.economagic.com >

Economic Report of the President. *Annual*. Washington, D.C.: U. S. Government Printing Office.

Economy.com. 2004a. *Demographics*. West Chester, Pa.: Economy.com. <http://www.economy.com >

Economy.com. 2004b. *Homeownership Rates*. West Chester, Pa.: Economy.com <http://www.economy.com >

Farber, Henry S. 2003. "Job loss in the United States, 1981-2001." Industrial Relations Section Working Paper No. 471. Princeton, N.J.: Princeton University.

Farberman, Jason. R. 2004. "Gross jobs flows over the past two business cycles: Not all 'Recoveries' are created equal." Bureau of Labor Statistics, Office of Employment and Unemployment Statistics. Working Paper 372.

Federal Reserve Board. 2000. Recent changes in U. S. family finances: Results from the 1998 Survey of Consumer Finances. *Federal Reserve Bulletin*. January 2000, pp. 1-29

Federal Reserve Board. 2003. *Household Debt Burden*. Washington, D.C.: Board of Governors of the Federal Reserve System

Federal Reserve Board. 2004a. *Flow of Funds Accounts of the United States: Annual Flows and Outstandings*. Washington, D.C.: Board of Governors of the Federal Reserve System.

Federal Reserve Board. 2004b. *Flow of Funds Accounts of the United States: Annual Flows and Outstanding*. Washington, D.C.: Board of Governors of the Federal Reserve System.

Federal Reserve Board. 2004c. *Flow of Funds Accounts of the United States: Annual Flows and Outstanding.* Washington, D.C.: Board of Governors of the Federal Reserve System.

Federal Reserve Board. 2004. *Industrial Production: Market Industry Groups and Individual Series.* <http://www.federalreserve.gov/releases/g17/ipdisk/ip.sa>

Feenstra, Robert C. and Gordon H. Hanson. 2001. "Global production sharing and rising inequality: a survey of trade and wages" National Bureau of Economic Research Working Paper No. 8372. Cambridge, Mass.: NBER.

Forbes. 2004. *Forbes 400 List.* <www.forbes.com>

Freeman, Richard. 1991. "How much has de-unionization contributed to the rise in male earnings inequality?" National Bureau of Economic Research Working Paper No. 3826. Cambridge, Mass.: NBER.

Galinsky, Ellen, Stacy Kim, and James Bond. 2001. *Feeling Overworked: When Work Becomes Too Much.* New York, N.Y.: Families and Work Institute.

Gardner, Jennifer M. 1995. Worker displacement: A decade of change. *Monthly Labor Review.* Vol. 118, No. 4, pp. 45-57.

Glyn, Andrew. 2001. "Inequalities of Employment and Wages in OECD Countries." Oxford University, Department of Economics. Unpublished.

Gundersen, Bethney. 2003 "Unions and the well-being of low-skill workers." George Warren Brown School of Social Work. Washington University. Ph.D. dissertation.

Hecker, Daniel E. 2004. Occupational employment projection to 2012. *Monthly Labor Review.* February.

Hertz, Thomas. Forthcoming. "Rags, Riches, and Race: The Intergenerational Mobility of Black and White Families in the United States." In Samuel Bowles, Herbert Gintis, and Melissa Osborne, eds., *Unequal Chances: Family Background and Economic Success.* Princeton, N.J.: Princeton University Press.

Hirsch, Barry T., and David A. Macpherson. 1997. *Union Membership and Earnings Data Book: Compilations from the Current Population Survey (1997 edition).* Washington, D.C.: Bureau of National Affairs.

Kalleberg, Arne, Edith Rasell, Naomi Cassirer, Barbara F. Reskin, Ken Hudson, David Webster, Eileen Appelbaum, and Robert M. Spalter-Roth. 1997. *Nonstandard Work, Substandard Jobs.* Washington, D.C.: Economic Policy Institute and Women's Research & Education Institute.

Koopman, Siem Jan, Andrew C. Harvey, Jurgen A. Doornik, and Neil Shepard. 2000. *STAMP, Structural Time Series Analyser, Modeller, and Predictor.* London: Timberlake Consultants, Ltd,.

Luxembourg Income Study. 2004a. *Income Inequality Measures*. Luxembourg: Luxembourg Income Study. <http://lisweb.ceps.lu/keyfigures/ineqtable.htm>

Luxembourg Income Study. 2004b. *Relative Poverty Rates for the Total Population, Children and the Elderly*. Luxembourg: Luxembourg Income Study. <http://lisweb.ceps.lu/keyfigures/povertytable.htm>

McCrate, Elaine. 2002. *Working Mothers in a Double Bind.* Washington, D.C.: Economic Policy Institute.

Mishel, Lawrence. 2003. *How Unions Help All Workers.* Washington, D.C.: Economic Policy Institute.

Mishel, Lawrence, Jared Bernstein, and Heather Boushey. 2002. *The State of Working America, 2002-03.* Ithaca, N.Y.: Cornell University Press.

Murphy, Kevin, and Finis Welch. 1989. "Recent trends in real wages: Evidence from household data." Paper prepared for the Health Care Financing Administration of the U.S. Department of Health and Human Services. Chicago, Ill.: University of Chicago.

Organization for Economic Cooperation and Development (OECD). 1998. *Economic Outlook.* Paris: OECD.

Organization for Economic Cooperation and Development (OECD). 1999a. *National Accounts of OECD Countries. Main Aggregates Volume I. 1960-1996.* Paris: OECD.

Organization for Economic Cooperation and Development (OECD). 1999b. *Economic Outlook.* Paris: OECD.

Organization for Economic Cooperation and Development (OECD). 2001a. *National Accounts of OECD Countries. Main Aggregates Volume I. 1989-2000.* Paris: OECD.

Organization for Economic Cooperation and Development (OECD). 2001b. *OECD in Figures.* Paris: OECD.

Organization for Economic Cooperation and Development (OECD). 2001c. *OECD Science, Technology and Industry Scoreboard 2001: Towards a Knowledge-Based Economy.* Paris: OECD

Organization for Economic Cooperation and Development (OECD). 2001d. *Economic Outlook.* Paris: OECD.

Organization for Economic Cooperation and Development (OECD). 2001e. *Employment Outlook.* June 2001. Paris: OECD.

Organization for Economic Cooperation and Development (OECD). 2001f. *Purchasing Power Parities (PPPs) for OECD Countries 1970-2001.* Paris: OECD.

Organization for Economic Cooperation and Development (OECD). 2001g. *Society at a Glance, 2001*. Paris: OECD.

Organization for Economic Cooperation and Development (OECD). 2001h. *Main Economic Indicators*. Paris: OECD.

Organization for Economic Cooperation and Development (OECD). 2002. *Source OECD Website: The OECD Online Library of Book, Periodicals, and Statistics*. Paris: OECD. <http://www.sourceoecd.org/content/html/index.htm>

Organization for Economic Cooperation and Development (OECD). 2003a. *Economic Outlook*. Paris: OECD.

Organization for Economic Cooperation and Development (OECD). 2003b. *Employment Outlook*. Paris: OECD.

Organization for Economic Cooperation and Development (OECD). 2003c. *OECD Science and Technology: Towards a Knowledge Based Economy*. Paris: OECD.

Penn World. 2004. *Penn World Table*. <http://pwt.econ.upenn.edu/>

Pierce, Brooks. 1999b. "Compensation inequality." Office of Compensation and working Conditions, Department of Labor Working Paper No. 323.

Piketty, Thomas. 2001. "Income inequality in France, 1901-1998." CEPR Discussion Paper No. 2876. London, U.K.: Center for Economic Policy Research.

Piketty, Thomas, and Saez Emmanuel. 2001. "Income inequality in the United States, 1913 to 1998." Working paper no: 8467. National Bureau of Economic Research (NBER). http://www.nber.org./papers/w8467

Polivka, Anne E., and Stephen M. Miller. 1995. "The CPS after the redesign: Refocusing the economic lens." Washington, D.C.: Bureau of Labor Statistics. Unpublished paper. March.

Roper Center for Public Opinion Research. 2004. *General Social Science Surveys, 1978-2002*. The Roper Center for Public Opinion and Research, University of Connecticut.

Scott, Robert E., Thea Lee, and John Schmitt. 1997. *Trading Away Good Jobs: An Examination of Employment and Wages in the U.S., 1979-94*. Briefing Paper. Washington, D.C.: Economic Policy Institute.

Shapiro, Isaac. 1987. *No Escape: The Minimum Wage and Poverty*. Washington, D.C.: Center on Budget and Policy Priorities.

Smeeding, Timothy. 2002. "Real standards of living and public support for children: A cross-national comparison." Paper prepared for The Bocconi Workshop "Income Distribution and Welfare." May 30.

Smeeding, Timothy. 2004. *Public Policy and Economic Inequality: The United States in Comparative Perspective*. Unpublished draft.

Smeeding, Timothy, and Lee Rainwater. 2001. "Comparing living standards across nations: Real incomes at the top, the bottom, and the middle." Luxembourg Income Study Working Paper. Luxembourg: Luxembourg Income Study.

Solon, Gary. 2002. Cross-country differences in intergenerational earnings mobility. *Journal of Economic Perspectives*. Vol. 16, Summer, pp. 59-66.

Stewart, Jay. 2003. *Recent Trends in Job Stability and Job Security: Evidence from the March CPS*. Washington, D.C.: Office of Employment Research and Program Development, U.S. Bureau of Labor Statistics.

Stewart, Jay. 2004. "Recent trends in job stability and job security: Evidence from the March CPS." BLS Working Paper #356, Washington, D.C.: Office of Employment Research and Program Development, U.S. Bureau of Labor Statistics.

Towers Perrin. 2004. *Worldwide Total Remuneration*. www.towersperrin.com

University of Groningen and The Conference Board. 2002. *GGDC Total Economy Database, 2002.* <http://www.eco.rug.nl/ggdc>

U.S. Department of Commerce, Bureau of the Census. 1999. *American Housing Survey*. <http://www.census.gov/hhes/www/housing/ahs/ahs99/ahs99.html>

U.S. Department of Commerce, Bureau of the Census. 2003. *Housing Vacancy Survey. Housing Vacancies and Homeownership Annual Statistics: 2003.* Washington, D.C.: U.S. Government Printing Office.

U.S. Department of Commerce, Bureau of Economic Analysis (BEA). 2002. *National Income and Product Accounts Tables*. Washington, D.C.: U.S. Government Printing Office.

U.S. Department of Commerce, Bureau of Economic Analysis (BEA). 2004a. *National Economic Accounts*. Washington, D.C.: U.S. Government Printing Office.

U.S. Department of Commerce, Bureau of Economic Analysis (BEA). 2004b. *National Income and Product Accounts*. Washington, D.C.: U.S. Government Printing Office.

U.S. Department of Labor, Bureau of Labor Statistics (BLS). 1997. *New Data on Multiple Job Holdings Available From the CPS*. Washington, D.C.: U.S. Government Printing Office.

U.S. Department of Labor, Bureau of Labor Statistics (BLS). 2000. *International Comparisons of Hourly Compensation Costs for Production Workers in Manufacturing, 1975-1998*. Washington, D.C.: Bureau of Labor Statistics.

U.S. Department of Labor, Bureau of Labor Statistics (BLS). 2001a. *International Comparisons of Hourly Compensation Costs for Production Workers in Manufacturing, 1997-2000*. Washington, D.C.: Bureau of Labor Statistics.

U.S. Department of Labor, Bureau of Labor Statistics (BLS). 2001b. *International Comparisons of Labor Productivity and Unit Labor Costs in Manufacturing, 2000.* Washington, D.C.: Bureau of Labor Statistics.

U.S. Department of Labor, Bureau of Labor Statistics (BLS) 2001c. *International Comparisons of Hourly Compensation Costs for Production Workers in Manufacturing, 2000.* Washington, D.C.: Bureau of Labor Statistics.

U.S. Department of Labor, Bureau of Labor Statistics (BLS). 2001d. *Comparative Civilian Labor Force Statistics, Ten Countries, 1959-2001.* Washington, D.C.: Bureau of Labor Statistics.

U.S. Department of Labor, Bureau of Labor Statistics. 2001. *Employee Benefits in Private Industry, 1999.* Washington, D.C.: Bureau of Labor Statistics.

U. S. Department of Labor, Bureau of Labor Statistics (BLS). 2003. *International Comparison of Hourly Compensation Costs for Production Workers in Manufacturing, 1975-2002.* Washington D.C.: Bureau of Labor Statistics.

U. S. Department of Labor, Bureau of Labor Statistics (BLS). 2004. *Comparative Civilian Labor Force Statistics, Ten Countries, 1959-2002.* Washington, D.C.: Bureau of Labor Statistics.

U.S. Department of Labor, Bureau of Labor Statistics. (BLS) 2004. *Employer Cost for Employee Compensation Historical Listing (Quarterly), 2002-2003.* Washington, D.C.: Bureau of Labor Statistics.

U.S. Department of Labor. Bureau of Labor Statistics (BLS). 2004a. *Table A-13. Persons not in the Labor Force and Multiple Jobholders by Sex, not Seasonally Adjusted.* Washington, DC: U.S. Government Printing Office. <http://www.bls.gov/webapps/legacy/cpsatab13.htm>

U.S. Department of Labor. Bureau of Labor Statistics (BLS). 2004b. *Employee Benefits in Private Industry, 2003.* USDL: 01-473 Washington, D.C.: U.S. Government Printing Office.

U.S. Department of Labor. Bureau of Labor Statistics (BLS). 2004c. *Current Population Survey.* Washington, D.C.: U.S. Government Printing Office.

U.S. Department of Labor. Bureau of Labor Statistics (BLS). 2004d. *Current Employment Statistics.* Washington, D.C.: U.S. Government Printing Office.

U. S. Department of Labor, Bureau of Labor Statistics (BLS). 2004e. *Labor Force and Employment Estimates Smoothed for Population Adjustments, 1990-2003.* Washington, D.C.: Division of Labor Statistics.

U. S. Department of Labor, Bureau of Labor Statistics. (BLS) 2004f. *Business Employment Dynamics.* Washington, D.C.: U.S. Government Printing Office.

Waldfogel, Jane. 2004. *Early Childhood Policy: A Comparative Perspective.* Forthcoming publication.

469

Wall Street Journal. 2003. The boss's pay: The WSJ/Mercer 2003 compensation survey. *Wall Street Journal*, April 12.

Wenger, Jeffrey. 2001. *The Continuing Problems With Part-time Jobs.* Issue Brief #155, Washington, D.C.: Economic Policy Institute.

Wenger, Jeffery. 2002. Unpublished tables on nonstandard work. Washington D.C.: Economic Policy Institute

Wolff, Edward. 2004. Unpublished analysis of Survey of Consumer Finances (SCF) dataprepared in 2004 for the Economic Policy Institute.

Index

About EPI

The Economic Policy Institute was founded in 1986 to widen the debate about policies to achieve healthy economic growth, prosperity, and opportunity.

Today, despite rapid growth in the U.S. economy in the latter part of the 1990s, inequality in wealth, wages, and income remains historically high. Expanding global competition, changes in the nature of work, and rapid technological advances are altering economic reality. Yet many of our policies, attitudes, and institutions are based on assumptions that no longer reflect real world conditions.

With the support of leaders from labor, business, and the foundation world, the Institute has sponsored research and public discussion of a wide variety of topics: globalization; fiscal policy; trends in wages, incomes, and prices; education; the causes of the productivity slowdown; labor market problems; rural and urban policies; inflation; state-level economic development strategies; comparative international economic performance; and studies of the overall health of the U.S. manufacturing sector and of specific key industries.

The Institute works with a growing network of innovative economists and other social science researchers in universities and research centers all over the country who are willing to go beyond the conventional wisdom in considering strategies for public policy.

Founding scholars of the Institute include Jeff Faux, former EPI president; Lester Thurow, Sloan School of Management, MIT; Ray Marshall, former U.S. secretary of labor, professor at the LBJ School of Public Affairs, University of Texas; Barry Bluestone, Northeastern University; Robert Reich, former U.S. secretary of labor; and Robert Kuttner, author, editor of *The American Prospect,* and columnist for *Business Week* and the Washington Post Writers Group.

For additional information about the Institute, contact EPI at 1660 L Street NW, Suite 1200, Washington, DC 20036, (202) 775-8810, or visit www.epinet.org.

About the authors

LAWRENCE MISHEL is president of the Economic Policy Institute and was the research director from 1987 to 1999. He is the co-author of the previous versions of *The State of Working America*. He holds a Ph.D. in economics from the University of Wisconsin, and his articles have appeared in a variety of academic and non-academic journals. His areas of research are labor economics, wage and income distribution, industrial relations, productivity growth, and the economics of education.

JARED BERNSTEIN joined the Economic Policy Institute as a labor economist in 1992 and is currently the director of the Living Standards Program. Between 1995 and 1996, he held the post of deputy chief economist at the U.S. Department of Labor, where, among other topics, he worked on the initiative to raise the minimum wage. He is co-author of five previous editions of *The State of Working America* and co-author (with Dean Baker) of the book *The Benefits of Full Employment*. He specializes in the analysis of wage and income inequality, poverty, and low-wage labor markets, and his writings have appeared in popular and academic journals. Mr. Bernstein holds a Ph.D. in social welfare from Columbia University.

SYLVIA ALLEGRETTO joined the Economic Policy Institute in 2003 after receiving her Ph.D. in economics from the University of Colorado at Boulder. Her areas of interest included income inequality, family budgets, unemployment, unions, and collective bargaining. She is co-author of the forthcoming EPI book *How Does Teacher Pay Compare?*